MADAME VESTRIS

A THEATRICAL BIOGRAPHY

MADAME VESTRIS, 1838

Madame Vestris

-a theatrical biography

CLIFFORD JOHN WILLIAMS

SIDGWICK & JACKSON

LONDON

First published in Great Britain 1973
Copyright © 1973 by Clifford John Williams

I.S.B.N, 0.283.97829.5

Printed in Great Britain by
William Clowes and Sons Limited
London, Colchester and Beccles
for Sidgwick and Jackson Limited
1 Tavistock Chambers, Bloomsbury Way
London WC1A 2SG

Acknowledgements

―――――――――――

Lucy Elizabeth Vestris was European in origin, technique, and temperament. She was not happy in the New World, but American scholarship has done its best to make amends to the lady, and American institutions are the custodians of many items that relate to her.

Through the kind offices of Mr Ronald C. Kern, I enjoyed the hospitality of Ohio State University for five months, as lecturer, actor, and director. In addition to the use of their own Theatre Collection, they also made it possible for me to visit other collections in the United States. My debt to Mr James H. Butler's two important articles is as appreciated as it is obvious. More personally I acknowledge the kindness of Mr Clair O. Haugen in allowing me to read his thesis for Wisconsin, following our meetings and talks; and of Miss Mary Ann Jensen, Librarian of the Theatre Collection of Princeton University.

Here at home, the Leverhulme Trust provided a Research Award, enabling me to work in Paris and London. The courtesy and quiet scholarship of Madame S. Chevally, Librarian of the Comédie Française, and the interest and help of Mrs D. Anderson, Librarian of the Garrick Club, are happily remembered. At the London Library I have been fortunate in the friendship and the services of Miss Joan Bailey and, untimely gone, the late Hamish MacDowell. The interest and advice of Mr Anthony Latham of the Enthoven Collection at the Victoria and Albert Museum is reflected in the range and variety of the illustrative material.

Many other faces, late and living, are called to mind by reflection upon the time that the book has been a-gathering. All deserve mention, but being, for the most part, theatre people, they will understand that to overplay a call – to milk it – is to kill it and, on this occasion, let the scholars and the librarians take the stage.

C. J. W.

Contents

List of Illustrations

(Note: various posters and other printed items which are reproduced are not included in the following list.)

xi

'. . . since which period no one has ever appeared possessing that peculiar combination of personal attractions and professional ability, which, for so many years, made her the most popular actress and manager of her day.' — PLANCHÉ, *Recollections and Reflections*

NOTE

Madame Vestris was known under various names at different times in her career and was also called – and called herself – different names. I have tried to tie particular names to their particular times and contexts. She was baptized Lucy Elizabeth and signed her marriage certificate thus. To her family and friends she was variously Lucy, Lizzie, and Lizzy. As she became established she usually used Eliza Lucy and/or Eliza. From the Olympic management onwards she was professionally and publicly known as Madame Vestris.

Introduction

To attempt a biography of Madame Vestris is to do her an injustice. This might be said of any theatrical person who held the affectionate regard and admiration of the public, but it is particularly true in the case of an artist such as Madame Vestris. With a 'legitimate' actress, for example Mrs Siddons, we are on surer ground. The plays in which such players appeared are still with us as yardsticks and challenges. From comparative criticisms, eyewitness accounts and other sources we may reconstruct something of the style and the impact of great tragedians and, to a lesser extent, those who excelled in the enduring comedies. Such performers are in what may be called the great tradition of dramatic presentation: the themes and intentions have been similar since the Greeks, however flexible the means of realizing them. The manner has been subject to fashion; the matter has been uniform. Vehicles equal to the greatest talent, the great roles are there to aspire to.

When the talent has been perfected through a personality that found its challenges and triumphs outside any enduring means of comparison or measurement, then assessment is inevitably replaced by speculation. And so it is with Madame Vestris.

Although I have suggested, for instance in the case of her Ophelia, that Vestris might have made a respectable career in a 'classical' company, I cannot really believe that such a life would have been right for her or for the theatre. For she was not in the great tradition. However much she enjoyed the trappings and the suits of royal and respectable approval, her talents, as continental as her blood, were derived from those performers of no fixed abode who wandered through Europe for as long as, if not longer than, their more settled but none the less related 'legitimate' brethren.

Early contemporary accounts trying to pin down that ephemeral phenomenon, Madame Vestris, emphasized her personal charms and sexual prowess. Charles E. Pearce, in his *Madame Vestris and her Times* (London 1923) gallantly defended the lady, setting her alongside similarly slandered ladies, excusing her lapses by reference to the standards of her time, and drawing attention to her theatrical achievements. It was good to have a general account of one who was known vaguely (except to addicts and theatre historians) as a rather saucy lady who was on the stage. The scarcity of references and the lack of a bibliography indicated a work intended for popular and unaugmented reading, a piece of high-class reporting by Mr. Pearce.

Since 1923 there have been well-authenticated accounts and assessments of various aspects of Madame Vestris's career. Most of these have been from the United States and the emphasis has been, quite rightly, upon Madame Vestris as manageress and innovator. Many of her innovations survived and developed and some are still with us. The consideration of them is therefore a primary concern of theatre historians.

Scholarly contributions to theatrical history are happily and readily acknowledged by theatre people, students, and addicts. They have both illuminated and inspired theatrical practice to no small extent; provided performers with an enlightened and articulate minority in the audience, and afforded performers their only hope of an informed memorial.

Playwrights make their own memorials. An increasing number of plays are soon published, with a Preface – following Shaw in practice if not in extent. Some are published in annotated school editions having had no more than comparatively limited runs to mainly coterie audiences. Programme notes have been developed, embalming the serious tone of the German originals of such things in the glib, easily digested, smart commercialism of the colour supplements. It all adds to the sense of occasion, and provides a souvenir.

Actors know, as they have always known, that they are pioneering for playwrights and not the other way around: even while interpreting one playwright they are experimenting with the forms and styles that will provide the materials for playwrights to come. They don't announce or record the fact. It is something that every executant artist does as an integral part of practising his craft, something so integral that most of them give it no conscious thought or expression.

Eliza and her Armand and her Charley were all performers. But she knew the game better and played it more vigorously than her men. Nothing in her story is more telling than the episode recorded by Planché and quoted on page 108. There is something of Medea about it and something of Mother Courage, but essentially it is the strolling player methodically packing up the cart and working out how to present the failure as a success story for the next town.

The fascination of the lady herself was, and is, in the fusion and confusion of the passionate woman and the disciplined manageress. In considering her as a performer and/or manageress these two facets are inseparable, accounting for her skill as a performer and her extravagance as a manageress, and finding their common ground in her style.

2

It cannot be claimed for this study, as Madame could claim for some of her productions, that the intention to achieve 'an harmonious whole' has been realized. I have been concerned to discover clues to those influences that might have contributed to the making of her particular style of acting and management, and to the displaying of these in the theatre.

Without pandering to the preoccupations of the morbid, a theatrical biography must take account of the social and amoral preferences of a lady who conducted so long and so successful a flirtation with her audiences. The change in her later professional style may be attributed in part to time and to illness, but the influence of the late and damaging entrance of love into her life in the person of Edward Thynne should also be considered. These aspects of her life have been referred to as and when relevant to her professional life.

At the risk of seeming, like *Hamlet*, 'full of quotations', I have included as many first-hand accounts of Vestris in the theatre, as actress and manageress, as seemed informative and imaginatively descriptive. There are not a great many such. For the most part there is fulsome, even infatuated, praise or spiteful and partial denigration. As will be seen, *The Times* has proved the most rewarding of all the many sources that have been worked through, and I remain yet another debtor to those anonymous contributors.

The fragile immediacy of a great artist would be denied if we could capture it, even at first hand. The truth of this consoles a biographer. To take a modern instance: there is no way of conveying, accurately and for everyone, the style and elegance of Vivien Leigh's first entrance in *Duel of Angels*, a simple walk from backstage right. Those who did experience this exclusively theatrical moment at the Apollo Theatre, London in 1958, or in New York or Australia in the early 1960s, are in some state of grace: they may get an inkling of the texture of the pleasure that was conveyed by Madame Vestris's entrance on to a stage.

1

The Name

'John Tillitson Curate' solemnized the marriage between Armand Vestris and Lucy Bartolozzi reported in the fashionable *Gentleman's Magazine*:

> 'Jan. 28 (1813) At St. Martin's in the Fields, the celebrated Mr. A. Vestris, to Miss Bartolozzi, dau. of Mr. G. B. the artist, and granddaughter of F. B. the eminent engraver.'

Lucy's father gave consent and signed the register, which was also witnessed by Lucy Elizabeth Tomkins and one 'Cecilia Violet'. Their Christian names being the same, it is possible that Lucy Elizabeth Tomkins was the bride's godmother.

The nice distinction between the 'celebrated' bridegroom and the 'eminent' grandfather of the bride was aptly made. The sixteen-year-old bride was to become far more celebrated than her twenty-six-year-old groom, though eminence would be far too staid an adjective to apply to her at any stage of her life.

Oxberry's comment on the wedding is less elegant but more succinct, if mistaken about the status of the parson: '. . . on the 28th of January, 1813, the rector of St. Martin in the Fields performed the marriage ceremony, and joined these extraordinary individuals'.

Although celebrated in his own right, Armand Vestris, like Miss Bartolozzi, enjoyed the reflected glory of an Italian grandfather. A member of the Florentine family of da Vestri, Gaëtano Vestris became 'Le Dieu de la Danse' for Parisian audiences during the middle years of the eighteenth century. He retired in 1782, survived the Revolution and the Empire, and died, aged seventy-nine, in 1808.

His illegitimate son Auguste, whose mother was the dancer Mlle Allard, was born in London in 1760. Auguste retired in 1816. As much distinguished as a teacher as a dancer, he numbered among his pupils Bournonville and Fanny Elssler.

Armand, the bridegroom of 1813, was born in Paris on 3 May 1787. (Among other errors in connection with this family, the *Enciclopedia dello spettacolo* gives the date as 1795.) A child of the Revolution, Armand's style of dancing and of living was very different from his grandfather's. On stage, he stirred hearts and turned heads with Spanish fandangos and other romantically inspired numbers, partnering Mme Angiolini. Off stage, he led the wild and fashionably 'artistic' life of the new age — a life that seems to have taken toll of his face and figure long before he was out of his twenties: 'He was known as a man of pleasure, and dissipation was stamped upon his features.' (Grinsted in *Bentley's Miscellany* 1856.)

It is the rake rather than the dancer that most surviving accounts of Armand are concerned to present. Without denying the possible effect of his private pursuits on his professional life, it is as well to remember that Lucy was not making, either in the eyes of her family or in the eyes of the public, a misalliance. She was the bride of the leading dancer of the day with a responsible position at the first theatre in London.

From both French and English accounts of his dancing, Armand seems to have had immense style in his work. In their different ways, and in their various theatrical fields, all the large Vestris family and the marital partners they chose had a great sense of style. Allied to this family attribute, each Vestris evolved individual and unique attributes that made each of them 'stars' in their own right.

In the sphere of the dance, Armand's grandfather Gaëtano seemed to convey in dancing dramatic and disciplined impressions and intensities that had previously been the prerogative of acting and singing. Armand's father Auguste had a taste, dignity, and gracefulness of contour that commented upon rather than presented themes and emotions.

Armand's strong individual points were a lightness (often evoking the adjective 'exquisite' from reviewers) and a power that dazzled audiences. Comments on his dancing are often in the same vein as later comments on Nijinsky. *The Times* commented on his pirouettes: 'Vestris whirls about with a rapidity which top-whipping urchins would do well to imitate.' The considerable amount of choreography for which he was responsible for both ballets and operas was always admired and often revived.

If he was selfish in private life and professionally jealous, it was not always so. For his ageing, but still accomplished, father he revived one of his own successes for the season of 1816 at the King's Theatre. The review in the *New Monthly Magazine* indicates that the son's confidence in his father was fully justified. A later reference will further bear out Armand's unselfish professional conduct.

Perhaps it was the fashionable, romantic, talented but doomed youth himself who attracted Miss Bartolozzi, just sixteen and eager to be a woman of the world. But there was also the glamour of the name, easier on the tongue and less 'eminent' than Bartolozzi, carrying the expectation of Paris with the surety of acceptance in that first city of Europe.

For Miss Bartolozzi was a European child. Francesco Bartolozzi, her grandfather, left Italy and his family to spend his most profitable years in London. The mistaken notion that Lucy was the daughter, rather than the granddaughter, of Francesco became a common error. Apparently begun by Oxberry in 1826, it was repeated in Madame Vestris's obituary in the *Annual Register* for 1856 (though Grinsted in *Bentley's Miscellany* for the same year gets things right). The error is often met with, for instance in Duncombe and even in E. B. Watson (1926). That she was 'the daughter of the great Bartolozzi' seems to have been the impression among younger actors in Lucy's later years. George Vandenhoff so describes her, referring to Francesco as 'the sculptor'.

Gaëtano, the only survivor of Francesco's several children, followed his father to London. He had been named after his father's close friend, the painter Gaëtano Gondolfi, and he inherited something of his father's talent for engraving. But it was a different art that delighted him. Music was his passion and he seems to have had a gift for it, especially for the tenor violin. According to Andrew Tuer, 'He wasted a great deal of the time that ought to have been devoted to business in the society of congenial, convivial, and especially of musical companions.'

This same passion led him into matrimony. Miss Teresa Jansen, of German origin, daughter of a dancing master of Aix-la-Chappelle, and the star pupil of the composer and pianist Clementi, married Gaëtano Bartolozzi in 1795. Reputedly a vain woman, and Germanic in her tendency to corpulence and floral headgear, she had sufficient German practicality to be the breadwinner for a commercially indolent husband and their two daughters.

With their mother's music lessons and their father's musical gatherings Lucy and her sister Josephine absorbed quite a musical education. And Oxberry records that Lucy became proficient in French and Italian as well as English. (Presumably the mother had picked up French at Aix-la-Chappelle; there seems to be no evidence that Mme Vestris was familiar with German.) '. . . both her parents', says Oxberry, 'dealt in that kind of small talk that may be termed Mezzo-English.'

John Coleman, in *Players and Playwrights I Have Known*, cites the evidence of 'a servant of the Bartolozzi family', Madame Mariotti, whose account was originally quoted by 'Old Stager' (Matthew Mackintosh) in 1866. She gives 1800 as the year of Lucy's birth and Marylebone as the place. More importantly, she mentions London's 'foreign schools, where it was customary to have a play performed by the pupils in French or Italian every Saturday in the presence of their

'the eminent engraver' by Lemuel Francis Abbot (Tate Gallery). It is difficult to 'analyse the characteristics of Bartolozzi as a draughtsman and engraver, for his efforts were necessarily governed and contracted by the spirit of the age in which he lived. . . . The production of his engravings was chiefly controlled by the print-sellers . . . and they in turn were governed by the taste of the art patrons of the period. . . . It is hopeless to attempt to describe the subtle power and fascinating charm of the results he achieved'. (Andrew Tuer: *Bartolozzi and His Works*)

parents and guardians.' There seems no reason to doubt this evidence. Mme Mariotti adds that

> 'At the age of fourteen she entered the school of His Majesty's Theatre, and danced in the ballet there for a season. She then went to the Académie in Paris for the winter; and on her return to London became a pupil of the ballet-master, whose name she afterwards bore, Armand Vestris. Her instructor kept her hard at work for twelve months, and then brought her out . . . '

If this is true (though the account is frequently inaccurate and unconvincing), Lucy might well have met Armand in Paris. She was brought out at her début as 'a pupil of Mr Corri' who was the singing coach at the King's Theatre. Armand himself took care of the dancing lessons. If Mme Mariotti is to be relied upon at all the success of Lucy at her début was backed by experience in technical training and stage business.

The Bartolozzi family lived at 73 Dean Street, Soho, afterwards the site of the Royalty Theatre. The 'amusements of the metropolis' (Oxberry) were on the doorstep and the Bartolozzis were not the kind of family to ignore them, nor to be ignored by them. Oxberry's assertion that by the winter of 1811, then aged fourteen, Lucy's 'interesting features might be seen nightly at concerts, balls, the opera, etc.' is probably correct. Oxberry states firmly that Lucy was 'NOT intended for the stage', and this in spite of the above evidence, might have been her parents feelings. Possibly they hoped that all the gadding about would result in a well-to-do husband, if not a Regency Buck. Accounts nearer in time than that of 'Old Stager' indicate that, beyond teaching her to play the piano pleasingly and to sing, no great pains were taken by the family to train her professionally. 'She was from infancy impatient of control', declared Oxberry!

Eligible gentlemen and personable rogues must have presented themselves by the dozen. If we may believe the essence rather than the indulgence of the so-called 'biographies' issued in her early life (which number the Prince Regent among her admirers) many well-turned legs and heads of Hyacinthine curls must have bent for her.

'Le Dieu de la Danse' once answered the charge that he was demanding a salary in excess of that allowed the king's marshals with 'Under those circumstances, I should advise His Majesty to make his marshalls dance – if they can.' The capacity to dance, to embody the romantic attitudes in her father's and grandfather's engravings and the passionate lyrics of Italian songs, must have been a trump card for Armand Vestris in the play for Lucy's heart. The titles of many of the ballets could have been themes for Bartolozzi engravings: *Les Petits braconniers*, *Le Prince troubadour*, *L'Amour et le poison*. A child of her time, and from such a background, her choice of Armand Vestris is not surprising.

Two examples of Bartolozzi's work. His grand-daughter was to inherit the pictorial sense and natural grace shown in such works: in her own style and appearance and, as manageress, in the detail and pastoral charm of many of her stage pictures. All three of Bartolozzi's illustrations for this edition of Milton's poem provide a clue for the inspiration that made *The Dream* such a visual delight. Note the 'cue' for lighting.

'Adam and Eve' from *Paradise Lost*, 1802

'Sheep Shearing' from Thompson's *The Seasons*, 1814

The honeymoon period was soon over, a fact that probably surprised no one. But if personally there was little to be said for the marriage for young Mme Vestris, professionally it not only provided her with a conspicuous début and a definite career; it also determined the direction that that career would take, both immediately and subsequently.

The marriage had also given her a name to conjure with in the European as well as the English theatre, a name whose glory she was to extend and enhance. By upbringing and temperament she was a European, and always remained one. That was part of her appeal for the British public, for it gave her an uninhibited zeal and zest that, in performance, might well have redeemed much of the vulgarity of, for example, *Giovanni in London*, and it also lent an elegance to the insipid gentility of some of the later pieces in which she appeared.

The European attitudes inherited from her background and the sensibilities developed by her European experience are the clues to the professional life of Lucy Vestris.

2

Début

Armand Vestris made his début in Paris in 1800. He had made many unofficial débuts before his official one. As a male Vestris he must have been in training from a very tender age, and training involved at first occasional and later frequent involvement in theatrical performance. As he outgrew pages, train-bearers and Cupids, there would be attendants upon deities, potentates, and shepherdesses.

Armand's official début was a memorable one, for, in compliment to his grandson, Gaëtano Vestris came out of retirement, so that the Parisian public saw three generations in one performance. Armand was an immediate success, no slight achievement with an audience well experienced and highly critical in everything concerning *la dance*.

Nine years later, at the age of twenty-two, Armand left France: anxious for new laurels? to escape the family? to escape from one or more amorous entanglements? He went to Italy, then to Portugal, and finally came to London, returning only briefly to Paris.

Lucy Vestris made her début at the King's Theatre in the Haymarket on 20 July 1815. The extravagant Armand, according to the 1826 memoir of Lucy in *Oxberry's Dramatic Biography*, saw a possible capital asset in his attractive young wife, and brought her out on the occasion of his own Benefit. With few exceptions, this theory has been echoed by subsequent writers, including Pearce. Perhaps that was the way of it, but it seems more likely that one of two things, or something of both, determined the début.

Either two and a half years as a fashionable young matron had been too frustrating for the future manageress, or she had always intended to use her married status as a means of making her début and had been preparing herself for the opportunity. Shortage of money provided a means of seizing the opportunity when it arose, and that excuse would also give both poignancy — and publicity — to the first public appearance of an eighteen-year-old charmer.

Whatever the reasons, the role and the place could not have been better chosen for the occasion. An opera known to the public for eleven years, containing many familiar airs, Peter von Winter's *Il Ratto di Proserpina* provided an effective vehicle without making any real vocal demands on the performers. A theatre, the most fashionable in London and one of the most fashionable in Europe, filled for the Benefit of her husband, provided a sympathetic setting for young Madame Vestris.

J. F. Godelet pinx.^t.   H. Meyer sculp.

ARMAND VESTRIS

just before his twenty-second birthday, in costume for a ballet. The costume, especially the hat, is little different from those seen in nineteenth-century ballets in our own time.

13

Her Majesty's Theatre and New Zealand House now occupy the site, at the foot of the Haymarket, of the Italian Opera House, as the King's Theatre was also called. A fragment of the old house still remains. Known as the Royal Opera Arcade, it runs behind the present buildings, connecting Charles II Street and Pall Mall. One of the most evocative links with London's past, the Arcade stands witness for many things that influenced the girl making her début. Practical, discreetly commercial, and coolly elegant, the Arcade has magnificent style. It was designed, like the whole of the Opera House, as a setting for a fashionable clientèle at one of those comparatively rare moments in social history when fashion was synonymous with good taste. The chauvinistic excesses and eccentricities of dress from the French Revolution had been tempered both by the innate French sense of style, a characteristic far more profound and valuable than their politics, and by the lessons that the Greek Revival had imported and adapted.

The Greek Revival in architecture presumed the presence of people, just as the so-called Regency style of dress implied or presented the human body inside it. The Battle of Waterloo had been fought some five weeks before Lucy's début. This affected both the mood and the composition of the audience, which, for this season, was probably more European than it ever had been. (The Coronation season of 1937 was a comparable event in the present century.)

The Royal Opera Arcade anticipates people as surely as a well-designed stage setting awaits actors. The series of arches invites entry and the central wrought-iron lamps dip gracefully along the centre. The slightly bowed windows of the shops that line the sides of the arcade invite but do not press inspection. An overall simplicity of line and plainness of finish set off the tracery of the lamps and the movement of people, a feature shown to greater effect at the time the arcade was built, when fabrics were light for ladies and cloaks long and full for gentlemen.

Fashionable dress was *de rigeur* for the audience. Without it they were refused admission.

'There were strict regulations in force respecting evening costume. Full dress consisted of a long-tailed coat with ruffles at the wrists; white cravat, with stand-up shirt collar; small-clothes [knee-breeches] with gold or diamond buckles; silk stockings, shoes, a waistcoat open, to show the shirt-front or frill, and white kid gloves. A cocked hat, called a *chapeau bras*, because usually carried under the arm, and a sword at the side, completed the costume. The hair was always carefully dressed. Thus attired every gentleman was obliged to present himself, till trousers superseded breeches, and boots, shoes. The round was adopted instead of the top hat, and the sword abandoned to those who intended to make it a weapon rather than an ornament.' (Duncombe, Vol. 1, p. 174)

The theatre was divided into pit (now stalls), boxes and gallery. In the pit was 'Fops' Alley', where a gentleman was displayed rather than absorbed into his seat. Ladies occupied the boxes, while the gallery was primarily intended for the servants of the patrons in the pit and boxes. The *New Monthly Magazine* gives a contemporary account of the impression made by the auditorium for the season of 1815:

'The fronts of the boxes, as well as the inside, are tastefully painted, and are uncommonly rich and warm in the color [*sic*]. The cold blue and silver have given place to red and gold, the effect of which, added to the new brilliant chandeliers, is worthy the saloon of the finest circle of boxes in Europe — for after all the new buildings, there is no theatre in any country, the plan and *coup d'oeil* of which are comparable to those of the English Opera. The new drop curtain harmonises with the general tone of color, and gives a delightful ensemble to the view. It is in truth the best curtain we ever saw . . . There is an additional large and beautiful chandelier placed in the gallery, by which that part of the theatre is rendered as light as the pit; and an essential improvement has taken place in placing the lustres; for now not one of the boxes on the two sides of the house will have the view of the stage intercepted by the glare of the lights. Another most material alteration will facilitate the exit of the box company to their carriages, as the opening to the vestibule is enlarged, and, with the ante-room, elegantly fitted up for their accommodation, till the carriages draw up.'

Wellington and Blücher might have been victorious on the battlefield but Paris remained the dictator of fashion and the arbiter of taste, even to the turns of phrase used in reporting.

Napoleonic red and gold had replaced the Bourbon blue and silver, just as it had done in the theatre at Versailles (now restored to its Bourbon splendour) and elsewhere in France, despite the fact that the patrons of the King's Theatre shared far more tradition and sensibility with the fallen monarchy and rejoiced in the defeat of Bonaparte.

The financial affairs of the Opera House were mainly dependent on the Subscription List, a practice still used for this 'exotic and irrational entertainment', as Dr Johnson called it. Patrons, mostly members of the aristocracy (for although the times were changing, land remained the basis of wealth) subscribed for an entire season. Of some 197 boxes, 68 were private property until 1825. They belonged to those whose contributions had made it possible to build the theatre on Crown-land. Thus 129 boxes remained for annual letting. Subscriptions for these amounted to £33,340 a year. Door receipts averaged some £11,000. Other income came from rentings for concerts, masquerades, etc., and from the rents charged to those selling fruit and refreshments. Expenses for the sixty-odd performances a year came to something like £33,000. It will be seen

15

that without the subscribers, no manager could plan a season or engage a company.

Generally speaking, Italian singers and French dancers were the artists demanded by patrons of the opera house. The personal, and to some extent, social, prestige of these performers was the main asset, as well as a perennial headache, for a manager, and comparatively small attention was given to staging and presentation. This is not to say that the visual effect was neglected: spectacle and mechanical devices were expected and provided, but the pattern followed was the earlier eighteenth-century practice, and seems not to have been influenced by the experiments in staging and lighting made, for example, by David Garrick, and in the staging of German and French plays.

Visual effect was exploited more imaginatively in ballet than in opera. Originally only an embellishment and a foil for singing, ballet had, by the time of Lucy's début, evolved as a *genre* in its own right. While a good singer could command a full house it was the ballet that was generally popular. In other words, the situation was roughly the same then as now.

The Parisian craze for ballet, for it was a popular as well as a fashionable phenomenon, developed rapidly during and after the Revolution. More easily

THE ITALIAN OPERA HOUSE

assimilated than opera, the dance could give definition to romantic aspirations without requiring much in the way of musical intelligence or subtlety of expression. The 'high astounding terms' of what Professor Dent aptly named 'dynastic opera' were alien, in intention and in execution, to the citizens of the new Republic, who gave their indiscriminate enthusiasm to the more immediate sensations offered by the dance.

English visitors to Paris followed the fashion, rather than considered the motive, and demanded similar fare from their own opera house. The mixed feelings of those who deplored the fashion but welcomed the patronage are well conveyed in the following item in the *Lady's Magazine* at the end of the 1816 season:

'It is a mortification to which the lovers of music have long been forced to submit, that the opera is attended chiefly for the sake of the ballet: and their only revenge lies in the consideration, that the ballet itself is indebted for support to the caprice of fashion, rather than to a taste for dancing. Our native gentry who have returned from abroad, after their several excursions, have some of them acquired, and more of them learned to affect, that foreign penchant, which sends every living thing in Paris and elsewhere to some theatre or other the moment they have dined. This has had a visible effect in giving bustle and brilliance to all our play-houses, as well as to the opera itself, of which they were hopeless for many preceding seasons; and the tastes imported by our travellers have propagated themselves widely among the English who have not travelled.'

Subscribers to the opera had certain privileges – the house resembled, in some ways, a fashionable club – and it is highly probable that many gentlemen subscribed and/or attended in order to meet the young dancers off the stage. From the level of the boxes there was direct access to behind the scenes (the green-room was not at this time established) where presentations and assignations could very easily be arranged. Thus, an attractive young person who obtained an engagement for the opera season had an automatic entry into, at least, certain circles and aspects of society in a comparatively respectable manner.

While it may be less true today, it was certainly the case until not so long ago that such a beginning was the real source of social, artistic and intellectual education for those without other means of obtaining it. It was real education, in that it was apprehended in experience rather than acquired from instruction. 'I believe that actors are made as well as born and theatres are the proper schools of their making,' said Madame Vestris at the end of her first Covent Garden season in 1840. The place where they begin to be made has a lasting professional influence.

As a young and highly intelligent beginner at the King's Theatre in 1815, Lucy had certain advantages. In addition to looks, grace and vitality she also had a husband 'in the business' and was well acquainted with, and doubtless well known by, a wide circle of performers and patrons. With an exceptional musical education and some years' experience as a theatregoer, she knew the tastes and the tendencies of the times and the city in which she was playing.

Working at the King's taught, or confirmed, various theatrical home truths: fashion usually determines what is successful. Fashion is instigated and endorsed by money, however acquired, and position. Talent is as dependent as fashion on the patronage of money, but usually has greater difficulty in getting patronage.

The precariousness and the competitiveness of work in the theatre makes it among the roughest of human games. Largely, though not entirely, because of this, performers are hypersensitive about their status in a company or in the public standing and jealous of their prerogatives, and are often required, possibly reluctantly, to insist upon those prerogatives. In the days before such bodies as British Actors' Equity, the battle for such rights as they thought were their due was fought by the performers themselves.

The company gathered on the stage of the King's Theatre depended for their salaries on the occupants of the pit and the boxes, not the gallery. In order to face that audience they had driven a hard bargain with the management and hoped that the management would be able to come through with the salaries. (It was a common enough thing for there to be less money in the box office than was promised on the contracts.)

Socially, the truths to be gleaned by the young beginner were immediately more agreeable, if eventually as tiresome as the theatrical points. The emphasis on dress for the audience has been noted. This emphasis was, as ever, echoed throughout fashionable and theatrical society. (The distinction might be made between the two kinds in that the fashionable people are, largely, demonstrating what they are able to buy, while actors are displaying what they hope to sell.)

To the natural and quite laudable concern of a young performer to present herself as charmingly as possible was added, for the young Madame Vestris, the professional necessity of presenting an elegant front as the wife of a principal French dancer, thus deterring the bailiffs who beset that extravagant husband. The taste acquired and the habit formed for such things is not easily abandoned. It becomes a part of the total professional image of oneself and can be defended, from that standpoint, more plausibly than other extravagances and indulgences. But the maintenance of elegance, though remembered now when the bills are forgotten, was to be an item that frequently left Eliza Lucy and her husbands with empty pockets.

The début was, then, the official 'coming out' of a young woman who was already part of the professional and social life of the Opera House. It is doubtful if she could have made it any other way. Unlike the theatre, opera and ballet make certain generally accepted technical demands on a performer that youth and charm may enhance but cannot supersede. It has not been uncommon for someone unknown to make their 'first time' in a play — an opportunity that has been secured by various means. But while there have been disastrous and ludicrous operatic débuts, they are comparatively rare. Singing and dancing are exact arts and sciences. Acting, in general, should be, but it has no accepted score or choreography to discipline it or to measure it by.

It was also the Benefit night for Armand Vestris. Whatever the eventual assessment, now congealed into encyclopaedias, there can be no doubt about his charm for his contemporaries and his skill and popularity as a dancer. *The Times* records that 'every part of the house was crowded.' With the programme offered plus Vestris's Benefit a full house could be expected. The début of the young wife, for whatever reason — and it takes little imagination to guess the range and kind of comment and gossip that must have beguiled the waiting moments — simply added a piquancy, and element of surprise and novelty, to the evening's entertainment.

Von Winter's opera, together with his other work, is now quite neglected. He is not mentioned in most dictionaries of music and *The Oxford Companion to Music* does not include him. The history of music since the early nineteenth century has been so momentous that it is hardly surprising that von Winter has been long since overwhelmed. But in 1815 he was much admired and *Il Ratto di Proserpina* an established favourite. *The Times* praised the 'nerve, science, and musical feeling that pervades it'.

The main objections to a revival of von Winter's operas today would be, technically, his failure to master counterpoint, and commercially, the lack of dramatic power and inevitability of good operatic composition. But he is not lacking in theatricality and in what might be called ritualistic sensibility: things that were so admired and looked for in both the theatre and the opera house in the early 1800s. He provided situations and opportunities for singers to 'make their points', as leading actors 'made their points' in Shakespeare. Though the instrumentation is rich, it is never allowed to swamp the voices, which are given charming melodies well fitted to the demands of the diction. (the librettist was Mozart's Lorenzo da Ponte.)

Such a work gave such an audience a comfortable and comforting evening. A reaffirmation of standards and styles that had been rudely disturbed by all that business in France that, by the defeat of Bonaparte, had deservedly met its Waterloo. Vulgar aspirations had been put down, land was safe and trading optimistic. Civilized, romantically tinged pleasures gave an elegant turn to the smugness of new-found security.

The role in which Lucy appeared seems, in retrospect, to have given the cue for much that was to come in her theatrical life; a fashionable comment on a mythological theme; individual set numbers in a musical presentation; scope for an effective and anticipated entrance, and for the revelation of her technical control of naturally graceful movement — which latter might be offered as a partial definition of style. All these things were to recur in the stage life of our heroine.

Whoever wrote the notice for *The Times* for the morning after that Thursday evening was obviously enchanted:

'It has a further, and we speak after due deliberation when we say a higher claim to public favour, from the various talent and exquisite attraction of a performer whom it introduced to our notice last night when Mme. Vestris . . . came forward for her husband's benefit, in the character of Proserpina, a most arduous undertaking for a novice. We much regret that the late hour at which the performance ended will enable us to give but a very slight and imperfect picture of the degree to which we were pleased, captivated and astonished. This lady, not more than 16 years of age, has a form of perfect symmetry, with a beautiful countenance, capable of the most animated expression – into which spirit and energy may be called up when she will – but in which, while unexcited, feminine delicacy prevails. Her voice is a 'contre alto' of the finest order. Young as she is, it has all the mellow richness of Grassini's – perhaps we might without exaggeration say, that it possesses more of that quality than Grassini could boast of in the zenith of her fame, and it indisputably possesses a greater compass, reaching far beyond her in the upper notes . . . The wife of Vestris may naturally be presumed to move with grace; but there is a keeping in her movement – an adaptation of it to the sense – an association of the step and gesture to the superior faculties of mind and voice, which appeared to us to complete the image of the most faultless and bewitching debutante that we have ever seen . . .'

The one regret of the reviewer was that she had come out so late in the season.

The literary drawbacks of newspaper criticism are also its theatrical strengths for the reader and historian. Restrictions of space and time; the extremes of praise or blame engendered by the immediacy of the experience: such things are often of greater value theatrically than accounts of performances recollected in tranquillity.

Critics of music, opera and ballet may be presumed to know something of the technical side of the work they are reviewing. (The presumption is dashed in certain instances but in general it is justified.) Their integrity may be assessed from where they were published; from the style and tone of the writing and from evidence of some knowledge of the work being performed and of theatrical and musical convention.

The remarkable standard of writing, criticism and reporting maintained by *The Times* throughout the nineteenth century, especially the earlier decades, is insufficiently acknowledged, though often exploited. Generally speaking, the dramatic critics of *The Times* reported (or were instructed to report?) *what they saw*. Their descriptions implied not only what they thought but why they were moved so to think. While it is true that the reader was often given simply a bald description with no comment — except from silence, sometimes in itself telling — this is of more value historically than comment without evidence, which is so often what one meets in more modern reviewing.

We are not here concerned with the scant, chatty, uninformed and largely uninformative summaries, from trite entries in Entertainment Guides to the few well-spaced, and often banner-headlined, scraps of opinion offered by much of the press. Grub Street has always had its share of such; Mme Vestris was never free of them. They tell us something of human envy and susceptibility and a lot about Grub Street. Smaller factual notices can be valuable as evidence; the *Morning Post* for 21 July 1815, for instance, confirms the tenor of the review in *The Times*: 'M. A. Vestris gave us an exquisite treat last night at his Benefit, but we have no room at present for particulars. Madame Vestris (pupil to Mr. Corri) made her début on this occasion; and her performance was such as leaves no doubt of her becoming a splendid acquisition to this theatre.'

The Times reviewers were anonymous. Today critics are better known, by name and face, than dramatists and most actors. They seem mainly concerned (under instruction?) to tell *what they think*, but give few clues concerning how the performance determined such thoughts. Even on the simplest technical level, in measuring audibility for instance, there seems no generally accepted standard or concern.

Both *The Times* and the *Morning Post* reported the second performance two days later:

'. . . a crowded and fashionable audience; the whole of the *beau monde* left in town at this late season having assembled, as it would appear, to greet the beautiful and accomplished singer whose *entrée* on Thursday last, for her husband's Benefit, we announced to the lovers of Italian song. Madame Vestris improves upon the eye and ear. The just encouragement held out to her on her first appearance, has had its due effect in a more distinct and vigorous development of the powers of her voice, and the graces of her action.'

Thus *The Times*, which also added details of the ballet omitted from the first notice. Armand's bolero was commended, as was the 'vast pomp and bodily dignity' of his father.

'Madame Vestris's second appearance' (wrote the *Morning Post*) 'received the most extraordinary marks of approbation; in fact her reception was almost beyond all precedent. Her voice is a contr'alto, and from its compass capable of all the most touching and delicious influences of music; her skill seems sufficiently practised; time may be required and her youth has much to give for the perfect development of her powers; but even in their present state they are attractive in the extreme.'

The *Theatrical Inquisitor* was equally delighted, making the same points and concluding: 'It appears extraordinary that the managers should not have brought this lady forward at an earlier period of the season; it would undoubtedly have been more to their advantage . . . we presume she is permanently engaged.'

Such a reception could leave the Vestrises in no doubt that they had made the right decision concerning Lucy's début. More was to follow. The *Theatrical Inquisitor* reported the final performance in almost excessive terms, and *Il Ratto* is perhaps unique in having been reviewed, for one production, no less than three times. The third notice appeared in *The Times* on Monday 14 August, the season having ended on the previous Saturday. It read: 'Madame Vestris sung with the taste, simplicity, and delicacy that have procured her so much admiration since the first night of her appearance. She has evidently become better assured of her own powers, and easier in their display.'

The audience, 'if not the most brilliant, was among the most crowded that we have ever seen'. George IV (did anyone, reading the comparison with Grassini, speculate upon the possibility of the young singer making the same arrangement with His Majesty as Grassini had with Napoleon?) was prevented from attending by gout. A substantial form of apology arrived in gold, and the social disappointment was relieved by the presence of his daughter Princess Charlotte, at the second performance, when her enthusiasm got her to her feet and her fan banged approval on the edge of her box. The following day she sent £50 to Lucy.

It is as well to set against this royal, fashionable and journalistic response the comments of someone 'in the trade'. William Oxberry, who was to act with Lucy at Drury Lane, was by all accounts a useful, if limited, actor, a better publisher, and at his best as 'landlord of a chop house'. In 1825 and 1826 his widow brought out *Oxberry's Dramatic Biography*, an account, in several volumes, of the most celebrated performers of the time.

The 'Memoir' of Madame Vestris that appears in the *Dramatic Biography* may not have been written by Oxberry himself, but it seems probable that it was. 'We have met, we shall never meet again . . . ' declares the author of this strange mixture of admiration – even fascination – sharp observation and piously phrased viciousness. The tone is unmistakable to anyone who has heard it: it is that of the small-part actor, in his late thirties, who has possibly tried and failed to make the lady on the ascendant or has not had the courage to try.

But yet, jaundiced or petty though they may be, in dealing with professional points Oxberry's accounts have a recognizable core of theatrical truth embedded in the lubricious mass. While acknowledging Lucy's success, Oxberry states that at this stage of her career 'the talents of the young performer' were not 'of a very striking order': 'Her voice by no means possessed that richness and volume it has since acquired, and her acting was still less admirable; being limited to crossing her arms gracefully upon her bosom, looking like a pretty piece of still life, or giving an occasional gentle wave of the right hand, during the execution of a song.'

The overall picture, from 'in front' and from backstage, is recognizable. The two extremes, of the press and of the supporting actor, hold somewhere between them the true assessment. Youth, good looks, a trim figure and sufficient experience of deportment and music, in a glamorous setting and allied to the name of Vestris, had given the eighteen-year-old Lucy a fortunate beginning to her career. The début must have reassured her parents that the marriage had been a good venture professionally, however it might have looked domestically.

3

Le Beau Monde

Between the close of the 1815 season and the following December the Vestrises went to Paris. It may well be, as the scurrilous 'lives' assert, that the marriage was not holding up too well; that Madame's temper and Monsieur's roving eye emphasized the differences of temperament between them. Madame was now confirmed in confidence in her ability to attract the public in her own right, a consideration that has terminated more than one theatrical marriage.

On 20 December 1815 the couple were announced among the principal performers for the 1816 season at the King's Theatre. Among the 'poets' for the opera company a Stephano Vestris is listed. Among the dancers for the ballet there appears, in addition to Armand (who also had separate billing as Ballet Master), a Monsieur C. Vestris. Thus the family was almost as powerfully represented in London as it had been in Paris.

On paper, as far as the operatic side was concerned, the season looked as though it might be less brilliant than some earlier ones. The *London Chronicle* commented on 'the miserable prospect' presented when the season opened on 3 February. *Il Ratto* was on the opening bill, with Mme Fodor as Ceres to Lucy's Proserpina. If not as rapturous as the earlier ones, the reviews were again favourable, *The Times* finding that Lucy was 'less overpowered by Mme Fodor than by the piercing treble of Mme Sessi' last season.

The *Lady's Magazine* for February noted: 'Her voice is much improved in strength and fulness, and she performed the part in a delightful manner, a task of no trifling difficulty, after Grassini, whose elegant notes and exquisite pathos all must remember.'

The *Morning Post* indicated that work was still to be done, though 'her skill will enable her to make progress with time', but within a few days it had

24

KING's THEATRE,

December 20, 1815.

THE NOBILITY, Subscribers to the OPERA, and the Public, are most respectfully informed that this Theatre will Open on Saturday, **13th January, 1816.**

The following Principal Performers are engaged,

For the Opera.

Madame MAINVILLE FODOR, *Her First Appearance in this Country.*
Signor BRAHAM, *His First Appearance these Ten Years.*
Signor N A L D I.

Signora LEDONI, *Her 1st Appearance.*	Signor GENI.
Madame MARCONI, *Her 1st Appearance*	Signor BEGRI, *His 1st Appearance.*
Madame VESTRIS.	Signor LE VASSEUR
Signora GALLI, *Her 1st Appearance.*	Signor ROSQUELLI, *His 1st Appearance.*
Signora MARZETTI, *Her 1st Appearance.*	Signor RIGHI.

Signor G. ROVIDINO.   Signor DI GIOVANNI.   Signor DEVILLE, &c. &c.
Composer, Signor LIVERATI. **Poets,** Signors CARAVITA and STEPHANO VESTRIS.
Leader, Signor SPAGNIOLETTI.

For the Ballet.

Madame DUPONT, *Her 1st Appearance.*	Monsieur A. VESTRIS.
Mademoiselle MILANIE.	Monsieur BAPTISTE.
Madame LEON.	Monsieur LEON,
Mademoiselle MANGIN.	Monsieur C. VESTRIS.
Mademoiselle NARCISSE.	Monsieur OSCAR BYRNE.
Mademoiselle MORI.	Monsieur BOURDIN.
Mademoiselle TWAMLEY.	Monsieur BOISGERARD.

Monsieur CAPELLE.   Mademoiselles COLSON, MARIANETTE, HARRISON, MORI, &c. &c.

Ballet Master, Monsieur A. VESTRIS.   **Leader,** Monsieur MORI.
Stage Manager, Mr. KELLY.   **Deputy,** Signor DI GIOVANNI.
Bankers, Messrs. MORLAND, RANSOM, and Co.

MR. WATERS, in submitting this List to the Nobility, Subscribers
to the Opera, and the Public, begs to draw their attention to the number
and eminent talent of the Company. Since the close of last season,

Programme of King's Theatre

occasion to warn: 'Madame Vestris, with a fine natural talent sometimes loses its advantages by languor; she should learn that sweetness is not incompatible with spirit and that monotony is fatal to the finest tones.'

Possibly Lucy was becoming bored with a role that gave her less scope for her vitality than she would have liked, and until she became manageress there were to be many instances of the effects of such an attitude.

In her defence, it must be emphasized that she was but aping, usually to a lesser extent, the manners and moods of the leading singers and dancers with whom she first appeared. Later, in the theatre, it was often part of the battle that any spirited performer always had to wage to hold their own against managements and 'star' performers.

It may be, too, that even as early as this there were symptoms of the illness that was often given as a reason for her non-appearances and which brought a comparatively early end to her career. While the plea of illness is often made the excuse for absence from work, such excuses over a long period of time are only plausible if supported by some evidence, and no one seems ever to have challenged the validity of Madame Vestris's absences on the grounds of ill health. There are, on the other hand, references to her being vocally or otherwise tired in performance.

If it was von Winter she was weary of, she got him again within a fortnight of the revival of *Il Ratto* (a predictable managerial ploy). *Zaira*, which opened on Saturday, 17 February, is the most important of von Winter's operas and is generally of a higher musical standard than *Il Ratto*. The overture, taken from *Maria von Montalban*, was familiar and is the kind of music calculated to set a house in a good and a receptive mood, and the evening was declared a success.

Lucy, in the title role, had to cope with a more exacting score and a presentation that was not as dramatically effective as her veiled and anticipated appearance in *Il Ratto*. She took the challenge, *The Times* noting 'more power' in her singing and the *Lady's Magazine* allowing that she 'acquitted herself in a very favourable manner'. The more cautious note was probably justified. It was one thing to charm as a promising newcomer. Now she must justify her place in the company of one of the principal opera houses of Europe.

Zaira was given seven times during the season and *Il Ratto* five times (with an extra performance of Act One in a mixed bill).

The main balletic event of the season was *Gonsalvo de Cordova*, which opened, after several postponements, on Saturday, 6 April. It is gratifying to have a lengthy notice of this event in *The Times*, for it gives an assessment of Armand's professional abilities that explains his international reputation and popularity and puts the glib, and usually derived, denigrations of him in a light that confirms both their ignorance and their bias.

The Times review indicates a choreographer and ballet master aware of the demands of his fashionable audience and of the resources and limitations of his

An early nineteenth-century ballet, supposedly at the King's, but the details are inaccurate (see above).
Despite the errors, the picture conveys a good impression of audience, musicians, and performers for
a 'heroic' subject. Such subjects were favoured by the male dancers for they provided excuses for
athletic display. The ladies in the boxes welcomed the display and the greater freedom that the 'classical'
costumes gave to their favourites. *And*, such ballets were the rage in Paris.

27

company. It also reveals an even rarer phenomenon: a star dancer subordinating himself to the general effect rather than exploiting the general expectation.

Following a long paragraph giving the story of the ballet, *The Times* notice continues:

> ' . . . the new ballet, which is, we are of opinion, beyond all comparison, by much the most splendid, interesting, and attractive that had ever within our memory been brought forward at the King's theatre . . . The scenery . . . must be allowed the praise of extraordinary richness and beauty. The dancers all exerted themselves with infinite success . . . The younger Vestris, the most promising performer of the present day, in the highest attainments of his profession, had little to do, but did it marvellously well.'

The notice includes details of individual dances, *pas de deux*, *pas de trois* and ensemble work.

Whatever has been written or may be conjectured about the personal aspect of the marriage, there can be no doubt about Lucy's professional good fortune (and her awareness of this) in beginning her career with such a man to guide and present her. No English husband could have offered her the style that the European tradition had evolved, nor the technical means to maintain it. It should perhaps be added that it is doubtful if any English husband would have tolerated the tantrums and the extravagance for the sake of the undeveloped talents of young Miss Bartolozzi.

Lucy's first experience of a Command Performance was on 4 May of this season. Commanded by George IV as part of the celebration of the marriage between Princess Charlotte and Leopold of Belgium, it was a grand occasion of the kind that still lingers when Covent Garden puts on a gala performance for the monarch to entertain a visiting Head of State. The spectacle presented by the audience somewhat eclipses the efforts of the official performers, who, for once, are glad of reflected glory.

Madame Fodor was the operatic star of the evening as she was of the season, but Lucy got a 'featured' moment when, with Braham, she sang the National Anthem with two extra stanzas and was 'universally encored', says *The Times*.

Whatever doubts there may be about the instability of the Vestris marriage, there are none about the marriage of George IV and Caroline of Brunswick. Her Majesty, excluded from the Command Performance as she had been from the Coronation, attended the first performance of *Una Cosa Rara* on 18 May. Lucy appeared in this charming opera by Martin y Soler, with a libretto by da Ponte, but the Queen's visit stole the thunder and the notices, although commending the performances, were mainly concerned to report Her Majesty's presence.

28

Her Royal Highness   *His Royal Highness*

Princess Charlotte   *Prince Leopold*
of Wales

PRINCESS CHARLOTTE AND PRINCE LEOPOLD

A delightful picture (in the Victoria and Albert Museum) of two of the first royal and fashionable admirers of Eliza in their box at the King's. The Princess's enthusiasm was widely reported and established young Madame Vestris as a favourite of the 'haut ton'.

Una Cosa Rara stayed in the bill for the rest of the season, playing five times. The music was very popular. Kelly's *Reminiscences* report that the duet 'Pace, caro mio sposo', sung by Lucy, was 'completely the rage all over Ireland, England and Scotland for many years'; it was the first of many pieces with which Lucy was to be associated. The playbill for Kelly's Benefit on 3 June gives 'Songs by Madame Vestris' as one of the items. In the midst of Italian opera and an international company began Lucy's 'second string' career as a singer of songs, a talent that was to make her name and features nationally famous.

On 20 June 'M. et Mme Vestris' took a Benefit. It was, of course, as the wife of Armand Vestris that Lucy was included. She could not yet have expected one in her own right as a junior member of an opera company.

The Benefit system, whereby one or more performers 'benefited' from the proceeds of a performance specially planned to show them to advantage, had had many variations since it had begun as a special 'indulgence' to Mrs Barry in about 1686. By the beginning of the eighteenth century the particular indulgence had become general practice, raising an endless succession of problems, jealousies and disputes between actors and managers. Scrupulous managers were given the invidious task of negotiating and arranging for the times and kinds of benefits to be given to the actors they were signing up. Commercial managers, concerned solely with profits, were given the happy opportunity of

A Benefit Ticket. Although from a season some years after her first years at the King's, this ticket belongs here with other items connected with the same theatre. The artist's signature prevented tickets being sold by unauthorized persons and also meant that the artists themselves could keep a check upon how much they should be making on the evening. (It also meant that patrons would have a souvenir of the occasion, for it seems that they were allowed to keep these tickets, new designs being printed for each Benefit.)

keeping salaries low by the promise of all or some of the proceeds of a Benefit which cost the management nothing.

As far as actors were concerned, the gamble was worth taking. It was a lottery that might give them a bit of capital, or a clearance of debt. From the response to their Benefit – and they had to make all the arrangements and meet all expenses, sometimes even to the printing of the tickets – actors could also get some indication of their standing with the public, a consideration that could substantially affect subsequent dealings with London and provincial managers.

Performers of a certain standing had Benefits written into their contracts and Armand Vestris, both as performer and as Ballet Master, would naturally have been accorded one. Lucy had made her début at her husband's 1815 Benefit, and had made a success. It was therefore understandable that she should not only appear for, but share with Armand, the 1816 Benefit.

Among other things they chose *Le Nozze di Figaro* in which Lucy sang Susanna. It was a part that she was often to repeat, both in the Italian and the English versions, at this and other theatres. This first essay was received, according to *The Times*, with 'enormous approbation', but the reference is to the whole evening's entertainment. Although it was well within her acting powers, an overall view of her reception in the part over the next decades suggests that musically it was beyond her. Temperamentally and technically she must have grown into an excellent Susanna as she matured as a performer, but it is doubtful if her vocal apparatus was really of sufficient calibre to do full justice to Mozart.

But the evening was what was known as 'a bumper', so much so that the programme was repeated the following evening – an unusual compliment. And *Figaro* stayed in the bill, Lucy giving her Susanna five times in all before the season ended on 10 August. A 'brilliant and protracted season', according to the *Theatrical Inquisitor*, it was dominated by Mme Fodor; Lucy appeared some twenty-nine times, a respectable record for one still a novice. The gloomy prediction of the *London Chronicle* was confounded. The *Lady's Magazine* thought it a season which, 'if we might judge from the nightly appearance of the pit and boxes . . . must have been by far the most lucrative within our recollection. The opera, in its brightest day, never drew such a series of crowded audiences as during the season just brought to its close. The ballet, indeed, has reached an extraordinary pitch of elegance and maturity . . . '

Indebted as the season might have been to the ballet, it seems likely that Armand was indebted too heavily off the stage and had to serve a fashionable season in a debtors' prison, though other evidence suggests that bankruptcy and a swift departure for Paris resolved the immediate problem.

The year 1816 had introduced Eliza Lucy to two permanent facets of her life: professional success and financial embarrassment.

4

Comme il Faut

How long the resolution of their financial problems kept the Vestrises in London after the end of the season is an unanswered question. The winter of 1816 was a very hard one: 'the poor were hourly crying out for food' (Thomas Dibdin), and even the gentlemanly section of the debtor's prison must have been grim if Armand had to be there until the cold struck. Eliza Lucy, presumably, was with her family.

Eventually they went to Paris, probably some time in November, and Lucy made her Parisian début at the Théâtre Italien on 7 December.

Taking no chances, Vestris presented his wife to Paris in the same vehicle as had served so well for her in London: von Winter's *Il Ratto di Proserpina*. Once again the choice proved wise and the French were indulgent and susceptible to the European child.

Evidence concerning this Parisian début is from British publications. Time and many violent hours have left Parisian theatrical records, other than those of the Comédie-Française, sadly depleted, especially as regards the early decades of the nineteenth century. There is, in many cases, no evidence of what must have existed. The collection of material in the British Museum – officially somewhat neglected – relevant to theatre history of this time is also sadly depleted. But the catalogues at least record the sometime existence of those many items 'destroyed by bombing in the war'. The destructive agents in Paris were more numerous in kind and swifter in time.

The Parisian début in December 1816 was reported in an 'Extract from a letter from Paris' in the January 1817 issue of the *British Stage and Literary Cabinet*, whose six volumes survive because they were bound, and so presumably more safely housed than unbound periodicals. The extract is interesting on many counts, and seems to be the original source of the date and place of the début.

In 1821 when the same periodical published quite an extended memoir on Madame Vestris (then 'taking the town' in *Giovanni in London*), details of the Parisian début were taken from the extract. *Oxberry's Dramatic Biography* (1825–6), repeats these details and he in turn is taken up, though unacknowledged, by subsequent writers of memoirs, anecdotes and obituaries.

Because of this, and because there is apparently no French evidence to call upon, the extract is worth quoting at length:

'Most of the fashionable gentry who last season frequented the King's Theatre, must doubtless remember the appearance of this lady, in the character of Proserpina, in July 1815, and many who were drawn to the personal attractions will be rejoiced to hear that their little favourite had been received at Paris with all the applause to which such attractions entitle her. On the 7th of December last, she made her début, in the same character, at the Theatre Royal Italien; and she has since continued playing at that house with success. Many encomiums have been passed on her singing, which are by no means commensurate with the nature of her acquirements in that art. The French critics, like their English brethren, appear to have been deluded by her personal charms, and, to have mistaken a proficiency in one particular part for real musical genius.

'Madame Vestris is certainly gifted with a good voice, and she sings one or two songs in a pleasing manner: so, a man may have a good flute, and perchance he may by exhausting his breath and annoying his neighbour, contrive to play a tune or two upon it; but it requires something more to constitute real talent; and the performer, even with the aid of his good instrument, must eventually disgust by a too frequent repetition of the same air. So it is with Madame Vestris; at first, for a short time, she will please, but upon a more intimate acquaintance (I speak only of her musical powers) she will gradually become less attractive. The criticisms on her appearance have been universally favourable, but if the correctness of judgment on the part of the writers, is to be measured by their knowledge with regard to her origin, the result will not be very favourable to the fair actress herself, for it was gravely asserted that "Madame-Bartolozzi-Vestris, niece of the great engraver, is in every respect a *veritable Italienne*, since Venice gave her birth".'

It will be seen that Lucy obviously repeated her popular London reception, that she aroused sufficient interest to merit some remarks on her origin (however inaccurate) and that to the musically discerning it was apparent that success was mainly dependent upon the great personal charm and grace of the performer, as it had been in London.

There was also, for Parisians, the benefit of her experience of two London seasons, the second one offering chances and challenges that must have given her a far greater assurance in all that she did.

Such added assurance was desirable. Even more than in London the magic of the name Vestris would have conjured up an audience in Paris, but the audience at the Théâtre Italien was very different from that at the King's. The London 'fashionables' taking their sexual and sartorial cues from the Prince Regent, now George IV, were a very different audience, in temperament and influence, from the citizens by whose consent the brother of the late guillotined monarch occupied the Tuileries. The political motives that had brought about the coronation of Louis XVIII in 1814 had been resurrected after Waterloo, but the emotional confusion still lingering from the Revolution and the exploits of its child, Napoleon, chiefly influenced the moods and manners of theatre audiences.

Beyond the above extract which records popular success, there is regrettably no positive evidence of the two to three years that Lucy spent in Paris. Her activities on, but more extensively off, the stage are variously reported in later 'memoirs' and from comments by other actors who might have got their information from the lady herself.

There are accounts of visits, with or without Armand, to Italy for singing engagements in Naples — where Armand eventually settled as ballet master — and elsewhere, and there are accounts of her performing, not very often or very prominently, at the Théâtre Italien and also at other Parisian theatres, such as the Ambigu and the Opéra Comique.

For none of these things can French contemporary evidence be found, but it may be reasonably presumed that there was such experience for the young wife of Vestris during her stay in France. Something kept her abroad until the winter of 1819. She returned and took up an engagement offered her to perform the kind of parts that demanded some experience and address in lighter musical theatrical pieces. Her immediate success in London in 1820 suggests that she was no novice in such things. From this time too begin the references to certain mannerisms that were to become part of her stock in trade, the raw material from which she built a highly skilled technique of performing. These things will be seen to amount to an adroit and individual manipulation of considerable personal charm and magnetism; in sum, all that creates what the French term an *artiste* rather than an *actrice*.

There is a story — it was almost a tradition by the time it was entered unquestioned in the *Enciclopedia dello spettacolo* — that Lucy played at the Comédie-Française as Camille in *Les Horaces*, thus performing with Talma. While it is possible that, at a private party or a special performance elsewhere, Lucy and Talma were involved in a reading or an acted excerpt from the Corneille play, it is not possible that such a performance was ever given at the Comédie-Française. The Constitution of that theatre does not allow foreign players to perform in the national repertory.

34

A full perusal of the well-kept records of performances in the library of the Comédie (in the vain hope of finding that, as the wife of a Vestris, she might not have counted as a foreigner) was fruitless. Every performance and every performer is recorded for the years in question and Lucy's name never appears, either as Camille or as anything else. The odd surviving numbers of journals that might report any special gala or event during the years 1817 to 1819 where, by chance, she might have performed with Talma record nothing of the kind.

Little Pickle in 'The Spoiled Child'. Madame Vestris opened in this at Drury Lane on 5 December, 1820. The picture could equally well represent a French performer of either sex in the Boulevard Theatres of Paris at the time.

A late confirmation of negative research can be found in *Our Recent Actors* (1888), where Westland Marston, an eye-witness of so many of Madame's performances, and not unresponsive to her charm, comments that 'one cannot read the statement that she once played Camille in *Les Horaces*, to Talma, at the Théâtre Française, without a smile.' The smile must remain, though it must be remembered that the Madame Vestris he knew was a mature woman using an assured technique in pieces tailor-made to exploit that technique. There are hints in earlier work and in the last appearances that suggest other, if never developed, possibilities in the lady.

If research on the French years is unrewarding concerning the person and the performances of Madame Vestris, it is highly informative about theatrical usage and atmosphere that must have made a lasting impression, both consciously and unconsciously, on the future manageress.

The Napoleonic decree of 1809 which closed all but eight theatres in Paris had been ignored or forgotten by 1816. Always an impractical decree in a city whose people were more avid in their demands for theatrical entertainment than those in any other capital, it became both politically and socially necessary for the government of Louis XVIII to wink at the opening or re-opening of additional theatres.

The large popular audience was not inclined to listen to the classical repertoire, tragic or comic, offered by the 'official' theatres. Action and spectacle were expected from entertainment in less formal surroundings than the staid auditorium of the Comédie-Française. Words had been discredited, for the literate and illiterate, by persistent abuse since 1789. They would come back in some ten years, heralded by Victor Hugo's preface to *Cromwell* in 1827, setting the 'Romantic' form on all the indigest of the years between.

Meanwhile, the illiterate made up the most enthusiastic audiences in Paris, keeping most of the theatres open and encouraging the opening of more. Parisians seemed to think no day properly ended without a visit to the theatre – a phenomenon often commented upon by visitors to the city – for, since the early years of the Revolution, theatres had often been the equivalent of clubs, newspapers and political platforms. (Something of this spirit still survives in Parisian audiences especially during first performances of new and controversial plays, for example, *Les Mains Sales* and *Les Paravents*.)

Words, in such a time, and for such a theatre, were functional things, serving to explain or to underline action: unsubtle signposts in settings that left little to the imagination. Playwrights had no alternative to the use of language in these terms, for it was the only language that could be 'understood of the people'.

French theatrical language, in both comedy and tragedy, had developed from the patronage of the salons. It assumed literacy and a certain kind of education in its audience. French language, theatrical and other, in the new and swiftly changing climate was totally unconcerned with tradition or even with

36

establishing a new tradition: its aim was to catch the popular ear forcefully enough to evoke an emotive reaction that would assist a political end made effective before reason could intervene. With such language the new rulers set about the 'education' of the French people.

Subtle distinctions of diction or tone according to place and theme had no place in a language which was common to the market place, the Convention, the clubs, the Parisian *sections* and the theatre. All extremes are lies, and even untrained minds eventually became aware of the hollowness behind the sonorous tones of their demagogues and came to suspect all words. To have offered discourses and philosophical comment from the stage would have been to court disaster. To catch the eye and divert the imagination into exotic and irrelevant themes was to ensure a response that was as enthusiastic as it was relieved.

Le Trois Quartiers. The second of three scenes for this Parisian production of Picard's play. It shows Le Salon due banquier de la Chaussee d'Antin. Opening at the Theatre Franchais on 31 May, 1872, this example of a setting with a ceiling over a box-set plus openings into other areas is by no means the earliest French example. I was unable to find pictorial evidence from Eliza's years of residence in Paris, though there must be some if time allowed a proper search. This antedates the opening of the Olympic by a few years. It is from a small brochure published in Paris in 1827: '*Indications generales et observations* pour la mise en scene de *La Trois Quartiers* par Solome, directeur de la scene au Théâtre Français'. A detailed notice in *Le Courrier des Theatres* for 4 June, 1827 confirms the three-dimensional nature of the setting and the good use made of the rear part of the stage.

37

During the years that Lucy Vestris was in Paris melodrama was still dominated by its virtual founder, Guilbert de Pixerécourt. Nicknamed 'le Napoléon du boulevard' by his enemies and 'le Corneille du boulevard' by his admirers, he had evolved a theatrical formula that became international and that continues as an influence that some of its imitators as well as its detractors underestimate. It was perceptive jesting that prompted certain of his more educated friends and admirers to address Pixerécourt as 'Mon cher Shakespierécourt' and refer to his 'irritabilité Shakespierienne', for it could be argued that his sensitive reaction to the stimulus of his times and the theatrical conditions available to him, was as keen and as popular as Shakespeare's had been.

It is the working methods and theatres of Pixerécourt that are worth considering in connection with Lucy Vestris's life in the theatre. This is not to deny the influence of Pixerécourt melodrama-formulas on many of the plays in which she was to appear and that she was to present, but it is the manner rather than the matter of his work that was reflected in her theatrical usage and policy. She was to appear in some plays, such as *The Haunted Tower*, derived from the 'gothic' 'comédie héroïque' that preceded and prepared the way for Pixerécourt – theatrical manifestations of the vogue for the unnatural and the supernatural that still commands a following – but, as far as her English stage life was concerned, she did not appear in melodrama as evolved by Pixerécourt.

Although generally familiar, an outline of the Pixerécourt formula will be useful as both a reference and a starting point for considering methods of production.

Paul Ginisty, in his excellent study *Mélodrame*, (Paris 1910) analysed the 'laws' of Pixerécourt's formula most lucidly. What follows is my rough translation and adaptation of his analysis:

There are four essential characters: a highly virtuous and unhappy woman; a hero to protect her innocence: a simple comic; a tyrannical and treacherous persecutor of the heroine. The hero, with the help of the comic, contrives the deliverance of the heroine and justice is seen to be done on the villain. The dialogue is liberally sprinkled with moral maxims and sententious phrases. Generally speaking, there are three acts: the first dedicated to love, the second to strife and the third to the triumph of virtue and the punishment of vice. Opportunity is usually made for dancing at some point, and a fight is an indispensable part of the formula. Music links everything together, introducing characters, underlining situations, enhancing emotions and developing atmosphere.

From this outline two main points may be seen. Firstly, such a formula is an excellent theatrical device, capable of endless variation and improvisation; and secondly, music does both its own work and that of indisposed speech.

Pixerécourt was correct in claiming classical authority for his formula. For different reasons, usually practical and only later made theatrical and/or academic, dramatic writing and convention has devised formulas from which to work. Numbers and kinds of actors and numbers and kinds of audiences largely determined the formulas evolved in ancient, medieval and renaissance theatrical practices, both occidental and oriental. Pixerécourt, observing the kinds of boulevard acting that had evolved from the demands for lively images of the patriot virtues overcoming patrician vices, concocted a flexible formula on classical lines. He justified his insistence on dancing and combat as part of the formula by reference to ancient models. His formula is classical in another sense in that it led to and established a lasting theatrical form.

The uses and abuses of music in this and subsequent forms of melodrama are too familiar to need enlarging upon. Like the formula of which it is a vital part, it releases an audience from responsibility. The excitement of how? replaces the anxiety of what? in a story whose end is a foregone conclusion. The indulgence of 'feeling' replaces the exercise of 'thinking' in situations where music insinuates the heroine's virtue and makes obvious the villain's tyranny.

Ginisty does not refer to Pixerécourt's claim to classical inspiration, neither does he make one other important point insisted upon by Pixerécourt himself and well demonstrated by Willie Hartog in his book *Guilbert de Pixerécourt* (Paris 1913). There was not a single word or plot that could shock the young and innocent. He might have been 'king' of the 'boulevard du Crime' but sex and violence (as opposed to combat) never find a place in his writing. In his later life he was shocked and afraid of the new 'Romantic' drama with its themes of adultery, violence, incest and prostitution. He had considered it part of his mission to present noble and virtuous models for the education of the new society. He aimed for natural speech, a true and simple style, heartfelt sentiments, and a *mélange heureux* composed of amusement and interest and sensibility! But, at the head of things he insists on a subject *dramatique et moral*. For some three decades he achieved these aims but 'Helas! ce temps est passé!'

Classical models and educational precepts having been declared and a formula arrived at, Pixerécourt spent comparatively little time in writing his numerous plays. Far more time and energy were spent on the presentation, casting and acting, and especially in the synchronization of music and acting. He could not call upon the talents of the 'official' theatres of Paris for such trained and skilled actors would have rejected such texts as Pixerécourt had to offer. The 'rogue and vagabond' type of performer (*les enfants du paradis* they liked to call themselves: *les prisonniers du rêves* they were more accurately called), was the only one available. Schooled, for the most part, in showmanship, in exploitation rather than interpretation, many of these actors were versatile enough to perform with circuses, with mime troupes, as ballad singers, fortune tellers, etc., and the range of individual talent was as varied in degree as it was in kind.

The better of these performers had played in theatres such as the Émulation and the Ambigu, the latter with its mock-medieval auditorium, which had offered lavish spectacles made up of pantomimes, parades, fights: anything to entertain, like the old Roman circuses. Of Ribié, a theatrical impresario of the time, it was said that he invented 'monstrous posters and huge productions'.

Pixerécourt played the same game but played it more meticulously and, unlike his competitors, he had one invaluable asset: a mission that he believed in, that gave purpose and vitality to all that he did. He concerned himself with every aspect of a production. Having written the play, he auditioned the actors, approved (and often designed) settings, properties and costumes, took rehearsals and kept a sharp eye on the front of the house. More important perhaps was his insistence upon the accuracy of settings and costumes in relation to each other and to the whole ensemble. He demanded simple, clear speaking and sensitive interplaying between actors. Though some of his actors became 'stars', he never employed them as such. Rehearsals, he believed, were for the education of the actors. Performances were for the education of the audience.

That the educational process was intended to be as informative and instructional as it was moral and emotional may be seen in the care that was given to historical research. In October 1814 Pixerécourt wrote and presented *Charles le Téméraire ou Le Siège de Nancy*. The play was set at the time of the Battle of Nancy in 1471. Dedicated '*à la Ville de Nancy*', the text of the play in the *Théâtre Choisi* (Tme 2 1842) is preceded by (i) the Dedication, (ii) an address to the people of Nancy (iii) a '*lettre stratégique*' to Pixerécourt from Général Jomini, (iv) an historical preface with a map, and (v) a section on décor and costumes.

From quoted notices we learn that the greatest care was given to the presentation and the music (by Piccinni) of this dramatized history lesson.

Pixerécourt's definition of melodrama, in which music expresses silent thoughts, fears, and so on, has long replaced the original German definition, wherein music accompanies the spoken word, in the public mind. His work was, and is, imitated, as much from desperation as from admiration, by French playwrights. Throughout Europe, and across both the Channel and the Atlantic, his work was imitated, plundered and exploited. He found a theatrical situation where effects, musical and visual, had replaced denied and unwanted words, and he made the situation work for him, as theatrical pioneers always do.

Most of those who thought that they were imitating Pixerécourt made musical and visual effect an end rather than a means. They used the recipe but lacked the experience or the concern behind it. The will o' the wisp of effect for effect's sake, and supposed imitation rather than acknowledged adaptation, has often turned into a bankrupt dinosaur for theatrical ventures, and historians and commentators are inclined to visit the sins of the children upon the fathers. Praise is often accorded to the better recorded and more 'respectable' sections of the theatre (as if the theatre had any business being respectable at all!). While the reforms, in matters of presentation generally and of costuming particularly, initiated by Talma at the Comédie Française should not be underestimated, they were basically academic rather than theatrical reforms. None the worse for

GUILBERT DE PIXERÉCOURT

The King of the Boulevards —
looking the part; large eyes, sensual
mouth, obstinate chin; plenty of imagination and energy. Modesty would
have got him nowhere, which was
perhaps another lesson Madame took
from him?

Madame Vestris in 1820, when she
returned to London to be established
as a popular favourite. A 'very French'
portrait. The hair style, hair ornament,
the monocle on a neck-chain, and the
shawl worn 'abandonné' were all 'la
mode' in the Paris she left at the end
of 1819.

that, perhaps, except that being linked with the National Theatre and having official approval, they have been given a prominence that they could not command from the majority of the theatre-going public of their time. That majority was applauding and approving the work, both practical and theoretical, of Guilbert de Pixerécourt.

It is reasonable to suppose that Madame Vestris attended and perhaps performed in the minor or secondary theatres of Paris between 1817 and 1819. Later scurrilous comment infers that she became the centre of 'a certain sort of society'. Whatever, we are supposed to infer from that statement that 'society' must have been largely made up of theatrical acquaintances connected, through the Vestris family, with the 'established' theatres as well as the minor houses. We have seen that traditions and regulations prevented her appearance at the major theatres. Her subsequent career, both as performer and manageress, more than suggests that she was familiar with both the work and the workings of the minors.

It would have been a pleasure to have ended this section with some evidence that Madame Vestris appeared in a piece by Pixerécourt. But there is no such evidence. He was unusually sparse in his output during her time in Paris, probably because of the gout that increasingly tormented him.

The years 1816 to 1819 were not, however, without some work to show for them. On 28 November 1816, within a week of Lucy's début, *Le Monastère abandonné, ou La Malédiction paternelle* opened at the Gaité – a house long associated, like the Ambigu, with the success of Pixerécourt. The music was again by Alexandre Piccinni. It was well received by the public and press, despite disturbances on the first night by, among others, actors who thought that they should have been included in the cast. The play ran for 267 performances in Paris and was to have 396 more in the provinces. In other words, it was quite a hit.

A M. Pellissier, introducing the play in the *Théâtre Choisi* (tme III 1842), makes a strong case for the merits of the event of the season. In this play, if she saw it, young Madame Vestris might have observed 'an interesting, and a moral plot; dramatic action; sustained interest; lively sub-plots; well-drawn characters and a denouement appropriate and satisfying . . . In short, this piece brings together the chief merits of its kind'.

A set of characters, well assorted in age and kind but predominantly male, are involved in a story of paternal pride and stubbornness in a French Alpine setting. The day is specified, the twenty-eighth of July, the year left vague. The directions for each setting are specific and detailed. The old assortment of gothic doors and an ancient monastery in an exotic setting are tellingly placed as the curtain rises on a peasant dance. (Those who saw an Italian opera company at Drury Lane in 1950 might wonder (a) if much has changed on the continent since then, and (b) how it was ever taken seriously. But in all such things we are really in Alice's situation after she had gone through the looking glass: we tend to judge things as if our view was the logical one. The difference between the 1816 and the 1950 settings was in the theatrical education of the audiences.)

The description of the second act gives a vivid picture of an elaborate romantic setting. We are inside the monastery. *Nuit profonde*, but we may discern through the door the frightening and dangerous route across the mountain. Most importantly, this route is *practical*, strongly enough constructed to take the weight of several actors. Much of the tension of the dramatic situations depends upon this bit of scene-building.

For the final act we are in the chapel – *demi-ruinée*, of course. As the tension heightens the setting closes in, becomes more concentrated. The Alpine pride of the father is humbled; man-made authority, even in the name of God, must decay, etc., etc. The sets have spread over three acts what the camera will eventually cover in three minutes, but the overall intention and effect is the same.

On 12 August 1818, again at the Gaité, *La Chapelle de Paris, ou Le Témoin invisible* opened and ran for 157 performances in Paris. On 10 December the more famous *Le Belvédère ou La Vallée d'Etna* opened at the Ambigu-Comique and ran for 198 Parisian performances. *Le Belvédère* has some affinities with *Le Chien de Montargis, ou La Forêt de Bondy* produced in Paris in 1814 and given, in an adaptation by Henry Harris, at Covent Garden on 30 September 1815 under the title, *The Forest of Bondy, or The Dog of Montargis*, a play that Lucy could have seen after her first season at the King's.

Whether or not she saw this or the Parisian productions of Pixerécourt, she was living and working in a theatrical milieu where these things were the principal topics for discussion and practice. The subsequent career of Madame Vestris indicates more than a passing interest, or unconscious absorbtion, of the theatres and practices of the *théâtres de boulevard* and, more especially, of Guilbert de Pixerécourt.

The theatre is not a democratic institution. It needs its Napoleons and its revolutions, both of which carry the possibilities of triumph and disaster. The dangers inherent in the visual reforms of dictators such as Pixerécourt in France and Madame Vestris in Britain were already evident in the year of Eliza's Parisian debut. On 5 March, the *Journal de Dame et des Modes* wrote up a production in terms that were as relevant for the Lyceum in the 1850s as they were for the Paris of 1817. In both cases illness and overwork had slackened the hold of the ruling spirits of the popular theatre of their time.

'Paris ce 4 Mar 1817

Le premier acte d'Aureng-Zeb offre une décoration tres pittoresque; le second, que represente l'interieur d'un bazar, est un fort bein effet; et le troisiéme surpasse encore les deux autres par la magnificence. Les costumes sont aussi tres riches et tres-brillans (sic) Voila à-peu-près a quoi réduit le mérite de ce nouveau mélodrame de la porte St. Martin dont les veritables auteurs sont . . . le peintre et le machiniste.'

5

The Popular Dictate

Under the management of Robert William Elliston at Drury Lane, Lucy was given once again a fine opportunity to display her talents. Musically and dramatically she was effectively provided for and, ironically, the least deserving of the pieces in which she appeared, *Giovanni in London*, was to establish her as a theatrical 'star'.

Elliston was what is known in theatrical parlance as 'a pro'. As Charles Lamb put it, 'Wherever Elliston walked, sat, or stood still, there was the theatre.' He knew the tricks of his trade and applied them skilfully. Turning a deaf ear to those who deplored his influence on 'the Drama' and his self-exploitation, Elliston used his instinct for showmanship to bring the public – and the money – into Drury Lane.

The word 'instinct' is important here. As with anything that depends upon intuition, there is always a risk involved: a risk that, in showmanship, usually makes for an extreme result. There is either a great success or a dismal failure, neither of them really providing a true estimate of the work done. The successes survive longer, are well recorded and become part of the common body of information. The failures, often more numerous, quickly fade and the surviving evidence is scant.

Elliston made many blunders in his choice of authors, as in the case of Captain Barlow, for whose *Virginius* Elliston paid £200, only to find that it ran for three performances, even with Edmund Kean in the lead; and in assessing the public mood, as in the case of *Giovanni in Ireland*. The size of the man can be gauged as much by the misses as by the hits. He was never just half committed.

It was this instinct for showmanship, and especially his genius for unscrupulous advertising, that prevented and still prevents his being admitted among 'the gentlemen of the profession'. Like Reinhardt, Diaghilev and C. B. Cochran in more recent times, he was unashamedly a showman, following a much older and in many ways more honest theatrical tradition than those who profess to despise the publicity they court but are not as successful in catching.

As far as advertising is concerned there is a point that is relevant to the professional history of our heroine. While there are strong grounds for the censuring of unscrupulous advertising of any kind, the general condemnation of such things has much to do with the pretensions of the public and, in the theatre, with changes in the social aspirations of the audience. It is more pleasing to human vanity to be flattered, however falsely, into thinking that our opinion is of consequence and our presence is desirable. The exclusive audiences of the Restoration, which moved into the opera house as the rising middle class moved into the theatres, were literally in a master–servant relationship with the actors. (The surviving dependence of the opera season upon advance subscriptions and permanent box-holders has already been noted.) But, as audiences grew more popular, the audience/master–actor/servant relationship became a game that both sides agreed to play. It made a living for the actors, whose trade makes them, as Hazlitt put it, 'honest hypocrites', and gave the audiences the opportunity of doing their own bit of acting.

To acknowledge this fact is not to deny the social advantages of the whole performance, for life runs more pleasantly on assumptions than on realities: bitterness is disciplined and thought given scope.

When she went into management Madame Vestris was to exploit the audiences' pretensions quite as much as Elliston. But she was to do it more elegantly, more subtly, guided by the divining-rod of her own social and feminine pretensions. The capacity for wonder – for wanting to say 'ah' as the fireworks went up – was the public propensity that Elliston was still able to exploit. Madame's London public, growing ever more cosmopolitan, were, paradoxically, more introvert. Their capacity for pretence was the propensity to be exploited.

Elliston, autocratic, often pompous and self-willed and a heavy drinker, was sufficiently an actor to be able to understand the foibles and the qualities of other actors (something that men like Macready never did or wanted to do.) Whatever one may think of the professional policies of such men, they are usually good managers to work for, for personal pretentiousness can usually be borne better than artistic pretentiousness. Unlike many managers who are more honoured in remembrance, Elliston engaged a company for their talents as individuals rather than as a setting to make him individual. (He had begun his Drury Lane management in 1814 with Edmund Kean's *Lear*.) For the subsequent career of Madame Vestris, as well as the subsequent development of the theatre, this was an important consideration.

Elliston was in his middle forties when he engaged Madame Vestris, though it is probable that they had met earlier. One of the best lovers on the stage (according to Leigh Hunt), unsurpassed as an actor of personable rogues, Elliston must have appreciated both the personal and the professional charms of young Eliza Lucy. He certainly gave her every opportunity and she justified his choice in a strong company.

On Saturday evening, 19 February 1820, Vestris opened as Lilla in *The Siege of Belgrade*. Once again, and as with so many things in which she appeared, the piece must be looked at in the context of the time and for its relevance to later developments.

The Siege of Belgrade, first brought out at Drury Lane in 1791, is a hodge-podge of a work on the printed page. To a libretto by James Cobb, Stephen Storace composed some music and compiled the rest from other composers, notably Martin y Soler. Always a popular piece with the public, it was evidently an agreeable piece to be involved with. Kelly (vol. 2) says that 'there was a good deal of beautiful original music in it' and William Parke, from a long experience as a theatre musician, says of *The Siege of Belgrade* that it was 'The first stage musical performance of moment to be given at our National theatres.' Its commercial value may be judged by the fact that the author received a copyright of £1,000. Then as now, the really big money was in a popular musical success.

George Raymond, in his *Memoirs of Elliston* records:

'On Saturday, the 19th February, Madame Vestris made her entrée on the English stage, at Drury Lane, in the part of Lilla, in *The Siege of Belgrade*. This lady was introduced by Corri. For the first few nights Madame Vestris did not appear to make any great impression on the audience, but, before the end of the season, she acquired that popularity, which she has since maintained undiminished.'

Whether or not she made an impression on the audience, the reviews on the Monday morning were enthusiastic. After noting that she was 'a splendid addition to the company' *The Times* continued:

'We remember her first at our own Italian theatre, when her chaste style, delicate expression, and superior perception of the beauties of Mozart, attracted the notice and admiration of all lovers of music . . . If we must hesitate to place her in the first rank of the profession, it is because her command of its mechanical difficulties is less complete than is required, her shake failing sometimes in brilliancy, and her execution in distinctness; but in all that constitutes the soul of the art, in grace, pathos, and just intonation, we may associate her with the greatest names of the day . . . Like many other singers in whom feeling and sensibility predominate, Madame Vestris in passages that have no merit in themselves, becomes careless of their execution; but when elevated by a passage she admires, and finds consonant to her own taste, she acquires a liquid sweetness, and enthusiastic force of expression, that must be numbered among the most delightful sensations the art can communicate.'

One member of the audience was certainly impressed:

' . . . I dined at Colliers and went to Drury Lane for the first time this season. I was better placed than usual. Though Braham's growing old he had lost none of his fascination in singing some two or three magnificent songs in

The Siege of Belgrade. But my admiration he shared with a new actress or rather singer, who will become I have no doubt, the darling of the public – a Madame Vestris – she is by birth English and her articulation is not that of a foreigner, but she looks, walks and gesticulates so very French that I almost thought myself in the Théâtre Feydeau. She has great feeling and naïveté in her acting and I am told she is a capital singer – I only know that she delighted me.' (Henry Crabb Robinson)

The periodicals gave more restrained, considered notices, and offered some advice:

' . . . though the popular dictate is not always to be relied upon, we think in this instance it well bear the test of confirmation. Though we cannot pay Madame Vestris, at this moment, the meed of proper attention, we are anxious for her professional welfare, and feel considerable apprehension that her efforts have been injured by some Italian teacher of English music, who neither knows nor cares about the due degree of accuracy with which her songs should be invested. Should this be the case, we intreat her to throw off the bondage of such worthless tuition, and appeal, if necessary, to the lessons of a more suitable master.' (*Theatrical Inquisitor*)

'She is a pretty, little, lively woman, with a peculiarly full-toned mellow voice, and no inconsiderable degree of science. We cannot, however, say that the feeling which some of the newspapers said she displayed in the execution of her songs, was very apparent to us. Her acting was as good or rather better than her singing . . . The house was excessively full, and she was more than once encored.' (*British Stage & Literary Cabinet*)

On 5 April Madame Vestris opened in the title role (which, however, is not the leading role) of *Artaxerxes*, a somewhat compressed version of Arne's opera. It had held the stage – defiantly British when Italian operatic pieces and singers were in fashionable demand – for some fifty years.

The role of Artaxerxes was written for a male soprano, and its 'moment' was the song 'In infancy our hopes and fears'. Madame Vestris was a popular success in this air, which she often sang as a number on its own during the next two decades, as well as in revivals of the opera.

The Times was kind: 'The song of "In infancy our hopes and fears" as given by her, was chaste and touching and may almost be adduced as a specimen of the true style of simple singing. The experience in recitative acquired by Madame Vestris in the Italian style, gave her a great advantage over the other performers . . .'

So which kind of teacher was she to choose?

The *Theatrical Inquisitor* was less kind but possibly more accurate, and, if pompously, makes a shrewd comment on the song:

'... the song ... does not afford a fair estimate of the singer's ability. It is too intrinsically congenial with the vulgar sense of things, to be either coolly received, or dispassionately considered; the audience catch at even the symphony, and – "no matter how it be in tune, so it make noise enough" –its

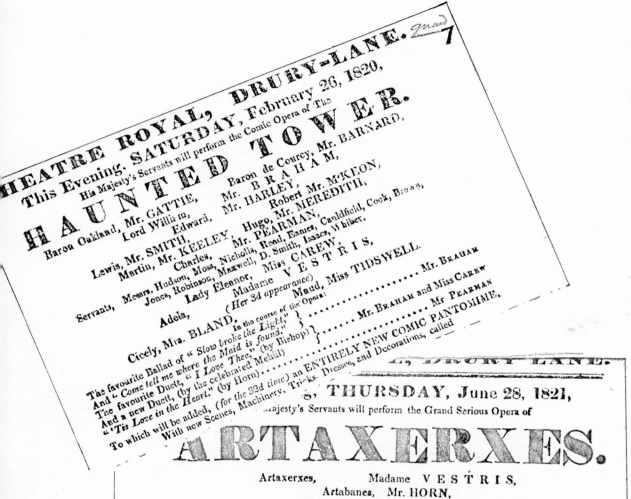

The Interior

The Exterior

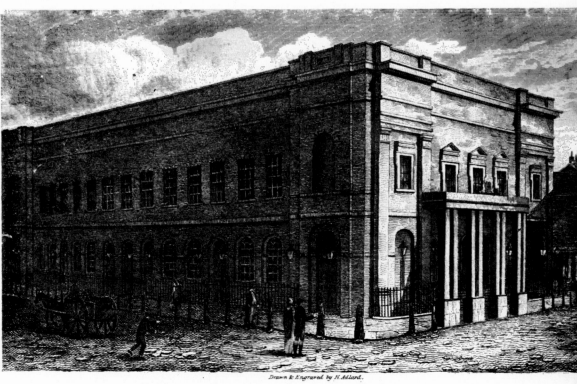

Drawn & Engraved by H. Adlard.

MADAME VESTRIS AS ARTAXERXES

The name part in his adaptation of the opera by Arne gave Vestris one of her 'standard numbers': the aria 'In infancy our hopes and fears'. Her rich contralto voice combined with her assurance and fine deportment made her a natural choice for roles originally written for male singers with a soprano and contralto range, the castrati for example.

repetition is sure to be vociferously demanded . . . Her singing is simplicity itself, for she cannot manage the most transient shake, or the slightest cadenza; and this we deeply regret, as there is a rawness in her higher notes which the greatest dexterity is wanted to conceal.'

One other notice is worth quoting, for it gives a more extended impression of her French style, and of her appearance in the part. The *London Chronicle* wrote:

> ' . . . The opera was understood to be brought out for the display of Madame Vestris, but it was probably for the display of her person, which, robed as it was in silk and gold of Persia, and surmounted by the handsomest of turbans, looked extremely riant and regal . . . she sang . . . with great purity, and a degree of expression unusual on the English stage. Hers has been a foreign school, and her style exhibits the grace of her model . . . In the recitatives she gave additional evidence of her foreign tuition for she modulated them with uncommon clearness, force, and truth. Her action was stately, and her aspect and performance, in general, entitled her to more than the habitual favour shown to the young and fair. Her voice is almost a soprano, but it has considerable compass . . . Its tone is, however, more French than Italian.'

Both *The Siege* and *Artaxerxes* were standard vehicles for Madame Vestris for many years to come. The reservations about her voice were also to recur, especially in reviews that were not written immediately following her performances. In these cases, where reflection had tempered the impact of an adroit and charming performer, there are two views that predominate — apart from the occasional taunts prompted by ignorance and/or envy: one that Madame Vestris had a good voice marred by Italianate training, and perhaps too little of any training, and too early a bringing forward to the public; and the other that there was no exceptional voice, but by training and skilful technique it was made to appear much better than it was.

There might well be something in both these theories. The facts are that she did appear between 1820 and 1830 in some twelve operatic pieces, including works by Rossini, Mozart and Arne, as well as in ballad operas. A song, or songs, were frequently offered in the course of evenings when plays filled the bills, and songs were given by Madame Vestris at concerts at Covent Garden and Vauxhall.

Mastery of the Italian language was, of course, a great asset at a time when Italian opera, and Italian librettos to opera from any country, were almost exclusively performed in London. But this, supported by musical skill, would not account for the amount of work Madame Vestris was given in this line.

A light contralto, well projected (we have to remember the size of those theatres she sang in) and intelligently used, is probably an impartial summing up of the available evidence on her voice. Whatever her limitations from the operatic point of view, there can be no doubt of how much she learnt about the 'putting over' of a number, about breath control, phrasing and enunciation, from working on Rossini and Mozart with the leading singers of the day, and these things she also applied to her more popular songs and shows.

Having opened in *Artaxerxes* on the Wednesday, Lucy showed the public a very different side on the Saturday. Elliston revived and adapted a two-act piece originally written by David Garrick in 1758, called *Harlequin's Invasion*. Elliston renamed it *Shakespeare versus Harlequin* for the 1820 production. Garrick had written it to ridicule the taste for pantomime which was depriving Shakespeare – and therefore Garrick – of audiences. William Boyce wrote the music, setting, among other songs, Garrick's 'Hearts of Oak' – an item from an eighteenth-century piece of theatrical nonsense that was to be part of the daily routine of Royal Naval barracks throughout the world.

The 1820 version takes the same outline: Harlequin arrives in England, is eventually defeated and 'King Shakespeare' restored.

Garrick's widow attended the First Night. *The Times* wrote: 'Mrs. Garrick, relict of the late David Garrick, Esq., visited Drury Lane Theatre on Saturday night, to witness the performance of the "Broad-farcical Pantomimical Drama, Shakespeare versus Harlequin", which was written by her celebrated husband. She was handed from her carriage to her box by Mr. Elliston.'

The same paper, the following Monday, gave as the main source of interest the variety of opportunities that the piece gave the excellent cast. It had little time for the piece, declaring it overlong and reporting unrest in the audience in the second half. Mrs Garrick's reaction is not recorded.

The Times responded happily to Madame Vestris, 'whose acting and singing all must acknowledge delightful . . . [She] is transformed into Columbine, and exhibits gracefully in one scene as a dancer'.

The character of Dolly Snip was the kind of bright, pert and versatile soubrette that was to be Lucy's most popular rôle for the next decade. In such parts she introduced many popular songs, including some still heard today (see page 73).

The periodicals, ungushing as ever, nevertheless approved of at least the acting of Dolly Snip:

'. . . though our opinion of her vocal poverty is rather ratified than removed, [she] evinced a spirit and a naïveté in Dolly Snip which were highly captivating, and if cultivated with zealous attention, will render her one of the most pleasing actresses it has ever been our enjoyment to applaud.' (*Theatrical Inquisitor*)

'. . . But, after all, the best attraction in the piece is the acting of the ladies, who perform the parts of Miss Snip and Miss Chitterlin, Madame

Vestris and Miss Povey, whose quarrelling scene is alone worth going to see. We know not which to prefer, the quality airs of Miss Snip – her inimitable tosses of the head – the careless grace "beyond the reach of art" with which she replies to the invitation of her lover to take a walk, "I don't know that I shall ever walk again", or the delightful spite of Miss Chitterlin who tries to provoke her.' (*New Monthly Magazine*)

It had a reasonable run. On the ninth performance, 'After the tragedy [Brutus] an apology was made by Russell for Mme. Vestris, who being *suddenly* attacked by a hoarseness begged permission to omit the songs usually sung by her in the pantomime.' (*British Stage & Literary Cabinet*)

Among those acting with Lucy in this pantomime was William Oxberry, already referred to. It is appropriate to mention here, in the chapter concerned with Elliston's management, Oxberry's biased assessment of that manager. *The Times* obituary for Elliston (1831) quoted Oxberry at length but added:

'We have omitted much that seemed to proceed from personal enmity, but still it will be seen that the above is from no friendly hand. Oxberry, most likely, had received some affront from Mr. Elliston, as manager of Drury Lane. No person has filled that situation within our remembrance, who did not temporarilly incur much odium in the profession.'

A few days later there was a letter from 'T.W.' refuting Oxberry and citing instances of Elliston's humanity and kindness.

Lilla in *The Siege*, Artaxerxes, and Dolly Snip proved for Elliston that he had picked a winner in Lucy Vestris, and he exploited this asset to the full in reviving *Giovanni in London*. It was during Elliston's management of the Olympic Theatre that this piece, called *Giovanni Let Loose* for the first four performances, was first produced, on Boxing Day 1817. The 'comic extravaganza entertainment' was brought out for 'Mrs Gould, late Miss Burrell'. She was a lady, according to Oxberry, 'of such masculine habits, as to bear the cognomen of "Joe Gould" throughout the country.' Perhaps this point lent a spicy novelty to the more usual reason for getting a woman to play a man's part at that time – the display of female legs.

Giovanni in London is a rather poor, if elaborate, romp on the theme of Don Giovanni. The idea – that Giovanni is sexually too hot for Hell and returns to a wickeder place, London, there to be redeemed by a good woman – is promising, and Planché or Gilbert might have made much of it. But beyond quite a clever use of well-known operatic airs and songs, the text stands mainly as a tribute to Madame Vestris for the success that her personality made of it.

For it was what would now be termed a 'smash hit'. It was part of the London theatrical scene for some three years and, although Vestris was not always in it, it was her success in it that established the slight piece.

A Portrait of Madame Vestris

The Green-Room, Drury Lane Theatre. Madame Vestris, like her fellow performers, still in costume for *Giovanni in London*, receiving some of her fashionable admirers

With the decline of Christmas pantomime, fewer and fewer people can be made aware of the effect of such travesty playing in the hands of a skilled actress. Probably the last to make her début in the line of Principal Boy actresses in the traditional style was the late Hy Hazell in *Babes in the Wood* at the Princes (now Shaftesbury) Theatre, London in 1950. Dorothy Ward, Fay Compton and Evelyn Laye were the great ones during the twenties, thirties and forties of this century.

Asked once how she managed to overcome the drawback of having most of her Principal Girls taller than herself, Miss Fay Compton replied, 'Authority, dear, authority.' Authority backed by projection, timing, deportment and an infinite sense of fun; of being part of the hoax and yet commenting upon it. These are the things that sustain and redeem a success in such a part, despite the elements of sensation and titillation that obviously drew a certain section of the town to *Giovanni in London*.

The best in this kind of travesty playing can provide a clue to the success of the boy players of the Elizabethan and Jacobean theatre. It shares with these, and with oriental male actors of female roles, the offering and accepting of a ritual, beyond the sexual element and profoundly theatrical.

There is no suggestion here that either Elliston or Vestris reasoned in such terms about the phenomenon. Elliston saw a money-spinner for his new actress in his old vehicle and she was persuaded to risk it. A risk it was. Society had applauded her début in a highly respectable and acceptable opera. Whatever her private life, Lucy's professional life had so far been within the bounds of propriety. She had appeared only at the King's and at Drury Lane, in opera and plays with music.

She was now asked to appear as a man in a piece that had been associated, just three years earlier, with a notorious actress. While it is true that the year was 1820, when the Prince Regent had just become George IV, there were certain things that ladies and gentleman 'didn't do', at least not publicly, and that might adversely affect their professional and social careers. Playing in *Giovanni* might, for example, have prevented Madame Vestris's appearing again at the King's, and at this stage of her career she was considered, and probably considered herself, as much a singer as an actress.

Raymond reports in the *Memoirs*:

'In May of this season, Elliston produced the most popular and successful afterpiece of his whole management, *Giovanni in London*. Madame Vestris, who was so attractive in the principal character, undertook it, in the first instance, with much reluctance; but the flattering reception which she nightly received, soon reconciled her to it, and constituted a great portion of that fame which has since been her freehold.'

That she decided to take the risk was probably due to a mixture of Elliston's powers of persuasion and of her own faith in her professional integrity, quite apart from financial considerations. Raymond records that the nightly half-price receipts, that is, the reduced entrance fee charged to those who came to the theatre just for the afterpiece, for *Giovanni*, averaged very nearly one hundred pounds.

The risk paid off, in every sense of the word. That it might not have done is evident from the review that appeared in the June 1820 issue of the *Theatrical Inquisitor*: 'We pity Madame Vestris, from every consideration from which her performance of Don Giovanni has been attended . . . we feel bound to treat it as a part which no female should assume till she has discarded every delicate scruple by which her mind or her person can be distinguished.'

Ever po-faced, but inclined to be indulgent and hopeful after *The Siege*, the *Inquisitor* becomes downright unpleasant and even threatening: 'Madame Vestris, it is true, from her mediocre talent, and moderate estimation, can possess but little or that influence which more lofty actresses are permitted to assert; but we counsel her to solicit the exemption she cannot command, and rather do anything than adhere to a task that is fraught with viler consequences than we shall venture to describe.'

Although written about her performance two years later in April 1822, Robinson's comment on Madame Vestris as the Don may serve as a counter to this in setting the competence of the actress against the innuendos of the vehicle: ' . . . Mrs Vestris is a fascinating creature and renders the Don as entertaining as possible and at the same time there is an air of irony and mere wanton and assumed wickedness which renders the piece harmless enough.'

Little noted by the daily papers – it was, after all, intended as no more than an afterpiece to 'send them home happy' – the public seem to have decided that Giovanni was what they wanted and the piece was given for the remaining thirty-five nights of the season, a phenomenal run for the time.

There is another circumstance that assisted the success of *Giovanni in London*. The risk referred to as far as Vestris was concerned had not been considered by Elliston as a problem for himself. His money was on the main item on the evening's bill, the *Virginius* already referred to. Edmund Kean starring in what seemed to Elliston a sure-fire vehicle for 'the Drury tragedian' made the success of the afterpiece desirable but not crucial. The swift collapse of his hopes for *Virginius* gave the manager a desperate interest in, and the public an expectantly hopeful anticipation of, the rest of the bill.

Her success made Vestris's name a household word. Rhymes, songs and tales about her (some of them of such a nature that they might well have been some of the 'viler consequences' that the *Inquisitor* warned against) were circulated and sung, and Tom Duncombe records that 'she was so much the rage that a modeller made a capital speculation by selling plaster casts of "*la jambe de Vestris*"'.

George Raymond was right in claiming for *Giovanni* the success that gave Vestris her 'subsequent freehold' in the theatre and with the public. She was not the first or the last performer to owe her fame to a vehicle that she probably despised and would rather not have been connected with. Many of her subsequent choices of plays, for acting and presentation, were probably to some extent determined by her desire to replace the public's association of her name with a *succès de scandale* with a more artistic image. She was to be persuaded to appear in one more such piece, *Giovanni in Ireland* (1822), a deserved flop, but that was the last of the lucrative but vulgar business.

Breeches, however, she did not abandon, but stepped into them for more commendable offerings, and the famous legs were to be displayed to advantage in mythological settings and comedies from the French.

The Drury Lane season ended on 8 July, and Vestris opened the summer season at the Haymarket on Saturday 22 July as Macheath in *The Beggar's Opera* – an almost inevitable choice in the circumstances.

'Madame Vestris personated the gay Captain with considerable éclat: she is a good actress, a respectable singer, and a pretty woman; but much of the force and energy is lost by its being represented by a female,' said the *British Stage & Literary Cabinet*, and that was the general reaction of considered criticism of her in the part over the next decade. On the other side there were those who were happy for any excuse to see the pretty woman. In 1824 The *Mirror of the Stage* records the popular reaction: 'Madame sings the music as well as any woman can sing it, and plays as well as any woman can play a MAN . . . "But then, Sir," says an old greyheaded dotard by the side of us "only think of her leg, Sir – there's shape – there's symmetry! Bravo! – Encore!" – And so goes the world.'

Madam Vestris's Legs.

Tune—" *Betsy Baker.*"

HAVE you heard about this piece of work
  All over London town, sir ?
It is all about an actress,
  A Lady of renown, sir ;
The case was heard at Marlborough-street,
  The truth I will tell you now, sir,
A man had stole the Lady's legs,
  Which caused a pretty row, sir.

CHORUS

Some villian stole my Lady's legs,
  We hope he will get justice,
Handsome just above the knee,
  The legs of Madam Vestris.

Mr. Papara, a gentleman,
  Of merit was, O fags, sir,
Went unto the Magistrate,
  About a pair of legs, sir ;
He says, kind sir, the legs were mine,
  And now I do want justice,
They were modelled from a Lady's legs,
  Whose name is Madam Vestris.

Then sir, says the laughing Magistrate,
  I now must ask you, whether
The legs of Madam Vestris,
  Could not be kept together.
I swear the handsome legs were mine,
  And hope you'll give the thief a dose,

Marlborough-Street Office, Thursday :
For it was not in my power,
  To keep the legs together close.

I am the man that made the legs,
  The model, sir, you now may see,
I made them like my Lady's own,
  Exactly just above the knee ;
And your worship must commit the man
  And I must ask you, whether
'Twas possible that I could keep,
  Such handsome legs together.

Oh ! then says the worthy Magistrate,
  This case I plainly see, sir,
The Legs of Madam Vestris,
  Are yours above the knee, sir ;
And I shall send the thief to jail,
  In spite of wind and weather,
When the trial does come on,
  Bring my Lady's legs together.

Now when the trial does come on,
  It's true what I report, sir,
You will laugh to see my Lady's legs,
  Come hopping into court, sir.
If the thief did steal my Lady's legs,
  I hope he will get justice,
Was it possible that it could be,
  The legs of Madam Vestris ?

Printed by T. BIRT, No. 10, Great St. Andrew-Street, Seven Dials.

As 'Maria Darlington' in *A Roland for an Oliver*, one of the characters regularly played by Madame Vestris during the 1820s, in a play that was a popular favourite.

Vestris played Macheath again in November at Drury Lane, and the reviewers made more or less the same points. The receipts went up £300 for the performance. The success spread beyond London and she established herself for a wider public between the London seasons of 1820. Manchester and Liverpool were personally and financially rewarding. The breeches parts, Giovanni and Macheath, were chiefly in demand. Extra prices were offered in the hope of a seat and the provincial managers were delighted. The manager at Manchester presented his star with roses 'out of which dropped a purse containing thirty guineas'. Smitten in the heart as well as braced in the pocket by the lady? The reply was teasing: 'Dear Sir, – I will play Cowslip tonight and tomorrow will take Don Giovanni. You are a queer fellow – I wish to oblige you. – Vestris.'

For the twenty-seven nights of her Liverpool engagement, Vestris seems to have given only her Macheath. Perhaps the resources, scenic and mechanical, could not rise to the boat on the Styx, the devil effects and the firework finale of *Giovanni in London*, or perhaps Vestris did not think that what could be offered was adequate. Perhaps, too, Liverpudlians were less inclined that Mancunians to respond to London taste. *The Beggar's Opera*, although set in London, did not have London in the title. More significantly, it was an established and popular piece, thus providing scope for making comparisons with earlier performers, a favourite and coveted habit of audiences then as now.

Madame Vestris seems to have stood the test of comparison. 'She was', says the *Gossip of the Country*, 'placarded on every wall and her likeness stuck in every window of every print shop. The town rang with her praises and for twenty-seven nights Macheath was received with cheers.'

Vestris ended the year 1820 back at Drury Lane. Almost twenty-four years old, she had had experience of many facets of work in the theatre. Beginning as the newest novelty for a fashionable and exclusive audience in the rarefied atmosphere of an international opera and ballet company, she had within five years (three of them away from the London stage) become a national and a popular performer who could negotiate her professional future, operatically and theatrically, as she chose.

6

The Freehold of Fame

By the end of 1820 Madame Vestris was an established theatrical figure in England. She had 'arrived', but she was far from considering herself as settled. During the next decade she sustained and increased her standing as a popular favourite, as much by her professionalism and hard work in a wide range of material as by her personal magnetism and the ceaseless interest that she provided for the gossip columnists and rumour-mongers.

Marriage had encouraged extravagance; Paris had defined taste: for both these propensities Madame Vestris was famous and both of them are expensive. From what is known of her professional earnings – her salaries at the King's Theatre, her approximate profits from Benefit performances, etc. – and from what may be conjectured concerning the various monetary gifts, and other benefits, from friends, lovers and admirers, Eliza Lucy could have lived pretty well, and supported her family, from either source. Despite professional frustrations and annoyances these were good years for her personally and financially. Even before her father's death in 1821, it is probable that she was the real breadwinner for the Bartolozzis. This she continued to be even to the extent of supporting her nieces after the death of her sister Josephine. For herself, money provided beautifully appointed houses in fashionable districts, a carriage, a numerous train of dressmakers, milliners, glovers, and shoemakers.

Theatrical clothing was, for the most part, the responsibility of the performer; at least, leading players often made it their responsibility rather than being obliged to appear in what was offered, a phenomenon not unknown today. The frequent reference to both the appropriateness and the elegance of Madame Vestris's stage clothing makes it obvious that she always made herself responsible for her appearance, thus beginning her ideas of 'educating an audience'.

Professionally, the decade involved so many kinds of performing for Madame Vestris that a chronological account would make confusing and tiresome reading. In most of these years there were appearances by Madame Vestris as an actress and as a singer, as well as a combination of both, and a clearer picture can be given by separate considerations of her work in various kinds.

OPERA

It was as an opera singer that Madame Vestris was introduced to the public in London and in Paris, and she had been well received. Her family background was a musical one and it is probable that she shared with them the thought that if she went into the theatre, it would be on the operatic and musical side.

She doubtless gathered from the notices on and following her début at the King's that it was her person and personality that had taken the town rather than her singing, which had been praised for its potential rather than its achievement. But, even when it became obvious that she was a singing actress rather than an acting songstress, she seems to have been reluctant to give up operatic work, unwilling indeed to make a definite decision in favour of one sphere or another.

By intuition and inclination she was a woman of the theatre, with an exceptional flair for knowing and managing her audience. She had an ear for a good tune and was well aware of the value of music as an asset for a performer, but there is no evidence of her having had any real interest of concern for opera; she seems, indeed, to have considered an opera as a series of opportunities to put over songs.

But opera at the King's was 'respectable' in a way that acting was yet to become and, perhaps more significantly, it was fashionable in a way that acting, even at Drury Lane and Covent Garden, was not. It was to be a decade or so before Madame Vestris was able to find a métier that gave scope for her talents and that attracted respectable and fashionable audiences. It may well be that she kept up her association with opera and the 'fashionables' in order to have the cachet of being offered contracts by the King's Theatre. With the popular, and vulgar, success of *Giovanni in London*, such an association was especially valuable to her, valuable enough to fight for. The *British Stage and Literary Cabinet* for April 1821 reports: 'Madame Vestris, by an arrangement with Mr. Elliston, concluded after much bickering, is to sing alternatively here [at the King's] and at Drury Lane. We cannot agree in opinion with those who think the Italian stage is her proper sphere.'

Eliza herself probably agreed with the *Theatrical Inquisitor*, which wrote: '. . . she will lose none of her great popularity by appearing on the stage where she was first heard.'

These 'arrangements' were made every year from 1821 to 1828, with the exception of 1826. They were always difficult to negotiate, for they meant that seasons had to be planned, by both the opera and the playhouse, to accommodate one actress. (A theatrical situation quite different from today's, where the run of a single play for each company makes such an arrangement impossible except for those companies which run repertories, such as the Royal Shakespeare Company and the National Theatre. In 1948 Robert Helpmann appeared as an actor at Stratford-on-Avon and as a dancer at Covent Garden in the same season.) The fact that managements were prepared, even if they had to be 'bickered' into it, to make such arrangements is evidence of Madame Vestris's drawing power in both operatic and dramatic pieces.

Quite apart from the social éclat of appearing on the stage of the King's Theatre, working conditions were much more agreeable in that building. She was treated as a Vestris; her contracts were drawn up in French; she was accorded, or might command, the symbols of her status as a leading member of the company: for example, a dressing room to herself and a proper allocation of wax candles rather than tallow.

Admiring members of her audience at the King's, especially the males, could, by their breeding and taste as well as by their means, offer Madame Vestris agreeable tokens of their esteem from ephemera such as flowers and supper parties to the more lasting evidence of trinkets and even jewels.

Conditions were as different as were the localities at Drury Lane and Covent Garden, and Madame Vestris must have looked forward to her nights at the King's, however gratifying the popular applause must have been at the other theatres. Actors are a more numerous species than singers (or, to be more accurate, more people are able to pass themselves off as actors), which means that backstage rivalries and jealousies, if not more intense, tend to be more numerous and lasting at a playhouse than at an opera house.

Understandably, but no less regrettably, the young and successful Madame Vestris often took her cue from the less admirable behaviour of the international prima donnas, of both sexes, who appeared at the King's. Her professional complaints, usually justified, were presented and argued in a manner that she might have thought 'fashionable' but was certainly vulgar. She employed the same tactics with the acting managers and companies from time to time, and occasionally with the audience.

Foolish behaviour of this kind deprived her of the experience of working with a singer who shared many of her more mature theories concerning staging. Giovanni Velluti came to London in 1825. He was among the last of the castrati, a type of singer that had been much in demand throughout Europe during the eighteenth century. Ebers, the manager of the King's, had been delighted to be able to get the services of Velluti when, owing to illness, the 1825 season looked like closing disastrously early.

It is possible that Velluti had, as a boy, been castrated by mistake or by a clerical trick, a circumstance that might well have led him to exploit his later

65

King's Theatre
Engagement

Entre nous soussignés Mons. John Ebers Entrepreneur et Administrateur du Théâtre du Roi, demeurant n° 27 Old Bond Street, d'une part —

Et Madame Lucia Vestri, artiste dramatique, demeurant n° 1. Curzon Street May Fair —

Sommes convenus de ce qui suit, savoir —

Que moi, Lucia Vestri, m'engage avec le dit Mons. John Ebers en le spécialité de chanteuse, pour les Opéra Séria, Sérieux Buffa, Oratorio, concert, concerts et Bénéfices qui seront donnés, par le dit Théâtre ou salle y appartenans, d'après les ordres du dit Mons. John Ebers, ou de son Délégué, comme aussi de me trouver aux heures indiqués, et toutes les répétitions qui seront convoqués, et contribuer en tout et par tout au bien être de l'Entreprise me conformant à-présent aux règlemens du Théâtre de la Sala et de Son Camerino. —

Et moi, John Ebers promets et m'engage de payer ou faire payer à Madame Lucia Vestri la somme de sept cent livres sterlings en trois payemens égaux, savoir ... de puiser après la vingtième Représentation, le deuxième après la ...

le dix Novembre prochain et finira le groupe pour
mil huit cent vingt trois. Le dit moment en outre
de lui faire fournir tous les costumes nécessaires
à sa volonté pour la susre reprise ou pour resette (?)
pour qui acrora a se charger —
Il est pareillement convenu que Mad. Vestry
est aussi engagé pour jouer le role en susdit pour
et que Mr John Ebers lui permettra de jour en doure
représentation au Théâtre Anglais, bien entendu
que ce ne sera pas les jours désirés pour l'Opera
Ils sont réservés en susdit Mad. Ebers
pour les cas ou suivis de Louca majesté — et après (?)
usage établi au dit Théâtre du Roi

Vertuit Jay le courant de mois de Mai et de Juin,
Jay le consentement de deux partis contractants sera
déjà à présent et pour l'acceptation, et pour le fait
a été dit ci desrit, engagent leurs revenons, leurs biens et
leurs héritiers avec en sadit qui seron moins de la somme
stipulée par le susdit engagement
fait double et de bonne consequence d'un tomoin

Londres ce 24. Mai 1822   R. f. 700.

John Ebers accorde sa signature à Mad.

successes with the kind of hysterical behaviour that was expected of castrati; but Velluti was an exception.

It was thirty years since London had seen or heard such a singer. Times had changed. The voice was of secondary concern as a news item; ridicule and gossip were much more diverted by the castration that had made the voice possible. Madame Vestris, swayed by this nonsense, refused to work with Velluti, thus losing the opportunity of working with an operatic star who was unusually concerned and skilled in stage business; who insisted on full rehearsals; who showed as great a concern for the work of the chorus as for that of the leading singers; and who, in his private life, was considerate and modest and concealed his private sadness from his friends.

The quality of his work as a singer, and as manager in the following years drowned the shrieks and the giggles, although they spoilt his working relations with the female chorus. Seeing the results of his work, especially in the moonlight scene in the last act of *Tebaldo ed Isolina*, Madame Vestris might well have regretted her tantrums as she absorbed a few more professional points.

More than her youth can be urged in her defence. It remains a sad truth in the so-called performing arts that ignorance, lack of integrity, pretentiousness, and incompetence, are often dealt with most quickly by methods in themselves regrettable. While it cannot be claimed for Madame Vestris that all her tantrums sprang from admirable motives, many of them did. To a large extent she was dealing with people who knew and cared considerably less than she did about the work in hand.

Madame Vestris's operatic experience was mostly in the works of Rossini, then at the height of his popularity. She sang in *Zelmira* at the London début of Rossini's wife, Isabella Colbran, and in his *Semiramide* she sang with Pasta. She was generally well received in Rossini, acquitting herself well beside the leading singers of the time.

Her work in Mozart, that is to say, in *Le Nozze di Figaro*, *Cosi Fan Tutte* and *Il Seraglio*, although admired, was obviously less accomplished than in Rossini, but her acting in Mozart was always praised. Her later habit of introducing one of more of her popular songs into operas in which she appeared was a piece of impertinence that many people particularly resented in Mozart. That she was generally able to get away with it is a back-handed kind of tribute to her popularity.

Her Rosina in *Il Barbiere di Siviglia* and her Susanna in *Figaro* were highly praised as acting performances, but the music was considered beyond her range.

In April 1826 Weber's *Oberon* was produced at Covent Garden. This event proved to be even more significant for theatrical than for operatic history. Its operatic importance was that it was expressly commissioned by a London management for a native cast singing an English text, not translated from any other language. It was also staged with more specific concern for detail than was usual at that time either for operas or for plays.

68

The theatrical importance of *Oberon* was that it began a professional relationship that gave Madame Vestris a perfect basis for all her talents and, through the exercise of these, gave a new impetus and standard to theatrical management and presentation.

The libretto for *Oberon, or The Elf King's Oath* was by James Robinson Planché. Born within a year of each other, Eliza and Planché were, in many ways unlikely associates. For Planché, 'theatricals' had been a childhood delight and an amateur diversion that had grown into a delightful recreation. Primarily a scholar, his work in heraldry had led him into studies that covered many branches of history. His acute sense of history, a rare enough attribute, was exceptional for its visual and pictorial imagination and insight. The *look* of the past fascinated him.

The first theatrical pieces that he wrote were not really intended for professional production but were put on at the invitation of theatre people who thought them amusing. These pieces, he records, cost him little labour and much amusement, and when they proved successful, he continued to turn them out at the rate of several a year. For the most part they were given at the minor theatres (principally at the Adelphi), which always asked for more, thus making Planché one of the most prolific writers for the theatre that England has known.

Plays for minor theatres meant plays with music, which in turn meant writers who were also librettists. Planché improved his natural ear for music and rhythm by theoretical study, becoming very knowledgeable in yet another field. In the year that saw the production of *Oberon* (1826) he was musical director of Vauxhall Pleasure Gardens.

Planché, always a charmingly modest man, did not rate his theatrical pieces highly and was surprised at their success. His own account of his first professional production is interesting on several counts. The modesty, humour and unpedantic scholarship of the man are nicely suggested. His writing has the same qualities in its ephemeral way, and these redeem it, to a considerable extent, from the smoking-concert atmosphere that pervades it.

The judgement of *The Oxford Companion to the Theatre*, that 'It appears to have no literary merit whatever, and divorced from its music and spectacular effects is quite unreadable' is a severe rather than a just estimate. Some of the lyrics, for example, are charming and Planché's libretto for *Oberon* is far better than the poorly edited, and often unmusical, text that was offered at the concert performance of the opera at the Royal Festival Hall in April 1970. Associated with the theatre from his teens, Planché knew what actors could speak and what singers could sing effectively in English. That was the secret of his success as a playwright and librettist.

In addition to music, the minor theatres wanted effects. The Parisian theatres showed Planché what could be achieved by mechanical ingenuity and many of the adaptations that he made from the French called for effects new to the London stage. Among these, in the early years, was the 'vampire trap', needed in 1820 for *The Vampyre, or The Bride of the Isles*, adapted by Planché from the French.

His hobby had led him into the minor theatres. His scholarship got him involved with the major ones a few years before his work on *Oberon*. In 1823 Charles Kemble had put on a revival of Shakespeare's *King John* at Covent Garden. Kemble asked Planché's advice and help with the staging and, especially, the costuming of the play. This led to Planché designing a set of costumes that were later published, and which for the first time in England gave an accurate general approximation to historical clothing. Particular costumes and items of costume had been worn bv leading players before this, but Planché was concerned that the overall picture should be as faithful as he could make it to the time of King John.

The Macready *King John* of 1842 (wonderfully recorded and reconstructed by Charles H. Shattuck) has, quite rightly, eclipsed Kemble's pioneer production in scholarly esteem and theatrical history, but it was the latter that laid the foundation for the professional and public acceptance of subsequent productions. The realization that accuracy of costume is not necessarily relevant to Shakespeare's history plays has eclipsed and challenged the theatrical practice that Planché's work had begun and that audiences came to expect. But from the standpoint of theatrical conditions, and Madame Vestris's place in those conditions, in 1826, Planché's work for Kemble cannot be overestimated.

John Warrack and Brian Trowell, in the programme notes to the concert version of *Oberon* already referred to, deplore Planché's libretto and sympathize with Weber's puzzlement and concern that 'the cut of an English opera is certainly very different from a German one', when he was faced with 'a libretto of at times stupifying banality'. (I have already commented on the edited version, which I followed with Planché's text alongside it.) The fact is, Planché knew his audience, and his management at Covent Garden. More important, he knew the performers and provided them with opportunities within their range and with a view to the general balance. In this context, this point should not be pursued beyond the fact that the part of Fatima was admirably suited to Madame Vestris, and that the opera was very well received, remained in the repertoire for the season, and was repeated in 1827 and 1829. Musically, Madame Vestris was highly commended, but once again it was her infectious personality and acting skill that were really memorable. The whole house was infected by her laughter when, in the last scene, she heard the sound of the magic horn.

Upon its revival next season, *The Times* wrote:

'Miss Paton, as Rezia, and Madame Vestris, as Fatima, sang with their accustomed excellence, and it is impossible to give them any higher praise. It was with difficulty that the audience excused them from going through all their songs twice over, and some pieces, in despite of an evident disposition to refrain from such demands, they were absolutely compelled to repeat.'

The setting and presentation generally were given more attention than was often the case, a circumstance that must have been mainly due to Planché.

Chorley, writing in the *Athenaeum* after Lucy's death, says: 'She was extremely bewitching, endowed with one of the most musical, easy, rich contralto voices ever bestowed on a singer, which retained its charm to the last, but full of taste and fancy for all that was luxurious she was either not willing, or unable, to learn beyond a certain depth.'

Perhaps not willing, more probably unable, Madame Vestris remained tempted by the challenge of opera. For her own and other people's benefit nights, throughout this decade, she sang an act or scene of opera, as in her Benefit as late as 1830 when she sang the heroine in the third act of Meyer's *Romeo e Giulietta*. There appears to have been no notice of the event.

CONCERTS AND ORATORIOS

As a member of the company at the King's and as a well-known singer of popular ballads it was inevitable that Madame Vestris should have been asked to sing in concerts and oratorios, especially those that were given at the theatres instead of plays during Holy Week. Concert versions of operas were sometimes given (especially *Der Freischütz*). Recitals and entertainments, at Vauxhall Gardens for instance, were good for publicity as well as financially and Madame Vestris was a popular choice.

Oratorio for her was, it seems, a mistake. In oratorio, unlike opera, musical inadequacy or weakness could not be redeemed by histrionic ability. The *Journal of Music and Drama* for 15 February 1823 made one of many similar comments on such things:

'The song of "He was despis'ed" devolved again upon Madame Vestris but as one of the newspapers had wit enough to perceive, it is not an effort that will promote her reputation. The cavatina in *Cyrus*, though indifferently sung, was not so gross a failure; the success however of this lady depends much more upon a pretty pair of legs, and we advise the ingenious director to contrive some expedient by which she may display them.'

The newspaper referred to was the *Morning Herald*.

SONGS

It was through her songs that Madame Vestris was generally known throughout the country. Song-sheets carrying her picture, often in costume, were sold everywhere and would be seen and bought by many people who never got

"Ei ei mein Lieber Augustin,"

The favorite Air,

Sung by

MADAME VESTRIS,

or the

Bavarian Girls Song, "Buy a Broom?"

Arranged with Variations for the

Piano Forte,

BY

I. L. WELLIN.

Ent. Sta. Hall.   Pr: 3

London, Published by MORI & LAVENU, 28, New Bond St. 1 Doors from Conduit Str.

to a theatre to see the lady in person. For those within reach of a theatre, the song-sheets had often been advance publicity as well as mementoes of performances. Certain songs were introduced in plays, either as part of the piece or sung during the course of the evening, whatever play was being offered. Others were sung between acts or between two plays being given on the same evening. Many remained popular for decades and some are still well known today. 'The Mountain Maid'; 'Hurrah for the Bonnets of Blue'; 'I've Been Roamin'; 'In the Month of Maying': these were regular items in Madame Vestris's repertoire. 'Cherry Ripe', from *Paul Pry*, and 'The Bavarian Girl's Song ('Buy a Broom' or 'Oh! My Little Augustine') have remained in the national repertoire, in schools and elsewhere.

Madame Vestris was fortunate in her songs, but there is no doubt that she excelled in putting them over. Here was the perfect middle ground for the combining of her great dramatic skill and limited musical range. Born later, she could well have been a star of the music hall, musical comedy and television.

Playbills of the years 1820 to 1830 show that on an increasing number of occasions Madame Vestris was given 'star billing' on a programme in which she appeared only to sing one or more of her songs. A bill of two or more plays would announce that 'In the Course of the Evening, MADAME VESTRIS will sing . . . a favourite air' or 'the last new and highly popular song', etc., and these occasions were sometimes noticed, along with the plays, in the press. The lyrics of the bigger successes were published in the theatrical and musical columns of the newspapers and periodicals.

It is probable that for these 'featured' songs some kind of setting was provided and, where appropriate, costume. The cover illustrations of sheet music, and prints and figurines provide evidence of this, not only in the case of Madame Vestris but as the usual thing for popular singers.

There is, for example, a ballad entitled 'When I knew He Was Married', sung 'with unanimous applause' by Mrs Waylett, (published, probably in 1820, by Lee), and sung at the New Royalty Theatre, the New English Opera House. The cover picture shows Mrs Waylett, fashionably and charmingly dressed, sitting in pensive mood on a Regency sofa in a detailed interior setting. While the picture might be simply an imaginative illustration of the song, certain details strongly suggest a stage setting. The open window with a pastoral view; the table with inkstand standing by the window; the painting on the wall: all these appear to be two-dimensional, i.e., painted on a backdrop, and lack the three-dimensional effect of the rest of the scene. One side of the setting is framed by a large, fringed curtain (probably a two-dimensional 'wing'), gathered up and half revealing one of those large ornamental urns on a monumental base often seen as a garden ornament and very familiar to anyone who has set up ballroom and palace scenes in Pollock's and other toy theatres.

Curtains as we know them were not used on the stage at the time. Some kind of backdrop had to be given a singer (it also provided a necessary screen for

THE BAVARIAN GIRL'S SONG

The Words by D. A. O'Meara.

Buy a Broom!

Sung (IN CHARACTER) by

MADAME VESTRIS,

With the most enthusiastic Applause.

Arranged expressly for her by

Alexander Lee.

Price 2

74

whatever might be being set up behind), and it may be that Mrs Waylett's background was a stock piece that had done service in many other contexts.

The many editions of Madame Vestris's 'hit' song, 'Buy a Broom' (the Bavarian Girl's song), show basically the same costume throughout with minor variations. The variations are slight but interesting. A simple, calf-length frock with a square neck edged, like her cuffs, with white; a neat cap tied under the chin, stockings with 'clocks' and simple shoes with small buckles make up the general costume. She always carries a sheaf of little brooms on her left arm and offers a single one with her right hand, and she is standing in the street in front of the shop of whatever publisher is represented in the sheet music.

The edition published by Mori and Lavenu (costing a shilling more than Mayhew and Company's two-shilling edition), shows an unusual angled view of the street and includes a lamp post by the kerb. Madame Vestris has what appears to be a gauze under-bodice with a high collar modestly augmenting her gown; a chain necklace with a cross, and a reticule. In a generally far more animated picture she is accompanied by two other performers, dressed almost identically. A small girl is holding her arm and a little way off there is the back view of another adult broom girl.

Obviously a street scene would have been provided but one wonders just how many variations and how much time and money was expended on putting over a song. Might publishers have paid for some kind of setting that would represent their shop, as advertisers later used the front drop cloths in so many theatres and now use programmes?

PLAYS WITH MUSIC

These, like the songs, were a regular and always popular part of Madame Vestris's repertoire. The play with music was another good setting for her, though there were very few such plays during the 1820s that could claim much for themselves as acting texts. More often than not it was Lucy who redeemed the piece rather than that the piece offered good opportunities for her.

Exceptions to this were *The Beggar's Opera*, *The Duenna* and, though in a different class, *Paul Pry*. The kind of notices, for and against, her performances as Macheath continued throughout the decade. At the end of the decade, in June 1830, for someone else's Benefit, she played Lucy Lockett for the first time. There is no notice of this performance, in which she should have been delightful and which she might well have played more often but for *Giovanni in London* which had created the demand for the display of her legs whenever possible.

It was in a male role (Don Carlos) that she appeared in *The Duenna* throughout these years. In this case, as with *Artaxerxes*, it was probably her contralto voice that was as much a determining factor as her legs.

This was also the time of the more exotic types of myth and fairy tales, such as *Midas; The Nymph of the Grotto* and *Pong Wong*, though these do have a more particular interest in that they were the kind of themes that Planché was to develop so ingeniously and successfully for Madame Vestris in her years as manageress.

Her playing of Phoebe in *Paul Pry* was not only famous for the singing of 'Cherry Ripe'. In this still rather charming piece, Madame Vestris was one of a fine cast which included notably John Liston. *Paul Pry* opened in September 1828, at the Haymarket Theatre. The Haymarket had a unique place in the London theatrical scene, for it was neither a major nor a minor, but rather a 'summer major': it was allowed to offer comedies and musical pieces during the months when Drury Lane and Covent Garden were closed. Many lighter pieces, originally given at the Haymarket, were later revived by the majors, despite objections from the minors that they *had* to produce such works and the majors should stick to their jealously guarded monopoly for plays.

THE NEW THEATRE ROYAL IN THE HAYMARKET

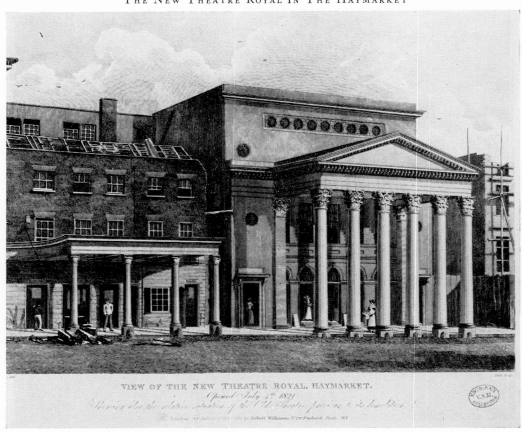

VIEW OF THE NEW THEATRE ROYAL, HAYMARKET.
Opened July 4th 1821.

It was at the Haymarket that Madame Vestris really evolved her own style and found her particular technique. A diary of her recorded performances for this decade indicates that she was at her busiest and happiest in this theatre opposite the King's. At times, she was engaged at both theatres for a season, having simply to remember which side of the road to go to, which Stage Door to enter: a leading singer entering the international ambience of the King's, or a popular comedienne/soubrette popping into the homely atmosphere of the Theatre Royal, Haymarket.

The Haymarket was, and is, a popular theatre with actors. The present building was opened during Madame Vestris's second season, her first having seen the last performance in the original theatre. It is small enough to allow for subtlety of effect and yet holds a large enough audience to offer a challenge and give a commercially viable return. Backstage conditions, necessarily more cramped than at Drury Lane or Covent Garden, were less daunting and expensive to keep clean and in good order with a reasonably small staff. Audiences, and payboxes, were easier to oversee and control, and the theatre shared with the King's a 'respectable' and agreeable locality.

The planning of a season and the presentation of plays at the Haymarket was not inhibited by either the size or the pretensions of the majors, where there was often more concern over the preservation of dignity than the entertainment of the public. The time of year helped too. At Drury Lane and Covent Garden audiences were often deterred by the cold, while the performers had to endure it.

For Madame Vestris the Haymarket was the setting for most of her popular successes of all kinds. Although busy in her Drury Lane and Covent Garden seasons, she was frequently the 'insurance' as it were, appearing in an afterpiece to make sure that, if the main play failed, some receipts would still come in. There were often weeks when she played these once or twice only (perhaps from her own choice) and there are many instances of illness and some of tantrums. Her record at the Haymarket, on the other hand, was rarely broken by illness or other causes and for many weeks at a time she was working every evening, there or at the King's — another house where her record of attendance is good.

There was congenial company at the Haymarket. Many performers who were to work under her management in the future, worked with her there, notably Mrs Glover, Liston and Farren.

Although they are really plays with songs rather than plays with music, 'romantic' dramas and historical pieces may be considered under this heading, for they undoubtedly had musical accompaniment and were sometimes largely attended because of the songs. These were often introduced quite inappropriately or an interlude was made for them during the evening. Often enough this did little damage to a poor text, however much the practice was deplored. Among such plays that held places in the bills were: *Lord of the Manor*, *The Haunted Tower*, *Rob Roy McGregor*, *The Castle of Andalusia*, and *The Pirate*, whose titles well enough convey their kind, a kind that was also to be regular fare in the cinema about a hundred years later.

Madame Vestris's acting was invariably commended in such pieces, though the bold romantic style, even bolder in those vast major theatres, cannot really have given her much satisfaction. Light comedy, and especially light comedy at the Haymarket, was obviously the work she really enjoyed and that brought her glowing tributes and enormous popularity.

She was fortunate in much of her material in this kind: *Secrets Worth Knowing*, *Sweethearts and Wives*, *Love Letters*, *My Grandmother*, and *The Wedding Day* are all quite well-made pieces providing acting opportunities both in the dialogue and in the cues for stage business — and for clothes for the leading lady. And for displaying herself and her talents in men's clothes there were besides *The Beggar's Opera* (and, of course, *Giovanni in London*), *The Invincibles*, *The Two Pages of Frederick the Great*, *The Epaulette*, and others.

Could they be played today? The success of one of Madame's later hits, *London Assurance*, by the Royal Shakespeare Company in 1970, prompts the question. Some, for example *Sweethearts and Wives*, might have a novelty value and could be valuable exercises for drama schools, but for the most part they have done their work and been superseded. The cinema has taken over the melodramas and extravaganzas to titivate the popular taste for spectacle, while the smart dialogue and witty style have found particular exponents for audiences who want entertainment for the mind as well as the eye.

Contemporary comments for the most part commend the manner rather than the matter of such plays as have been mentioned:

'*The Wedding Day*; in which Farren and Madame Vestris alone were enough to repay the trouble of coming to the theatre.'

'It . . . is a slight piece, in which Madame Vestris displays her powers and her person to great advantage: with such assistance *The Epaulette* could not fail of success.'

'*The Nymph of the Grotto* . . . The character which this lady fills is in itself very insignificant, and yet she managed to execute it so cleverly and gaily, as to make it the main support of the piece.'

The songs were praised in the theatrical columns: '. . . sang two songs in the piece very charmingly; she was encored in one, and ought to have been encored in both.' and given publicity in the music columns: '. . . many pretty novelties are making their way towards the patronage of the Haut Ton . . . 'In the Month of Maying' sung by Madame Vestris in *The Invincibles* now performing to overflowing houses at the Theatre Royal Covent Garden.' And her wardrobe was

Madame Vestris as Captain Macheath

always good for comment: '. . . played, and sang her songs extremely well: and wore a variety of fine clothes enough to satisfy almost any fine lady.'

In such things Madame Vestris could make her own style and mould the vehicle to suit her.

CLASSICAL PLAYS

When it was a question of tackling a good text from an established tradition, the result, although often commended, was not as uniformly successful. This is not as severe a reflection upon Madame Vestris as it may seem. She was evolving a style of acting, and would help evolve a new style of acting and presentation, that the public had yet to adjust to. The so-called 'classical' pieces, even those as recent as Sheridan, were, for the public, still associated with an acting style that had been evolved for the huge auditoria of the majors and for audiences who were familiar with the plays. They went to see what 'points' so and so would make in *Macbeth* rather than *Macbeth* itself, to make comparison between Princes of Denmark rather than a production of *Hamlet*.

The theatre in the early 1800s was going through changes not unlike our present theatre of the 1970s, where it is taking some time for a number of styles of playing and writing to resolve themselves into anything like a generally recognizable approach to acting that reflects our own time. Madame Vestris should have been just right for Lydia Languish, for Lady Teazle and for Letitia Hardy (in Hannah Cowley's *The Belle's Stratagem*), but, although never damned in them she was never more than faintly praised (except for one performance of Lydia at Farren's Benefit in 1827 when *The Times* described her performance as being 'in the true spirit of the author'). Her Lydia in 1828 was 'for want of a better, tolerable' (*The Times*); her Lady Teazle 'easy and spirited' but no more (*Theatrical Observer*). Though it was allowed that her very presence 'carries the house along with her' her characterization of Lititia Hardy receives no comment in *The Times* (1827).

If it is granted that Madame Vestris may not have subjected herself to properly detailed work on these few performances it must also be allowed that there must have been an odd mixture of styles of acting, of stock scenery and assorted costumes for her to perform with. Such plays depend upon a balance of performances which, in turn, means considerable rehearsal and sympathy between the actors involved. The theatrical conditions of the 1820s allowed little time for the working out of mutual business: it was more often a case of going through the lines and determining key moves, often on no more than one occasion.

In addition to Sheridan, Cowley, and Cibber, Madame Vestris also appeared in Goldsmith's *She Stoops to Conquer* for her Benefit at the Haymarket in November 1826. This is of interest because she played Mrs Hardcastle rather than Miss Hardcastle as might have been expected, despite the fact that she was now getting on for thirty. Actors and actresses often used Benefits as testing grounds for the kind of parts they had not tried before. If they failed, it was for that one performance only and no real harm done. If they succeeded it was a clue to the kind of things they might do in the future. Mrs Hardcastle, or ladies of her kind, did not enter Madame's repertoire, so presumably that particular experiment did not satisfy the lady and/or the public, who wanted their favourite's charms revealed rather than concealed by the characters she played. It was as difficult then as now for a performer, especially a female performer, to defy successfully the popular image that she originally created.

Diana in *Lionel and Clarissa* was another character tried in a Benefit but not followed up, nor was *The Way to Keep Him*. She was more successful in *The Wife's Stratagem* (adapted from Shirley's *The Gamesters*) in the 1827 season at Covent Garden. But none of these better written comedies gave her the sustained successes in which she could be depended upon to fill the theatre.

SHAKESPEARE

During this decade Madame Vestris appeared in five of Shakespeare's plays. It is not surprising that an appealing young actress who could sing should have tried her hand at Ophelia, at Drury Lane in 1822. The Prince of Denmark was Charles Mayne Young, a delightful person and an actor of the kind that is sometimes referred to as 'accomplished', by which is meant a good all-round actor, invaluable to a company and popular with the public without being a star. It was fifteen years since his first success as Hamlet in London, and the house was 'ill attended' for the forty-five year old actor in 1822.

The Ophelia, however, surprised the critics:

'. . . sang prettily in Ophelia, and went through that character with more pathos and simplicity than we had expected, judging from her ordinary style of acting.' *The Times*

'Though her talents have been hitherto confined principally to the most dashing line of comedy, her Ophelia was far from being deficient in feeling as far as the acting was concerned, and her execution of the plaintive airs afforded the utmost satisfaction.' *London Chronicle*

Two years later, in the same theatre, Edmund Kean was her prince: 'Kean's Hamlet was as vivid and as careless as ever. Ophelia was a pleasing and affective piece of acting.' *Mirror of the Stage*

Not enough evidence here to convince one that there was a Shakespearian actress in the making, but sufficient to indicate that the depth and sensibility that were noted in the last appearances of her career were not solely the result of maturity, experience and an awareness that the end was approaching.

There were three other Shakespearian roles in 1824: brief encounters with Ariel in *The Tempest* for a Benefit in May, Luciana in *The Comedy of Errors*, in June (the prompt book of this production is in the University of Nebraska; the so-called 'operatic' version was used giving scope for the expected songs), and the first encounter with *The Merry Wives of Windsor*.

In *The Merry Wives*, Madame Vestris found, at last, a Shakespearian play to give her a popular showing. She played in it at Drury Lane and at the Haymarket (1824/1825) and at Covent Garden (1828/1829). She began as Mrs Page in February 1824, but for a few performances at the end of the Haymarket season in October she changed to Mrs Ford and kept this part for the 1825 Haymarket season. For the Covent Garden revivals she again changed to Mrs Page. Perhaps Mrs Ford goes better in a smaller house and Mrs Page in a larger one? (The detailed, if messy, prompt book of the 1824 Drury Lane production is also with the University of Nebraska.)

During May and June 1825 Madame Vestris played for seven performances as Rosalind in *As You Like It* at the Haymarket. She was probably not the first and certainly not the last to find that female charms are doubtful assets when playing parts written for trained boy actors. It may be that this is what the critic of *The Age* meant when he said that: 'Madame Vestris cannot play Shakespeare because she cannot comprehend Shakespeare.' In the 1826 season at the Haymarket, Rosalind was tried again, but wisely given up after one performance (4 October).

Something of the range of work done between 1820 and 1830 has been indicated above. In all Madame Vestris appeared in about eighty different pieces of one kind and another, excluding concerts, oratorios and the presentation of songs. Quite apart from the achievements, the energy of the lady was phenomenal. Throughout these years her comings and goings, amorous and domestic as well as professional, were always news, in London and on her regular tours, in Ireland as well as in Britain. A glamorous and unpredictable personality, her box office appeal was tempting enough for managers to put up with a lady who could be as obstinate as she could be charming, and who knew her own value. But, though jealous of her position, she was a generally welcome member of a company, most of whom recognized the professionalism that was the real basis of her success.

In many ways she was too professional. The theatres had poor material and little money for the most part during this decade, and the larger houses were spending all they could spare in the doomed hope of competing with the spectacular effects offered by the smaller theatres which were so much cheaper to run, and more popular. (Poorer folk living out in the ever-growing extremities of London had neither the time, money nor inclination to walk great distances to pay major theatre prices when the minors were satisfying them cheaply round the corner.)

By 1829 excessive rent and bankruptcies had crippled Drury Lane; Covent Garden was closed in June, so deeply in debt that a fund was started to help it; and there was a deficit of some £13,000 at the end of the season at the King's Theatre.

7

The Leasehold of Freedom

To help Covent Garden, Madame Vestris sent £40 to the fund. She accepted a contract for the Drury Lane season and relieved the depression there by giving them a success. It is doubtful if she would have considered working at the Lane again had it not been for the mutual admiration and respect that working on *Oberon* had created between Planché and herself.

Planché, adapting a French success, wrote the 'book' for a play with music called *Hofer, the Tell of Tyrol*. The role of Josephine was made for Madame Vestris in her most popular soubrette line, with ample cues for song and a plot that obliged her to appear for a time in trousers.

Really too light-weight a piece for a theatre such as Drury Lane, it was Vestris together with the music that carried it through regular performances during the month of May. *The Times* commented: '. . . though great scope is given for the display of her vocal powers, very little opportunity is afforded for the exercise of her fine talents as an actress.' (Another of those tantalizing references, raising yet again the question of what the lady might have been capable of, given different theatrical circumstances. *The Times* added that she '. . . executed her portion of the music delightfully. Her air "sweetly on the wings of morning" commanded the only encore of the evening'.

The further comment that the scenery was 'exceedingly good' makes it a safe bet that Planché, and perhaps Planché and Eliza together, was involved in this aspect of the production. It was good to make a success of *Hofer* but it did not really resolve either the theatre's problem or that of Madame Vestris. Bored with revived pieces, or new pieces that felt like revivals, and frustrated by unimaginative, incompetent or indifferent presentations, Madame Vestris began to lose interest in her work. It could not offer her the creative impetus that her energy and talents needed. It obviously affected her private life and regrettably did not prevent her domestic problems and her amorous concerns from damaging her work and her reputation.

Armand died in 1825 in Italy. It is doubtful if the couple had met again after he left Lucy in Paris, taking another little fascinator with him to Italy, though Lucy was quite a frequent visitor to Paris either visiting or being given a break by a gentleman friend or, as in 1825, nursing her sick mother who seems to have been mainly resident in Paris. The parting might have been by mutual agreement and they might have met again and/or remained on good terms. For Lucy, as for Armand, the marriage and any obligation it involved was over and they behaved as single people.

Never lacking admirers, Lucy showed good judgement in her selection of particular ones, choosing gentlemen who were well-endowed both physically and financially, and who were discreet. Of course there was gossip; there were innuendoes in the press; there were obscene elaborations of fragments of fact and gobbets of scandal printed as 'Memoirs'. There was also some blackmail, which for a time she, or someone, paid off. All these things at first failed to daunt her; scurrility she wisely ignored, accepting it as a kind of compliment to her fame.

Entering her thirties and with no indication of the kind of professional future that she might face, other than declining into character and 'grande dame' parts, was depressing enough. There was also the financial problem of keeping not only herself but her mother and sister who were both dependent on her.

Sister Josephine had some talent, light-weight perhaps, but quite appealing, and Lucy had got her engagements, billed as Miss Bartolozzi, at the Haymarket. Josephine was being courted in 1830 by James Anderson, an actor and singer who was later to marry her (and give a power of trouble). For his engagement at Drury Lane he was apparently indebted to Madame Vestris. Temperamentally, Josephine's lover did not hit it off with Lucy. Regrettably their domestic squabbles were carried into their working relationship. Whatever the motive the breach of behaviour was Lucy's.

Two years earlier *The Times* had found occasion to warn: 'This lady has taken it into her head lately to make speeches to the audience whenever she is hissed, which, indeed, is not oftener than she deserves it. She did so last Saturday, and was laughed at; last night she came on a little later than she ought to have done, and was again hissed accordingly. She immediately advanced to the lamps, and resolutely remonstrated with the audience, insisting that it was not her fault, and that she ought not to be hissed. It is probable that she may try the patience of the pit too far; and if she will be well advised, notwithstanding that she is to a certain extent a favourite, she will refrain from abusing the precarious influence.'

The quarrel with Anderson on 20 April 1830 was a bad business. The action of *Guy Mannering* was first interrupted by the sudden dropping of the text and a resumption of a quarrel that had been going on off-stage. This quickly passed, was apologized for, and the love scene(!) proceeded according to the script. But Madame Vestris again resumed the quarrel and walked off the stage, later sending a message that she was too indisposed to continue the performance.

The audience was understandably annoyed and *The Times* reported and censured the event among its news rather than its theatrical items, a shift of emphasis and implication which was certainly deserved.

After a few weeks of at any rate public peace Lucy took a successful Benefit on 4 June which included an act from *Guy Mannering* with Anderson. The same play was the main offering for the following evening but Lucy was advertised as prevented by illness from appearing. A week later when Anderson took his Benefit we find her appearing on his behalf, her first appearance as Lucy in *The Beggar's Opera*.

The ups and downs of the family quarrels do not really matter, and should never have been made public business, but they provide substantial evidence of Lucy's restiveness at this time. There were offers from America, that oft-maligned but much used haven for artists in voluntary or compelled exile, and it seemed that she would go. It might well have been personal reasons that made her decide not to cross the Atlantic but to accept provincial offers instead: 'Madame Vestris does not got to America. She is at present engaged on a provincial tour. She performs at Leamington on the 30th inst., from where she proceeds to Manchester, to fulfil an engagement there.' (*The Times*, 26 July 1830)

Returning to London after a successful tour, Lucy found that, with other leading players, she was 'unplaced' for the coming season at either major theatre. From the managers' point of view, Madame Vestris was expensive and had become increasingly particular about the pieces she appeared in and the way they were presented. Knowing her popularity, she turned the tables on the majors by accepting an engagement with a minor theatre, the Tottenham Street Theatre (later to be the site of the Scala, Charlotte Street, demolished in 1969).

The Tottenham Street season ran from 15 November to 11 December 1830. This little season has been referred to as offering Madame Vestris nothing new and as being undertaken for the money. The little evidence that still exists suggests that this is an unfair summing-up.

During this season Madame Vestris took possession of the Olympic Theatre. The government option on the Olympic (discussed below) was not abandoned until quite late in 1830. When the Tottenham Street season was negotiated Madame Vestris must have either been hoping for, or more probably, have entered into the business of acquiring the Olympic. The brief season was a practical and business-like move even apart from the financial considerations: first, by this means she was introduced back into the London theatrical scene, and so already 'in the news', secondly, she could test the public response to herself in a minor theatre, without the caché of a fashionable or a patented house, and third, she could have a 'try-out' or two.

The season opened with *Lord of the Manor* and *John of Paris*. She had been playing Annette since 1820. In *John of Paris* she played the male singing lead. Thus the two most popular images and types of song were offered to launch the season. A version of *Don Giovanni* was given a few nights later. A new piece,

TOTTENHAM STREET THEATRE, 1830

A sketch that indicates the neighbourhood as well as the theatre, and explains why Vestris was considered to be 'slumming' when she appeared here, having been a star of the major theatres.

The Stratagem, was presented on 20 November. There are unfortunately no notices to be found for this (or for the season). The title suggests a story of ends achieved by feminine wiles, another familiar Vestris theme.

On 24 November for the '1st time in this country' was presented *Fra Diavolo, or The Inn of Terracina*, with Vestris in the male lead (despite the fact that it was written for a tenor!). This proved interesting enough for Madame to include it for three performances in the first Olympic season.

The third new piece was *The Sultan and the Slave* (9 December), the title of which again indicates a familiar kind, which was to be completely transformed by Planché.

Not a very exciting season of plays perhaps, but the majors were offering no better attractions and the public followed their favourite, bringing the shabby little theatre and scruffy district more visitors and takings than it had ever received. In her costume as Don Giovanni Madame Vestris took her last bow at the Tottenham Street Theatre. William Vining gave the Farewell Address, acknowledging the success of a leading lady who was also his new employer, for Madame had signed him up for the Olympic.

On 21 September 1829 *The Times* carried the following advertisement above its theatre announcements:

ROYAL OLYMPIC Theatre to be DISPOSED OF. This theatre is held for a long term of years, at a small ground rent, and is in excellent condition. The stage, saloon, and audience part, which are very large and commodious,

As 'Olivia' in *John of Paris*. This collection of songs and a meagre linking plot was certainly more genteel than *Giovanni in London* but it will be seen that, though the attitude is more subdued the same popular 'charms' are displayed, set off by elegant little boots.

MADAME VESTRIS as DON GIOVANNI.

As 'Don Giovanni' in *Giovanni in London*. My personal favourite from among the many extant pictures of Vestris in the part that made her a national figure. No two pictures show her in quite the same costume. During the long run and the many revivals her wardrobe was frequently renewed. The settings seem to have been re-done several times too but it is difficult to tell this with any certainty from the pictures.

Apollo.   Olympic game, at Whist,   Hebe,   Jupiter,   Cu

Vulcan,   Pandora, & Cupid,   Apollo, Kneeling to Pandora,   Cupid.

Mercury, & Swifs Boy,   Prometheus, & Pandora,

Olympic Revels. The inclusion of a production in t

90

Bacchus, & Pan,   *Neptune,*   *Piutus,*   *Momus,*

o, enraged at Pandora,   *Mercury, bearing Pandora; to Earth,*

rva,   *Hope,*   *Pandora Pleading to Jupiter,*   *Prometheus devoured by a Vult*

by toy theatres was a sure sign of popular success.

THE OLYMPIC THEATRE

are splendidly fitted with chandeliers and lamps, to be lighted with gas, and the house abounds with a profusion of new and effective scenery, on a large scale, the theatre having been built by Mr. Philip Astley, and the stage fitted to receive the scenery of the Royal Amphitheatre, which was removed into and used by him therein during his winter season. There is also a useful wardrobe of stage dresses and abundance of properties. The theatre is remarkably well attended, and, with good management, there is no doubt but an ample fortune would be made in a short time. There are no incumbrances on this theatre, and immediate possession may be had. For particulars inquire personally of Messrs. Smith and Buckerfield, solicitors, of Red Lion Square; if by letter, post paid.'

Although often described as 'a pretty little theatre', the Olympic had never enjoyed a smart reputation. It was situated in a network of little streets around Drury Lane, streets that have since been cleaned up, rearranged and in some cases renamed. A generally notorious area, it housed brothels, thieves' kitchens, and drinking houses with so dubious a clientele that even the authorities steered clear of them as much as possible.

Philip Astley, despite objections from the nearby majors, opened his Olympic Pavilion in 1806. As building materials he used a captured French warship bought from the Admiralty. Pitched and tarred canvas covered the tin roof of what had been properly called a pavilion and was intended for horse shows and pantomimes. This unique building underwent many changes of name and fortune before its demolition in 1899. Elliston had owned and managed it before he took Drury Lane (and was prevented by the terms of the patent from running other theatres at the same time). *Giovanni in London* had first appeared at the Olympic under the Elliston management. He had redecorated the interior and managed to attract a regular as well as quite a fashionable audience. Since his time a succession of managements had tried and failed to make a living, let alone a fortune, until the theatre declined into a home of cheap melodrama for audiences far from fashionable.

The government put a reservation on the building and negotiated for a purchase. They wanted it for conversion into a police barracks as headquarters of the New Police. They obviously had an eye on the cleaning up of the neighbourhood as well as housing for the Force. Over some months they tried to beat down the £2,000 that the manager, Scott, was asking. Scott held out; the government withdrew and the next news the public had of it was that Madame Vestris was negotiating a purchase.

Committed at last, Madame Vestris could channel her tremendous energy and organizing flair, and events moved fast. There was a company to recruit — actors and staff, plays to find, scenery and costumes to make or muster, publicity to arrange and rehearsals to get under way, quite apart from the legal business of determining whether, as a woman, she could be granted a licence. As a widow she could negotiate a lease, but she had to use all her influence as a long-established darling of the fashionables, on and off the stage, to get the business of the licence resolved. An old admirer, the Duke of Devonshire, then Lord Chamberlain, settled the matter in her favour: 'There is your licence. I cannot refuse to Madame Vestris what would have been granted to any person of less powerful attractions. I shall come and see you often and bring all my friends, and I have no doubt your speculation will prove eminently successful.'

It was not until St Nicholas's Day, 6 December 1830 that Eliza became Madame of the Royal Olympic Theatre. The decision was taken quickly, going straight from the agent's office in the Strand to Messrs Coutts and back again with the deposit. The lady was not usually 'in funds' but sufficient were found for the venture.

Within a calendar month, by 3 January 1831, the house had been refurbished and the season opened. Whether this prodigious amount of work was all done within so short a time is difficult to determine. Actors might have been sounded out earlier, but she could not have got much done in a practical way until she took possession.

Perhaps she had not intended to open so soon but she stopped her carriage when she saw Planché one day, told him that she had just taken the Olympic and asked him if he had anything ready to produce immediately and also whether he

THE 'FAIR LESSEE'

Madame Vestris at about the time she took over the Olympic Theatre.

Below are the two authors mostly responsible for keeping the Olympic well supplied with what was wanted by Madame's public.

CHARLES DANCE   JAMES R. PLANCH

would advise and assist the new venture. Planché at once accepted both offers. With the assistance of Charles Dance 'in two or three evenings' he brushed up an 'oft rejected' old classical burlesque he had written years before, renamed it *Olympic Revels, or Prometheus and Pandora*, and gave it to Madame Vestris for the opening bill, herself to play Pandora.

As adviser and assistant he had Madame's willing co-operation for his ideas of costuming. It was usual for burlesques and extravaganzas and the like to be dressed in what can best be termed 'fancy dress', a conglomeration of styles that bore no relation to each other but were often put together even on a single character. Planché knew his manageress. She needed no persuading to adopt Planché's suggestion that the costumes should be designed individually and collectively to a picturesque and coherent overall scheme.

Scenically, however much she wished it, she could not give Planché all he would have liked. Time being short and money going out but not yet coming in, prime consideration was given to the settings for the other items on the bill that were to feature the leading players who had joined her rather than herself. The setting for *Olympic Revels* was limited to 'a few clouds, the interior of a cottage, and a well-used modern street, which was made a joke in the bill to anticipate criticism', an idea that took the public fancy so well that comic references and puns on the settings became a regular feature of the playbills for Planché pieces.

Members of the technical staff were recruited from working experience, in London and on tour. The success of the Olympic years depended a great deal on the backstage supervision of Frank Raymond and later James Vining, on the musical direction of Wagstaff and the scene painting of Hilliard, which, as soon as money was available, rapidly replaced the crude work inherited from Scott's melodramas.

Recruiting a company was not difficult with so many talented discontents about. It must have seemed like old times when 'all persons engaged' were 'requested to meet in the Green-Room on Monday morning at eleven' and met so many Haymarket colleagues. Most of the cast of *Paul Pry* were in the first Olympic season, including Liston himself, Madame's trump card among the gentlemen, and Frank Raymond and the Vining brothers. The 'mother of the company' was Mrs Glover, an old friend as well as a colleague and one of the most popular, esteemed and affectionately regarded actresses of her time. Her presence in the company, quite apart from her talent, gave status and tone to the venture, of invaluable assistance in countering the surroundings, and the sneers of the major managements. Mrs Glover brought other acting members of her family with her.

As 'straight' leading lady the Olympic could boast Maria Foote who, from the moment she heard of the idea was so enthusiastic in her support that the press assumed that she was taking the theatre jointly with Madame.

The simple business of finding the leading players was followed by the more complicated business of sorting out the rest of the company and other employees:

> 'The morning following the appearance of the "announced" bills, the stage-door was surrounded by a motley group composed of almost every grade in the profession, from the 'decayed Hamlet' downwards, all applying for situations. There were heavy fathers and ditto villains, utility men, chambermaids, chorus singers, ballet girls, etc. – not forgetting the material for organising an army of "sandwich men" or board bearers. The names of the most likely of the lot were taken down by Ireland, the copyist of the theatre, and a selection made from the list by Madame herself.'

The first bill was planned to give particular opportunities to Liston, Mrs Glover and Maria Foote. Madame was to speak the specially written Prologue and to pop up through a trapdoor in *Olympic Revels*. The part chosen for Maria Foote was Maria Darlington in *A Roland for an Oliver*, an effective but very familiar piece. The management of Covent Garden claimed the copyright of this piece and their claim was legally upheld. With time so short, this was a blow but it proved to be another setback that was turned to advantage.

Mary, Queen of Scots, 'a new historical burletta' was got up for Miss Foote. The hand of Planché in this choice is obvious and with this setting he could begin to realize his dreams.

Madame herself would have liked to have had time and means to attend to the decoration of the auditorium. As things were she had what there was thoroughly cleaned and repainted including the ceiling. Flowers and cupids were the principal motifs, taking up the style of 'that eminent artist', Madame's grandfather, some of whose work was reproduced on the panels dividing the first tier of boxes.

Surrounded by actors, sempstresses, carpenters, painters and workmen, and with the smell of size and paint, timber and varnish, Madame and Planché could delight in one of the most satisfying games devised by man – the preparation of a theatrical season, especially when accompanied by the knowledge that the demand for seats exceeds the supply. Fashionable admirers from the King's, and popular admirers from Drury Lane, Covent Garden and the Haymarket, and probably a few new admirers from the Tottenham Street Theatre, all hoping for a much-needed change of theatrical fare, were looking forward to the Fair Lessee's second début – as the first of a new species: an actress/manageress in London.

8

Madame

'The nobility and public in general' were advised of the opening of Madame's first Olympic season on 3 January 1831. Arriving at a reasonable hour the nobility found that the public in general had anticipated them by some hours and had brought about such a rush for admittance that it had been difficult to control. Madame's doings were always news and publicity had got under way within a day of her taking the Olympic. Posters were printed and distributed with more than modern speed announcing her new venture. The Tottenham Street season had kept up her personal publicity. Fashionable gentlemen were loyal to 'fascinating little Vestris'. Ladies were intrigued with the new ground that had been broken for their sex in regard to the licensing laws. The public in general welcomed a promising new diversion. The 'locals', who liked to see 'Missis Westris', wondered if she would give them melodramas again 'as good as the gaff in blood and guts square'.

On the first day of 1831 every thing was as ready as it could be in the time allotted. Before they went away, doubtless looking forward to the free Sunday ahead, all members of the company were quietly sent for, one by one, and given a week's salary in advance.

On the Monday morning there was a complete dress rehearsal, including the National Anthem (then, more than now, a feature of the evening), all of which was controlled, watch in hand, by Madame who sat at the footlights, presumably in her Pandora costume, perhaps protected by a wrap. This rehearsal ended at two, giving a good break until the evening performance.

Thus before the season had opened Madame Vestris began to change theatre practice in Britain. The paying of salaries in advance was regarded by other managers as a further example of the extravagance for which Madame Vestris

'Pandora'. The most charming of the many 'Penny Plain' portraits of Madame in her first Olympic role.

was notorious. When the season became a success the tune changed. What had that woman begun? Where would it end, this betrayal of managerial thrift and confidence? In other words, they were afraid, and correctly so, that this might all lead exactly where it has led: both to a reappraisal by actors of their status in a theatrical venture and their rights as employees, and hence to the British Actors' Equity Association; and to Equity's present ruling that, before launching upon any theatrical venture, two weeks' salary for each member of the company must be lodged with Equity so that there is some remuneration and compensation for performers if it all comes to nothing.

The timing and supervision of final rehearsals (themselves timed to provide reasonable breaks between rehearsal and performance for actors) was adopted and adapted by Madame Vestris from her knowledge of the successful practices of Pixerécourt, who had also invited first the sneers and later the envy of other managers.

These three facets of managerial concern for a company: financial assurance, the proper regulation of working hours and breaks, and consideration for the personal dignity and welfare of all those working in the theatre, were always important to Madame. The emphasis in later commentaries on the lady has been mostly upon her work in changing the public and professional attitude to stage setting and theatrical conduct, on both sides of the curtain, and upon her personal fascination as an artist.

It is not belittling Madame's achievement to remember that the straws were already in the wind in the matter of what may be called atmospheric – or, to be currently fashionable, 'environmental' – settings. David Garrick had imported initial attempts from France, and we have noted the Kemble/Planché *King John*. Madame's great contribution was to apply these things, again from French experience, to comedy and plays of ordinary life though the full significance of this development would not become apparent until after her death. It must be added that the practical application of these things was brought to a hitherto undreamt of perfection under her supervision.

There was, however, no sign of considerate management in the wind. The old notion of a 'company of players' had, in London and to a large extent elsewhere, long since been replaced by individual performers trying to outdo each other in order to get employed by a management that had to make enough money to pay those who owned the land the theatre stood on. Thus the only people who could not lose were those who had least to do with the business that kept them. There were instances of interested, and even theatrical, people among the landlords and patent holders, but basically they were primarily concerned with the quantitative rather than the qualitative yield of their investment.

There had been benevolent management of a sort, under the unchallenged authority of a star performer who could show a paternal concern for those who provided the setting for his centre-of-the-stage position and paid due respect to his status and pronouncements off the stage. In the case of Macready this public benevolence was backed by a private contempt of the trade that birth and circumstances had led him to.

Madame introduced considerate management, a proposition that was naturally deemed to be financially disastrous and theatrically dangerous. 'Stars' brought in money and there were always more than enough people to fill in the supporting roles. No one knew this better than Madame, who had had more than a few squabbles about her own star status, but to the invaluable and irreplaceable asset of her own theatrical experience were added three other considerations: the depressed condition of the major theatres was the cause as much as the result of the scarcity of stars and the public neglect; the happier state of the minor theatres indicated that any new developments would be in their direction, but, with the number of minor theatres that already existed, any new venture was a gamble, and a contented company would make that gamble more likely to succeed.

The situation resembled that of the Boulevard theatres (between themselves and between them and the National French companies) and although in a stronger position than Pixérécourt as far as her recruits were concerned, Madame shared his attitudes and working premises in her dealings with actors and staff. Authority was delegated and responsibility assumed unless and until it proved either misplaced or diminished. Good manners and efficient work were presumed. Individual cases of distress, professional or personal, were brought to the notice of the management and help given.

Instances of all these things are found in the reminiscences and anecdotes recorded by those who worked with Madame under all her periods of management. Whatever they might have felt about Madame personally or as an actress, for instance Vandenhoff's dislike, all agree that there was no more agreeable or reliable management to work for. Planché, in his preface to his *Puss in Boots* (1837), records kindnesses to Emma Murray, at the Olympic and later at Covent Garden when Miss Murray had been forced out of early retirement by unjust treatment, and there are many other indications that this was not an exceptional case. Companies and staff were always paid in preference to other creditors and often when the actress/manageress took no salary herself, for example in the third Covent Garden season.

Unlike Pixerécourt, Madame Vestris was a performer as well as a manageress, and the public wanted to see her perform – she was a star. This complicated to some extent the democratic theatrical attitudes that her management fostered and it made problems, as has been noted, for those who had no high opinion of the star but appreciated the manageress. The difference of sex also complicated things. For Lucy Eliza fascinated many gentlemen and some who had no hope of gaining admittance to the bedroom hoped that they might at least get into the office. When they did not they got spiteful.

Molloy Westmacott, a journalist, or more accurately a gossip writer and theatrical reviewer, had for some time appointed himself in his columns as Madame's admiring adviser. He was indignant that any other gentleman should be chosen as adviser for the new manageress and a campaign was launched, in *The Age*, against both Madame and Planché. The fair lessee was not without her defenders and champions (notably 'Handsome' Jack Phillipson) and the press generally made much of the business. The trouble made by Westmacott is now only of interest as an indication of some of the problems that life as a manageress brought for a woman.

There is, however, one happy result of Westmacott's muck-raking and slander. It was the means of recording for us the name by which Planché was known to the stage staff, and given him, no doubt affectionately rather than viciously, by the Olympic carpenters: Plank.

An unhappy result was that Westmacott's false picture of declining houses in the mid-thirties at the Olympic has helped to endorse the general feeling that the whole venture was a financial failure, seeming to prove that management on Madame's lines was impractical.

Both Pixerécourt and Madame Vestris died short of funds, despite years in which they had been earning thousands. The destruction of his theatre by fire ruined Pixerécourt, in the days before insurance. Personal combined with professional extravagance has usually been given as Madame's financial dowfall. It would be fairer to say that lack of sound financial advice was the real problem. Her head followed Planché who just went on designing prettier, cleverer, and more expensive toys, whose manufacture might have been curbed or adapted by a shrewd and resourceful Production Manager (a type then unknown); while her heart, more disastrously, followed one who *The Times* was to call a 'noble dupe' to the bankruptcy discussed below. These things, like the fire in Paris, consumed the money, not the kind of management that was attempted.

A sound financial adviser could also have prevented or checked the abuses of trust that her good intentions exposed her to. She was cheated by her box-keeper, Norton, and by her brother-in-law, Anderson. The Anderson business was all part of the bankruptcy mess. In the case of Norton she might have reflected that she would have done better to emulate her predecessor as a lady manager, one Mrs Baker, mentioned by a Kent paper quoted in *The Times* ten days after the Olympic season began. This lady was the mother-in-law of the actor, William Dowton, and she leased and managed theatres in Tunbridge Wells, Maidstone, Rochester and Canterbury. At all these theatres she was always present for performances and took the money in person!

On the opening night of her management, after three rounds of applause from the over-crowded house, Eliza Lucy spoke the Opening Address. It was written by John Hamilton Reynolds at the request of Planché. It was frequently interrupted by applause:

> 'Noble and Gentle-Matrons-Patrons-Friends!
> Before you here a venturous woman bends!
> A warrior woman – that in strife embarks,
> The first of all dramatic Joan of Arcs.
> Cheer on the enterprise, thus dared by me!
> The first that ever led a company!
> What though, until this very hour and age,
> A lessee-lady never owned a stage!
> I'm that Belle Sauvage – only rather quieter,
> Like Mrs Nelson,* turned a stage proprietor!
> Welcome each early and each late arriver –
> This is my omnibus, and I'm the driver!
> Sure is my venture, for all honest folk,
> Who love a tune, or can enjoy a joke,
> Will know, whene'er they have an hour of leisure,
> Wych Street is best to come to for their pleasure.
> The laughter and the lamps, with equal share,
> Shall make this house a LIGHT-house against care.
> This is our home! 'Tis yours as well as mine;
> Here Joy may pay her homage at Mirth's shrine;
> Song, Whim, and Fancy jocund rounds shall dance,
> And lure for you light Vaudeville from France.

* A lady well known to the coaching men of the day.

Humour and Wit encourage my intent,
And Music means to help me pay my rent.
'Tis not mere promise — I appeal to facts;
Henceforward judge me only by my ACTS!
In this, my purpose, stand I not alone —
All women sigh for houses of their own;
And I was weary of perpetual dodging
From house to house, in search of board and lodging!
Faint was my heart, but, with Pandora's scope,
I find in every BOX a lurking hope;
My dancing spirits know of no decline,
Here's the first TIER you've ever seen of mine.
Oh, my kind friends! befriend me still, as you
Have in the bygone times been wont to do;
Make me your ward against each ill designer,
And prove Lord Chancellor to a female MINOR.
Cheer on my comrades, too, in their career;
Some of your favourites are around me here.
Give them — give me — the smiles of approbation,
In this Olympic game of speculation;
Still aid the petticoat on old, kind principles,
And make me yet a Captain of INVINCIBLES*!'

This light but very accurate summing up of the situation written for the one occasion was followed, when the applause finally subsided, by the singing of the National Anthem led by the fair lessee.

The first item on the 'four piece bill' was a two-act play that, because of the Monopoly, had to be termed a 'burlesque', called *Mary, Queen of Scots or, The Escape from Loch Leven*, by W. H. Murray. This featured Maria Foote, a great public favourite, especially admired for, and skilled in, portrayals of damsels (royal and otherwise) in distress and gentlewomen of good manners but sterling and staunch character. Madame Vestris could not have had a better opposite number on the female side, they balanced each other splendidly as colleagues and friends.

The first visual surprise of the evening had been the auditorium. Externally there had been no real alteration to the building, but the inside had been as thoroughly cleaned and overhauled as the limited time had allowed. The effect pleased, but such redecoration by a new management and for a new season was not unusual — Elliston had also redecorated the Olympic when he managed it and the work was much praised. The pleasure given by the appearance of the Olympic in 1831 was due to the feminine touch that had been introduced.

* A farce that had been one of her big successes at Covent Garden.

The second visual surprise was the new curtain that had replaced the old green baize one, modelled on the curtains at the majors. These green baize curtains were gathered up rather than drawn up, by the several threads running from top to bottom, a method that left a looped pelmet effect framing the top of the proscenium arch. The new curtain for the Olympic parted in the middle to be lifted out of sight on either side, French fashion, like the curtain of the Royal Opera House, Covent Garden today. Such a curtain gives much more elegance and intimacy, especially to a small auditorium, than the more traditional kind, though more expensive to buy and more difficult to install — two considerations that were secondary with Madame.

By Permission of the Lord Chamberlain.

Madame VESTRIS'
Royal Olympic Theatre,
Newcastle Street, Strand.

Madame VESTRIS begs leave most respectfully to announce to the Nobility, and Public in general, that having become SOLE LESSEE of the above Establishment, it will open for the Season,

ON MONDAY, JANUARY 3rd, 1831,
WHEN
AN OCCASIONAL ADDRESS
Will be spoken by Madame VESTRIS.
Which, will be immediately succeeded by
"God save the King!" Verse & Chorus, by all the Company.

The whole of the Scenery painted by Mr ALLEN, Mr. ROBERTS, & Assistants.—The Dresses, by Mr. SMITHERS & Miss IRELAND.

The Performances will commence with an entirely New Historical Burletta, called

MARY, QUEEN of SCOTS

Lord George Douglas, Mr. FREDERICKS;   Lord Lindsay, Mr. BROUGHAM,
Sir Robert Melville, Mr. WORRELL, Lord Ruthven, Mr. BECKWITH, Roland, Mr. RAYMOND,
Drysdale, Mr. NEWCOMBE,   Sandy, Mr. J. KNIGHT.
Officers, Messrs. DURAND and W. YOUNG.   Servants, Messrs. G. BRADY and NEALE.

Mary Stuart, (Queen of Scots) Miss FOOTE,
(Who has kindly given her valuable services for a limited number of Nights.)
Lady Douglas, Mrs. KNIGHT,   Catherine Seyton, Miss PINCOTT,   Lady Fleming, Miss KING,
Mattie, Miss KIBREY,   Moggy, Miss LANGLEY,   Jenny, Miss SLATER.

To which will be added (FOR THE FIRST TIME) a Grand Allegorical Burlesque Burletta, in One Act, *not translated from the French,* but borrowed from the *English* of George Colman, the Younger, the HEADS being taken from that Gentleman's TALE of "*The Sun Poker,*" in his "*Eccentricities for Edinburg,*" and humbly offered in a new shape, as "*Laughables for London,*" under the title of

OLYMPIC REVELS!
Or, PROMETHEUS AND PANDORA.
Previous to which, an OVERTURE, composed by J. N. HUMMEL.
MORTALS.

Prometheus, *(an eminent Man-ufacturer)* Mr. J. COOPER, Swiss Boy, *(a great Anachronism)* Mr. BECKWITH,

Pandora, { *a Mettlesome Lady, forged by Vulcan to be passed upon Prometheus, and pleading guilty to the minor offence of UTTERING NOTES for her own Benefit.* } **Madme. VESTRIS.**

IMMORTALS—OLYMPIC REVELLERS.
" In their habits as they lived," and with the habits they've contracted.

Jupiter, Mr. J. KNIGHT,   Neptune, Mr. W. YOUNG,   Hercules, Mr. WORRELL,
Plutus, Mr. PAGET,   Vulcan, Mr. BROWN,
Apollo, Miss MELBOURNE,   Bacchus, Mr. W. VINING,
Momus, Mr. D. SMITH, Esculapius, Mr. COATES, Somnus, Mr. JAMES, Mars, Mr. BROUGHAM,
Cupid, Miss JOSEPHINE,   Mercury, Mr. NEWCOMBE.
Ganymede, Miss GREENER, Minerva, Mrs. THOMAS, Juno. Miss STUART, Hope, Miss LANGLEY.
THE NEW SCENERY WILL EXHIBIT
THE SUMMIT OF OLYMPUS, with an Olympic Game (AT WHIST.)
A STREET, ON EARTH, (as unlike Regent Street as possible.)
Prometheus' Work Shop, in *Body* colours, with *the Devil to Pay* for Peeping.

To be followed by Comic Burletta, call The

The third visual surprise came when 'Queen Mary's room in Loch Leven Castle' was revealed. Planché had had a field day. Old furniture and curio shops had been sought out to find authentic looking items for this setting. Where genuine carved oak could not be found for an item, wood was carved and stained to resemble carved oak, nothing two-dimensional was allowed in the furnishings. Presumably the back drop was painted – from necessity rather than desire! The arms of Stuart were seen on every item of furniture and the motif was repeated on candlesticks and even cutlery. The carpet on the floor carried the same motif. Planché's aim was to transport the audience into a 'real' Stuart room, to present an accurate historic picture, which then came to life.

Thus, within half an hour of the opening of the season, Madame had pioneered another theatrical practice for Britain: the design and execution of a setting immediately and exclusively related to the matter of the play. This tradition is now so taken for granted that it is difficult to imagine the impact that such things had on the first audiences that saw them. And if we could see that first Olympic setting it might well remind us of the settings for some of the earliest silent films, with the important differences of actuality and a third dimension.

Size had something to do with the initial impact of the setting. Converting the small stage of the Olympic into Mary Stuart's room was a very different matter, financially and practically, from attempting a similar effect at Covent Garden or Drury Lane. From the available evidence it seems probable that before later alterations the acting area at the Olympic was between a quarter and a third of the acting area at either of the patent theatres. The difference in height, of settings and facilities, was even greater. In such an intimate theatre, with the audience so close to the stage, there must have been a feeling of being drawn into the setting. The motifs on the candlesticks, for example, could be seen by a good many of the audience. At Drury Lane they would hardly have been distinguishable to any.

Maria Foote acquitted herself well as the 'tragic queen'. It would be fascinating to know how the lady felt, how she reacted and responded as an actress to the advantages and the drawbacks of the setting. The text is a routine but quite effective piece of historical romance making no specific demands of the set and no concessions to language or turns of phrase that would parallel the authentic atmosphere of the setting. (The same mixture of 'period' dialogue – often ludicrous and sometimes impossible – and authenticity of setting is still found in films.)

We are going through a time now when the designer of stage settings often assumes an authority far beyond his real importance and that all too often works against the play and the actors. This danger was already apparent at the Olympic and in Madame's subsequent managerial ventures. Although his comments on Madame Vestris and other performers are always charming and grateful, it is very clear that Planché was primarily interested in the setting and presentation of his and other pieces. He rendered great service to the theatre and to the education of the public. He was a true 'amateur' who found a highly professional playmate to interpret his theories in theatrical terms; not practical terms, for, as has been noted, the treasury was often embarrassed by Madame's desire to realize the charming dreams of Planché.

To recognize this is not to deny the value and the importance of Planché's work to the theatre and especially to playwrighting. For his ideas as realized by Madame made the audience look at the stage and *see* what they were looking at. Having seen the look of those Stuart pieces grouped together around those Stuart dresses, *Mary, Queen of Scots* would have a lasting pictorial effect on the audience — an effect that would lead them to query anything less 'correct' in the future. It was a long process, over a few decades, and involved the growth of a new school of acting that recognized and worked within the discipline of a restricted setting, but it eventually produced audiences that, trained to look, began to listen and to relate behaviour to surroundings and language to atmosphere. So much established, dramatists could let dialogue explore motives, leaving the setting and costumes to take care of behaviour, comically as in Wilde and Shaw, or tragically as in Ibsen and O'Neill, to name extremes.

Maria Foote coped with Planché's Stuart competition, and neither she nor her audience were concerning themselves with decades ahead. Planché was enjoying the successful transfer of his historical imagination from the study to the stage. Madame was probably keeping one eye on the stage and the other on her (doubtless pretty and expensive) watch. She was under the stage, waiting to pop up through her trapdoor, as the enthusiastic reception broke in waves over Maria.

Reference to the playbills will have shown the first members of the cast of *Olympic Revels* as follows:

MORTALS

PROMETHEUS (an eminent *Man*-ufacturer) Mr. J. Cooper
SWISS BOY (A *Great* Anachronism. . .) Mr. Beckwith
PANDORA (a Mettlesome Lady, forged by
Vulcan to be passed upon Prometheus,
and pleading guilty to the minor
offence of uttering notes for her
own Benefit)   Madame Vestris

The rest of the cast, some seventeen of them, are listed without comment, but these punning programmes were to become a regular feature of this type of entertainment up to the present day.

Olympic Revels was an engaging romp in the old tradition, costuming being left to do the educating in this case, all very intimate and introvert in its puns, jokes and merry allusions to the new manageress. She was called upon to offer her established stage personality and charm, never more winningly displayed than in her verse in the final song:

'Ye belles and ye beaux,
Who adorn our low rows
Ye gods, who preside in the high ones;
Ye critics who sit
All so snug in the pit, —
An assemblage of clever and sly ones!
Let the smile of content
On our efforts be bent;
Hope anxiously waits an encora;
In the fate-dooming scale,
Oh! let mercy prevail,
And be kind to poor little Pandora.'

It is perhaps of interest to note that Madame did not have the last word or verse – this was left to Mr Knight as Jupiter.

The next two pieces were for the senior players in the company: *The Little Jockey* for John Liston and, 'top of the bill', *Clarissa Harlowe* for Mrs Glover. There was nothing new in these and the audience would not have liked it if there had been. Things to come might have been casting their shadows earlier in the evening but, for the end, folk wanted some laughter and sentiment to see them happily on their way, and Madame was shrewd enough to know this.

It is greatly to the credit of Lucy Eliza that she treated such established actors as Liston and Mrs Glover with consideration and respect. It was a major point of policy to take care of the dignity and the comfort of her employees in whatever department and, with the younger members, to train them in her ways. But even when established practices might be contrary to her convictions she did not prevent good older performers from following them if they wished. An example of this is the Benefit that was given to Mrs Glover when, by substituting the payment of fixed and regular salaries, Madame had abolished Benefits for her company.

The first evening, like the short season that followed it, was a success. The nobility and the public in general filled the house every night and the Olympic Theatre found itself in the novel position of being *the* smart place to be seen:

'Amongst the numerous visitors of the Olympic Theatre we noticed (in the course of the week) the following fashionables:– Duke of Richmond, Lord and Lady Mountcharles, Lady Georgina Paget, Lady Agnes Byng, Earl Mountedgcumbe, Lord and Lady Edward Thynne, Lord and Lady Rendlesham, Lady Knatchbull, Lord Adolphus Fitzclarence, Honourable Mrs Mulgrave, Lord Bolingbroke, etc., etc., etc.'

106

On St Valentine's Day, *The Times* carried a tribute from a fashionable beau and old acquaintance:

STANZAS
ON MADAME VESTRIS HAVING ESTABLISHED
A THEATRE OF HER OWN
BY SIR LUMLEY SKEFFINGTON

'Now Vestris, the tenth of the Muses,
To Mirth rears a fanciful dome,
We mark, while delight she infuses,
The Graces find Beauty at home.
In her eye such vivacity glitters,
To her voice such perfection belongs,
That care and the life it embitters,
Find Balm in the sweets of her song.
When monarchs o'er vallies are ranging,
A court is transferr'd to the green,
And flowers, transplanted, are changing
Not fragrance, but merely the scene.
'Tis circumstance dignifies places;
A desert is charming with Spring!
And pleasure finds twenty new graces,
Wherever the Vestris may sing.'

Fourteen new productions were given between 3 January and 26 March, Madame appearing in four of them, in three male roles and Pandora – thus 'displaying her charms' as well as her talents. It cannot be said that any of the pieces offered are worth consideration as any more than ephemeral pieces designed (except for *Diavolo* which had only three performances) expressly for the Olympic. The season was generally felt to be, like the decorations in the auditorium, a triumph of feminine charm and ability:

'OLYMPIC THEATRE. –Wych-Street ought to change its name, and henceforth be called Witch-Street, for great is the enchantment of Vestris and Foote. The two principal actresses are excellent; the pieces diverting; but the male performers are not to be written of, for very pity. The ladies have resolved on keeping all the merit to themselves; and as there is so much, and so prettily displayed, we will not quarrel with them for the monopoly. Miss Foote makes a beautiful and elegant *Mary of Scotland* and Madame Vestris, in *Pandora*, will fill more boxes than she empties. The only fault of her boxes is, that there is no hope, at the bottom, of getting into them. The house is nightly crammed.'

Madame's first lease terminated on 10 April. By 13 February she had applied for a new one for five years, so quickly had success been established: 'The Olympic closes to-night, after a season that can scarcely have failed to be as profitable as it must have been pleasant to its lively entrepreneuse.'

Before the season ended another important innovation had been introduced, again by chance. As the idea originated with Planché, his own account of it, from his *Recollections and Reflections*, is worth quoting:

'Its sudden removal (*Mary, Queen of Scots*) for some cause or other, occasioned the performances of that evening to terminate at eleven instead of twelve. Dance and I, going out with the crowd, heard several expressions of gratification at the prospect of getting home at a rational hour, and the fact favourably contrasted with the practice at other theatres of prolonging the performance till long past midnight, so that persons living at any distance could not possibly be in their beds before the small hours in the morning. The following day therefore, when Madame Vestris consulted us as to what should be the programme for the following week, we advised her strongly to take advantage of the circumstance, and instead of substituting any drama for the one withdrawn, to announce in the bills that the performances for the future would be so arranged as to terminate every evening as nearly as possible at eleven o'clock.

'Our advice was taken. The new arrangement gave general satisfaction, and continued during the whole period of Madame Vestris' lessee-ship, one of the many agreeable features that distinguished the Olympic Theatre. The lines in the finale to the *Olympic Devils*,

"Since home at eleven you take yourselves,
It cannot be said that you rake yourselves,"

were invariably received with applause as well as laughter by the audience.'

But old habits die hard and, in 1872, he is still having to make his point: 'It ought surely to be a self-evident fact that nothing can be more injurious to a theatre than the exhaustion of the actors and the wearying of the public by the spinning out of the performances to so late an hour as is still too frequently the practice at more than one theatre.'

The 'entrepreneuse' gave her farewell address to a house 'crowded almost to suffocation':

'Ladies and Gentlemen – The last night of our little season has already arrived, and I appear before you to say "Farewell!" At its commencement I had recourse to poetry in my address to you, the better to describe the hopes and fears which actuated me. Circumstances are now changed. I have tried, and I have succeeded! (LOUD APPLAUSE FROM ALL PARTS OF THE

108

HOUSE.) Fiction must, therefore, be laid aside and truth, in its own honest prose, express the heartfelt gratitude of this first female lessee. Woman is said to be a contradiction – this I, for one, dare not deny; for I own that I stand here a thoroughly contented manager (APPLAUSE). We have done the best which the suddeness of the undertaking permitted, to deserve your support. We have produced several new pieces, some of which have been eminently successful – *none* of which have failed. We have introduced to you several new faces, whom three short months have served to convert into old friends. Thus much I may speak for the past – the future shall speak for itself. I leave you with the sincerest wishes of a grateful heart for your health and happiness, until our next October Meeting; and when the gloom of winter shall again be on your heads, come to the Olympic, and it shall go hard but we will kindle a summer of merriment in your hearts. At all events, no exertion shall be spared on my part to win from you an admission, that, *"the women are the best Managers after all"* (LOUD CHEERING) – I have now only to offer you the sincere thanks of the performers generally, for the kind encouragement they have met with. Be assured, they all feel it as they ought. In fact, Ladies and Gentlemen, the *heart* of the Establishment is full, and the *head* of the Establishment is here to say so. As *Fanny Bolton*, the Captain of Grenadiers (PLACING HER HAND TO HER FOREHEAD), I salute my company in the pit. As *Julian*, the Page, I pay respectful duty to the boxes; and as *Pandora*, I drop my curtsey to the gods.

'Madame Vestris then curtsied three times and retired, the audience giving her three rounds of applause.'

(The *British Stage; or Dramatic Censor*, April 1831)

9

Love and Marriage

Madame ran the Olympic for nine years, from 3 January 1831 to 31 May 1839. She began the venture as the widow Vestris and ended it as Mrs Charles Mathews, but professionally she was always Madame and for the public she was always Vestris.

It was during the second Olympic season that the first contact was made between Madame and Charles James Mathews – though Madame did not, in fact, know with whom she was corresponding. Mathews had asked John Liston to offer a play for consideration. Although the son of the celebrated comedian, Charles Mathews, young Charles did not intend to be an actor. In the early 1830s he was something of a gentleman of leisure, still dabbling in various things and enjoying frequent visits to great houses and noble persons, in Britain and abroad. His hosts and hostesses appreciated his charm and he was invaluable for charades and amateur performances 'got up' for diversion and sometimes for the support of charitable causes. Among his hosts were Lady Blessington and Count d'Orsay.

Madame's reply was encouraging:

'Olympic Theatre, Monday, 12th Dec., 1831

'Sir,

I received your letter this morning, and have read your piece, "Pyramus and Thisbe", which I approve of much, as well as Mr. Liston, who has also read it.

'My usual terms for a one-act piece are twenty-five pounds, and if this meets your views I shall be glad to hear from you immediately, as I shall put it into hand without loss of time.

'Your request as to the *nom de guerre* shall be most faithfully attended to.

I am, Sir,

Your very obedient Servant,

E. VESTRIS'

Mathews's desire for anonymity might have been due to his reluctance to let his mother know that he was attempting to get a play on with that lady at the Olympic. The play was not, in fact, done and it was another four years before he decided upon the theatre as a living and began the period of his life described under the heading 'Difficulties 1835–1858' in his autobiography, and which demonstrated for him 'how easy are the stages by which a man may descend from the airy empyrean of poetry, music, and painting, to the heavy slough of pounds, shillings and pence'.

Mathews does not say whether it was before or after the submission of his play that the following incident occurred:

'. . . my last return from Italy. When slowly recovering from my long illness, I paid a visit to the Olympic with my father and mother. At the end of the performance I was carried down from the box in the arms of my Italian servant, and we were invited to wait in the little treasury of the theatre, in order to escape the crowd at the doors. After our departure a lady remarked to the stage-manager, looking after me as I was lifted into the carriage: "Ah! poor young man! it's all over with him – he's not long for this world!"

'How astonished would that lady have been had she been told that she would be my wife for eighteen years, which, however, turned out to be the case.'

By the time Mathews joined the company the Olympic had established itself as the most successful theatre in London. Envied and imitated but not surpassed, it became a model of efficient management and high-class entertainment. Production followed production, all of them sustaining a standard of presentation that left the reviewers at a loss to find new superlatives and expressions of delighted surprise. The constant praise reads tediously but is indisputable evidence of Madame's achievement.

No less than sixty-eight new pieces were put on during the first five seasons, covering some twenty-seven calendar months. Madame appeared in twenty-five of these and supervised them all, as well as going on tours between the seasons.

Westland Marston remembered these years in *Our Recent Actors* (1888). The distance of fifty years may be expected to lend a certain enchantment to his memories, but his analysis of acting suggests that he probably recorded many of

A Cast List, 1835

his impressions immediately. His account of Madame Vestris's handling of an audience is invaluable evidence. It provides clues to the praises of the press, and also explains why that praise was general rather than specific.

It is worth preceding Marston's account of Madame with his description of the effect of a London evening on a young man when the Olympic seasons were established as a part of London life:

'An evening in the summer of 1835 still lives distinctly in my memory. It was the height of the seaon, and when, between five and six o'clock, I found myself in Piccadilly, opposite the Green Park (having probably made my way to this point from the grand old trees of Kensington Gardens), the road was still crowded with lines of carriages and equestrians bound to or returning from Hyde Park. To a lad's eye the scene was, of course, enchanting. How delightful the fresh green of the trees, the brightness of the evening, the effects of sunlight on harness or emblazoned panel, or the glimpse of grace and beauty as some fair Amazon dashed by. Then, on nearing Regent Street, how brilliant the shops with their glittering windows, where more than the

112

treasures of an Eastern bazaar were displayed. These, with the shops of Regent Street itself, had probably offered me many temptations to linger, to say nothing of an episodic seduction in the shape of the Burlington Arcade, with its cool, mysterious shade, its treasures of French nick-nacks, its fascinations in haberdashery, its imitation jewellery, and its autographed likenesses of reigning celebrities in opera and ballet.'

He gives the following account of Vestris at the Olympic. He thinks the year was 1836, but the reference to *Olympic Revels* indicates an earlier date:

'. . . her charm was not the less that it is rather difficult to define it . . . That she had no title . . . to claim an eminent position either as vocalist or actress, seems to have been the general impression. She had, however, with playgoers, such great popularity, that to seek for the grounds of it may not be uninteresting.

'In the first place, though she could not boast the highest qualifications for her profession, she had some that stand the owner in even better stead. Her voice in a ballad had great expression, and, to use Leigh Hunt's words, "all the ripeness of the South in it". She was charmingly arch and vivacious, with a happy carelessness which helped effect, with an occasional air of playful *mutinerie* that increased public favour by her evident consciousness of it. Let it be added that she never failed to give her personal attraction the advantage of rich and tasteful costume, and that she was such a votary of elegance in dress, that she would display it even in rustic or humble characters. That a silk skirt, a lace-edged petticoat, a silk stocking, a shoe of satin or patent leather, would never have been worn by some of the characters she personated, was of no more concern to her on the ground of consistency than were their rich attires to Marie Antoinette and the ladies of her court, when they masqueraded as shepherdesses and milkmaids in the grounds of the Petit Trianon. . . . she cultivated a personal understanding with her audience. It was, I fancy, her practice of taking the house into her confidence, combined with her coquetry and personal attractions, that rendered Vestris so bewitching to the public. When she sang, she looked with a questioning archness at her audience, as if to ask, "Do you enjoy that as I do? Did I give it with tolerable effect?" and though in the delivery of dialogue she could hardly be called keen or brilliant, she knew what mischief and retort meant. When she had given a sting to the latter, she would glance round, as to ask for approval, with a smile that seemed to say, "I was a little severe there. He felt that, I suppose?" She had on the stage, either real or assumed, the abstraction of a spoiled favourite. Thus, on the night of my first seeing her — as Psyche, I think, in *Olympic Revels* — she would at times seem absorbed in contemplating her dress, in adjusting a sleeve or a fold of the skirt, or she would drop her eye in reverie upon the point of her pink satin *bottine*. Of a sudden she would affect to wake to consciousness, and cast a trustful and appealing glance on the house, then become demure and staid, as one who felt that she had taxed indulgence. She had skill enough not to carry these little pantomimic contrasts too far, and to enchance them by fits of reserve.'

This certainly describes an 'artiste' rather than an 'actrice', perfectly suited to a theatre such as the Olympic. It describes what today would be called cabaret technique, which might or might not work on television.

At the same time that Vestris was making productions she was also making actors. Stylized and broadly defined movement, based mainly on the head, arms, and legs, evolved to complement — and to counter — two-dimensional scenery and large theatres, was deprived of its excuses and reduced to absurdity in three-dimensional settings in a small theatre. Greater flexibility, based on the whole body and features, had to be acquired to convey subtler points related to an intimate setting. Working in the freedom of her own theatre and against the restrictions of the theatrical laws of the time, Madame pioneered the practical basis for the revival of playwrighting and the education of actors and audiences who could respond to the great European dramatists that she would never know.

In the theatre it is always the performers who do the pioneering work and the playwrights who follow on and build. To make this point often provokes an unease in academic rather than practical persons interested in theatre history, as if the achievement of, for example, *A Doll's House* should have made a style of playing rather than the other way around. Potential Norahs and Torvalds were being made at the Olympic in the 1830s.

It is true that on paper there is little to show for it. There is really no play worth reviving from those Olympic seasons, and little enough of anything original that Madame ever put on. The immediacy that gives theatrical performance its great poignancy and charm eludes satisfactory recording and the memory of one occasion is soon eclipsed or distorted by succeeding ones so that, without a major playwright to distil the essence of the achievement, pioneers such as Madame Vestris have no lasting monument.

Again, it must be emphasized that no claim is being made for Madame Vestris as a conscious pioneer, as an earlier and feminine Copeau, for example. The Drama with a capital D had never brought her much success and was associated, for her, with acting and management that was pompous, and unpopular with her admirers both among the nobility and the public in general. In setting up shop at the Olympic she was as concerned as Macready to gather a company that would be responsive to the mood and style of the leader of the company. But her style of acting and of presentation required *inter*acting for its best effects combined with an intimacy with the audience that had made the Boulevard actors so popular. The fascination and the pleasure of such a style

114

comes from true theatrical irony: immense care is taken to deceive the eye at the same time as the mind is being asked to enjoy the deceit.

Like clowning, which also demonstrates the absurdity that balances the human condition, such an acting style is at least as dependent upon physical as upon verbal dexterity. 'The wife of Vestris may naturally be presumed to move with grace', and her subsequent career had endorsed the early training and observation, and it is probable that her work at the Olympic was mainly concerned with getting greater physical flexibility from her company.

But for the Olympic Charles Mathews would not have been lured into the theatre:

'I had no passion for what was called the "regular drama". I had no respect for traditional acting, and had no notion of taking a "line of business", as it is called — that is, undertaking for so much per week all the characters in comedy and tragedy, whether fitting or not, played by Mr. Charles Kemble, or Mr. Jones, or Mr. Elliston, whose every movement was registered in the prompt-book, and from whose "business", as it is technically termed, no deviation was allowed. The lighter phase of comedy, representing the more natural and laboured school of modern life, and holding the mirror up to nature without regard to the conventionalities of the theatre, was the aim I had in view. The Olympic was then the only house where this could be achieved, and to the Olympic I at once attached myself. There was introduced for the first time in England that reform in all theatrical matters which has since been adopted in every theatre in the kingdom. Drawing rooms were fitted up like drawing rooms, and furnished with care and taste. Two chairs no longer indicated that two persons were to be seated, the two chairs being removed indicating that the two persons were not to be seated. A claret-coloured coat, salmon-coloured trowsers with a broad black stripe, a sky-blue neckcloth with a large paste brooch, and a cut-steel eye-glass with a pink ribbon no longer marked the "light comedy gentlemen", and the public at once recognized and appreciated the change.'

It was almost certainly John Liston, an old friend of the elder Mathews and his wife, who introduced young Charles, this time under his own name, to Madame. She agreed with Liston's estimate of the young man and they persuaded him to give up his idea of a time in the provinces and to make his début at the Olympic.

An easy, graceful manner of performing was not the only talent that recommended Charles James to the management. Personally he was slim, tall, good-looking, by nature and by education a 'gentleman'; socially, he had a wide and impressive circle of friends and acquaintances who made his début one of the events of the fashionable as well as the theatrical season; professionally, he had a flair for dancing, some ability in singing, a facility for writing light dialogue in a witty manner, and an excellent judgement for assessing and editing scripts. Such a congenial and useful new recruit, so well recommended and a disciple of her own theatrical faith, was inevitably much in demand by the manageress. That his professional collaboration should eventually be extended into a personal liaison with Madame was perhaps just as inevitable.

Charles James made a début on 7 December 1835, that was as enthusiastically received as Lucy's had been, and almost as aristocratically attended. The sailor king, William IV, did not lead a society as brilliant, or as brittle, as had the Prince Regent. The 'romantic' mood, losing some of its cruder manifestations in crossing the Channel, was in the ascendant, not a little indebted to the old affinity between France and Scotland (that opening piece for Maria Foote was timely done).

Having seen him safely launched, Madame appeared with her new recruit in his next part. *One Hour, or A Carnival Ball*, by T. H. Bayly, opened on 11 January 1836.

Matthew Mackintosh, who had impressed Madame by his sympathetic efficiency during one of her Scottish tours, had taken her at her word when she said, 'If ever you come to London be sure to give me a call. I may have a theatre of my own one day'. She engaged him as carpenter for the Olympic from the second season. He published his *Stage Reminiscences* in 1866. His account of Madame's earlier years is wildly inaccurate – though not scurrilous – but his record of 'perhaps the happiest period of my theatrical career' at the Olympic reads authentically. Mackintosh records the opening of *One Hour* and his description is evocative and informative:

> 'On the first night of "One Hour", when he commenced the song he sings to Julia, accompanied by himself on the guitar, his courage seemed somehow to forsake him. Whether it were owing to the fact that it was his first musical effort on the stage, or to some other cause, I don't know, but his voice faltered and he broke down. An experienced general was at his elbow, however. Without appearing in the least disconcerted at his dilemma, Madame smilingly said to him, "Try it again – you did very well indeed at rehearsal this morning." This was said in hearing of the audience, and the round of cheering which it evoked seemed to break the spell that bound him. A fresh attempt was completely successful, and the song was heartily encored.'

Note Madame's absolute assurance and awareness of her personal power over the audience, as well as her concern for Charles. Mackintosh goes on to mention the tarantella that Mathews danced in the 'superbly got up and managed' ball-room scene in the same play, and adds: 'The veteran Oscar Byrne arranged all the dancing business, and so anxious was that accomplished professor that nothing should go wrong, with the tarantella especially, that he went

116

CHARLES JAMES MATHEWS, 1835

Madame's second husband-to-be as he appeared at his Olympic début on 7 December. An elegant and charming addition to the company, just what Madame needed to give a new lift to the sixth Olympic Season. The play was the *Humpbacked Lover* and the character was George Rattleton.

on the stage, made up as a Neapolitan fisherman, and beat time to it on a tambourine himself . . .' a good clue to the atmosphere that made the company such a successful working unit. Westland Marston rates *One Hour*, 'an insipid piece, which owed everything to her manner and the mercurial spirit of Mr. C. Mathews.'

The advent of a new leading man at the Olympic who was also something of a playwright made no difference to the type of material that was written and produced for the Olympic. The output went up: seventy-two new productions in

MADAME VESTRIS'
Royal Olympic Theatre,

ONE HOUR, EVERY EVENING.

This Evening, TUESDAY, January 12th, 1836,
Will be presented (Seventeenth Time) a BURLETTA, entitled

BARBERS AT COURT.

Charles the Second, - Mr. HOOPER,	Rochester, - Mr. JAMES VINING,
Maximus Hogsflesh, (*the Court Barber*) Mr LISTON,	Magnus, (*his Son*) Mr. KEELEY,
The Queen, - - - Miss PAGET,	Catherine, - - - Mrs. ANDERSON.

After which, an **ORIGINAL BURLETTA**, by the Author of "*Perfection*," "*Comfortable Service*," &c. entitled

ONE HOUR!
OR,
A CARNIVAL BALL.

The New Scenery by Mr. Hilliard and Assistants.—The Dresses by Miss Glover, Miss Ireland, and Assistants.

Mr. Charles Swiftly, - Mr. CHARLES MATHEWS,
In which he will introduce **A NATIONAL AIR.**

O'Leary, Mr. BROUGHAM,   **Mr. Smith, Mr. HUGHES,**

Mrs. Bevil, Mrs. KNIGHT,   **Mrs. Smith, Miss PAGET,**

Miss Dalton, · Madame VESTRIS,
who will sing an entirely **NEW SONG**, called

"LOVE IS THE THEME OF THE MINSTREL,"
(Composed by Mr. TULLY).—And

A NEAPOLITAN AIR.

Characters at the Ball.—Mr. W. Vining, Mr. Wyman, Mr. Collier, Mr. Brayne, Mr. Dubochet. Mr. Hughes, Mr. Kerridge, Mr. Ireland Mr. Connell. Mr. Huggins, Mr. Tully, Mr. Hitchinson, Mr. Morgan,—Mrs. Anderson, Miss Malcolm, Miss Eliza Lee. Miss Goward, Miss Greener, Miss Norman, Miss Lebatt, Miss Holmes, Miss Brothers, Miss M. Lee, Miss Kendall, Miss Paris, Miss Julia Carr, Miss Maxwell, Miss Somerville, Miss F. Kendall, Miss E. Bartlett, Miss Bartlett, Miss Ireland, Miss M. Kendall.

In the course of the Piece **THE NATIONAL DANCE** of

THE TARANTELLA,
By Mr. CHARLES MATHEWS and Miss FITZWALTER.

To which will be added (**25th Time**) an **Original Burletta**, entitled The

OLD AND YOUNG STAGER

Sir Pompadour Puffendale, Mr. F. MATTHEWS,	Mr. Clement, ... (*his Son*) .... Mr. JAMES VINING,
Topple, (*Sir Pompadour's Coachman*) Mr. LISTON,	
Tim, ... (*his Son, and Tiger to Mr. Clement*) .... Mr. CHARLES MATHEWS,	
Slang'em, (*a Bow Street Officer*) Mr. SALTER,	Mr. Stocks, Mr. WYMAN, James, Mr. COLLIER, Dick, Master RYAN,
Lady Puffendale, Mrs. MACNAMARA,	Laura, Miss MALCOLM,
Lu , ... Miss PAGE	Susan ... Miss GOWARD, Miss Lu Stocks, Miss NOR

the sixth to ninth seasons, and the company was increased. The number of plays and the general standard of presentation are a tribute to the organization and ingenuity of Madame and her team of technicians. Similar resourcefulness with limited facilities has been seen in our time at the little Player's Theatre in London for their pantomimes adapted from nineteenth-century Christmas entertainments. But these were once yearly events, whereas the Olympic was open for six-month seasons at a time, and there were several items given on each evening's bill.

Looking through the lists, the theatrical gossip columns, and the notices of the Olympic years, prompts the question whether such ceaseless activity and the constant provision of new novelties did not become a rather desperate pursuit. In its own way it has something of the anxiety behind most serials and comedy series on television.

In Madame's case the laws prevented the use of all that skill and hard work for the benefit of great pieces of comic writing from the past, and we have noted the incompatibility of style and the kind of talent that would have prevented success with these. The same laws had kept any more recent and contemporary potential playwrights from the theatre, where the financial gamble was daunting enough without the political and legal ones being added to it. The material that was available could only be expected to last for a short while, however splendidly served up, before being replaced by a further variation on the standard formula.

The problem of a working formula was a trickier business for Madame and Planché than it had been for Pixerécourt. His audiences were largely illiterate, supposedly equal and politically hopeful. Themes and sights that would alleviate the first condition while encouraging belief in the other two were happily taken in, with the usual dose of morality, by the Boulevard audiences. The nobility and the public in general in the right little, tight little, island were largely ignorant, considered themselves anything but equal and were politically stagnant. One must never presume to educate the British – though you may inform them, preferably in a diverting fashion. Foreigners are 'violent' and 'emotional', the British 'indignant' and 'eccentric' in their extremes. Their moral integrity may be presumed or questioned in jest. Fortunately for the Olympic, these beliefs are common to all classes, together with the British genius that redeems the race – its delight in fun and laughter even at the expense of itself.

With these things in mind, Planché and Charles Dance, with Madame constantly at hand applying Miss Mae West's celebrated maxim: 'It's not what you do, it's the way that you do it', devised a formula. You take a slice of life and show it to be such – you more than imagine that you are there, you are persuaded that you are there in person. Attention is focused on certain individuals in the passing show and we are invited to consider their story. The story might be comically or seriously told, more probably, 'like life', it will have a mixture of both laughter and reflection and even a few tears. The resolution of the story

Madame Vestris and Charles J. Mathews in *One Hour or A Carnival Ball*, 11 January, 1836, their first joint success. The pictures convey the care and tasteful detail in costumes and in setting.

will involve a misunderstanding and a reconciliation, or a revelation and a rejection, these things being effected by means of the most obvious to the most subtle. The characters return to the passing show and the box of tricks closes as the audience reflects that 'there, but for the grace of God . . .' and leaves with a feeling of benevolence and of heightened understanding. Next day they will say how good it was and talk about the scenery and the dresses.

The formula may be used for other times and other manners. Be-wigged and be-spanielled for the Stuarts, or draped and garlanded for Ancient Greece, it can look quite a different thing, but the ingredients will be found to be the same. For the audience are invited to look at, and not into, what they see. Behaviour, not motive, is being presented. Judgement may be made but it is certainly not being required.

Planché and Dance provided more plays for the Olympic than any other authors (Mrs Planché also contributed six), and they set the pattern.

Generally speaking, the mythological and historical pieces were the work of Planché. Dance, when not in collaboration with Planché or anyone else, provided contemporary vignettes of family and, more usually, lovers' feuds and stratagems, liberally supplied with 'authentic' servants, workmen and other familiar types setting off the main protagonists. Disguise, mistaken identity, overheard schemes, songs, contrasting exterior and interior, humble and noble scenes, with dresses to match and effects when necessary: these were regular things found in Dance's 'modern' pieces and in the work of other writers in his kind.

Much of the work, for example Dance's *The Water Party* and *Naval Engagements*, most of Planché's and some others, is skilfully written for its place and cast. The company's talents are well displayed and the dialogue, however flat it may now appear on the page, can be seen as having worked in action at the time. For example the flimsy pretext for *The Water Party* – a boat trip to Richmond with the accidents invariably attending such an outing – is sustained virtually plotless through two acts, by repartee and situations that must have been tailor-made for the performers concerned.

A little contretemps between Madame and Charles Dance in 1835 is worth recording for the professional implications. Dance wrote songs in their own right as well as those for his plays. One of these he asked Madame to sing – to 'plug' as more recent jargon has it. Madame agreed to sing it for a fee of £20, a modest sum considering the singer's popularity and influence. Dance, considering that, as a colleague, she ought to sing for nothing, and hoping, no doubt, to get some free publicity, wrote to *The Times* complaining of Madame's treatment and enclosing a copy of the song.

Dance had made the wrong move. On 5 February under the heading, 'Madame Vestris and Mr. Dance', *The Times* commended Madame's generosity and offered its own opinion that '£1,000 could hardly compensate a rational being for singing such trash in public.'

OLYMPIC SETTINGS

Three examples (shown on this page and the next) from the seventh season (September 1836 to 31 May, 1837), of Olympic sets that are probably much closer to the general scale of things at that theatre than the impression given by the *One Hour* illustrations.

The proscenium can be no real guide to the Olympic. The kind of thing shown here was more or less standard framing for illustrations in published texts at the time.

Above: *The Two Figaros* (30 November), called for practica stairs, a checkered pavement between grass walks, overhangin branches (in this case surely a drop-cloth?), and that elevatio at the middle distance set up in front of the backdrop that wa a three-dimensional construction used by the actors in the piec

At left: *Court Favour* (29 September), shows an interior 'box set complete with floor covering, practical entrances, as muc as the set will tastefully allow in furnishings, and, above all ceiling supporting a chandelier and painted decorations at th corners to prove that it is the real thing and not a row of to drops.

Tailor-made for Madame were parts that followed her established types but which were gradually remade more subtly, with more maturity and with more sentimentality than had previously been the case. With her thirties passing more swiftly than those of the century, her legs were more often skirted – but oh! how elegantly! – than revealed in trousers or tights. She and Charles evolved a style of acting, or rather of apparently not acting, that in the initial stages was better served by the tailor-made texts than it might have been by more established ones. Charles and Eliza were the first of many couples in modern comedy and 'naturalistic' playing. In our own time we have had the Lunts. It is the kind of playing that anyone not in the theatre thinks they could do given the chance, and it has led to deluded amateur couples in their thousands (in and out of the theatre) attempting to emulate it. The real thing is a rare phenomenon.

Planché had given Madame historical sense and sensibility. She gave Charles assurance and breadth of technique. Charles gave Madame refinement of technique and effect, together with the additional dimension gained by working in with, rather than simply with, another performer.

Tailor-made for everyone who appeared on the Olympic stage were the costumes they wore, as were the sets, after the first season, tailor-made for that stage. The stage was remodelled after a French idea. It was in fact a number of small stages, all independent but all joining together to make up the complete one. Each little stage was on its own lift and could be taken up and down, by itself or with others. This meant that changes of scenes, properties and even characters could be effected without the falling of the curtain or the appearance

Riquet With the Tuft, a scene in Planché and Dance's piece for Boxing Day 1836, showing the use of older styles when appropriate. The rows of cut-out rocks, ready to be 'transformed' in a twinkling, are augmented with three-dimensional sections for climbing up and sitting down.

of stage hands. The effects moved as if by themselves, rising and sinking with nothing to disturb the kaleidoscopic illusion.

Whatever could be achieved on that stage was achieved and, short of pulling the old naval timbers and the tin roof about their ears, even the fabric of the backstage building was tinkered with. A perspective scene of the Mall was needed for *The Court Beauties*. None of your painted, two-dimensional old things! A passage led from the back of the building to Madame's offices in Craven Buildings. One hundred feet long, it was the obvious answer, and the show was stopped by the applause for the caged singing birds (hired from the bird market in St Giles) suspended between the trees; stopped further by the reception for Mr Hooper as Charles II, with his court all dressed 'authentically for the first time on the stage and accompanied by no less than twelve King Charles's spaniels; and stopped yet further by Madame, as the king's favourite page, leading on two buck hounds specially borrowed from the royal kennel at Windsor! Pixerécourt might have wondered. Elliston would have been de-delighted. And how useful that remodelled passage would be, for instance for *The Burlington Arcade* a couple of years later, as well as other things.

Royalty was again called to assist, giving permission for Hampton Court paintings to be reproduced for *The Court Beauties* and sanctioning the sale of tapestries from Carlton House and, for £8, the old curtain that had draped the original Hampton Court pictures. All this information was passed on to the public.

The zeal was excessive in this and other cases, but the crusade launched by Madame as Planché's confederate and General, almost justified it, though we are still reaping more of the excess than the reform.

Less immediately spectacular, but more important, were the attempts to get 'real' walls and a roof on to rooms on the Olympic stage. *The Conquering Game* in 1832 and *Court Favour, or Private and Confidential* in 1836 (both with Madame in the casts and with quite good scripts) certainly seem to have achieved the 'box' effect, and there were others. The box set eventually became the accepted and only logical setting to go with 'real' properties etc., and only in recent times has there been (for reasons of finance, staffing and so on as much as for novelty) a general departure from such settings. Then, they must have been the crowning glory for the 'natural' crusaders.

The arrival of Charles Mathews had given a lift to the sixth Olympic season and confirmed the Olympic's standing as the home of the new school of acting. The end of the seventh season saw the retirement of John Liston. It should have been Madame who led him forward and spoke the Farewell Address for the season. But, after the tumult of applause acknowledging an evening of Liston at his best, it was James Vining who spoke for the manageress to her hushed auditorium:

'Aware how much less graceful is my bow than Madame Vestris's courtesy, I would willingly have escaped from being her deputy upon the present occasion. To the causes which have led to my being so, it is not her wish that I should make more allusion than to express to you her deep sense of your generous sympathy and support at a most trying period. She will ever be delighted to share with you the hours of her merriment, but she is unwilling to intrude upon you her moments of depression. Most truly cheering has it been to her, and to all of us, that the two months' extra season has brought with it two months' extra success. The gracious condescension of His Majesty by permitting the extension of the present season has hastened the approach of the next, and for four months, therefore, ladies and gentlemen, instead of six, in the name of Madame Vestris, and of a company which feels justly proud of its female captain, I respectfully and most gratefully bid you farewell.'

The extension of the season had been the sympathetic response of the Lord Chamberlain to the financial and personal difficulties in which the most successful theatrical person in London found herself. Once again the lady's private problems were brought before the public. This time it was not professional tantrums, and her theatrical work was not allowed to suffer, although she herself was 'off' for some time while personal bankruptcy was declared, heard, and eventually cleared. Hence her absence on Liston's last appearance. The first official news broke in April 1837. On Shakespeare's birthday the papers carried the following statement:

MADAME VESTRIS TO THE PUBLIC

'Gratitude for the unceasing favour bestowed upon my efforts as actress and manageress will not suffer me to remain silent while an event on the result of which my character depends is made known to you through other channels.

'Painful but mature consideration has convinced me that this address is called for by respect for you – by respect for myself.

'An unfortunate entanglement in a series of bill transactions, the first step in which no one can regret more than myself, has lately drawn itself so closely round me as to preclude all hope of extrication by private means, though none which honour, honesty, and self-sacrifice could dictate have been left untried and my name is about to appear in the *Gazette* as a bankrupt.

'I shall carefully and respectfully abstain from all attempt to forestall or to influence the result of the coming enquiry, but calumny will doubtless be busy with my name and I ask you, the kind dispensers of the popularity I enjoy, to suspend your judgment and to protect me against the penalties to which your envied favour is sure to expose me.

'The two reports most obvious for malevolence to fix on are – personal extravagance and failure of the Olympic Theatre, and these I shall briefly answer by anticipation.

'My *bona fide* creditors have shown every confidence in me and have cheerfully and unanimously agreed to every proposition made with a view to my avoiding the step now forced upon me, and with a full knowledge of the receipts and expenditure of the theatre they have been willing to allow me an ample annual income out of the profits and to receive the remainder and gradual liquidation of their claims.

'These are facts and enquiry cannot shake them. Their intentions for my good and for their own have been frustrated by persons who have purchased my acceptances which I was incautious enough to sign in blank. Indeed to such an extent has misplaced confidence blinded me that I await the coming investigation to ascertain their number and amount.

'My first impulse was to withdraw myself from the stage until the ordeal should have been passed through, but the claims of all those who are dependent on the theatre remaining open — claims which, be it remembered, have never been one hour in arrear, came forcibly to my mind and I did not hesitate to sacrifice my private feelings to my public duty.

'You will, I am assured, put the most generous construction on my motives. You will remember when I present myself before you that I am labouring for others in a field where I must not reap for myself and you will receive me not only with your usual kindness, but with all needful indulgence.

ELIZA L. VESTRIS

Story's Gate, April 19th, 1837.'

If the lady doth protest somewhat it is understandable. Such an open letter, with its almost regal tone and manner, is of interest from the point of view of theatre history, as evidence of both the confidence of the lady and of the degree of popularity that must have inspired that confidence.

The transactions referred to had involved her brother-in-law Anderson again, as well as traders and moneylenders. Always irresponsible and impractical as far as money was concerned, Madame was an easy prey for sharp practice. In Anderson's case it had been misappropriation and a touch of embezzlement. Tradesmen had had a field-day presenting bills for goods that had either not been delivered or delivered but never ordered. The situation had been generally aggravated by a love affair. For about four years — crowded professional years — Madame's emotional life had been dominated by a young married nobleman. Reference back to the list of fashionable attenders during the first Olympic season will show Lord and Lady Edward Thynne among their number. Though known as 'Lord' he was in fact the Honourable Edward Thynne, a younger son of the Marquess of Bath.

Separated from his wife (who, fortunately for her, had her own house and income) he had exhausted his own fortune and was heavily in debt when his youthful charm overwhelmed Eliza. Her infatuation cost her a fortune in money, not only in gifts and 'loans', but in the earnings lost by missing tours and other engagements.

The long, happy round of lovers and their tributes had ended, and the actress still playing the Queen of Hearts so skilfully in her own theatre was giving her newly-found commitment to a lover who was quite unable to realize the value of her tribute. A miserable hide-and-seek with the law ended with Edward's imprisonment in March as an outlaw.

The Times for 3 May 1837 gives a vivid picture of the scene in the Court of Bankruptcy the day before. The key points are the densely packed court room, the courtesy that was extended to Madame (reflecting the general public sympathy evidenced in other newspapers as well as *The Times*), the clarity of her replies, her leaving with her solicitor and 'several friends', followed by the swift emptying of the court room. 'Proved' debts amounted to only £1,387 9s. 8d., though several creditors who were called did not appear – some couldn't get through the crowd!

A private hearing on 10 May led eventually to an annulment on 2 June, her creditors having accepted five shillings in the pound. On 24 June, in an edition heavily bordered in black for the death of William IV, *The Times* noted that on the morning of 22 June: '. . . the sale of furniture and effects of Madame Vestris commenced under the direction of Mr. Foster, at her late residence, No. 2 Chesham-place, Belgrave Square. The auction was most numerously and fashionably attended. We noticed several persons of distinction. The articles disposed of fetched good prices. The sale terminated yesterday.'

Anderson also faced the Bankruptcy Court to receive a far less courteous reception and a longer wait for annulment. Lord Edward, after several petitions and legal debates concerning whether an outlaw *could* file a petition, got a hearing on 1 December and was discharged. An indignant *Times* followed its report on the hearing with the following: 'A dastardly scamp who complained yesterday of our omission of this case must have known it had not been heard when he sent his anonymous letter. We suppose the fellow is one of the fleecing creditors of the noble dupe.'

Madame returned to the Olympic to begin her eighth season in a pleasing new piece written for her by Charles Dance, *The Country Squire*. It turned out to be one of the successes of the season, but it is noticeable that Madame did not appear as frequently as she had done. Very active in management and presentation, she left most of the acting to Charles and her now well-trained company.

She had a personal and managerial success with *Naval Engagements* in May 1838 when London was filling up with visitors for the Coronation of Victoria in June. From America came handsome James Wallack and Stephen Price. Price had managed Drury Lane from 1826 to 1830 and so was well known to Madame. Both these gentlemen wanted to present Madame and Charles in America. Terms were discussed and it was decided that Price's $20,000, with the possibility of more to be made, was the better offer.

A HANDSOME GROOM

Charles Mathews at about the time of his marriage to Madame. The boyish charm of the early Olympic pictures is no longer as evident, but the portrait conveys the irrepressible good humour and attraction of the man.

Madame's Benefit before going to the States was held at Covent Garden in order to accommodate her well-wishers and the evening brought her about £1,000.

She did one other thing before going to the States. She went with Charles to Kensington Church and they were married on 18 July. Mackintosh gives this as a condition insisted upon by Price. George Vandenhoff, who later acted with Madame, records: 'Price, the old Park Theatre manager had them married as a necessary preliminary sort of purification before their being admitted to the rarified atmosphere of New York'.

Whatever the reason, the marriage itself worked. He was no more business-like than she but he did know those whom he could refer to with confidence. The married status was socially and professionally desirable in the changing climate of opinion that the new Queen would direct. They achieved great things together and his surviving letters to her show a tender regard and concern for her.

As soon as the news of the impending marriage got about the press could not resist indulging in the current style of smut and innuendo. The genteel rompery of the *Court Magazine* takes on a grotesque fascination if, as was probably the case, it was written up by a male reporter:

'Last month the YOUNG widow had not brought new supplies for the theatrical market, but no sooner had the new month commenced, than she MARCHED forward with increased force, and produced the new burletta entitled *You Can't Marry Your Grandmother*. We should like to know if this is a quiz upon Charles Mathews, who we hear has, or is about to lead Madame to the hymeneal altar! . . . Another amusing trifle is a burletta, from the pen of Mr. Oxenford, entitled *What have I done?* which, if it be true that Charles has married his grandmother, ought to have been uttered by him instead of Farren.'

There were, in fact, between five and six years' difference between Eliza and Charles.

Although there were the Covent Garden Benefit and some Haymarket appearances to come before sailing to America the Olympic season's end was the 'official' farewell:

'Ladies and Gentlemen: it has been my practice to address a few words to you on the last night of each season; it would ill become me to omit doing so when we are about to part for a longer time than usual.

'Offers of so liberal a nature have been made to me from America, that no one who labours for ultimate independence would be justified in declining them.

'Eight seasons of continuous success, unexampled, I really believe, in theatrical annals, major or minor, have stamped with an indelible mark of public approbation the system I had the honour to introduce in this theatre.

'That system was simply to set before you in the best manner, and as far as the Lord Chamberlain's license would admit, the best entertainments I could procure, to realize the illusion of the scene by an unflinching outlay upon proper costume, and careful attention to the decorations of the stage. Your constant attendance has shown that efforts however humble, to elevate the dramatic art, are not wasted upon a British public, and liberality has proved the best economy.

'Great as has been the favour which I have ever experienced at your hands, and highly as you have been pleased to estimate whatever requisite for the stage I may possess, I am convinced that the great success of the Olympic is more owing to the manageress than to the actress; and I have, therefore, no fear that Madame Vestris's Theatre will lack support in Madame Vestris's absence, especially when it shall be found that the Olympic is conducted precisely on the same principles, and that it will boast next season a comic company adequate in point of numbers to all its wants, and not to be surpassed in point of individual excellence by the united theatres of the metropolis.

'I have great pleasure in adding, that I am promised the best exertions of all those dramatic writers of whose works you have been accustomed to approve. And now that I have told you what you have to expect, promise me that when the cat's away you will come and see the mice play.

'Seriously, and in conclusion, I wish you, ladies and gentlemen, earnestly and sincerely that good fortune, which I am sure you wish me, and I bid you for a season respectfully and most gratefully farewell.'

It was Madame's first time away, and legally she had changed from Madame to Mrs. Both these things called for some token from the company. Probably it was James Vining, perhaps Planché, who placed the order with Messrs Makepeace and Walford, of Lincoln's Inn Fields. They had decided against recording the journey or the marriage. As the curtains met for the last time after her speech, Eliza Lucy turned to find herself presented with a peridot and brilliant bracelet engraved 'To Madame Vestris, a token of affectionate regard, from the company of the Royal Olympic Theatre, May 31, 1838.'

10

Stars and Stripes

They sailed from Liverpool. The experiment was to be tried at last, after many invitations, and after Eliza had once been actually announced as appearing. *The Times* on 26 September 1828 reported under *Theatrical News*:

'"The enterprising manager of the Bowery Theatre has induced the celebrated Madame Vestris, one of the most distinguished performers of Europe, to visit this country. She makes her first appearance in America at that theatre this evening." New York paper Aug. 30. This must have been some trick practised on our American friends. Clever as Vestris is, we suppose she could hardly contrive to be at the same time at Cheltenham and N.Y.; and that she was at Ch. about the time here spoken of, she could adduce a very distinguished visitor of her pretty cottage to prove. The great person alluded to should, by the way, be more cautious.'

Many similar items, seizing upon any professional news as a means of introducing a salacious anecdote, had made regular appearances in the press. We may understand Price's apprehension and his proviso concerning the marriage. He hoped that the ceremony might help to deaden the image that had crossed the Atlantic for more than a decade: Madame Vestris flitting, generously and gaily among 'Handsome Jacks', 'Lord Edwards' and 'Honourable Horatios', to name a few of those more frequently alluded to, with the occasional hint of a 'great person'.

It was her personal past rather than her professional appearance that was to dash the hopes of the American tour. The Mathewses were comparatively early victims of misrepresentation by a certain kind of American journalism which is now as prevalent in Europe as in America. Facts are of no interest in such journalism, being replaced by biased opinion set out as 'news'. Assuming that any Vestris must be in the ballet, the *New York Morning Herald* referred to Madame Vestris 'the celebrated danseuse'. Charles is not 'news' enough to mention, but his account of their attempt to get away from the New York heat for a spell is a good piece of reporting in its own right:

'The heat even here (Poughkeepsie) was intolerable, and we were advised to remove again to the Mountain House, a summer retreat on the top of the Catskill Mountains; and after a long steamboat run, were bumped and jolted up a half-made road of miles, in a half-made carriage crammed full of people, to the monster hotel at the top, where we arrived, with aching bones, just at nightfall, in search of cool and repose. Sounds of revelry met our ears as we approached, and on reaching the house, tired to death with our fatiguing journey, and covered with dust from head to foot, we had to make our way through a blaze of light and a host of elegantly-dressed men and women, who abandoned the illuminated ball-room, and lined the piazzas and corridors, to inspect the new arrivals. Through this bevy of strangers we sneaked as quickly as we could, in search of a room. A room! What an idea! The whole place was brimful and over-full, and every bed doubly occupied. Sitting rooms were unknown; the public saloons were the only resorts for meals and conversation, and repose and quiet were things never even inquired for. After writing our names in the book, for public inspection, the whole party was in a state of tumult, and "The Mathooses!" travelled from mouth to mouth with electric speed. A small bedroom was given up by one of the officials of the house. It was divided by a scanty Venetian blind from the public corridor, or piazza as they called it; and we were allowed, on the plea of ill-health, to have a cup of tea in it alone. This, it appeared, gave great offence; and there is no doubt we were greatly to blame in not at once putting on our ball dresses and joining the dancers.

'It was clear that this was no place for us, and a carriage was ordered to be ready immediately after breakfast, to bump us down again. This was not to be done privately. The guests were all up in arms and indignation. At the moment of departure, as we sallied forth into the corridor, we found it lined on each side, with eager faces turned toward us, to get at least one good stare at parting. We retreated for a moment to hold a council of war, when a sympathizing coloured waiter grinned with delight as he beckoned us down a back staircase to a lower corridor, through which we passed, leaving the mob of starers over our heads, popped into the carriage and off we drove.'

Getting the place and the motive wrong — and so making more 'news', the *New York Morning Herald* squealed: 'We understand, from a good theatrical gossip, that the facts of the affair about Madame Vestris and her servants at

Saratoga, are these: Vestris and her Charley could not condescend to sit at the public table; they had their meals in a private room, and sent their servants to dine at the table d'hote with generals, admirals, governors, secretaries of state, id genus omne! "that is the way the row began".' (Monday 20 August 1838).

Public behaviour having been impugned, the way was open for private morality to be questioned, loudly published in the name of 'private opinion' in a 'free country': 'We presume that it is not a piece of presumption for unpresuming people, in this free country, to have and to hold an opinion of their own. Our own private opinion is, that these two people . . . are not married. Major Noah labors to be severe upon those who dare to doubt the fact. Now we can assure the major that a near relation of his, and one of his intimate friends, doubts the fact — nay, more asserts positively they are not married — at any rate we think it bad taste to send her, after leading the notorious life which she has for years. We are curious to see whether she will be announced as Mrs. Mathews, or Madame Vestris.' (Monday 20 August 1838).

The next step, having introduced righteous titillation, is to invite salacious embroidery on pornographic anecdotes of the lady's past. It is to be hoped that the evidence that suggests that Wallack was, at least partly, responsible for the publication of an obscene pamphlet (based on much earlier London items) is unfounded, though rivalry in theatrical management is no less open to dirty dealing than any other kind of management.

The final move, having impeached a lady's reputation and implied her indecency, is to gloat over the loss of that which all the preceding ploys have been suggesting as an excuse for her indulgence and others' fascination: her personal charms: '. . . Time, that unsparing monster, has passed his icy finger over her brow, and although she looks uncommonly well in face and figure, and her constitution appears to have breasted all the shocks of a long theatrical life, still it is evident that Madame Vestris could not possibly be in 1838 what she had been in 1818.' (*New York Evening Star*, 13 November).

A more respectable journalist, in *The Knickerbocker*, went 'all round the houses' to express what might well have been a general feeling as genteelly as possible: 'She was known in this country as much from the fame of the peculiar charm which it was said belonged to her delineations of male characters, as by any superiority which attached either to her acting, or singing, in personations of her own sex. Now whether it was altogether from a high sense of the refined delicacy of the Americans, which in her opinion might not brook the metamorphosis in which she had so often appeared to admiring audiences at home, or whether she was guided by a just regard for that respectability with which the marriage-rites had so lately graced her condition, we are unable to decide; but however doubtful the motive, it is true that the result was a complete omission of all male personations in her American engagement. Bachelor though we be, we confess to a reverential horror for ladies in pantaloons, actually or figuratively, in real life; yet if, by assuming these much-abused garments upon the stage, they can for an

133

hour give a fictious charm to manhood, by softening down the rough asperities of the masculine gender, we are inclined to applaud the fascinating delusion. One great attraction of Mme VESTRIS' art was thus entirely abandoned.' (April 1839).

Neither the Mathewses nor Price would have even thought of such an appearance for Madame, but, she was known, after all, as 'Madame Vestris' in the States. The stories that were reported of her were concerned with pieces like *Giovanni in London* and social gossip. They knew little or nothing of Madame at the Olympic and even less about Mrs Mathews. She should have taken one of those earlier offers to cross the Atlantic. Then she might have been welcomed back, even if style had changed. As it was, the American public was led to expect one kind of performer and got instead two performers acting in a style that was still unique even in London where they had had some years to establish it.

It was shortsighted of Price and the Mathewses not to realize that the house style of the Olympic could not be transplanted without taking the whole company, and even then it could not be the same without the Olympic audience. Those slight plays, so delicately, and often affectionately, satirizing ladies and gentlemen, their servants and their way of life: what could they convey to a New York audience?

The *Herald* again: 'Their fashionable movements and affections we despise – their pride of place elsewhere honored, we ridicule. How then by a display of, to us, artificial life could she hope to succeed?' (22 November 1838).

American actors, too, must have found it impossible to adjust to the new style in the time available, a style that the more discerning of the American critics acknowledged, even if they were looking for something bolder:

'Mrs. Mathews never appears the character she would personate. She never steadily gazes at the audience, betraying signs that she knows there are persons before her. . . . No actress could be more perfect – though others may be more fascinating . . . The style of her acting is such that persons who wish to see something beyond nature had better not witness her performances – such persons can see just such acting every day in a lady's parlor without paying a dollar, if they have only the happiness of being introduced into good society. Mrs. Mathews, then, is only to be admired by those who have a good taste for the dramatic art and those who have never seen much of life – those who prefer to view it at the theatre than search for it in the actual world.' (*Ladies' Companion*, December 1838).

The Morning Courier and New York Enquirer got to the heart of the matter:

'Here is the most finished specimen of acting in her peculiar line, that has ever been exhibited either here or in Europe; and it really appears, that the

134

…e printing of such items as reproduced here and … the next page assisted the dirty work in the …nited States, of native journalists there in their …ccessful spoiling of the Mathewses 1838 tour.

MEMOIRS,

Public & Private

Life, Adventures,

AND

SECRET AMOURS,

OF

Mrs. C. M. late Mad. V.

Of the Royal Olympic Theatre,

WITH

INTERESTING & CURIOUS ANECDOTES OF CELE-
BRATED & DISTINGUISHED CHARACTERS
IN THE FASHIONABLE WORLD;

DETAILING

AN INTERESTING VARIETY

OF

Singular, Curious, and Amusing SCENES,

As performed before and behind the Curtain, &c.

TO WHICH IS ADDED, THE

EXTRAORDINARY AND SECRET AMOURS

OF

Mrs. HONEY.

————

Published by J. THOMPSON, 51, Gloucester Street, Oakley Street,
Lambeth.

ELLIOT, Printer, 14, Holywell-street, Strand.

very perfection to which she has brought her art — the chasteness and inimitable excellence of her personifications — her being literally true to nature —
has caused her to be less attractive than if she had exhibited SOME faults
and attempted to catch the public voice by mere clap trap. To be properly
estimated she must be seen frequently . . . Those who really admire excellence and perfection in acting will avail themselves of the few opportunities
left them to see Vestris.' (6 November 1838).

Let us hope she saw that notice.
Even without the mud-slinging it seems doubtful if the tour could have
been a success, but it might have stood a better chance of being assessed for
what it was rather than for what it was expected to be.

MADAME V——, AND HER YOUNG TIGER.

136

CHUBBS GENUINE EDITION.

MEMOIRS

OF THE

PUBLIC AND PRIVATE

LIFE,

ADVENTURES AND WONDERFUL EXPLOITS OF

Madame Vestris,

THE

FEMALE GIOVANNI, MACHEATH,

AND

DON JUAN

OF THE PRESENT DAY.

INCLUDING NUMEROUS

INTERESTING AND CURIOUS ANECDOTES.

Hence, ye prudish matrons ! hence,
Squeamish maids devoid of sense !
And shall these in loving dare
With my pretty dame compare !
She, who in the bard will prize
What she'll in his lays despise ;
Wantonness with love agrees,
But reserve in verse must please.

LONDON:
PRINTED AND PUBLISHED BY WILLIAM CHUBB
At the JOHN BULL Printing Office,
48, HOLYWELL STREET, STRAND.

Within three months they were home. They had given forty performances in America, twenty-eight in New York and twelve in Philadelphia, all in Olympic pieces interspersed by little American pieces in which they did not appear.

An evening or two of songs or excerpts from her old favourites might have eased the atmosphere, and if they had worked up an American playlet or two they might have appeared less 'grand'. The matrimonial gentility was such a contrast with the legend. But it is doubtful if Eliza was either in the mood or the state of health to work on such projects. She was not really over the bankruptcy business and the emotional turmoil that surrounded it when the gutter press got at her across the Atlantic. She must have been glad of 'her Charley' to champion her before they sailed away:

'The New York Albion, November 19 1838

PARK THEATRE

'The last appearance of Mr. and Mrs. Charles Mathews in America took place here on Tuesday night. The favourite pieces of *One Hour*, *My Eleventh Day*, and the *Old and Young Stager*, kept the audience in continued laughter from beginning to end. Mrs. Mathews was in better voice and spirits than usual. The brilliant appearance of a house crowded in every part, the boxes containing an overwhelming majority of ladies, and perhaps the feeling that the period of her mortification and annoyance was at an end, all combined to produce this happy effect. She was called forth at the conclusion of the *Eleventh Day*, and received the rapturous applause of the house. At the termination of the evening's performance Mr. Mathews received the same compliment. After the first cheers had subsided, the audience resumed their seats, and a dead silence prevailed. Mr. Mathews then delivered with great energy and vigour the following address, which we give as it was written out for us, with the sanction of Mr. Mathews, and which was listened to with marked attention, and cheered throughout with the most enthusiastic plaudits.

"Ladies and Gentlemen, – This is the first time I have ever addressed an audience in my own character, and I certainly had not the slightest intention of doing so now; but, being assured that on the last night of our engagement it would be taken as a mark of disrespect were I to remain wholly silent, I am determined that that imputation at least shall not be cast upon me; and indeed I should be most ungrateful were I to refuse a few words to those kind friends who have given us such a "bumper at parting". (APPLAUSE)

"In consideration of the lateness of the hour, I will be as brief as possible in what I have to say, though, as this, ladies and gentlemen, is our last interview, and as in all probability we may never meet again, I do hope you will not deny me your patient attention for a few minutes. Our story is soon told and easily understood, and if I have hitherto refrained from troubling you with a single word, upon the several occasions when I have had the honour of being called forward to receive your flattering applause, I have so refrained purposely, from the fear that as my own independent spirit would not allow me to offer unqualified thanks for a partial success, some unguarded expression might be seized upon as conveying intentional offence to the American public. I can now, however, speak without danger of being accused of interested motives, inasmuch as we have appeared before you professionally for the last time, and our immediate return to Europe is already determined on.

"We set sail for this country, ladies and gentlemen, as upon a trip of pleasure. Steam reduced the voyage to a mere nothing, and though it is true we were obliged to make many sacrifices in leaving home, friends, and unvarying professional success, to risk a doubtful reception among strangers, still we did so with light hearts and perfect reliance on the well-known hospitality of the people we were about to visit, backed by a thorough confidence in our own good intentions, and the conviction that, as we set out with the determination to spare no effort to please, our endeavours must be met, if not with brilliant success, at all events with the usual indulgence and protection so notoriously extended to British actors. We set foot then on these shores, resolved to be pleased with everything; and to the question of "How do you like our country?" so universally asked by all persons here upon a first introduction (A SLIGHT MURMUR), we readily answered in terms of the highest praise, as fortunately we were then honestly and conscientiously able to do.

"Two days after our arrival in this city, the weather being insufferably hot, we were advised to proceed at once to the Catskill Mountains. We did so, with the intention of passing there our few weeks of leisure in cool retirement; but after being jolted, at the hazard of our necks, up to that "cloud-capt" hotel called the Mountain House (where we arrived between nine and ten o'clock at night), we found it a gay, noisy, fashionable hotel, anything but adapted for those who sought quiet and retirement; and therefore at an early hour next day, at the still greater hazard of our necks, we were jolted down again. (LAUGHTER) Our intention was to return at once to New York; but that same night, chance lodged us at the Exchange House at Poughkeepsie, where we found all the quiet that we had been taught to expect at the Mountain House; there we at once installed ourselves, and there we remained for three weeks as retired as possible, literally confined to our apartments, with the exception of our usual drive in the cool of the evening.

"Little did we expect, ladies and gentlemen, while applauding ourselves for our politic conduct in retiring altogether from the public eye, and thereby avoiding, as we supposed, all the possibility of offence, that at that very moment we were insulting the whole American nation – that the press was teeming far and near with comments on our atrocious behaviour, and that a fatal prejudice was rapidly gaining ground against us.

"Of all this we remained in a state of happy ignorance till our return to New York. I was then informed that we had given serious offence at Saratoga Springs, on our way to the Falls of Niagara – that we had refused to sit at the public table, but at the same time had insisted that our servants should be admitted there, and that the visitors to the hotel, disgusted at the gross outrage, had been compelled to rise and leave the table.

"I could only smile at this absurd accusation, and deemed it one of the gossiping and ephemeral paragraphs of a newspaper, the subject of an hour's chit-chat, and then to be forgotten. I therefore replied, jestingly, that there were were seventeen reasons why the alleged offence at Saratoga could not have been committed – the first was, that we had never been there. (LAUGHTER) I presumed that the other sixteen reasons would not be required – (GREAT LAUGHTER) – but I was mistaken. The report was not suffered to die a natural death; it was resuscitated day by day, nourished and amplified hour by hour, till at last the conviction was forced upon me, that what I had at first looked upon as a harmless mistake, was, on the contrary, a regularly organised deliberate falsehood, systematically planned and persevered in, for the purpose of creating a rancorous feeling against us in the public mind, and thus, at once, irreparably injuring us on our first appearance in this theatre. I asked advice as to the propriety of openly contradicting these reports, but was assured that such a step was quite uncalled for. I thought so myself, but I was wrong again. The night of our first appearance arrived. The theatre was crowded to the ceiling, chiefly with gentlemen; hundreds were turned away from the doors, but very few ladies had dared to venture within them – in short, it was clear that a riot was anticipated. When Mrs. Mathews appeared upon the stage, the cheers were enthusiastic, but the ominous sounds of disapprobation were also to be heard – a deafening shout of applause, however, from the more liberal portion of the audience, at once silenced these sounds. On the symphony of her first song being played, disapprobation again manifested itself, and was again checked as before. I was thunderstruck, and made up my mind that the torrent of ill-feeling was only stemmed, from motives of gallantry, until my appearance, which would doubtless be the signal for a general tumult. Judge then, of my surprise, ladies and gentlemen, at meeting with the most cordial welcome, without a single dissentient voice. How was this? Was not I the proper person to have been attacked, rather than my wife? Was not I the person answerable for the misconduct alleged against us? No – hers was the talent they sought to disparage. The secret was at once explained – the disapprobation had just as much to do with our conduct in America as it had to do with the late general election. (LAUGHTER AND CHEERS)

"I must not trespass too much upon your patience, ladies and gentlemen, by entering into more detail. Suffice it to say, that since the failure of this

139

attempt to mar our first appearance and drive us from your stage, no efforts have been left untried to bring about the same end by other means. The press (that is, a portion of it) has been industriously employed in writing us down. Why, or by whom instigated, I do not wish here to inquire; but if it be any triumph to them to know it, I beg to assure them that they have fully succeeded. They have not only utterly destroyed our professional prospects, but have undermined the health and spirits of the lady they have chosen to make the object of their unmanly attack. . . . We have fought up against the attack with all our strength, but the enemy has proved too much for us, and, at length, after mature deliberation, we are compelled to abandon the field. In the name of Mrs. Mathews and myself, allow me, ladies and gentlemen, to bid you, and for ever, most respectfully, Farewell."

Mr. Mathews then bowed and retired amidst the hearty cheers and long continued applause of the whole house.'

*   *   *

Planché had run the theatre while the Mathewses were away in America. It had been quite a good season, but it was clear, from the press and from the takings, that Madame and Charles were missed. Madame's official return to her stage on 2 January in 1839 was thus noticed in *The Times*:

'. . . Long before the opening of the doors Wyche-street was filled both by carriages and foot-passengers, and long before the rising of the curtain for the first piece there was not one unoccupied nook in the Olympic Theatre; even a door was broken down by the rush of the crowd . . . As she entered to the tune of "Home Sweet Home", the immense mass of people burst out in one continuous shout of applause, and a large bouquet was thrown upon the stage. This was almost too much for her; and she clasped her hands, curtsied to the public with a look expressive of the deepest feeling, then caught up the flowers and kissed them, and as the applause increased turned back, as if seeking someone to support her. Then she appeared to make one great effort, she stepped into her part, and went through it with resolution; not that she ever completely recovered her self-possession, but what she lost in self command she gained in feeling, and her song of "My Old House at Home" was most exquisitely touching.'

She had come home, and from this time she is treated by the press as an established and respectable matron. Mrs Charles Mathews is no longer the target of innuendoes and personal anecdotes about Madame Vestris — a title that is now used only of her managerial and performing activities.

The new dignity was somewhat shaken by a Regency rumble that was reported by *The Times* on 13 March 1839:

'A respectably dressed youth, named Edward Purday, called on Sunday last at the house of Mrs. Mathews at Elm Grove, Notting Hill, Kensington, and desired an interview with that lady, which being granted, the youth immediately said he was her son, and he had come to claim her as his mother, as also some property which had been left him by his father, the Duke of Cumberland. Mr. Mathews, who was in the apartment at the time, immediately sent for a constable. The youth begged he might not be taken into custody, but upon being told he would, he said, "Well, I was told five years ago, by a man named Harrogan, that I was the son of Madame Vestris and the Duke of Cumberland." Upon being questioned, he said, "If it was not the Duke of Cumberland, it was Lord Harrington who was my father," but he was sure Madame Vestris was his mother. Mr. Mathews having given the youth in charge, he was taken on Monday before the magistrates at Queen Square, when it was clearly proved that the boy was of unsound mind. His father, who is a respectable tradesman at Richmond, having promised to keep his son in future under proper restraint, the prisoner was liberated.'

They had returned to find the Olympic in 'a fainting state' writes Mathews. Despite the large sums he had sent over from the States, receipts were down sufficiently to cause an ever-mounting debt. Within a short while of their topping the bill again the press reported: 'This temple of the Muses continues to be well attended; Madame's return is, we are glad to say, pulling up wonderfully the resources of this Establishment; showing after all, that one person, who has been, and is, a favourite, will still attract and fill a theatre, while twenty perhaps equally valuable persons, not having rooted that kindred affection in the people's hearts, failed to have half filled it.'

But they had to face the fact that, in so small a theatre, the losses accrued during their absence could not hope to be made up. As a less generous journalist commented, 'the late catastrophe has not ended in America' and noted 'care marked' in Madame's features. She probably realized that it was the end of the Olympic. She had done her job too well, demonstrated her theories too efficiently: other managements had eventually caught on and set their houses and their stages in order. A large number of variations of Madame's methods were to be seen in other London theatres. The crusade was successful and the crusaders were broke.

With a boldness that must have struck many as lunacy, Charles Mathews accepted the offer of Covent Garden when Macready resigned it. They decided to move the company and all the stock up the road from the Olympic and carry the crusade into the majors: 'As the season draws to a conclusion, the state of affairs improve and the public appear resolved to make hay while the sun shines, and enjoy the entertainments of this theatre while yet they may. "Meet me by Moonlight", (and who wouldn't meet the Olympic "Fairies" by that, or any other light) "The Dream of the Future" etc., are pieces now in favour. It is true that Madame Vestris has become the lessee of the Covent Garden. Mr. Bentley will be stage-manager, and Emden, prompter. It is whispered, that comedies got up after Madame's own style, will form part of the arrangements. We are inclined to think that this will answer, for they form no inconsiderable part of the beauties of the stage.'

With 'the most sanguine hopes of success' (Mathews) they ended the last Olympic season and Madame spoke the Farewell:

'. . . though it must be confessed that the mode in which you manifested your regret at my absence was more calculated to feed my vanity than my treasury, your kindness since my return has left the latter nothing to complain of.

'Encouraged by the approbation my managerial efforts have received, we have became lessees of the Theatre Royal, Covent Garden. I am aware that we shall have many difficulties to contend with. We propose to face them manfully and womanfully — to preserve the good points of former managements and reject the bad — to take with us the best results of my experience here, and to trust to the public to do the rest.

'Some kind friends have already prophesied that I shall not succeed there. My only answer is, that nine years ago they said I should never succeed here.

'The most absurb reports are in circulation about the characters which we mean to appropriate to ourselves: two of them, and two only, I shall notice, for if allowed to remain uncontradicted they may do us serious injury — Mr. Mathews will not play Macbeth, and I have positively refused Queen Catherine. . . . the great increase of our business having justified us in taking more extensive premises . . . I entreat a continuance of your custom and recommendation for the house of Mathews, Vestris, and Company.

To preserve the good points of former managements and reject the bad . . . to take with us the best results of my experience here, — a brave intention, followed by the fond 'trust to the public to do the rest.'

There were to be fine things done at Covent Garden and at the Lyceum, and the Mathewses' management was to continue to make as great a contribution as any — and more than most — to the climate of opinion that, in 1843, did away with the Monopoly of 1662 and the Licensing Act of 1737. But the really important years were over before Eliza and Charles sailed for America. They built on those foundations with their usual brilliance and taste, and with their usual extravagance, and with their admirable courage. Their last new production at the Olympic was Dance's *A Dream of the Future*, but they were no longer, to use a title from the second Olympic season, 'The Young Hopefuls'.

It is fitting to give the last word on the Olympic to Planché. His play *The Two Figaros* was produced in November 1836. For the published text he wrote a letter to Madame Vestris as a dedication. The letter sums up what Planché

MADAME VESTRIS,

AS SINGING

MY HEART'S TRUE BLUE.

calls Madame's 'Golden Rules'. It is an author's comment to set alongside the audiences' viewpoint given by Marston, and the performers' feelings as demonstrated by their presentation to Madame:

'. . . As a very humble member of that body [The Dramatic Authors' Society] I therefore take this public opportunity of expressing the opinion which I, in common with many of my brethren, entertain of your management of the Olympic Theatre, and of the beneficial effects likely to result from it to the whole dramatic community.

'In a time of unexampled peril to the best interests of the Drama — whilst theatrical property was at the lowest ebb, the larger theatres changing hands continually, and the ruin of their lessees involving that of hundreds of their unfortunate dependents, — the little Olympic, the most despised nook in the dramatic world, became not only one of the most popular and fashionable theatres London ever saw, but served as a life-boat to the respectability of the stage, which was fast sinking in the general wreck. Your success is a matter of notoriety; not so, however, the principal causes of your success; which also constitute the claims you have upon the good wishes of all who regard the true interests of the English Stage. To those causes thousands are blind, and none perhaps so blind as the very persons who are most concerned in clearly perceiving and reflecting on them; I allude to the majority of Theatrical Managers, Provincial as well as Metropolitan.

'In the first place, you have never allowed a temporary decline of attraction to scare you into the destructive system of filling your Boxes with orders.

'Secondly — You have never suffered your Play-bill to be disgraced by a puff, but rigidly restricted it to the simple announcement of the Performances.

'Thirdly — In the production of EVERY drama, without regard to its comparative importance, the most scrupulous attention has been paid to all those accessories which form the peculiar charm of Theatrical Representation, by perfecting the illusion of the scene, and consequently at the same time every possible chance of success has been afforded to the author.

'Fourthly — That if, notwithstanding such aid, a Drama has occasionally failed, it has been as soon as possible withdrawn in deference to the opinion of the public.

'Fifthly — That the advantage of early hours was first perceived by the audiences of the Olympic, the performances having been generally so regulated as to enable families to reach their homes before midnight.

'It is to these few "Golden Rules" which you have had the good taste and sound policy to adopt and persevere in, more even than to your deserved popularity as an Actress, that you owe your unequalled success, and when by the adoption of similar measures, similar prosperity shall attend other Theatrical Speculations, and the benefit of that prosperity be felt throughout the various branches of the Dramatic Profession, I trust it will not be forgotten that the laudable experiment was first made by Madame Vestris . . .

'Fortunately for yourself, perhaps, your exertions have been confined to a Theatre the direction of which is a creation, more than a labour; but the model is not less instructive because it is made on so small a scale and preserved in the cabinet of a lady. That great good will eventually, and not far distantly arise to the Drama from your example, is the firm belief of many for whose judgement I have great respect, and that you may continue to deserve their "golden opinions", and live to enjoy an ample harvest reaped from the practice of your "golden rules", is the wish of,

My dear Madame Vestris,
Your sincere Friend,
J. R. PLANCHÉ

Brompton Crescent,
Dec. 19th, 1836.'

11

Theatre Royal

'It is not a fitting spectacle – the national drama in the hands of Mrs. Vestris and Mr. Charles Mathews', was Macready's reaction, recorded in his diary, to the Mathewses taking over at Covent Garden.

In the light of his own theatrical dream, and in the long view, Macready was right. The trouble was that his dream was out of touch with reality, too ambitious to be realized in one man's lifetime, let alone a few seasons in a dinosaur of a theatre to administer and to finance. His ideas concerning the presentation and the textual accuracy of Shakespearian tragedy began the long haul to reform in these things, His brave attempts to get good writing into the theatre were limited by solemnity and mistaken about style, but absolutely right in intention.

The snags were a private contempt for the theatre as he found it and for those performers he considered less enlightened than himself, and a professional aloofness that prevented a practical – and humorous – understanding of the necessity of beginning reforms from the bottom upwards instead of vice versa. His own dignity was his prime concern – a preoccupation that has nothing to do with the theatre, except as a target.

But Macready's self-appointed task of restoring the purity of the national drama and making Covent Garden theatre a respectable and suitable home for it, was a laudable one, and discriminating people supported him. Undiscriminating people, being far more numerous, found purity and respectability none the less boring for being flaunted so boldly. Given more than two seasons the crusade might have been able to adjust itself and regroup its resources, but the opportunity was denied. The high rent was demanded in full. Macready, saving every penny for retirement as soon as possible, gave up the fight.

146

The proprietors of Covent Garden at this time were Charles Kemble, W. J. Surman, Captain John Forbes, and John S. Willett, the last two administering the shares belonging to their wives, daughters of an earlier shareholder. These four gentlemen, representatives of the kind of theatrical ownership that has crippled and killed many a true theatrical enterprise, had set a £7,000 a year rent on Covent Garden.

High rents for the majors were justified according to the proprietors by the monopoly and the size, which made higher receipts possible. At this stage of the game it was a hollow justification. Minors had been openly flouting the law for some time and, as the Olympic so amply proves, had been doing far better at the Box Office than the patent theatres.

In 1843 the special status of patent theatres was to be ended and the long and unjust business of the monopoly came to an end. Commercial landlords never die of course, they simply fade from publicity and let the theatre people dance to their tune.

In the case of the Covent Garden proprietors, it will have been noted that an actor was among them, Charles Kemble, whose *King John* has been referred to. A member of a great theatrical family (which included Sarah Siddons), Charles Kemble had experienced the problems of theatrical management, and had been rescued from them by his daughter, Frances (Fanny) Kemble's success. As an actor he had been at his best in romantic, witty parts such as Benedick, Romeo, Mercutio and Charles Surface. Although his range was far greater, his acting style, relying more on the head than on the heart, was an earlier version of the style of Charles James Mathews.

Perhaps this similarity of style lent, at any rate for a time, an ease to the professional relationship between Kemble and Mathews. It was most probably Kemble who talked the other proprietors into the 'gentleman's agreement' about the rent. The 'most advantageous terms' (Mathews), were that the rent stayed the same, but that if Mathews paid £5,000, they would not haggle about the other £2,000. It might have seemed generous to Mathews, though it was in fact still leaving him with a rent about half as much again as the Olympic plus considerably increased overheads and salaries.

The 'gentleman's agreement' was a further snub to Macready, who considered Mathews no gentleman anyway and Madame Vestris in no sense a lady. Kemble might have agreed, privately, with Macready, but, together with the other proprietors and employees of the theatre, he found Macready's obstinacy infuriating and his general manner upsetting for the establishment.

Denigration and scandalous comment were old bugbears for Madame and she had weathered them, usually, by ignoring them. Charles, who was jealous of his standing, by education and by acquaintance, as a gentleman was less serene about affronts to his manners, and there were frequent and bitter exchanges between the 'brash and offensive' young comedian and the 'arrogant' tragedian.

147

The differences of professional style and personal temperament were as evident in the business of management. Macready, from the hard experience of getting his father's acting company on its financial feet again, and of trying to carry the principles and atmosphere of his broken Rugby schooling into a seedy and profligate 'profession', was a shrewd business man. He kept careful accounts and kept a wary eye on the behaviour and reputation of his company. It must have seemed, indeed, a 'school' of acting under his management. And, alongside his professional caution, he kept up a steady routine of personal saving, and retired comfortably at the age of forty.

Vestris (for although Mathews was the lessee, Madame was still the manageress) from her experience of living for the moment and always before having found a friend in need, brought into management the manners and the attitudes of the elegant occupants of the boxes who had first applauded her.

Macready, seeing the irrational pair of burletta performers taking over his theatre, was understandably bitter. The fact that they were to give the public what it wanted was no satisfaction since, in his eyes, the public wanted the wrong things.

From their point of view as performers Covent Garden was not right for Madame and Charley, but the alternatives were depressing: to try and rally the Olympic again on the old lines when it was so obvious that the 'moment' was gone, or to work for another management. Mathews might have done this, as he did do for most of his long professional life, but Madame would have opted for any risk to remain a manageress.

Quite apart from the habit of being her own boss for almost a decade there was also the grim fact that the decade had carried her into her forties, and to the fading of those physical charms and the health that had served her so well (not that she ever lost her trim figure and great charm of appearance and manner). The later Olympic seasons had seen a discreet withdrawal from performing while maintaining a strong interest in management and presentation.

As for the proprietors of Covent Garden, they made their offer to the most consistently successful management of recent years. It was not quite like offering the lease to a minor management, since Vestris had always been associated with the majors before the brief Tottenham Street season and the Olympic. Her name had after all been made at the major houses.

The misalliance having been contracted, the Olympic revellers moved into the sacred precincts of the National Drama and put on appropriately serious faces. Despite their merry disclaimers, they appear to have hoped to have carried on Macready's work in a more lavish and enlightened manner. Of course they were concerned to make a profit, but they certainly began at Covent Garden with an air of knowing their 'duty' to the claims of a major theatre.

There was a big drawback to such grand and respectable ends: there was no performer who could play the great Shakespearian male leads. Macready was out of the question, (though they tried a spell of working with him later).

MADAME VESTRIS

Charles Kean and Samuel Phelps might have been possible bets, but, although I have a notion that Phelps and Madame might have got on quite well, Mathews did not care for him nor for Kean, and they themselves tended to share Macready's view of the 'light comedy gentleman'.

After a stupid attempt to get Macready's leading lady (and pupil) Helen Faucit, they engaged Ellen Tree as a leading actress, but on her own terms: Mathews wrote to John Harley in November 1839: 'Of course Miss Tree knows that the whole range of the Drama is at her command at Covent Garden, in short that she may have her own way in everything.' This meant that, with tours and other commitments that she thought fit to take, they had to arrange things around her and lost that exclusive control of the bills that they had enjoyed at the Olympic. (Madame was getting the other end of an old stick that she had troubled managers with in her earlier days.) A further aggravation was that, without a suitable male lead the plays they could present with Ellen Tree were limited in number.

Understandably, their company for comedy was as brilliant as could be found at the time. This did not prevent them trying to coax Liston out of retirement, another silly move that Liston wisely resisted. This mixed quality was augmented by quantity. From a company of something around forty for the last Olympic season, they more than doubled their payroll for Covent Garden on the acting side. But this was only the tip of the theatrical mountain that they had involved themselves with. In Mathews's *Life* there is a return of all those working for them at Covent Garden at the end of 1840. It is worth giving in full for it provides a clear picture of the responsibilities of management at the time, especially for a management trying to live up to its reputation for perfection in presentation and considerateness as employers. It was an enormous – and inevitably doomed – business undertaking in the circumstances.

'THEATRE ROYAL, COVENT GARDEN

A Return of all Persons engaged in this Establishment during the Week ending 26th December, 1840.

Company – Gentlemen		38
,, Chorus Singers		8
,, Ladies		34
Band		32
Officers		9
Box-keepers		2
Check and Money takers		15
Bradwell's Department:		
Workers	.60	
Supers	.22 = 82	82
Scenery Department (Painting-room)		10

Sloman's Department:
Carpenters	.26	
For working Pantomime	.80	
Cassidy	. 1 = 107 .	107

Gentlemen's Wardrobe:
Workers	.24	
Dressers	.14	
Extras	.18 = 56 .	56

Ladies' Wardrobe:
Workers	.42	
Dressers	.14	
Attendants	. 2	
Mrs. Thomas and Mrs. Lewis	. 2 = 60 .	60

Supers (per Horner):
"Midsummer Night's Dream"	.52	
Pantomime	.37. = 89	89

Extra Chorus and Band	13
Property Department	4
Printers, Billstickers, Upholsterers, Housekeeper, etc	57
Watch and Fire men	5
Police	4

Attendants at Bar, etc., in Drysdale's employment:
Boxes	.16	
Pit	.18	
Gallery	. 8 = 42 .	42

Place-keepers	7
Box-keepers (Deputies)	10
total	684'

Although at the beginning of the season the numbers were not up to this total, they still began with a very large number, certainly around six hundred. It was imprudent to begin with so large an expenditure on the company and on scenery and costumes that demanded so large a staff. They were planning as if they were over a hundred years ahead and on a regular subsidy. The *Theatrical Journal* for 28 December 1839 noted that the 'expenses of Madame Vestris at Covent Garden are half as much again as those of [her predecessors] partly accounted for by the great number of performers engaged — many of whom are seldom required to play'.

Even allowing for the fact that it was a sizeable theatre the accommodation problems backstage must have been pretty grim. Such problems also point up the importance of the day-to-day atmosphere in such an entertainment factory.

Covent Garden Theatre   from Bow Street

he Interior

The cue 'from the top' in such conditions determines the general response and interest in the work done. Small snippets of items give glimpses of backstage conditions and the reactions of the workpeople. Whatever Macready might have thought of Madame's easy-going nature, she saw to it that there was no question of who was in charge at Covent Garden: '*New Theatrical Etiquette* – When Madame Vestris attends rehearsals, immediately on her carriage reaching the Stage door, all the workmen, carpenters, etc., cease operations, make their humble obeisance as she passes, and do not resume their labours till Madame is again beyond hearing.' A respect paid the more willingly in that it was known that: 'Mr. and Mrs. Mathews are at the theatre all week. Sunday is the only day they have leisure to see a friend.' (The *Theatrical Journal*, 18 January 1840).

Managers come and go but certain theatre people go on for ever – fewer than used to be the case, but there are still some, for example stage door-keepers and the staff of established national companies. One such old hand at Covent Garden was the keeper of the properties, Mr Rye. An eccentric character, he always wore blue and white 'gentleman's stockings' as he called them, and was never known to wear a hat or cap. After forty years at Covent Garden he died, in October 1840, after just over a year of Madame's management. He was found to have left a considerable sum. Among things bequeathed was a handsome gold ring to Madame Vestris.

Relations between the new management and the poorer section of the public were less successful in the auditorium. Perhaps Madame's concern to get the front-of-house behaviour into something resembling Olympic good manners prompted the closing of the top gallery. This meant that the cheapest price for admission was a shilling and sixpence instead of the old shilling minimum. There were other price changes but these were in parts of the houses patronized by people who would not be greatly affected by a shilling here or there and who appreciated the improved conditions made for them in the house. For, in the more expensive parts, there was a general improvement: new decoration and more comfortable seating. The annoyance of the galleryites was not eased by the new lobby, entrance and staircase that made the Dress Circle and the boxes a completely exclusive area.

The reaction was predictable. Urging that prevention was better than cure, The *Observer* for 25 September 1839 warned:

'It is said that the shilling gallery has been closed up, and is to be done away with. If this report be correct, the proceeding will be nothing less than a sentence against a class whose only fault is their poverty. All classes are interested in the preservation of the shilling gallery: the poor, because by its extinction, they will be wantonly driven to an inferior description of amusement; the rich, because the poor will be degraded; the actors, because a class of persons will be excluded from the performances whose feelings excited applause.'

154

This question eclipsed other comment on the new management, comment that was watchful and curious rather than enthusiastic, but that wished the 'indefatigable lady' well.

Another mistake was in the choice of play in which to open. Somewhat overplaying their hand in trying to prove that they were fitting custodians of the National Drama, the Mathewses chose *Love's Labour's Lost*. The choice of Shakespeare is understandable if not inevitable. The choice of play is rather insanely commendable, and anyone can see the arguments that led to it: a play not performed since Shakespeare's own time; a play not calling for a leading actor that they had not got; a play depending on the team work that they had always fostered and worked for, and a play giving Planché a fine opportunity for some costume lessons.

Their new status had befuddled them and they were 'doing a Macready', that is putting the cart before the horse and asking the public to accept something it had not yet learned to understand. An assembly of skilled and popular comedians dressed in Planché's authentic designs against the beautiful scene painting of John Henderson Grieve and his two sons (Grieve had been Kemble's painter for *King John*), and smoothly managed by George Bartley as stage manager and accompanied by M. R. Bishop's musicians could not set right the managerial mistake in the choice of play.

The season began on 30 September 1839 and gave Madame the worst moment in her career. Poised centre stage to give her Opening Address, she found that the rising of the curtain did not bring the expected quiet in the auditorium. Instead, the noise increased. She began her speech, hoping that the house would settle, but the hope was confounded.

The speech was not recorded in the press but, at Princeton University, there is a piece in Mathews's handwriting (in the Mathews Family Papers) that was intended to be the text of the address. Little of it was heard, and it is not worth quoting here. From the *Morning Advertiser* of 1 October 1839 we learn that the noise rose to a tumult at Madame's mention of the Olympic pieces that were to be part of the repertoire, the howls of derision from the pit and gallery being finally overwhelmed by applause from the 'exclusive' boxes and dress circle, whose occupants also urged the fetching of the police to put out the ruffians. Mathews led an overwhelmed and shaken Madame off the stage. He faced the crowd and attempted a compromise with the galleryites and, at length, the performance proper began. Had it been the later production of *A Midsummer Night's Dream* the evening would probably have been saved. Even *The Merry Wives of Windsor* might have eased and calmed the ruffled atmosphere. As it was, *Love's Labour's Lost* fell beautiful and flat on a bewildered pit and gallery and politely attentive dress circle and boxes.

The notices were generally enchanted with the 'exquisite', 'splendid and elegant' costumes and the décor 'in the best drawing-room style of the Olympic' (a strange commendation for the setting of the play). The choice of play was regretted though 'respectably and evenly acted'. Only *The Times* commended the play and blamed the lack of gaiety and skill in managing the conceits of language and adding that it was 'encumbered rather than relieved by the scenery and decorations.' The *Chronicle's* advice came too late: 'The management will do well to get up some other of Shakespeare's comedies with the same attention they have bestowed on this.' (1 October 1839)

It was given eight more times before it was taken out of the bills.

These two initial blunders, in the auditorium and on the stage, indicate the confusion in the London theatre generally at that time and the confusion of aim that had led to bad judgement by a performer and a manager as experienced as Madame Vestris. She was trying to offer a grander version of her fashionable little house, dressed in the redesigned draperies of the handmaid of the dramatic muses. Thus, Covent Garden might be made the dramatic equivalent of the operatic King's.

I suspect that she was encouraged in these high falutin' thoughts by Planché, as well as by the feeling that she ought to live up to what was expected of her position. There was also the desire to disprove the misgivings and the doubts of Macready.

Her style, temperament and practicality were those of a popular and skilled soubrette — a true sister of the European tradition of performing found, as already emphasized, in the Boulevard theatres. There she had picked up her basic and individual technique that set off her personality and made her so popular with the general public.

The public did not expect *Drama* from 'Missis Westris' — and the nobility were really happier without it, having never shared with their European counterparts either the inclination or any pretensions to culture. They all enjoyed the pretty things she could show them but were somewhat disconcerted if she expected them to listen seriously.

Before considering the brave attempts that Madame made to reconcile her status with her temperament, a contemporary account of the kind of audience who were making all the noise on the opening night will be in order here. Although both the majors are in the title the scene is, as will be seen from the context, at Drury Lane. Such were a large number of those whose morals were the despair of Macready and whose manners were the despair of Madame Vestris. Both he and she would have given much to be independent of them.

'DRURY-LANE & COVENT-GARDEN
12 o'clock at Night

'. . . no sooner are the actors on the stage placing themselves in a row, at the conclusion of the last piece, than the audience begin to move, in box, pit and gallery; but in the latter they are not always contented with moving, for as the curtain drops, a tremendous whistling is frequently heard. The women who are in the habit of selling bills of the play and fruit, may be seen looking under the seats in pit and boxes, for any article that may have been dropped or left behind; it is no uncommon thing for them to pick up pocket handkerchiefs, shawls, gloves, snuff-boxes, reticules, &c. No sooner do the audience arrive at the box entrance, than a number of men, commonly called "cads" salute you with, "a coach, your honour? a cab marm? clear the way! first coach! — where to? a good four wheeler here, sir! open the door, Jim! now marm; take care, Miss". "Yes, sir;" "Pull up, Joe! stand on one side, you sleepy people," &c. when up comes another driver, who declares he was the man who brought "this here" party from Oxford-street, and they promised to go back with him; and after a few words that shall be nameless, you get out of the clutches of both parties and perhaps do not obtain a vehicle at all! The pit door is somewhat different, although you go under the same ceremony; and, in consequence of getting intermixed with the audience at the box door, you frequently lose your friends; and not thinking of your pockets, when you get home, or perhaps before, find the contents that were deposited therein taken away, to the great mortification of yourself and the ridicule of your friends: if you happen to miss anything at the time you are at the doors, and make any observation in the hearing of these cads, they are sure to turn everything you say to account, and laugh heartily at your misfortunes, by observing, "Sir, have you lost anything? sure, did you bring it with you? what will his mother say, Ned? does your mother know you're out, sir? I vish I vos your keeper, if you had any thing, don't you think I knows how to take care of it for the gemmon, Bill: shall I get a policeman, or will you advertize first, sir?" while at the same time he is talking in this manner, his companions are very likely picking the pocket of your friend, and a third is bawling "coach, yo're hired! three shillings to Vest-minster bridge; and two shillings and a saxpence to St. Paul's, 'cos its a rainy night. I beg your pardon, marm, I did'nt go for to splash your stockings; but its all to oblige you, I assure you, marm: what! only a Joey! you should stand saxpence this here vet night, marm! then if you von't stand saxpence, I hopes your supper will be cold before you gets home, that's what I wishes." At the gallery door it is sometimes very amusing to follow some of the younger branches, and hear their conversation; as soon as they get out, the first question is generally — "I say, Bill, what's the clock, aye?" "a quarter-past eleven; no more than that there: I shan't come here again, why Common-garden ain't over till half-past twelve!" "besides I don't like all this here tragedy stuff; I wish they would play the pantomimes again that's summut like!" "then there was that singing covey! I could'nt tell the tune at all, nor a word that he said!" "where's Harry and Charley, call them will you?" "now suppose we goes and has some alamode-beef and porter?" "I ain't pleased at all with my night's diversion; it ain't half so good as Astley's — why the horses going once round the ring is worth a dozen of that chap's songs." "Sue, did you like it?" "I liked nothing

but them there women's dresses, and the cupids holding up the torches!"
"did'nt you like the music?" "oh, no! only where that chap played the symbols,
that was grand."

   'The streets are soon cleared, and the taverns round the theatres full; thus
ends an evening at a Theatre Royal.' (The *Theatrical Journal and Stranger's
Guide*, 17 October 1840).

   It was largely the opposition of the pit and the gallery that blighted another
managerial hope. It was planned that Saturday nights were to be *Olympic Nights*,
in the belief that, once a week at least, there would be a popular attraction. It
was the old problem of square pegs and round holes again. Just as performers
could not suddenly be expected to stretch their minds to *Love's Labour's Lost*
and their physical, Olympic, style to the vastnesses of Covent Garden, so the
frail and intimate little diversions that had such charm at the Olympic could not
be expected to survive the 'blowing up' necessary to get them over. The masking-
in (to reduce the proscenium opening) and the various compromises necessary
to make the Olympic scenery work at Covent Garden only served to increase the
incongruity. Mathews had quite a personal success with his patter songs in
Patter vs. Clatter, but there was either little or hostile response to the smart
little vignettes in such surroundings. Some, for example *Naval Engagements*,
The Ringdoves, and a few more, survived as afterpieces, but the *Olympic Nights*
were given up in November.

   The School For Scandal opened on 10 October, the bills drawing attention
to something that was to become an establishment policy with 'classical' pieces:
'The dresses and decoration will be of the date of the production of the play –
1777.' A good idea and, naturally, carried out with beautiful effect. Though
'it was apparent that although all was beautifully got up, there was no desire of
rendering it subservient to scenic effect' (*The Times*) it was the scenic effect that
drew unanimous praise from the press generally and, historically speaking, this
is what made the production memorable. The acting got a mixed reception,
Mathews coming in for everything from condescending approval to definite
dislike, mainly because of his inability to adapt his modern style to Charles Surface.
Despite his recorded objection to being 'typed', all the evidence suggests that he
was an actor who imposed his own 'line' on each role rather than attempting to
adjust himself to the demands of the play.

   The *European*, whose reviews in general make one wish that more than one
issue had survived (or maybe it had only one issue?) records that *The School For
Scandal* 'brought good, sympathetic and gratified audiences to her theatre', and
goes on to say of Madame herself: '. . . if we have any fault to find with the
Lady Teazle of the representation, it is, that it is a personation somewhat too
matronly'.

   Was she carrying her 'responsible' Theatre Royal manner into her acting?
Mrs Nisbett was the obvious choice for the part, but it is understandable that

158

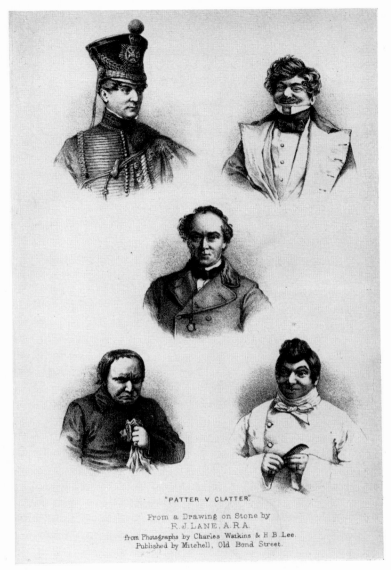

"PATTER V CLATTER"

From a Drawing on Stone by
R. J. LANE, A R A.
from Photographs by Charles Watkins & H B Lee.
Published by Mitchell, Old Bond Street.

Patter v. Clatter. Charles Mathews's virtuoso piece in which he played five parts and which was a standard and popular item in his repertoire for the whole of his long career.

Madame should wish to try her hand again. The play stayed in the Mathews' repertoire from this time on.

George Vandenhoff joined the company at about this time. In his *An Actor's Notebook or The Green Room and Stage* (1859), he recalls his taking his first job at Covent Garden in October 1839. Mrs Glover watching a rehearsal, '. . . saying aloud in her brusque, semi-Johnsonian infallibility of style, — "Well, he's sure to be heard, at all events; and has plenty of confidence; voice enough, and face enough, he'll do!"'

He speaks highly of Madame's earlier triumphs: 'She was the best soubrette *chantante* of her day; self-possession, archness, grace, coqueterie, seemed natural to her; these, with her charming voice, excellent taste in music, fine eyes, and exquisite form, made her the most fascinating and, (joined to her *esprit d'intrigue*) the most dangerous actress of her time. Believe it, reader, no actress that we have now can give you an idea of the attractions, the fascinations, the witcheries of Madame Vestris in the hey-day of her charms,' but he descends to feline and effeminate comments on her marriage to Mathews when, he says, she was 'already in the "sere" with a good deal of the "yellow leaf" visible; that is, when the blanc and rouge were off, and allowed "The native hue and colour" to be seen', a piece of nastiness that is only worth quoting as a sample of the gossip that was put about concerning Madame's 'painting'. She was even said to enamel herself and then sit by the fire to set it! The *Cornhill Magazine* in February 1863 carried an article headed: 'Aids to Beauty, Real and Artificial' which mocks this nonsense and states that, although on the stage she used rouge and pearl powder 'prodigally employed', 'Those who know that agreeable and accomplished actress off the stage are aware that she allowed the brown of her brunette complexion to appear undisguised, however liberally she may have applied rouge and pearl powder when on the stage.'

Having relieved his feelings and displayed his ignorance of things that were not his concern, Vandenhoff, from his own experience, admits to the pleasure of working with Madame:

'Let it be recorded, to Vestris's honour, that she was not only scrupulously careful not to offend propriety by word or action, but she knew very well how to repress any attempt at *double-entendre* or doubtful insinuation in others. The Green-Room in Covent Garden Theatre was a most agreeable lounging-place, a divan adorned with beauties, where one could pass a pleasant hour in the society of charming women and men of gentlemanly manners, and from which was banished every word or allusion that would not be tolerated in a drawing-room.

'It must be understood that in Covent Garden and Drury Lane Theatres, there were a first and second Green-Room: the first, exclusively set aside for the *corps dramatique* proper, – the actors and actresses of a certain position; the second, belonging to the *corps de ballet*, the pantomimists, and all engaged in that line of business – what are called the little people – except the principal male and female dancer, who had the privilege of the first Green-Room.

'. . . the first Green-Room at Covent Garden Theatre was a withdrawing room, carpeted and papered elegantly; with a handsome chandelier in the centre, several globe lights at the sides, a comfortable divan, covered in figured damask, running round the whole room, large pier and mantel-glasses on the walls, and a full-length movable swing-glass; so that, on entering from his dressing-room, an actor could see himself from head to foot at one view, and get back, front, and side views by reflection, all round.

'The Green-Room was exceedingly comfortable during the Mathews and Vestris management. Indeed I must pay them the compliment of saying that their arrangements generally for the convenience of their company, the courtesy of their behaviour to the actors, and the consideration for their comforts, formed an example well worthy to be followed by managers in general; who are not, I am sorry to say, usually remarkable for those qualities. In fact, the reign of Vestris and her husband might be distinguished as the drawing-room management. On special occasions – the opening night of the season, for example, or a "Queen's visit", – tea and coffee were served in the Green-Room; and frequently between the acts, some officers of the guard, or gentlemen in attendance on the royal party, would be introduced, which led, of course, to agreeable and sometimes advantageous aquaintances.'

There is an anecdote about the opening night of *Rule a Wife and Have a Wife* that provides a glimpse of the friendly atmosphere under the Mathews' management as well as Eliza and Charley 'off duty':

'. . . entered the Green-Room cool and self-possessed. There was Charles Mathews, dressed for Perez, and also Madame Vestris. On my replying to their enquiries that I felt perfectly at ease, Mathews, placing his hand on my left breast, said, "Let's see; let's feel!" He kept his hand there a moment, then withdrawing it, exclaimed to Vestris, – "By Jove, Liz, it's as calm as a child's!"

'"Now then," said I, "let me feel how yours goes."

'"O, no!" said he, "I'm as nervous as I can be!"'

Rule a Wife and Have a Wife was, like *Love's Labour's Lost*, really beyond most of the actors. If the National Drama was going to do it then something should have been done to rescue at least the last scene from Garrick's 'judicious alterations'. It was probably with an eye on propriety, for the dress circle and boxes, that the cuts were retained and the old woman and her daughter played by men (though the latter device could claim 'authenticity'). Surviving only five performances the play did little to help the worrying position at the box office.

That old mainstay *Artaxerxes* helped a bit. True, 'whole scenes had been cut out. And why? Because English singers are incapable of operatic recitative' declared the *European*. But, 'real, ancient Persians, of the times of winged horses, peaked beards, and Babylonian bricks' rescued the piece long enough for some pennies to be earned from it.

It was to *Love*, a new play by the popular Sheridan Knowles, and starring Ellen Tree, that the management were looking for financial salvation. On the strength of that author, and one of his lady-catching titles (there had been

Love-Chase; *Woman's Wit, or Love's Disguises*) they had borrowed money to keep up their standard of presentation.

It proved a success and enjoyed Royal patronage, but it was not the resounding financial success that was needed for that ever-demanding monster of a theatre. Furthermore, Miss Tree took herself off on her customary tour after thirty-seven performances so the run had to be suspended.

Mathews read the writing on the wall, consulted his old family solicitor and agreed with him that the accounts should be made up with a view to following Macready and throwing up the game.

While Mathews was in the counting house, Madame was in the wardrobe and the paint-shop, supervising more 'original costumes' and watching the Grieves rebuild Newgate Prison for the afterpiece that was to follow *Love* on 18 November.

The Beggar's Opera was hardly an original choice and it was not particularly well acted but it saved the season – or lured the management on to ruin, however one likes to look at it. Its great success paid a lot of bills and persuaded the Mathews that they could still make the project work. The way in which it might work was the way in which *The Beggar's Opera* worked, and it was the road to disaster: expensive presentation based on a policy of newly designed and made costumes and settings for every production.

The Beggar's Opera was given in 1728 costume (which meant an entirely new collection), the prologue was restored as well as more 'authentic' dances than more recent efforts. Madame as Lucy, in a text that was not as 'original' as the costumes, was giving a happy public the Vestris it knew and wanted. The rival production that opened at Drury Lane proved no competition.

The ruthless business of play after play to keep everyone paid went on unabated, despite the comparative success of *Love* and the great success of *The Beggar's Opera*, and even Madame began to show signs of flagging. *The Times'* penetrating eye observed that *The Rivals* (28 November) lacked the 'minute care in the decorative department which distinguished *The School for Scandal*'. The Christmas pantomime, *The Great Bed of Ware*, made extensive and wonder-making use of the large mechanical resources of Covent Garden, but there were mishaps that would never have occurred at the Olympic. On a few occasions the towering scenery got stuck in the course of transformations and there were other backstage headaches. Another shot at Sheridan, *The Duenna* made only about a third as many performances as either of the other two. 'Very picturesque moonlight' by means of Covent Garden's expensive limelight, was about the best thing that could be said about the few performances of *Hamlet* (Moore), though the audiences who did attend were kind, and *The Clandestine Marriage* fared no better.

Midwinter was cheered by the company being called to the Green-Room to hear Leigh Hunt read his 'elegant and poetical play of *The Legend of Florence*' (Vandenhoff). Hunt records that it made Ellen Tree and Planché weep. Madame got it up with her old flair and the piece did quite well, socially as well as financially. Midwinter was further cheered by the gradual support for and appreciation of what the new management were trying to do, by the more discriminating press.

The *Theatrical Journal* and *Musical Intelligencer* were among the supporters. On 4 January, it its third issue, the *Theatrical Journal* reprinted a notice that it had found of Madame's début. Where it was found or which newspaper originally printed it is unfortunately not indicated, but it belongs here rather than in Chapter Two. The *Theatrical Journal* took as its motto: 'A well-governed Stage is an ornament to Society, an encouragement to Wit and Learning, and a School of Virtue, Modesty, and good Manners. CHESTERFIELD'

It must have given Madame cause for a modest smile – perhaps accompanied by a hint of the old 'espieglerie' in the eyes – to see her name in large letters under the *mot* of his Lordship:

'MADAME VESTRIS

'Our readers may perhaps be amused by the following notice of the first appearance of Madame Vestris on any stage, and they will perceive that the critic on his reviewal of the fair debutante was pretty correct in his prophecies of her future career. "Madame Vestris, wife of the celebrated ballet master, on Thursday July 20th 1815, appeared for the first time on any stage in the character of Proserpina, and seldom have the votaries of Terpsichore experienced a greater treat. This lady possesses a richness of tone, and correctness of delivery, without the affectation of execution, which at best can but astonish, without finding the way to the heart; added to a melodious voice, nature has gifted her with an elegant person and a lovely countenance; since her infancy she has received instruction from the first masters, and from her successful début we may congratulate the frequenters of the Opera, upon having so valuable an acquisition added to that establishment. Upon her entrance she was greeted with the applause of ENCOURAGEMENT which during the performance increased, and called forth that of general SATISFACTION. It would be difficult to select any particular part without being guilty of an injustice to the rest, the whole being uniformly excellent; we shall not on the present occasion enter minutely into the merit of her performance as we shall no doubt at a future period have occasion to notice her more particularly. The curtain fell before an excessively crowded house, much to the satifaction of the audience, and we trust equally so, to the feelings of the fair debutante and her husband."

'Four-and-twenty years have elapsed since the above critique was written, and yet it might be copied into any of the prints of the present day, as referring in all its particulars, except the first appearance, to the lady for whom it was written, as a notice of her present acting, and her attractive influence.'

The next issue, a week later, gave a perceptive summing up of recent considered opinion:

'At the beginning, public opinion was not in her favour, many stood aloft watching the progress of things rather than encouraging her first attempts to please, and not till the new play of *Love*, and the accession of Miss Ellen Tree to the company turned the scale, did the public generally appear in her favour, and then the current being turned decided at once she must do and the public crowded to support one who for four and twenty years had been so great an idol of attraction. Madame Vestris will not easily be induced to resign Covent Garden, and if life and breath be spared her, we may look forward to her retaining this Theatre for many succeeding years. Nor can we as public journalists have the least wish to the contrary, but rather feel great pleasure at the prospect, as, under her direction we may rest assured, that taste and elegance combined will always be apparent in her exertions. It is right that the national and patent theatres should be under the guidance and direction of some one who is fully aware of the responsibility of conducting and managing the only houses in which we can look for the success of the legitimate drama . . .

'Although the season at Covent Garden is yet but in its infancy, still, great things have been done, and every one must allow that the management has been good, new talent has been produced, and a renewed vigour given to the profession, which on the relinquishment of the Theatre by Macready, it was expected, would languish like an unhealthy and sickly plant. We have noticed that a little hesitation on the part of the public to crowd the house was observable at its opening, and we are glad of it, and why? for this reason; it clearly proves that it was not because Vestris had the Theatre that people patronised it, but as soon as the productions were worthy of extensive patronage, then and not till then, does a discerning public enter the doors. Let all managers learn from this . . .'

To this goodwill were added two further events that boosted the remaining months of the season; the Royal Marriage, and Charles Kemble's return to the stage. By Royal command theatres were opened free of charge to the public for Her Majesty's nuptials on 10 February 1840. Planché wrote a 'masque', *The Fortunate Isles, or The Triumph of Britannia*, produced on the 12th. Nobody understood it, but there was a very pretty effect at the end:

'. . . an elaborate piece of mechanism, which opens as it enlarges, and discovers the word "Victoria" in brilliant letters, surrounded by smaller revolving stars. A hymeneal altar rises, heraldic cupids fly about the air, and the piece terminates.' (*The Times*, 13 February 1840)

For the visit of the royal pair on 28 February it seemed appropriate to offer *Love*, though it was remarked that Her Majesty seemed especially taken with Charles Mathews in *Patter vs. Clatter* (the afterpiece). Victoria and Albert were back within two weeks for *The Legend of Florence*. Kemble's return was enough to draw a good house, but the incognito arrival of the royal couple for a third visit made it a bumper night. The Queen asked to see Kemble as Mercutio, returning not only for that but also on several other occasions.

Madame was in her element preparing for the reception of the visitors. How fortunate that, despite that unpleasantness, the house had been altered so that the royal bride and groom could be tastefully and exclusively received. But for the chance of death the arrangements would have been for Madame's old admirer, Charlotte and her Leopold. This was a more solemn, a more genteel pair.

The Bed of Ware having provided the 'unavoidable' Harlequinade at Christmas, the 'fairy piece', which had become an institution under Madame's régime, was postponed until Easter. Planché's charming version of *The Sleeping Beauty* was the first of a number of similar pieces that he was to write for Vestris. It was well received, though again the first performance was hampered by scenic problems — and Madame Beauty was dropped by her Prince Charming! A natural, rather than a mechanical, hitch stopped the show and convulsed Madame and the audience with laughter: the parrot — real of course — on her shoulder decided to join in her song!

The Merry Wives of Windsor with Madame as Mrs Page 'looking younger than her daughter', brought healthy noises to the box office. It was still the version that gave ample scope for songs, and the best of the notices were, again, for the 'getting up'. There was, however, a difference, for the period chosen was Shakespeare's own and not that in which the play was set. Was it simply that Madame did not greatly care for the ideas Planché gave her from the reign of Henry IV? Or was *The Times* right in guessing that: ' . . . it was probably considered that . . . Shakespeare designed the comedy as a representation of his own period.' (1 May 1840). The implications of this are, I think, wider than we should apply to Vestris. There is no other evidence in her work that the *mood* or *intent* rather than the time of the action of a play should determine its setting.

Moore left before the end of the season, early in May. He probably felt that Madame's régime was not the kind to appreciate the tragedian he felt himself to be. The management probably felt that his engagement had been an expensive mistake. He was, however, back next season.

About a week before the season closed, Madame cleared about £400 for her Benefit. The boxes, on this occasion, held a nicely balanced assortment of old memories and new manners: Lady Blessington and Count D'Orsay, Lord Chesterfield, Prince Napoleon, Lady Montefiore, Lady Charles Bentinck . . .

Some sixty-three productions had been mounted in eight months. The

Farewell Address on 29 May was the last such speech that Madame was to make:

> '. . . We cannot always comprehend . . . first-rate talent, but we have endeavoured in the representation of plays, to look to the production of an harmonious picture rather than to the prominence of an individual figure . . . an actor is not fit until after arduous study and long practice. I pray you, then, to support our national schools, that they may produce you good actors . . .'

A brave notion, if not really a possible one at that time or in that theatre, and raising points that are still the subject of anything but rational discussion. The *Satirist* made no bones about stating a widely held opinion: 'The times are against her. There is a lack of dramatic impulse though not perhaps of dramatic feeling in the country. The public want something better than second – and third-rate actors placed in first-rate parts . . . Madame Vestris must seek for an O'Neill, a Cooke, or a Kean ere she can command success in her future management . . . People are sick of the fustian of Macready and the mechanical imitation and croaking imbecility of Charles Kean . . .'

But 'until September next' they could take some rest before beginning a successful tour at Liverpool after, all things considered, a good season. A mixture of hard work and lucky breaks had saved the enterprise for a while. An average nightly loss of about £22 had to be set against the fact that there were good pieces 'in stock' for re-presentation, and the house was still looking spick and span from the face-lift they had given it last September.

12

The Dream and the Awakening

To help fill its columns between seasons the *Theatrical Journal* gave another of its little pictures of life around theatres, on 18 July 1840:

'THE STAGE DOOR

ON THE FIRST NIGHT OF THE SEASON

'Those persons who are not much acquainted with theatricals, can have no idea of the multiplicity of persons who are seen at this door, the whole of the day, prior to a first night's performance: all is bustle and sometimes great confusion. It would seem to a stranger, that this door was only used for the actors, musicians, &c. But it will be found there are a great number of others connected with a theatre — such as scene shifters, carpenters, tailors, painters, machinists, dressers, box keepers, money takers, firemen, watchmen, property men, and a great number of others with no property at all; who all enter at this door. About 11 o'clock in the morning the throng begins, the actors come to the rehearsal; their friends will be waiting in great numbers, when up comes a principal actor, and is accosted by his friend, "Good morning, Mr. F., I called at your house, and was told you was come to the theatre. Can you oblige me with a ticket to go on the stage when God Save the Queen is sung?"

'MR. F. — "Why really you have come so late, and I have so many to oblige, — let me see, door-keeper, have you any letters for me?"

'DOOR KEEPER. — "Yes, sir, twelve."

'MR. F. — "Oh! what was it, an order? how is Mrs. P. and the children? has Mr. B. come, door-keeper?"

'D.K. — "Yes, sir, he has been asking for you."

'MR. F. — "John, take the phaeton back, and say I shall be home at four."

'FRIEND. — "Can you oblige me, Mr. F?"

'MR. F. — "I had quite forgot you! I can't say exactly — oh, an order! — I am afraid not, the first night. It's a fine day, Mr. Simpkins. I don't think I can do that for you, come again at six; stay, I'll see Mr. B., wait a few moments."

'His friend waits at the door all the time the rehearsal is on, when out comes Mr. F.

'MR. F. — "Oh! the manager is so busy I could not get to ask that question; good day, sir!"

'D.K. — "What do you want?"

'Stranger. — "The manager."

'D.K. — "What's your business?"

'STRAN. — "I want to see the manager, and I can't tell you my business."

'D.K. — "You had better write, I can't go bothering him now."

'STRAN. — "You are a saucy fellow, and I'll tell the manager of your behaviour."

'D.K. — "Oh! you must get to see him first before you can do that; you must not stop here, crowding the place, if you have anything to say write so — come, right about."

'STRAN. — "I wish I could see the manager! I know he would turn you away for such behaviour. I'll mark your pretty doings; what a Jack in office!"

'D.K. — "Stand on one side there — what's your business?"

'2 STRAN. — "Do you know Mr. Bustle, sir?"

'D.K. — "Yes; you can't see him now, he's on stage: why don't you go to his lodging? what do you come here for? have you any letters? I can't keep talking to you all day, stand aside. Mr. Chatter here's a parcel and some letters for you, and four ladies and a lad wanted you."

'MR. C. — "Oh! if they come again say what you like, to get rid of them. Botheration! because I dined with them last Sunday, and borrowed a sovereign, they all want a ticket to go on the stage, to hear the national anthem sung. Tell them to come at half-past six, then you'll know how to get rid of them."

'D.K. — Mr. W., Mr. W., sir! sir! I did not like to call you by your name; there's been two men enquiring for you: I know who they are! the same fellows that were looking after you on the last night of last season; shabby genteel chaps. They are the same I'm sure that you took lodgings of, at a certain place over the water; who prevented you going to Scotland last season, to fill your engagement."

'MR. W. — "The devil they are! they might let me receive a week's salary first. Can you manage to get me in some other way for a few nights — it's very unlucky!"

'D.K. — "I'll ask Sligo, sir! If you would only consent to be brought in in a sack, we can make it all right between us."

168

'MR. W. — "To be sure I will; fetch me from the Garrick about half-past five. You know I shall stand something handsome. (aside) At least I may as well promise."

'D.K. — "Miss T. madam! there has been three ladies in a carriage enquiring for you: they stopped nearly an hour, they said you promised to meet them here; they would not believe me when I told them you was not come."

'MISS T. — (hastily) "Indeed! who did they look like? was it a yellow carriage? were the ladies stout or thin? had one a red face? was she tall? did any of them wear a veil? did they leave any message? was there a man with them? — no man! monsters! tell them, if they come again, either to write or come to Pimlico."

'STRANGER. — "Is the manager in? I mean Mr. C. or Madame V. Have you a note directed 'Publicola.'"

'D.K. — "Have you any letters? you can't see them. There's no letter for that name."

'STRAN. — "Take in my name, I belong to the press, and expect an answer about the free list: I must have an answer."

'D.K. — "Oh, sir! I will send to Mr. C., what name? Publicola did you say? please to walk this way."

'STRAN. — "Pray can I see someone belonging to the house, door-keeper?"

'D.K. — "Who did you want?"

'STRAN. — "Some person in office."

'D.K. — "I am in office. Do you see that board with writing on it — read that."

'STRAN. — "'No person admitted here except on business, and all letters to be given to the hall-keeper.' Why, door-keeper, I am on business."

'D.K. — "Yes, sir: but you have no business here. I must beg you will clear the way, gentlemen."

'The hall is cleared, the rehearsal over. A succession of the same enquiries takes place again, about six o'clock, and so continues till the end of the season. What an enviable situation is a stage door-keeper, at a Theatre Royal!'

The second season began early, on 7 September. They began prudently, for them, and perhaps realized that the lucky breaks that had got them through last season could not be looked for again.

They reduced the company and more than halved the new productions that were done. Attempts to strengthen the acting company were unsuccessful. They offered £50 a night to Charles Kean (a sum originally demanded by his father, Edmund, and now insisted upon by his far less talented son), but lost him to the Haymarket because of their principle of not giving Benefits. Kean might well have raised the point that Madame had taken one herself in May.

169

Ellen Tree was re-engaged and Moore came back again, but comedians again dominated the company. No tragedies and very little Shakespeare at all was done during this or the following season, but the prospects were as well as could be expected, 'making due allowance' as The *Morning Herald* said on 8 September 'for the lowered conditions of the market'.

They opened with no competition from Drury Lane which was now given over to musical pieces (The *Herald* wondered if Shakespeare's bust in that theatre was to be replaced by Apollo playing a jews' harp!).

A fashionable, though not an excessively crowded, audience attended the opening bill of *The Merry Wives* and *The Sleeping Beauty*. Nothing new on stage, but one change in the auditorium, perhaps prompted by the royal visits of last season? The boxes were no longer linked with the dress circle — yet another dividing line had been introduced between the classes. Unfortunately for the management's good intentions in beginning the season early to make money, many of the box patrons had not yet come back to town, thus depriving the theatre of its best-paying customers.

Revivals of *The School for Scandal* and *The Rivals* and *Love* went not too well, but better than the *Twelfth Night* revived from May. It was for this *Twelfth Night* that the damaging device of transposing the first two scenes was introduced. (It has been done since, in our own time, when we ought to know better.)

Despite the hint that *Love* had given, not to back too heavily on a play by Knowles, Madame threw earlier prudence to the winds and squandered a vast amount of money and energy on *The Bride of Messina*. Despite the fact of its having really been written for Macready — a fact that Moore apparently tried to adjust by giving a regrettable imitation of that actor — and of its having a flat, tedious and pompous text, the play might have paid its way for it had a reasonable run only ended by the illness of Ellen Tree.

But it would have taken a phenomenal success to repay, let alone profit from, the expenditure and the running costs. Shades of Pixérécourt haunted the Covent Garden stage: classical ruins on a 'beautifully painted pavement' of a ground cloth; a grand wedding ball, and even Etna, across the Bay of Messina, moonlit, of course.

As production followed production, the refrain was the same from the press. 'The immense care bestowed on the production' and 'those elegant scenes in which the present manager so much excels' are examples of many such comments.

The full Olympic effects were achieved on Covent Garden scale in *The Fashionable Arrivals*. Smart dialogue and fashionable foibles set against, firstly, a breakfast room — a *real* meal in progress, and secondly a conservatory 'with the roof covering the stage, the view of the trees, the Chinese lamps, the mosaic pavement, and the opening into the drawing room, which is seen at the back' (*The Times* 30 September 1840). Madame had nibbled the mushroom and her Olympic doll's house had become a Gargantuan toy for her Wonderland. Despite a script not up to the best Olympic standard the toy attracted and was to justify its construction before the end of the season.

November 1840 brought two successful productions. *The Critic*, originally Sheridan's but so adapted (by stage tradition) by Mathews as to be close to an Olympic revel, gave Mathews, as Puff, his first real success in an older play, and a part for most of his acting life.

A Midsummer Night's Dream was much more faithful to its author. The accounts of this production, together with those of the later *Comus*, indicate a

THEATRE ROYAL
COVENT GARDEN
UNDER THE MANAGEMENT OF
Madame VESTRIS.

The FREE LIST (the Public Press excepted) will be Suspended This Evening.

This Evening, MONDAY, November 16, 1840,
WILL BE REVIVED
SHAKSPERE'S
MIDSUMMER NIGHT's DREAM

Preceded by MENDELSSOHN's celebrated OVERTURE.
The Music selected and arranged by Mr. T. COOKE,
who will preside in the Orchestra.
The Scenery by Mr. GRIEVE, Mr. T. GRIEVE, & Mr. W. GRIEVE·
The Decorations and Appointments by Mr. W. BRADWELL.
THE MACHINERY BY MR. H. SLOMAN.
THE COSTUMES BY MR. HEAD AND MISS IRELAND.
The Action, by Mr. OSCAR BYRNE.

Theseus, ... (*Duke of Athens*) .. .. Mr. COOPER,
Egeus, (*Father to Hermia*) Mr. DIDDEAR.
Lysander, ... } *in love with Hermia,* { .... Mr. JAMES VINING,
Demetrius, ... } { .... Mr. BRINDAL.
Philostrate. (*Master of the Revels to Theseus*) Mr. HEMMING. .
Quince, (*the Carpenter*) Mr. BARTLEY. .. Bottom. (*the Weaver*) Mr. HARLEY·
Flute, (*the Bellows Mender*) Mr. KEELEY, Snout, (*the Tinker*) Mr. MEADOWS.
Snug, (*the Joiner*) Mr. F. MATTHEWS. Starveling. (*the Tailor*) Mr. W.H. PAYNE.
Hippolyta, (*Queen of the Amazons, betrothed to Theseus*) Mrs. BROUGHAM.
Hermia, ... (*Daughter to Egeus, in love with Lysander*) .. .. Mrs. NISBETT.
Helena, (*in love with Demetrius*) Miss COOPER.
FAIRIES.
Oberon, ... (*King of the Fairies*) .. .. .. Madame VESTRIS,
Titania, (*Queen of the Fairies*) Mrs. W. LACY,
Puck, or Robin Goodfellow, (*a Fairy*) Miss MARSHALL,
First Fairy. Mr. .. NFAP H.

visual impact of a kind that was not to be experienced again until the London seasons put on by Diaghilev before the 1914–18 war. Madame, using her fine taste and technical skill, had mustered her forces and deployed them in a manner that gave form and pressure to the imagination of her time in regard to this play.

The organization involved boggles the imagination. Where did the extras – over seventy of them – dress? When was time found to rehearse the fourteen musical numbers, and when could Oscar Byrne have everyone for the production numbers? The rest of the season was, meantime, going on around mountains of canvas, gauze and cut-outs and umpteen properties ordered by Mr Rye, whose 'gentlemen's stockings' must have been sadly missed after his death in October.

Productions could be enlarged for Covent Garden, but actors could not be reduced for fairies, so Madame made the scenery effect the change. Extensive use of gauze, indirect lighting and moving scenery, together with the construction of scenic devices that could convey or reveal actors at any level, above or below the stage, were the means she used. Gliding panoramic scenery created effects that superimposed celluloid films were to give Walt Disney for his more romantic cartoon films. Mortals were firmly grounded in ancient Athens and the rustics performed in an 'archaeological reconstruction' of a Greek amphitheatre. 'Authenticity' excused and commended Hippolyta's knee-length tunic.

The press were full of praise for the production though one ominous note is sounded by *The Times* who mentioned 'the pauses incident to dramatic production'. Unusual for Madame, but something that was to become a deadly thing for many of her would-be imitators in her own day and later.

We may get a better estimate of what this production meant at the time if we note the reaction of a playgoer, known simply as E.R.W., who wrote his impressions for the *Theatrical Journal* for the edition of 1 May 1841:

'A FEW WORDS ON A MIDSUMMER NIGHT'S DREAM

As produced at Covent Garden.

'It was with no common feeling of pleasure, that I read the announcement of this beautiful poem being revived at the only royal theatre; especially as it would be presented to the public, under the unerring taste of the most fascinating woman of her day; I had a presentiment as to the effect which would be attempted, and rejoiced most heartily at the universal praise bestowed upon its "first night" by the press; yet so fearful was I lest it might not be exactly as my fancy pictured; I, child-like, reserved my visit, not wishing to dispel the illusion, till unable longer to repress my curiosity I entered the theatre; many readers may smile at this last remark, they will not on deliberation, for be assured, no pleasure on earth is equal to anticipation, it is the finest feeling of childhood, and clings to us all with equal tenacity of life. The curtain drew up: Athens as it stood in its palmy days was before me, the eye ranged over those magnificent buildings whose ruins are the wonder and the standard of taste to all succeeding times; I was electrified with delight, and most cordially thanked the Messrs. Grieves for availing themselves of the print lately published of "Athens as it was"; the very scene so calculated to raise one to a contemplation of the finer portion of the mind, was the prologue, or rather the stepping-stone to creation's realm; I was on classic ground; my step was among the habitations of the Gods; my thoughts already soared beyond the dull routine of mortality; the wand was waved, a fluttering and a buzz rang in my ear, and I almost saw the fairies; the characters entered; – what a Theseus! he the prototype of the deified! but stay, it is not in mortal's power to put the semblance of divinity, so let him pass; to make amends for this, we had the Amazonian Hippolyta; truly a queen, whose very step bespoke the royalty of her heart; the lovers, I did not like, and truly pitied the beauteous damsels their probation with two such cool passioned beings; Hermina (sic) the Greek girl, whose birth place seems writ on her fair form, and no less to be admired Helena; all dressed in the becoming style of the age, all true Athenians well mated to the scene; what a remembrance to the well stored mind, to see the glories of this city of the world called up upon his imagination, to be among them, to share their feelings, to be for awhile Greek in heart and hand.

'Now comes a different scene, the cottage of a mechanic, the would be player, Bottom, and most inimitably played; Quince, Flute, Snout, also well enacted; Snug, Starveling, hit off to the life with all their humorous conceits, and so ends the act; our impatience is at last set at rest, the act drop rises; a translucid lake hemmed round with trees, with here and there a break in the woody ring, thro' which you gaze on some grassy spot where tiny elves keep their midnight gambols, or shelving banks velvetted over with nature's softest greens, fit couches for the fairest forms to lay in dalliance sweet and lisp the amorous song, while above, the star bespangled sky shoots out its myriad lights, and the pale moon pours down her silver flood in a glittering hail on the water, and sleeps the charmed spot in so soft and mellowed a tone, that the mortal sense overcome with her spirit's influence parts with its grosser self, gives loose to nature's love, and feels at home once more in Eden's garden; the most imaginative of all creative forms, mischievous Puck, shoots up from the earth, other spirits come, – the mighty Oberon, Titania, and all their beauteous court, till so life-like all becomes, that we are in the fairy land, and mate with forms whose essence, light as the air, sport about in fantastic revelry, as leaves whirled round and round when caught by the summer's wind; the action of the poem goes on, the fairy quarrel is continued, the mortals love, and the fairy influence over it; Puck flies away; Oberon, waving his wand, melts with the scene from our sight, and leaves a forest glade with its carpet of green and line of trees, whose overspreading branches entwined one over the other, over arched the earth and jealously guarded the fairies' sleeping haunts from the rude gaze of the surrounding sky; truly, these two scenes are the most beautiful of their kind ever seen on the stage; it seems as if the poet had descended from high Olympus, and throwing his own essence into the painter's pencil, rewrit in colours the words that once sprang from his pen, they are his own as much as the poem; the people, the fairies, seem to have risen with each stroke of his pencil, they bear his own impress, have the pallas stamp born of this brain; are so mingled with the scenic effect as to appear one harmonious whole.

'The actors, the fairy mistake, the humorous transformation, quickly follow out the plot, till drawing towards the climax; we have another wood scene, this is at the outskirts, a lake with the distant country, hedged on one side with trees, by the side of which, a path winds its way far into the adjoining wood; a soft twilight overspreads the whole, and prepares the mind for the coming change; the plot is at its height, the turn to happiness has begun, night thickens, and as the actions begin to change, morning breaks down from his couch, the sun pours out his warmth and light, the lovers are made happy and the fairy quarrel is at an end; this is another felicitous effort, and as far as can be effected in representing the atmospheric changes is here done; the poetry of the nation deserves high commendation, and we can but regret, the feeling cannot be more happily carried out. Now comes the play; then the last scene, a hall in Theseus's house; one of those rich architectural compositions with galleries and flights of stairs, that have a most impressive effect on the stage; here assemble the entire body of fairies making merry over the triple nuptials, darting from side to side, flying round and round, now here, now there, on the ground, in the air, waving their tiny lamps till the entire place seems sparkling with the countless hues of light, and the delighted eye passing its thrill of pleasure to the tongue, one exclamation of delight springs from the beholders as down falls the curtain. Take it all together, I do believe a happier revival never took place on the stage, than in *The Midsummer Night's Dream*; the spirit of poetry seems to have actuated all concerned, and right merry am I, that the public has with a profuse hand tended their thanks to Madame for so dainty a fare: I do hope it will not for some time be set aside, and that a night at least per week will be devoted to its use, and if the public think as I think, they will visit the theatre night after night with the same thirst and veneration, as the poor Jew journeys to the Holy Land; for Shakespeare re-lives, and calls for homage, nations declare to be justly his. E. R. W.'

Shakespeare, that is *The Merry Wives* and *The Dream*, together with the Christmas piece, *The Castle of Otranto*, kept the public coming to Covent Garden for some months, until, at last, Madame accomplished her task of showing a piece tailor-made not only for her kind of presentation but for the company style of acting that she had always worked for. John Brougham, a member of the company for some time, had the original idea for *London Assurance*. What the project lacked was a part for Mathews, so the idea was bought from Brougham and Dionysius Boucicault (then calling himself Lee Moreton or Morton), reshaped it to include a part for Mathews. It is pretty clear that Mathews himself was responsible for a lot of editing and doctoring to get the play right for himself and the company. *The Times* commented on the fact that the parts fitted the actors perfectly and vice versa.

The notices, at last, commended the cast and presentation with the same enthusiasm. What more could they say of the settings? The *Athenaeum* found that: 'the stage in each instance presents rather a realization than a mimetic representation'!

London Assurance proved to be one of the big successes of the new style of acting, often revived until the 1914–18 war. It was revived again in 1970 by the Royal Shakespeare Company and enjoyed a good run in repertory, though Madame would have had misgivings about the presentation, thinking it tended to mimetic representation rather than a realization. It gave Eliza and Charles a good stock piece for themselves, and it justified what Madame had tried to do with *The Fashionable Arrivals*. For their second Covent Garden season the play topped the bill practically every night from its opening on 4 March until the season ended on 3 June.

London Assurance made the reputation of Dion Boucicault overnight – to apply an often misused but in this case correct phrase. The grapevine between theatres in the same town has something uncanny about it. News of success or failure is transmitted almost as it happens. Lester Wallack in his *Memories of Fifty Years* (New York 1889) describes how he was waiting in the wings of the Haymarket Theatre when: 'Some one came hurrying in and announced, "An enormous hit at Covent Garden; the third act is over and it is tremendous. If the other two acts go in the same way it is an immense go."'

The cries of 'Author' set off a backstage drama, for John Brougham and Boucicault were ready to be led forward. Madame, in her third charming ensemble as Grace Harkaway, swiftly changed her leading lady smile to a managerial frown and banished poor Brougham from her theatre. Resuming her smile, she led on the shy nineteen-year-old who, said *The Times*, was, understandably, 'eyeing the enthusiastic multitude with considerable nervousness'.

Brougham was, after a brief period at the Lyceum, to cross the Atlantic where he made a good corner for himself as Dazzle in *London Assurance*, the part he had *not* written for Mathews. Boucicault, as is the way of a successful youth, soon overcame his shyness and made a successful career for himself as the author of the English/Irish equivalent of the Boulevard authors' pieces, with their flair for ephemeral but shrewd theatricality.

Within a few days of the first night, before the charm of youthful delight had hardened into opportunism, he wrote his mother a letter that nicely conveys the still-sweet smell of success:

'My dear Mother,

'I dare say, before this has reached you, you will have heard of the triumph I have achieved. On Thursday last March 4, a comedy in 5 Acts written by me was played at Covent Garden Theatre, and has made an unparalleled hit, indeed so much so that it is played *every night* to crammed houses and it is expected to run the whole season. Today I was elected Member of the Dramatic Authors' Society. I enclose you fifteen pounds and by that you will come over to me immediately. I have now 5 pieces in Covent Garden, all accepted, the present piece "London Assurance", from which I shall get £300 – "Woman", a play in 5 Acts – £500, "Sharps the Word" a comedietta in 2 Acts, £100 – "The Old Guard" a Drama in 2 Acts, £150 – making a £150 independent of publishing which is worth about £300 more and other sundries. Believe me, I am not exaggerating. If you doubt me, look in any of last Sunday's papers. I am now looked upon as the great rising dramatic poet of the age. Lord Normanby and Mr. Fitzroy Stanhope were introduced to me on the first performance and said those very words. The Queen went to see it on Saturday night (third time of playing it) and after praising it in the highest terms as the best production that had seen the stage for the last fifty years, Her Majesty sent me a most gracious message by Lord Alfred Paget expressing her pleasure at seeing so young and promising an author, and hoping so early a success would not destroy my emulation and understanding.

'Pray my dear Mother, come over and share with me these honours and congratulations. Let me see you by me. I shall have no heart or mind to continue my labours till I see you at ease – do not lose one moment not one hour – but the instant you receive this – place your affairs in the hands of Mr. Ball or Wilson and come by the next packet with William. I have taken pleasant lodgings for you where you will be comfortable. I shall *expect* you here on Sunday evening at latest – as I suppose you will receive this by Saturday morning.'

His play, *Woman*, was the subject of an earlier letter to Mathews that indicates some of the problems and the foibles of managers:

'My dear Sir,

'I find on reflection that the minute I prepared for Mr. Macready of the statement made by me in the Green Room of Covent Garden Theatre – in reference to the play of "Woman" – is neither so full nor so correct as it ought to have been and I have taken the earliest opportunity of mentioning to Mr. Macready as I now do to you – that the words I used on that occasion were as nearly as I can recollect the following –

'"That I had sent a play called "Woman" to Mr. Macready — that he had read the same — Had explained his willingness to produce it — if I would transfer the speech in praise of Shakespeare from the woman's character to his own and that the conclusion of the play should be devoted to him — that I refusing this withdrew the manuscript"

'I have produced the letters which are now in Mr. Macready's possession on which I was induced to make the statement.'

The nightly loss on the season had dropped by half. Even allowing for the dangerously large dowry given to *The Bride of Messina*, it is a grim reflection on the theatrical problems of the time to note that the great successes of *The Dream* and *London Assurance* as well as other steady houses could not absorb the losses, let alone make a surplus.

Mathews gave the closing address for the 1840–41 season. He could promise nothing except a 'mysterious and melodramatic silence' with regard to the next season. An ominous note that heralded the disintegration of the company and the eventual end of the Covent Garden experiment under Madame.

It is not surprising, if sad, that the over-sized, over-worked toy should have eventually lost its impetus and its charm. Covent Garden and Drury Lane were each attempting to run organizations that are now divided into separate subsidized concerns in London: plays, operas, and dancing (a safer term than ballet for what was offered), plus extras such as pantomimes, burlesques, and fairy pieces. With both establishments attempting to attract with similar fare there was constant competitive bidding for performers, musicians and technicians.

Madame had no trouble getting the best people on the technical side and was pretty sure of securing the best comedians. But tragedians, or 'serious actors', were not too happy in the enlarged Olympic atmosphere. For the third season, the main supports in the 'serious' line, both male and female, had gone. Ellen Tree had married Charles Kean and Macready, preparing to take over Drury Lane (Apollo's jews' harp having lost its twang), had persuaded Anderson to join him.

It is not surprising to find evidence that Madame generally got on better with actors than with actresses, especially actresses of about her own age and younger. Allowing for the malice and invention of gossip, it is probable that she got tetchy and more than a touch imperious as she grew older and tired more easily. Such an undertaking as Covent Garden left little time for discussion and for countering opposition. She seemed to assume that her peers could understand and cope with her demands, and that they had her drive and meticulousness, and she saved her more considerate side for the 'smaller' people in the establishment — who were always loyal. The *Theatrical Joural* had commented, (30 January 1841) that 'Madame must have a constitution of iron to play and sing every night as she does' (though, in fact, she was cutting down her appearances).

177

Sounding its own prelude, it was opera that gave the Mathews' third Covent Garden season its main support. Ironically, it was not even native opera, a development that might have gone hand-in-hand with Madame's methods. It was a return to the thing she grew up with: Italian opera.

Before the opening of Bellini's *Norma* on 2 November there had been a desperate succession of pieces, old and new, that had shown to indifferent houses the management's dilemma: a shortage of the right actors for older good plays and no supplies of good plays for the actors available. Trying to divert attention from textual and acting shortcomings by dazzling the eye had outworn its effectiveness, and had brought things to such a pitch that comments began to be made about long waits for scene changes and even some shortcomings in the painting. Saddest of all was the *Athenaeum's* point, made after the opening of *The Old Maids* (Sheridan Knowles's attempt to please a genteel audience) that the play seemed 'to have been written at random . . . and with no thought beyond providing opportunities for Madame Vestris and Mr. Charles Mathews to display their talents'.

The play was generally commended for the costumes (Charles II again), and the sword fight between Mathews and Vandenhoff. 'It never missed fire' wrote Vandenhoff, 'Angelo, the great *maître d'armes*, was present at our last rehearsal of it, and we had the advantage of his suggestions and approval.'

Charles Kemble was especially fortunate in his daughters. Fanny (Frances Anne), who made her début aged twenty in 1829, rescued her father from bankruptcy and brought fame and fortune to Covent Garden for a spell. Adelaide, almost as talented operatically as Fanny was dramatically, made her début, aged twenty-seven, in 1841, in *Norma*.

For the four operas planned for Miss Kemble, Madame made the usual elaborate and careful preparation. There was no other way Madame *could* work. Unfortunately Miss Kemble's appearances were only decided upon when all the other arrangements for the season had been made. Opera, as with everything else that Madame did, could not be done on a shoestring, nor from stock, and moreover needed a far larger personnel than plays. Additional chorus (there were seventy in *Norma*) and an augmented orchestra had to be engaged. And Miss Kemble drove a hard bargain. A letter from Mathews in the Princeton collection tells the story. She won an initial eight weeks at £100 a week, being called upon to perform three nights a week and she was even given a Benefit. More expense was involved for a new director of music engaged at Miss Kemble's earnest request. She was able to bargain with two major assets to support her: the political fact that she was the daughter of a proprietor of the theatre and a member of a distinguished theatrical family, and the personal fact that she was Charles Mathews's maternal cousin.

The Times made comforting reading: 'The choruses are well disciplined, the scenery was beautiful and appropriate, and the groupings were effective and picturesque. How differently was the war-song of "Guerra, Guerra", given last

Madame Vestris as 'Oberon'

night by the crowd of warriors who mounted the sacred steps, and mingled their swords together in picturesque confusion, to the same song by the dull Celts who stand in semi-circular order at Her Majesty's Theatre! These trifles, this general attention to propriety in every particular, this dislike of defect in any one part of the exhibition, and the refusal to consider it compensated by the perfection of any other part, are the honourable characteristics of the Covent-garden management. Hitherto, this season, success has not crowned exertion, but the triumph of Miss Kemble last night may lead to a hope that a better period has arrived, and that attraction is at last found for the London public.'

The comfort faded when the realization came to Madame that the applause and the crowds were for Adelaide – a new personality to beguile the public, however much the discriminating few might realize the value of the management's contribution. She had been too long at the game not to realize the implications of the situation even before the proprietors themselves. Planché records:

'I dined with her and Mathews nearly every day, in their room in the theatre, George Bartley, the acting manager, making occasionally a fourth. One day when I was alone with them, and long before any calculation could be fairly made of the ultimate result of the season, Madame Vestris said, abruptly, after a short silence, "Charles! we shall not have this theatre next year." "What do you mean?" he and I exclaimed simultaneously. "Simply what I say." "But what reason," inquired Mathews, "can you possibly have for thinking so?" "No particular reason; but you'll see." "Have you heard any rumour to that effect?" I asked. "No; but we shall not have the theatre." "But who on earth will have it then?" we said, laughing at the idea; for we could imagine no possible competitor likely to pay so high a rent. "Charles Kemble," was her answer. "He will think that his daughter's talent and popularity will be quite sufficient, and we shall be turned out of the theatre. But," she continued, seeing us still incredulous, "three things may happen: Miss Kemble may be ill; Miss Kemble may not get another opera like 'Norma'; and Miss Kemble may marry." Every one of these predictions was fulfilled.'

Eliza and Charles were apparently dispensable at last; the masks were off and the toyshop confiscated. For, although the other three operas did not repeat the success of *Norma*, the proprietors decided that it was worth chancing that they would find another hit for Adelaide. They waited until a deficit on the season was obvious and, by the simple device of ignoring the 'gentleman's agreement' demanded the rent in full. A disgusted Planché, somewhat underestimating the deficit, wrote: '. . . there was a deficit of some £600 in the payment of the rent of as many thousands; and, with the usual liberality and good policy of the proprietors of theatres in general, Madame Vestris, who had raised Covent Garden once more to the rank it had held in the days of the Kembles, and paid her heavy rent to the shilling during two brilliant seasons, was denied the opportunity of recouping herself from losses caused by a most exceptional circumstance, and coolly bowed out of the building.'

The Mathewses made a brave end to the season and, if they could have found another *London Assurance* the proprietors would have been thwarted. But Boucicault's *The Irish Heiress*, as well cast and presented as his first success, failed to take the town. Nearer the mark was *Bubbles of the Day* by Douglas Jerrold (the ex-sailor and writer for *Punch* whose great success had been *Black Ey'd Susan* and who wrote *Paul Pry*) which, though poorly constructed, had the kind of characterization and 'realism' that went well with the Vestris style of acting.

The mutual dislike between Macready and Mathews blew up into an unpleasant public squabble as to who had the first idea for, and therefore the right to present, productions of *Comus* and *King Arthur*. A *Comus*, with other bits of Milton, parts of *King Arthur* and an assortment of music by Arne, Handel and Purcell, was put on at Covent Garden. Somewhat at sea with Milton's text, the cast had a happy time, sliding down waterfalls, travelling in jasper shells, rising in trembling bowers and parading as virtuous spirits in the opened skies (that *Dream* machine again), and the public responded to all those intellectual concepts turned to favour and to prettiness.

Planché whimsy, Madame's organization and Bradwell's machinery produced an Easter pantomime in *The White Cat*. Even Macready conceded, in his diary, that in this kind of entertainment the 'Covent Garden theatre people bear away the bell'.

As things turned out they could not bear away the bell or anything else. In their legal claim for cash or kind the proprietors were upheld in their demand for all that vast collection of scenery, costumes and properties, so carefully made and submitted for approval to Madame, some of them having been brought up the road from the Olympic.

When the news came out, the public reaction was one of shocked surprise and some indignation. On 29 April 1842, the day before the last night of the season, The *Morning Post* printed the following:

'Tomorrow night Madame Vestris takes (with a Benefit) her farewell of the Covent Garden stage – a stage she has both refined and adorned – and we will not suffer the occasion to pass without paying a valedictory tribute to her claims as a lady and an actress upon a public she has more delighted than any individual of her time.

'Preliminarily, however, let us state what we have heard as to the pecuniary disputes which have ended in this most-to-be-regretted result. The rent conditioned to be paid annually for the theatre was £7,500 with (we are informed) a verbal understanding that if the sum of £5,000 were actually paid each year, Mr. Mathews was not to be molested for the difference. More than £15,000 have positively been paid during the three years' lesseeship for rent, and in addition a sum little if any short of £14,000 for properties, the value of which, however much it may benefit the theatre itself, cannot in any way be converted to the advantage of Madame Vestris or her husband. Independently of these facts, we are given to understand that neither of them have drawn their own salaries, although everbody else in the establishment has been paid in full. We make this statement upon authority we deem to be conclusive of its truth, and we are sorry to be obliged to add that from the same source we hear that in violation of the fulfilled verbal agreement one of the proprietors of Covent Garden Theatre has sued Mr. Charles Mathews upon the legal document, a step which has compelled both himself and Madame Vestris to vacate their theatrical home and seek in a rival establishment the protection and support they ought to have found in their own.

'We will not anticipate the judgement of the public in this affair, but this we will state, that we know enough of its sympathies with justly established favourites to feel assured that a hearty and enthusiastic welcome awaits the appearance of Mr. and Mrs. Charles Mathews within the walls of Drury Lane Theatre, whither their new fortunes will shortly conduct them.

'What has not Madame Vestris done for the English stage? Let those who are close watchers of its phases answer. She has banished vulgarity, coarse manners, *double-entendre*, and impertinence from the boards over which she presided, and in their place has evoked the benefits that flow from a dramatic interpretation of polished manners, refinement, and politeness. Her green-room was the resort of the learned, the witty, and the wise, a miniature picture of polite and well-bred society whence a wholesome example spread itself on all within its influence. Once communicated to the stage, it became communicable to the public, and sure we are that a desirable tone of refinement both in manners and conversation has been extensively spread in private life by the lady-like deportment and acting of Madame Vestris.

'To art she gave an impulse of no mean importance. Witness the magnificent scenery, as appropriate as it was beautiful which her fine taste caused to be continually brought before the public. The *mise en scène* was never perfect until Madame Vestris taught her painters how to execute and the public how to appreciate her own pictorial conceptions, and to her judgement in this way the playgoing world has been indebted for much of its theatrical enjoyment.'

A crowded and affectionate audience filled Covent Garden on 30 April, and Mathews delivered the Farewell Address. There is a personal note in the reference to Thompson's *Seasons*, for Eliza's grandfather had done one of his most popular sets of engravings to illustrate this work.

'No season, excepting "Thompson's Seasons" are endowed with immortality, and ours having run the undeviating course marked out for it on the railroad of Time, has arrived at its terminus . . . My partner and I have been [the theatre's] directors for three years, during which we have endeavoured . . . to sow the seeds of that solid prosperity which would, we hoped, one day, manifest itself in permanent satisfaction to you, and a golden harvest to ourselves; but, alas! for "the mutability of human affairs"! Our first season was merely sowing – the second, little more than hoeing – and, though the third has been growing we must leave to other hands the fourth, which might have been our mowing. *Why* we have left these premises, I will not intrude upon you to explain. Suffice it to say, that in quitting them, we leave not only our business, but our good-will to our successor; and if, ladies and gentlemen, that successor should prove to be a gentleman – the admired representative of that thrice-honoured theatrical family . . . in that case, ladies and gentlemen, I can say that "as far as one manager *can* forgive another," it will afford us much consolation, should the change prove to be for his and your gain . . .'

Madame was vociferously called for and Charles led her on stage:

'. . . whereupon the whole audience rose *en masse* and vehemently cheered her. In a few minutes the stage was covered with chaplets of flowers, directed towards her from the boxes nearest the proscenium. Several of these she picked up, and pressed to her lips with an emotion that she could not conceal.' (*The Times*)

As Mathews wrote: 'we found ourselves adrift with nothing left but a piece of plate [presented by the company] and the debts of the concern.'

Covent Garden saw the fulfilment of Madame's predictions. In Planché's words: 'The theatre closed prematurely, and after an abortive attempt of Henry Wallack, and a brief and desperate struggle of Bunn, ceased to be a temple of the national drama.'

As a postscript to this section it should be noted that Queen Victoria had got the message from Planché and Madame. On 12 May 1842 she gave her first Costume Ball at Buckingham Palace. Desiring that the costumes should be historical and strictly accurate, she sent for Planché. Albert appeared as Edward III and Victoria as Queen Philippa, the rest of their entourage being dressed in the same period, according to their offices. Other folk might choose other periods but had to be as accurate as the monarch and her court – no 'fancy dress' was allowed.

13

Rogues and Vagabonds

Eliza and her Charley were out on the street. Transformed from host and hostess of the most elegant Green Room in Europe into rogues and vagabonds. Eliza's husband went the way of her lover: to prison as a bankrupt. Vagabondage had been arranged early, and in the provinces they were welcomed as always. They were still treading a Regency way in the new age – the Blessington-d'Orsay way, though Charles could not carry off bankruptcy with the éclat of that couple or of his wife, and was to complicate things still further by a Victorian attempt to save his good name.

A touch of that old society relieved his imprisonment. A young nobleman had been imprisoned for a spell over the Porter's Lodge and had had the room decorated and fitted up into 'a really elegant little boudoir'. Here Charles was lodged – a practical demonstration of the general sympathy that was extended to both the Mathewses at this time. After a week of confinement, Charles went with Eliza to the country for a few weeks, until the day when he was cleared of his financial problems and they were free to make a new life.

Experience had not taught him that neither heroic actions nor noble sentiments (that had lent a specious charm to Olympic plays) can be relied upon to produce happy endings in real life. He was always much more concerned about his status as a gentleman than Eliza was about other people's opinion concerning her claims to being a lady. Or perhaps it is more correct to say that their interpretations of such terms as 'lady' and 'gentleman' differed: her definition depended upon what she believed herself to be, his upon what others thought him to be.

Charles announced his intention of repaying those debts (of which he had been legally cleared) that had been personal as opposed to the official ones

184

incurred for Covent Garden. An honourable notion and one that he could have done by instalments as and when possible in due course. But, with a grand gesture, inappropriate for an actor in his 'line of business', he issued securities for the various amounts and so guaranteed his own ruin. When he could not meet the given dates, the interest mounted and eventually overwhelmed him again.

Madame must have felt this to be folly, but when Mathews got a notion he was inclined to follow it blindly. He had supported her loyally and courageously through her troubles and she gave him, at least, her silent support in this business.

Vagabondage was all right – indeed it was customary – for the summer months, but there had to be a return to London in the autumn, and they had arranged (as the reader will have gathered from the *Post's* comments) a few weeks before the end of the last Covent Garden season, an engagement to which to return.

An odd mixture of motives prompted Macready to offer them work at Drury Lane. The better side of him must have appreciated their professional dilemma and have recognized their hard work and integrity as managers. They had done better than he had at Covent Garden. But his meanness and vanity, linked with his fears, resented their professional and personal success – especially Madame's. A man who expected esteem from the public could not understand, and also envied, a woman who was given affection. It was unjust. These conflicting notions are conveyed in his diary entry for 1 May: 'Read Mr. Charles Mathews's speech on the closing of Covent Garden. It was worthy of Mr. C.M. and "the management of Madame Vestris". Players, poor players!'

They took his offer – what else could they do? – but insisted on their terms of £60 a week for two years and he gave it to them. It was possibly £70 in fact: £60 salary plus £10 for 'wardrobe', as they had at the Haymarket later. (Their stage clothes were in pawn, and they had to rent what they needed from them by the week.) The press suspected that Macready thought it was better for him to have them with him than as a threat to him elsewhere. He himself noted: 'It is a very great salary, but it is paid in consideration of enfeebling a position as well as adding to my own strength . . . Parted with them, they started off in their carriage, I in my shabby old hackney cab.'

It could never have worked. Macready took more professional liberties with Charles than he dared to take with Madame, for example he cast him as Roderigo in *Othello*. He got at Eliza by hardly ever putting her on the stage and keeping her name not only very subordinate to his own in the bills, but also reducing it to small print. The press reflected the public's reaction to a rising storm that could not be kept backstage. The *Age and Argus* exclaimed:

'Drury Lane will shortly be in a state of revolt if Mr. Macready does not relax from his habitual routine of tyranny . . . When Mr. Macready engaged

Madame Vestris, he ought to have had no other object in view than turning her great talents and popularity to account; but in the palpable spirit of wishing to crush her fame and wound her feelings she has become a comparative cypher . . . Mr. Charles Mathews has been thrust into Fag, and the name of his wife, that for some years has blazoned conspicuously in the *affiches* of all theatres, can only now be discovered in them by virtue of a magnifying glass.'

In addition to the personal affront, Madame's managerial ethics were shocked by the way things were done at Drury Lane. Especially disturbing was the old sharp practice of cancelling a performance on a badly attended night and deducting a percentage of the salaries of the performers – thus subsidizing managerial losses at the expense of the actors.

Things came to a head when for the projected production of Dryden's *King Arthur*, the obvious part for Vestris was given to Priscilla Horton, a quite talented but inexperienced singer, while the minor role of Venus was offered to Eliza. Not accepting the identification with the goddess as a compliment, Charles went to make a protest, about this and other things, and Madame followed him into Macready's office. According to Macready, there was 'much Billingsgate' from Eliza, and a press report says that she declared that she had 'often heard of the devil being painted blacker than he was, but she never knew his exact colour until she met with Macready'. Throwing the goddess of love back at him, she swept out with Charles, so ending the most tiresome and unhappy weeks of their professional career, and ending her association with the London theatre that had seen her establishment as a popular actress.

Webster soon engaged them, at the same salary, for the Haymarket, an arrangement that proved so agreeable to both sides that, on Christmas Eve, the *Theatrical Journal* announced that their contract had been renewed for twelve months. This arrangement allowed for provincial tours, and there was a very successful Edinburgh engagement in 1843.

The years from 1843 until 1847, when the Lyceum opened 'under the Management of Madame Vestris', have attracted little attention in accounts of Madame's life. These years were not, in fact, a time of professional uncertainty spent in reviving old successes in London and in the provinces. The events of these years not only made possible the Lyceum management but determined that it would be a different kind of management than those of the Olympic and Covent Garden.

Webster knew what was good for his box office and had no reservations about letting such public favourites as the Mathewses bring the audiences in as often as possible. They had a popular success at once with *The Little Devil*, giving them scope to exploit their individual and joint talents. It was on the bill with, among other things, *A Double-Bedded Room*, and like that piece made no pretentions to high art. They were probably relieved to get away from the

National Drama at last. *The Little Devil* had a good initial run and remained in the repertoire of the Haymarket for some years.

By May Covent Garden was in bad trouble. The proprietors were reaping the reward of their avarice. A wag commented, as he looked down from the gods: 'Well, I've often heard of the bottomless pit, but I've never seen it before!' By June the place was actually offered to Vestris again – a gesture that was confirmed by The *Theatrical Journal* for 8 July 1843.

All their stock and most of their staff were there. It must have been tempting. But Charles's knight errantry on behalf of his creditors and the happy success at the Haymarket probably combined to prevent them following up the offer.

At the end of June Eliza's mother died, aged eight-nine. It was quite a blow for Vestris and she did not appear for some two weeks. Madame Bartolozzi probably died in Paris where she preferred to live, and this would also account for Eliza's long absence from the stage in the midst of a new and successful engagement.

On 19 July *The Times* announced that a new play would be done at the Haymarket by: '. . . an authoress of rank and fashion connected with the first families in England. It is a perfect epitome of the sayings and doings in high life, and is exciting extraordinary interest in the circle where the lady is so well known for her wit and talent. It is read in the Green Room today . . .'

The play, *Moonshine*, opened on 3 August. The long notice in *The Times*, on the 4th is the reason for mentioning this otherwise uninteresting play. For the dutiful reading that an admitted addict undertakes when looking into the majority of the ephemeral pieces put on by the Mathewses in their capacity as managers or star performers, reveals that many of them could come under a similar – if not always so severe – censure. After dismissing the play as an 'utter failure', *The Times* continues: 'The merit of the piece . . . consists in some clever writing, the demerit in its thoroughly undramatic character. . . . Something more than mere literary talent is required to write plays – you may have a store of wit, you may put "good things" into the mouths of some half dozen personages – you may draw what you think characters, fashioning them after the manner of Theophrastos – you may make admirable reflections, but yet you shall make no play. The drama, besides being a branch of literature, is an art by itself, and it is no more a reproach to a literary man that he cannot write a play than it is to a painter that he cannot model a statue.'

The piece was 'most beautifully put upon the stage'. Webster was a manager who relied more upon his actors than his settings – one clue to his continued solvency as well as success. References to this and other felicities of presentation during the time the Mathewses were working for him indicate their influence (and Planché's) and also show the happy working relationship that existed, for a time, between Webster and his main attractions.

Moonshine, the 'utter failure', struggled on for about three weeks, 'compressed into three acts' after ten days, and supported by popular pieces – a run that strongly suggests guarantees against loss by the authoress of rank and fashion or her family.

'Most beautifully put upon the stage.' It was Paris that had stirred Madame's intuitive flair and led to the practical implementation of this dream at the Olympic. It was Paris that determined the next theatrical development in the London theatre. While Madame had been improving the modes and manners of the London minor theatres, the audiences of the Boulevard theatres had become more sophisticated in their tastes. The high moral intent of 'le mélodrame' justifying the sacrifices made for Revolutionary principles had lost its impetus as those principles were converted into individual pride of position. A social tone, inferring that indulgences, once the prerogative of the rich, were now objects of general aspiration, attracted audiences. A political and male dominated audience was being superseded by a social and female dominated audience.

French plays had been a main source of inspiration and adaptation at the Olympic. Vestris and Planché kept themselves well informed of developments in Paris. Planché was certainly a frequent visitor there, and it is possible that Madame was, too, as has been mentioned.

In between the Olympic seasons Madame rented the theatre to French companies and these visits became regular features of the London scene. English companies visited Paris as often, and the press in both capitals regularly reported each other's theatrical news. It was naturally the wealthier classes who made up the majority of the audiences for the French companies, the same well-to-do patrons who were the mainstay of Madame's seasons. There were a sufficient number of these to encourage John Mitchell to open the St James's in 1842 as a regular French theatre in London, a project that kept the place well filled for some twelve years.

The St James's seasons, whose success was so much indebted to the theatrical climate that Madame had created, provided the models for most theatrical writing in England for decades to come, for the kind of writing that was to revive playmaking by British authors. The 'frenchified ways' of an Italian/German pet of the British aristocracy had accidentally prepared for an invasion more subtle than that planned by Napoleon.

The end of the Covent Garden venture might have encouraged Mitchell to begin his St James's season, in that audiences deprived of Madame's productions would welcome his Théâtre Française.

One phenomenon that illustrates both the personal success of Madame Vestris and the growth of French influence generally with the public is the steady increase in the number of 'Madames', real and assumed, who appear in London from the late 1820s. By the mid 1840s an average of nine or ten 'Madames' were to be found in various fields of entertainment during the theatrical seasons. Many of them were no more 'to the manner born' than 'Miss Tinguet' was an English spinster when the pendulum had swung the other way several decades later.

188

It was entirely appropriate that Madame's Olympic novelty should be translated by Charles Mathews into an Anglo-French style of acting that would eventually resolve itself into the 'naturalistic' acting especially associated with English performers. (Further consideration of this point belongs in the next chapter.)

Eliza was delighted with the possibilities of a French musical play called *Trianon* by Bayard and Picard, and gave it to Planché to read. The bait was effective and Webster put on the adaptation on Tuesday, 22 August 1843, only too glad to get *Moonshine* off the boards no doubt. Under the English – and very Haymarket – title of *Who's Your Friend? or, The Queensberry Fête*, it proved a hit for everyone concerned and held the bill for weeks to crowded houses.

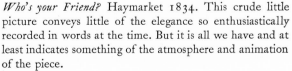

WHO'S YOUR FRIEND?

Who's your Friend? Haymarket 1834. This crude little picture conveys little of the elegance so enthusiastically recorded in words at the time. But it is all we have and at least indicates something of the atmosphere and animation of the piece.

The action of *Who's Your Friend?* had been transferred to the Duchess of Queensberry's villa at Richmond, but there was no doubt that the inspiration for the 1728 piece was the school of Watteau. *The Times* was delighted:

> '. . . he has approached the age of perriwigs with something of the tenderness of a lover . . . a complete Watteau picture in excellent taste, and we are much mistaken if we are not indebted to Mr. Planché as well for the tableau as for the drama.'

The opening moments showed ladies and gentlemen in pastoral costumes sitting about the gardens of the villa and others dancing. Vestris, in the guise of Amaryllis, a milkmaid (in 'reality' the Countess of Rosedale) entered with Mr Holl (Sir Felix Lovel as a miller), he in a white satin peasant suit; she in a lavender, green and puce silk dress with a white lace apron and flower-trimmed hat, – the crook is there, but it is manufactured in exquisite style.

> Countess: 'Can anything be more charming than this scene?'

and a crowded house responded with applause before she could continue her speech.

The two scenes (the second a 'salon in the Mansion of the Countess') are 'remarkable specimens of good taste' said *The Times*, 'fully reviving the best days of the Olympic theatre'. Vestris was at home again. Quite a slice of experience was behind two of her closing lines:

> 'It is an awkward question, by the way,
> For "Who's your friend?" 'tis sometimes hard to say.'

For Charles Mathews these Haymarket seasons were not so much a return home as a new departure. He found a confidence, a range and an independence of effect that gave his talent a new and stronger direction, largely because Eliza was no longer able to undertake the amount of new work that she had done.

The character of Giles in *Who's Your Friend?* was an early example of this bolder approach. Giles is a country bumpkin who gets involved in the Fête, is passed off as a foreign Baron incognito, and is eventually found to be the childhood friend of the Countess (all very 'egalité', royally dressed).

'There are not many occasions' said *The Times* 'when Mr. Mathews is completely drawn out, but this is one of them' and they were to increase.

In October 1843 *The School for Scandal* joined the season's offerings – the Mathewses as Lady Teazle and Charles Surface – and it, too, went successfully, alternating with *Who's Your Friend?* and other pieces, including some of Mathews's established afterpieces, especially *Patter vs. Clatter.*

This happy professional autumn clouded as the monetary assurances, given with such panache, became overdue and turned sour. With bankruptcy certain and prison probable for Charles, they panicked and resolved to leave England and settle in France. The resolve was not as mad as it sounds for they were both quite capable of taking engagements in Paris.

On 4 November they sold the furniture (chosen with such care and regardless of cost) of their cottage in the Harrow Road for £800. They had their current week's salary and more money for some plate that was pledged, and Mathews crossed the channel to avoid arrest. The following evening Eliza wrote to Josephine that she was going 'God knows where'. Setting off by train for Folkestone with seventeen or eighteen pieces of luggage, she found that the line went no further than Tonbridge! A coach was hired and, noting the amount of baggage, the coachman suggested adding two more horses to the two already harnessed and this was done. This 'omnibus and four' was to be made much of by the prosecution in the bankruptcy hearing.

They were in France for under a month – spending it seems, about £600! Realizing the grim truth that he could be arrested abroad for his English debts – and more harshly treated – Mathews decided to come home and appeal to the mercy of his creditors. 'Charles James Mathews, Westbourn Green, comedian' was among the bankrupts in *The Times* of 13 December 1843.

Webster took them back again and they appeared together in *The Little Devil* on Saturday 30 December. *The Times* on the following Monday recorded the fine welcome back for 'those two public favourites' who had not been on for a few weeks 'from reasons diversely explained by the "on dits" of the Sunday newspapers'.

After a revival of *Know Your Own Mind* on 4 January the next sustained Haymarket success was *The Merry Wives of Windsor* (Mrs Page and Slender) opening on 10 January, and continuing almost nightly for over a month.

The first of the bankruptcy hearings, all fully reported in *The Times*, was on 8 February and the final order was given on 4 April. Their Haymarket appearances were limited during these hearings to a few *Merry Wives*, but Mathews made a very good showing in the court room before a crowded audience of his professional colleagues and anyone else who could get in. The 'cast' for this real life drama was a good one. Mathews as the charming, if wayward, hero, defending himself and his lady in distress from a crowd of Thackeray-style creditors led by the lubricious brother-in-law, Anderson. Briefed as mercenaries were Chambers and Jones for Mathews (Chambers acquitting himself especially well) versus James.

The campaign proved of great theatrical interest. Sir C. F. Williams, presiding, prevented its descent into a sordid disinterment of old ghosts. Anderson declared that he knew Lizzie possessed 'five diamonds and other stones in a bracelet' that was 'a present from Lord Edward Thynne' and was firmly advised that it would be as well 'not to mention names if possible'. Chambers soon squashed an attempt by James to revive things from Madame's bankruptcy and, these two points disposed of, the hearing concentrated on professional matters and financial problems.

The involved circumstances that led to Anderson being a creditor showed that the Bartolozzi family problems had changed very little with the years, mother usually taking Lizzy's part and poor Josephine being caught between her family and her husband and trying to prevent trouble between them.

Madame's concern for real items rather than stage properties evidently extended to the jewels she wore on her stage. The beauty and the value of these were the basis of long exchanges in the court room, which indicated that Madame was no exception and that, especially for provincial female audiences,

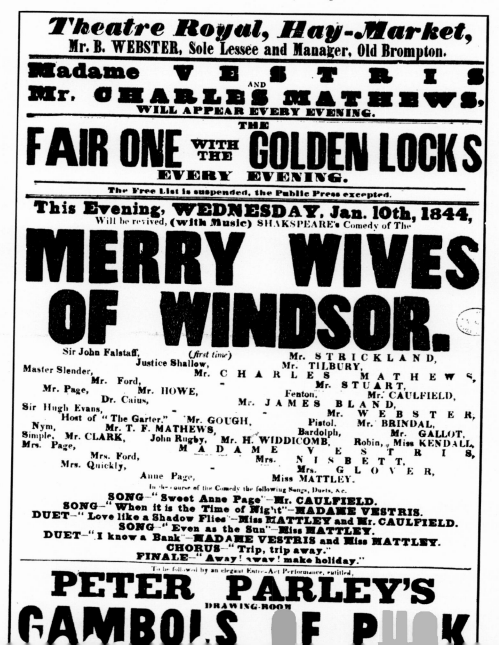

Theatre Royal, Hay-Market,
Mr. B. WEBSTER, Sole Lessee and Manager, Old Brompton.

Madame VESTRIS
AND
Mr. CHARLES MATHEWS,
WILL APPEAR EVERY EVENING.

FAIR ONE WITH THE GOLDEN LOCKS
EVERY EVENING.

The Free List is suspended, the Public Press excepted.

This Evening, WEDNESDAY, Jan. 10th, 1844,
Will be revived, (with Music) SHAKSPEARE's Comedy of The

MERRY WIVES OF WINDSOR.

Sir John Falstaff, *(first time)* Mr. STRICKLAND,
Justice Shallow, Mr. TILBURY,
Master Slender, Mr. CHARLES MATHEWS,
Mr. Ford, Mr. STUART,
Mr. Page, Mr. HOWE, Fenton, Mr. CAULFIELD,
Dr. Caius, Mr. JAMES BLAND,
Sir Hugh Evans, Mr. WEBSTER,
Host of "The Garter," Mr. GOUGH, Pistol, Mr. BRINDAL,
Nym, Mr. T. F. MATHEWS, Bardolph, Mr. GALLOT,
Simple, Mr. CLARK, John Rugby, Mr. H. WIDDICOMB, Robin, Miss KENDALL,
Mrs. Page, MADAME VESTRIS,
Mrs. Ford, Mrs. NISBETT,
Mrs. Quickly, Mrs. GLOVER,
Anne Page, Miss MATTLEY.

In the course of the Comedy the following Songs, Duets, &c.
SONG—"Sweet Anne Page"—Mr. CAULFIELD.
SONG—"When it is the Time of Night"—MADAME VESTRIS.
DUET—"Love like a Shadow Flies"—Miss MATTLEY and Mr. CAULFIELD.
SONG—"Even as the Sun"—Miss MATTLEY.
DUET—"I know a Bank"—MADAME VESTRIS and Miss MATTLEY.
CHORUS—"Trip, trip away."
FINALE—"Away! away! make holiday."

To be followed by an elegant Entre-Act Performance, entitled,

PETER PARLEY'S
DRAWING-ROOM
GAMBOLS OF PUCK

real jewels were part of a leading actress's stock in trade. If she did not own them then she hired them. The expenditure seems to have paid dividends. Earnings in Dublin for four weeks in 1843 were £610, while a season at Liverpool of similar length brought £1,700.

'James: . . . anyone accquainted with the celebrated career of Mrs. Mathews must well know the value of her jewels, which were at one time the admiration of Europe. (Loud laughter.) Chambers might smile but James imagined that Chambers had not often sat in the three front rows of the pit at the Haymarket, or else he could not have been ignorant of the cost of the decorations Mrs. M. possessed. (*Much laughter.*)

'Chambers: Some people go to look at other things besides jewels. There was a day when jewels did glisten, but they unfortunately do not now . . . Her diamonds had been attractive as well as her voice and person on the stage, but while she supported her character with dignity in her profession she had no diamonds, for the late speculation at Covent Garden theatre had sacrificed all that the insolvent had possessed in the world. His learned friend had said that Mrs. M. continued to display attractive jewellery on the stage; but was his learned friend so ignorant as not to know that the jewellery which was displayed at the drawing rooms of Her Majesty was by far the greater part borrowed for the occasion? Anyone knowing the course of high life in this world, must be aware that the jewellery which decorated some of the most distinguished personages in the land was no more their property than the horses and carriages which took them to those assemblagies.'

Mathews later explained that Madame's jewels cost £3 a week to hire. He asked for further hearings to be postponed until after the break in the Haymarket season (1 March) because of damage to Webster in that his season was being upset by the hearings and the unpredictability of Mathews's appearances. This was agreed to, despite some attempt by Anderson to prevent it.

Mathews undertook to give all earnings, in excess of immediate needs, to his creditors. His salary was £60 plus £10 for dress (the latter 'scarcely sufficed'). The Mathews's professional wardrobe, in pawn, was valued between £300 and £400. Asked for his expenses, Mathews said that he would need £10 a week for household, £10 a week for wardrobe, 5s. a week for carriage plus servants and theatre expenses.

James's suggestion that the carriage might be dispensed with (shades of Macready in his 'shabby hansom') was countered by Mathews who said that cabs were more expensive, adding that there was much travelling to be done: to the theatre by eleven a.m. until two, any shopping and home to dinner by three, to the theatre again by four-thirty for the performance. 'Fatigue required a conveyance home at night.' These points were agreed and the final settlement entailed about £1,300 a year to be repaid.

On 22 February 1844 Vestris had a personal success in *Grist to the Mill* at the Haymarket. Declaring her to be 'the support of the piece' *The Times* gives a glimpse of the effect of her personality: 'At her first entrance into the dilapidated old château, when the drama was moving somewhat slowly, her appearance was like a gleam of sunshine thrown on a dusky ruin.'

After a short break, and the last hearing of the bankruptcy, the Haymarket re-opened on Easter Monday 8 April 1844, with the Mathewses topping the bill: *Grist to the Mill* for her, *Used Up* for him. There is a suggestion, in the report of the last hearing, that Webster had felt obliged to make an adjustment in salary in view of the damage of the last weeks. Mathews said that the return from the Haymarket 'was low compared with usual terms but Mr. Webster had suffered much from their absences and other difficulties that Mathews felt almost bound to accept what was proposed.'

'. . . A part of the theatrical wardrobe of an eminent actor and actress' was up for auction on 23 April. It was no secret that it was the property of Vestris and Mathews. The 'large assortment of very elegant dresses, shawls, etc., which were worn by that eminent actress in some of her most celebrated characters' should have brought them a few hundreds. But, with their customary impracticality when it came to financial transactions 'there was very short notice of the sale, the effect of which was that there were but few of the theatrical corps present.'

The bulk of their wardrobe was still in pawn. These now offered for auction were those things still in their hands. *The Times* account of the sale gives an indication of the incredible amount that must have been spent over the years on dress alone, as well as inviting reflection upon the ultimate value of elegance:

'. . . 65 lots, amongst which were 36 dresses and 15 shawls, besides scarfs, riding habits, gowns etc., an embroidered cashmere cloak, a black velvet ditto, an Indian satin ditto. 12 muslin and cotton dresses sold for £2; a black satin dress and ditto embroidered shawl for £2.2s; an embroidered cashmere cloak and two slips for 19s; a very elegant velvet dress, richly trimmed, for £2; a piece of net muslin and lace, and a blonde skirt, which was stated to be worth about £10; for £1.5s; and various others at an average loss. A superfine court dress coat and a pair of breeches fetched only 18s; the auctioneer said that the coat was worth £5; the first bidding for it was 7s. The property produced about £76 which, it was stated, was not a fifth part of the value. The principal buyers were of the Hebrew persuasion.'

The season ran from 8 April to 7 August. *The School for Scandal* and *The Merry Wives* still attracting and a revival of Mrs Centlivre's *The Busybody* adding prestige rather than popularity to the bills. Vestris was praised in this, though it was felt that the part gave her too little scope, though it was probably just as much a case of Madame, like Charles, not being as happy in older pieces with more textual authority. The Duchesse de Chartres in *Follies of a Night*, by Planché, gave her more of her own kind of scope.

There are hints in this season of the break between the Mathews and the Haymarket that was to come next year, though Vestris's increasing bouts of illness also had something to do with events. *London Assurance* was put on (8 May) and *Secrets Worth Knowing* (25 May). Vestris appeared in neither of these plays so closely associated with her name. The public must have been especially intrigued to find Julia Bennet playing Grace Harkaway. Mathews, generally busier than Vestris, could hardly be replaced as Dazzle and had his usual success in it.

The Mathews's engagement ended on 31 July; thus the last week of the season was without them. On the 30th, the gentlemen of the company presented Webster with 'an elegant epergne', Mathews presumably being among the presenters. The success of the season, due in great part to the Mathewses, had been good enough for Webster to take over the Adelphi as well as the Haymarket in June. Madame Celeste made a success of that venture for him as well as enabling him to separate the two Madames who were, for a time, both in the Haymarket company.

In his Farewell Address on 7 August, Webster made no reference to *Who's Your Friend?*, to *Grist to the Mill* or to any other Olympic-style successes during the season, emphasizing instead other theatrical values nearer his heart: '. . . the highly successful production of Shakespeare's *Shrew* unmutilated and unaided by scenic effects, gratifyingly proved the public mind is still warmly alive to fine writing and a well-wrought play.'

Here is the first professional note of the theme hinted at in *The Times* in its comment (see page 156) on *Love's Labour's Lost*: '. . . encumbered rather than relieved by the scenery and decorations . . .'

The cry of actor versus scenery – Patter versus Clutter? – as old as acting, was to have a long wait to be heard again with any force, and it was through Shakespeare that it would emerge, when the distorted and parasitical growths that were bred from Madame's tasteful tidying up would be done away with for a spell. But Webster's early protest deserves to be remembered.

The Times took up the theme when the new season began, commenting on 1 October 1844:

'Theatricals are certainly looking up, theatres are opened, actors employed on all sides, and a fresh playgoing impulse seems to activate the public; nevertheless it is not probable that the cause of the declining drama, which has of late been so much bewailed, and for which such efforts have fruitlessly been made, will gain anything by this unwonted activity. Translations and dramatic novels, and burlesques, we fear, will still remain the staple commodity furnished. If, however, there be any home for the "legitimate" in any

195

shape, with the exception of Sadler's Wells, which may be considered as a sort of colonial settlement for the drama, it is certainly the Haymarket.'

There is something almost defiant about the new act drop for the Haymarket, painted 'again by Mr Marshall'. The picture of 'Old London' was painted over with 'an Italian scene, water, boat etc., according to the old school'.

Getting the message, Vanbrugh's *The Confederacy* opened on 2 October. *The Times* gave a very long notice to this 'first dramatic move of the season', but kept its loyalty to Vestris as well. As Flippanta, she scored one of her best *acting* as well as personality successes: '. . . delivered an exit speech, in which she compares her mistress's pulse to a pendulum, as well as speech was ever delivered yet. The length of Flippanta's part renders it no small charge to the memory . . .'

The School for Scandal and *The Busybody* joined *The Confederacy* to give some six weeks of very high-toned comedy (Madame's longest sustained spell of classical pieces) before Boucicault's new piece, *Old Heads and Young Hearts* opened on 18 November. The 'legitimate' was driven off the boards and the novelty triumphed for some eighty consecutive performances. It had been a rough road to the opening of the new play. Since their sponsoring of *London Assurance*, the Mathewses had not been too happy about their bumptious protegé. Webster had asked Boucicault to do some editing of *The Confederacy* and received a cry from the young man in August 1844: 'What am I to do about *The Confederacy*. The Mathewses want everything altered – their own and other people's parts. "Oh that mine————would write a play."'

With *The Confederacy* established in sight of the public, there were ructions backstage about the new script. Mathews, still it seems at Westbourn Green, wrote in an undated letter to Webster:

'My dear Webster,

'After the gross impertinence of Mr. Boucicault this morning in your presence you cannot be surprised at my returning the parts of "Lyttleton Coke and Lady Belle". His last words were these: "I want no one's opinion but my own as to the *consistency* of the characters I draw – your business is to utter what *I* create." As I differ *in toto* from this inflated view of the relative position of actor and dramatist I at once decline subscribing to it. I can only regret our not being in the comedy on account of any inconvenience it may cause you. It is of course a relief to escape from parts which, though they might be rendered consistent by dint of alteration, could never be rendered palatable to us.

'I am, my dear Webster, etc.'

But Webster was not Macready and knew how to handle, and even to reconcile, indignant actors and impertinent authors. By dint of alteration the parts were rendered palatable enough to reach an opening night with playbills carrying the names of the creator and his mediums despite their categorical negatives. Once on the boards, the Mathewses did the play proud: Vestris as Lady Alice, '. . . a dashing fine lady, a patroness . . . and a rage among the loungers at the opera, played with great spirit and acted really up to the mark . . .' which sounds like a good example of a vivid and lively memory being called into service.

On 4 December, there was 'much sprightly action' for Vestris in a new afterpiece to *Old Heads* called *Somebody Else*. Her song was encored (like old times) and both of them were called for at the curtain. Three days after this began another bout of illness for Vestris and Miss Woolgar replaced her in *Old Heads*.

It was to be like old times again on Easter Monday 1845. Planché had a success at Covent Garden with his version of *Antigone*. A Greek stage had been set up for this play — surely the same one still in stock from *The Dream?* — and everything was in the 'authentic' Planché manner, that is authentic except for the extended parody and loaded nineteenth-century humorous style.

The success of *Antigone* brought the suggestion that Webster might put on a similar thing as his Easter piece, and *The Golden Fleece* was the result. Euripides's *Medea* preceded by Planché's reconstruction of *Jason in Colchis*, gave Vestris an unusual rôle as Medea. With 'dishevelled hair' and 'immense spirit' she 'looked and acted admirably' (*The Times*). The austerity of the Greek theatre setting was relieved by its 'falling away' at the end of each part: first to discover the Argo under sail and finally for the departure of Medea's dragon chariot.

The most interesting thing about *The Golden Fleece* is the part that Mathews played. A century before Anouilh, Planché reduced — or rather transformed — the Chorus to one leading actor who establishes a personal relationship with the audience, guiding their response to the action while involving himself in it when necessary. This change not only overcomes the alienation and often boring and embarrassing problems of a chorus in an age that is no longer atuned to them: it has dramatic validity in that, since the Renaissance, audiences recognize and respond to individual rather than corporate expression.

'No one on the stage could have played this eccentric part like Mr. Mathews', commented *The Times*. He used 'pomp', 'dignity' and 'comic patter' all to excellent effect. George Henry Lewes used this performance as an excellent example of Mathews's skill as a performer:

'Probably few who saw Charles Mathews play the Chorus consider there was any art required so to play it; they can understand that to sing patter songs as he sings them may not be easy, but to be quiet and graceful and humorous, to make every line tell, and yet never show the stress of effort, will not seem wonderful. If they could see another actor in the part it would open their eyes.'

A month later there was another success: Douglas Jerrold's *Time Works Wonders*, with Vestris as Betsy Tulip from Trincomalee, full of pertness and

Still handsome, but the cares of management, bankruptcy, and a sick leading lady have taken their toll despite the prosperous appearance.

WESTBOURNE GREEN

At this time they had left the Haymarket and were giving their season at the Royal Surrey. Here, away from the fashionable districts that had once been Madame's haunts and habitats, Eliza and Charles lived through the trouble of bankruptcy, and the return to employment after years of management.

SURREY THEATRE, 1838

When the Mathewses appeared here, about seven years later, the monopoly had ended and it called itself The Royal Surrey Theatre. Mrs Davidge was manageress — another of Madame's precedents followed.

pleasantries. Although suffering from Jerrold's old problem of lack of construction, the characterization and writing in this play makes it among the best and most forward looking of his works. It has all the spontaneous charm of *Black-ey'd Susan* but there is greater theatrical sense and variety in the dialogue. The play was honoured by a royal visit on 26 May.

Exactly how and when the Mathewses left the Haymarket is a tantalizing mystery. The *Theatrical Journal* for 26 July mentions their secession and is inclined to rebuke them for it. They could not have had more success — especially Mathews, and Webster had been sympathetic throughout their troubles (although it must be remembered that it was in the interests of his box office to retain such favourites). The clue is surely in Madame's frustrated managerial hopes. Some thirteen years of being the boss — and a good boss — must have made any other working arrangement galling for her, and Charles took his cue from her. Old colleagues, tolerant Webster and the comforts of the Haymarket could not provide a lasting substitute for what was lost. The basically different principles in their approaches to presentation can never have made things particularly easy between Webster and Vestris when it came to the actual business of preparing something for the stage.

Whatever the cause, they went, and their going was an unkind blow to Webster as well as to themselves. It should be mentioned to his credit that there

199

was a social reconciliation in later years and he always had a respect for Mathews, who was to work for him again after Madame's death.

From 11 August to 13 September the Mathewses did a season of 'favourite pieces' at the Royal Surrey Theatre, which happily added to its advertising: 'NIGHTLY OVERFLOWS'. Then they went on tour with old and new

Note that this theatre is under female management

DAVIDGE'S ROYAL SURREY THEATRE

Under the Management of Mrs. FRANCES DAVIDGE, Lessee, No. 1, Davidge Terrace, Kennington Road, Surrey.
Licensed by the Lord High Chamberlain, under the Act 6 and 7 Vic. cap. 68.

Mrs. DAVIDGE has the greatest gratification in announcing that she has effected an Engagement (for 12 Nights only) with those Inimitable Artistes,

Madame VESTRIS
AND
Mr. CHAS. MATHEWS

During which they will appear in their most POPULAR and ATTRACTIVE CHARACTERS.

☞ **Notwithstanding the extent of the Expense attendant on this Extraordinary Novelty, the Prices will remain as heretofore.**

MONDAY, Aug. 11th, and during the Week,

The Performances will commence with a New Comic Drama, in Two Acts, written by
MR. CHARLES MATHEWS, entitled

USED UP!

Sir Charles Coldstream, Bart. Mr CHARLES MATHEWS
(His original character—played by him at the Hay-Market 77 Nights)
Sir Adonis Leech, Mr NEVILLE.
The Honorable Tom Saville, Mr FREDERICKS.
Wurzel, (a Farmer) Mr HESLOP, John Ironbrace, (a Blacksmith) Mr R. HONNER,
Mr Fennel, (a Lawyer) Mr LEWIS, James, Mr MORRISON,
Mary, — — — — Mrs R. HONNER,
Lady Clutterbuck, Miss MARTIN.

After which, on Monday, Tuesday and Wednesday, the popular Vaudeville of The

LOAN OF A LOVER!

Gertrude, (Her original Character) Madame VESTRIS,
Ernestine Rosendal, Mrs H. HUGHES,
Captain Amersfort, Mr FREDERICKS.
Peter Spyk, — Mr CHARLES MATHEWS,
Swyzel, Mr HESLOP. Delve, Mr LEWIS.

On Thursday, Friday, & Saturday, after "Used Up," the admired Vaudeville of The

SWISS COTTAGE.

Natz Fleck, — Mr CHARLES MATHEWS,
Corporal Max, Mr S. COWELL, First Soldier, Mr HAWKINS,
Lisette, — (Her original character) — Madame VESTRIS,
Louise, Mrs LEWIS. Janette, Mrs LAWLER.

On Monday, Tuesday, & Wednesday, after "The Loan of a Lover," the Farce of

PATTER versus CLATTER.

Captain Patter, Mr CHARLES MATHEWS,
(His original character)
Mr Pepper Parker, Mr HESLOP, Minheer Pierre Pytter, Mr HAWKINS,
Mr Percy Peuter, Mr PHELPS, Peter Perker, Mr LEWIS,

pieces, playing to an enthusiastic reception for three nights at Bristol and taking in other established dates in larger places. Vestris found it increasingly tiring to travel and for a few years past they had concentrated on the main touring dates and given up the smaller ones.

They were 'welcomed with enthusiasm' and Vestris 'received a bouquet amid loud acclamations' when they made their first appearance 'after a considerable absence' at the Princess's Theatre in Oxford Street, where they began a five-month season on 7 March 1846.

A new piece, *A Speaking Likeness* was in the popular Vestris manner, calling for a dual role and pretty frocks. 'Very pretty acting by Madame Vestris' declared *The Times* 'who contrasts the simple airs of Manette with the polished graces of the Marchioness'.

But these five months were really a proving ground for the establishment of Mathews as a solo artist in his strongly individual line. Regularly scattered among the expected *Busybody*, *Merry Wives* (an odd collection of folk they must have played with in that piece), *Belle's Stratagem*, *The Critic*, *One Hour*, etc., are

PRINCESS'S THEATRE, OXFORD STREET

How the Theatre looked some five years after the Mathewses played their seasonal to 'brilliant, fashionable, and overflowing houses'.

new pieces for, and often by, Mathews, and it is these pieces that get reviewed in the press.

None of these new pieces were any more than what were generally termed afterpieces, and it had not been the custom to review such items. There is no exceptional merit in Mathews's playlets: the attraction was Mathews himself with his fresh approach and lightness of heart, in the prime of life and having done his reputation a world of good by his conduct during the much publicized bankruptcy hearing.

The long struggle to end the monopoly had brought its looked-for reward. Most of the plays listed above could not have been done at the Princess's before 1843. The field was now open and some standards of writing could be expected to develop. Reviewers, too, might have been expected to give prominence to new productions of older pieces. The facts were otherwise. With few exceptions press and public followed personalities rather than plays, and would continue to do so.

The audiences that filled the Princess's for the Mathews's season must have been a wide cross-section of the public, ranging from Madame's old admirers through devotees of Olympic elegance and 'natural' dialogue to the mostly younger supporters of Mathews as an artist on his own.

How far their old scenic standards could be kept up at the Princess's is difficult to assess. For the most part, the pieces made no exceptional demands, though there was a *Sleeping Beauty* in July. Perhaps the original material, or some of it that would fit, was borrowed for the one occasion?

The season set them up, both professionally and financially, for a bit, but almost nightly performances, sometimes in two or three pieces, had taken toll of Eliza's health. After a rest they went on tour again, a tour that was to be a round of farewells for Vestris.

Her Farewell Address, at the end of January 1847, at Liverpool, a place where she had found 'favour nowhere greater than in this flourishing, opulent and liberal town', set the pattern for the following farewells. Although she was not as ancient as some people had supposed 'health rather than inclination' had led her to 'close her country accounts'. How long she would continue to appear in London she could not tell. 'Recommending to your cordial support my junior partner' she bid them 'respectfully and forever' farewell.

14

Le Finale Bien Fait

A graceful and comfortable retirement from the London stage would have been the right step for Vestris at this time, having made her mark and her contribution both as a performer and as a manageress.

Charles knew this as well as Eliza and probably they hoped that one more gamble with management might make such a thing possible. But it had to be undertaken together. There was no doubt of Charles's established personal success on the stage. But the name of Vestris was still the name to conjure with in management.

All the business arrangements, correspondence, contracts and so on were arranged and settled by and through Charles for the Lyceum, but the venture was launched 'under the management of Madame Vestris'.

Mathews's letters in the Enthoven Collection and the Garrick Club show that from the beginning of 1847, if not sooner, they had begun to sound out possible homes for their new venture. A Leicester Square scheme came to nothing, and by April the Lyceum had been fixed upon.

Although she had been ill in the spring, Madame set to work on the 'domestic' side with her old zeal, probably feeling that a new lease of life had been given her and determined to defy the onset of her fifty-first year.

Planché, just ending a contract with the Haymarket, was back as literary adviser. An Olympic-style company was assembled. Although there was now an unrestricted choice of plays, they were not inclined, with Mathews as the mainstay, to risk any more Shakespeare, and only for two performances in the second season did Sheridan get a showing (*School for Scandal*). Apart from this the only thing that could claim classical connections was *The Beggar's Opera*, given during the first three seasons.

204

The production and technical staff were largely the old crew: Oscar Byrne for the ballet, Bradwell for the decorations and many of her 'practical gentlemen' and sewing ladies from Covent Garden.

Buckstone, a comedian who was to be in the company, wrote to Mathews in April about the poor condition of the theatre, especially the poor lighting and the generally dull and dingy air of the place. Needless to say, Madame was to change all that, as well as to introduce some other innovations. The 'half-price' system, which had admitted to the afterpiece only for half price, had often been the way that the less welcome members of the public had got into the theatres. It was late in the evening and such patrons would often be in merry or belligerent mood. Madame abolished half prices.

'Performances commence at seven, and are arranged to terminate as near eleven o'clock as possible', said the bills, so the audiences and performers knew where they were.

A bolder move was the abolition of 'fees', those extras charged by box-keepers (in Paris such charges are still looked for). We have seen that Madame had problems with this kind of thing earlier. There were to be different problems, in the shape of many grumblings by the box-keepers and their minions, but Madame insisted, urging in advertisements that any incivility should be reported to her.

There were those who were professionally interested in the alterations being made to the Lyceum. The *Builder* published two articles on the work, during October 1847. There was also wide-spread curiosity concerning how Madame would delight the public this time. The transformation of the Lyceum was the most ambitious project of its kind that Madame had attempted. The impact of the new house was the more effective in that during four years, when she had no theatre to manage, her old achievements had become something of a legend. With the bankruptcy troubles and the professional to-ing and fro-ing of Eliza and Charles, it was generally assumed that any further managerial prospects were out of the question. By every logical consideration that should have been so, but their ventures, like their wardrobes, had never been daunted by possible costs and long-term disaster.

The considerable public support and sympathy that they continued to enjoy seemed insurance enough and it is remarkable that, despite three bankruptcies between them, they were able to spend so much of their professional lives as their own bosses. Remarkable, too, that the final fling at the Lyceum was to survive eight seasons. Seasons which ended with yet another financial collapse and a proper dose of prison for Charles, but which really ended because of Vestris's illness and retirement. Popular as Charles was (and was to continue to be through a long career) there was about Eliza a special mystique for the public: for older folk she evoked their youth in what seemed (as it always seems) merrier and more hopeful days; for the young she had the fascination of legend as well as the comfort that the usual symptoms of advancing years could apparently be defied and postponed.

Madame played to encourage just these reactions for as long as she was able, and as long as she was there the public continued to support the Lyceum.

The unanimous praise of the newly decorated house has about it a feeling of real pleasure and something of a relief that such things could still be done. The delicacy and the deployment of an impractical colour scheme for a public building lit by gas — pink, pale blue, white and crimson — was made even more impractical in that the paintwork was a largely unseen background for the lavish use of materials — of crimson damask and white lawn, three-dimensional white doves gathering up fabrics in their beaks, and fretted relief work applied liberally.

The descriptions of Madame's Lyceum remind a later reader of the kind of dreams that Ludwig II of Bavaria was to realize in his castles. And the Lyceum was Madame's last castle. The elegance of her own homes having been sold up and lost with no hope of recovery, she transferred her domestic tastes to her professional lodging.

A curtain, rather than a drop cloth, is surely something that Madame would have preferred. It was probably impossible, considering everything else that had to be paid for, to consider risking a further large amount of money on a fabric curtain. It had been expensive at the little Olympic. The Lyceum stage was closer to Covent Garden than to the Olympic. The *Builder* gives a proscenium opening of thirty-four feet across. The height must have been twenty-five feet or more. In other words an opening needing many lengths of cloth which would have to be of a good enough quality to stand comparison with the other stuffs in the auditorium. A finely painted drop cloth was the alternative, and was in the tradition of the best of the European theatres. It is my belief that it was only the suspension of any more credit from suppliers that prevented a larger version of the Olympic curtain being installed at the Lyceum.

The *Theatrical Journal* for Saturday 23 October 1847 provides a good, if by no means the fullest, example of the reaction to the house:

OPENING OF THE ROYAL LYCEUM

'The opening of this house has been looked for by all the play-going public with the greatest anxiety, they being well aware that the fair lessee, Madame Vestris, from her former management, would do things in no ordinary way; and on the opening of the doors, on Monday last, they soon discovered their anticipations were more than realised. The whole of the interior has undergone such a re-modelling that it is quite impossible to give even a faint idea of the exquisite beauty of the various designs which the artiste, Mr. Bradwell, has introduced; they must be seen to be appreciated. However, we will attempt an explanation. On entering the lobby previous to getting into the theatre, the various gas lights which are scattered about the staircase and passages are numerous; and independent of the chandeliers, are pedestals bearing lights of various forms, which have a novel and pleasing appearance, and prepare the eye of the visitor for the splendours of the interior, the prevailing colours of which are white, pale pink, and blue, but they are so blended together as to produce the greatest harmony. The old chandelier has been removed from the ceiling, which is now occupied by Venus and her attendants. The huge balcony has been removed from the dress-circle, and the fronts of the boxes are hung with crimson silk, each festoon being supported by a dove, who holds it in its beak. The fronts of the panels of the boxes have various devices, and have the appearance of embossed paper, with numerous emblematical figures. The chandeliers round the boxes are gilt, and are supported by Cupids of white and gold. The proscenium is chaste, elegant and classical, and Her Majesty's Arms are beautifully executed. Altogether the house has the appearance of enchantment. We have never seen anything that will bear a comparison to it, even in the royal apartments.'

The house was presented with the same care and theatricality as the stage. When the audience was settled in, and before the performance began, the lights, subdued until then, were gradually turned up and the full glory of the house revealed, prompting rounds of applause; although there were some who wondered how long and how well all that white would last and how many staff would be needed to keep the whole place looking so fresh and spruce. Some must have been surprised by the retention of the pit benches throughout the forty-eight foot area from the stage to the back wall of the auditorium. The Haymarket announced, in the winter of 1843: 'By a curtailment of the useless portion of the stage in front of the curtain, and advancing the orchestra and lights near the actors and scenic effects, the Lessee has been enabled to appropriate the portion so obtained, to form a certain number of Orchestra Stalls, which can be retained for the parties taking them for the whole of the evening.'

The experiment had proved agreeable to the public and profitable for the management. The inclusion of orchestra stalls in the new Lyceum scheme was to be expected, and it seems likely that Vestris would have approved of such a change. But the pit benches were retained, and even the few stalls that had been there were removed and replaced by pit benches. It was not a case of Madame doing a Cicero and refusing to follow what others had done, but a case of Mathews beginning his new authority. He had never approved of this particular change in the auditorium (an attitude that lasted all his life) for he felt that there should be ample provision for inexpensive seats in a theatre and a place where the young sparks could gather as if they were at a club. Madame's reaction to this is not recorded. She might have been ill when these decisions were made, or she might have agreed to the kind of arrangement for the audience that the leading attraction considered right. The main point is that it went through as his decision at the beginning of what was in fact to be his management rather than Eliza's.

At first her hand was both strong enough and sure enough to control events and she and Planché made as congenial a partnership as ever. He wrote an opening piece for her, *The Pride of the Market*. The applause on her entrance was such that it overwhelmed her, and Buckstone had to support her and encourage her before they could go on with their scene together. As her health deteriorated and her absences from the theatre became more frequent, more responsibility fell upon Charles. He was an easy prey for Bradwell's machinery and, later, Beverley's painting, and the management that had been responsible for reforming what was seen on the stage, and relating it to the action, was eventually swallowed up by scenery that virtually took over the action.

Planché, seeing what had become of his theories after the 'fair lessee' (though now the lessee was Mathews and she the manager) had become a largely absentee landlady, abandoned the struggle, deploring the scenic 'epidemic' which spread in all directions, 'it was no longer even painting; it was upholstery'. There was plenty of skill available but Madame could no longer leaven everything with her redeeming taste – a rare attribute that calls for energy and determination as well as flair. This state of affairs is the answer to some assertions that it was Planché who was really responsible for the theatrical changes that were introduced in Madame's managements. His contribution was enormous and valuable, but without her his ideas would have remained unproven and untheatrical. He wrote many charming things for the theatre but he did not really speak the language of the theatre: like George Henry Lewes he was a stage-struck literary gentleman rather than a man of the theatre.

As in their other theatres, the Mathewses put on a prodigious number of plays and playlets during the eight seasons at the Lyceum. Many of these were old favourites, for example *The Water Party, Ringdoves, Patter vs. Clatter, Follies of a Night, The Critic* (Mathews's version), *The Court Beauties* and *Used Up*. Others were new but on the old lines, giving Mathews especially plenty of good parts well suited to him, for instance *Box and Cox, A Day of Reckoning*, and *Cool as a Cucumber*. Some even older pieces make their return: *Sweethearts and Wives* and *Guy Mannering* for example.

One *Olympic Revels* came back and several *Olympic Devils* (though Madame surrendered Pandora to a younger actress, Julia St George). But the great successes were the extravaganzas and pantomimes and fairy pieces. *The Golden Branch* ran nightly through from Boxing Day to 7 April: seventy-three performances. Its ballets and set pieces 'a la Watteau' recalled the visual delights of *Who's Your Friend?* Madame sang 'Cherry Ripe' among other things, to great applause. The run was really too long for her, which must have been why the season was suspended until Easter.

Perhaps rashly she rehearsed and appeared as Theseus in Planché's Easter piece *Theseus and Ariadne*, still able to show a neater leg than any other performer, but then the playbill announced her absence 'in consequence of a domestic affliction'. This was the death on 1 May of her sister Josephine, Mrs Anderson, and so another phase in the anything but tranquil Bartolozzi family saga ended. Lizzy made the care of her two nieces her concern, thus assuming more responsibility than she had been relieved of by her mother's death. Madame was 'off' for nine days arranging and settling the sadly tiresome rigmarole that follows death.

She recovered sufficiently to bring her old vivacity to Lucy in *The Beggar's Opera*, and the first season could claim to have been a good new beginning by the time it closed on 31 July. They had been aiming 'to please' not 'to astonish', declared Mathews in the Farewell Address.

It was not until some seven weeks after the opening of the new season that Madame appeared again, on 20 November, in *The Merry Wives*. There was certainly nothing to astonish here but the audience was the distinguished and crowded one that always welcomed Vestris. The press gave up trying to find new adjectives for the production, the *Morning Post* saying that any reference to the 'perfect ensembles' and 'exquisite manner' of the production would 'be now superogatory'.

Perhaps encouraged by the fact that Madame had brought the comforts and the proprieties of the drawing-room into the theatre, Queen Victoria resolved to bring the pleasures and the properties of the theatre into her drawing-room.

'The Windsor Theatricals' under the initial supervision of Charles Kean were a mixed blessing to the professional performers. The prestige of being summoned to Windsor and the compliment of being received by the monarch, was offset by the loss of prestige that theatre-going itself suffered when the Royal Box was no longer in demand. The financial losses (for example the closing of their theatres while companies were at Windsor) were far from compensated for by the honorarium paid out from the castle.

Mathews's impression on Victoria had been a lasting one. After respectably recognizing the Drama with a Hamlet (Charles Kean), she enjoyed Mathews in *Used Up* and *Box and Cox* on 4 January 1849, the first of several visits that he was to make via the special train to Windsor.

Madame in her turn followed Victoria in that her presence became ever rarer at the theatre. During the fourth season, in 1851, it was necessary for Mathews to write to the press to refute the rumours that she would never appear again. She did appear again, but the presence of her name on the bills could never be taken as an assurance that she would be seen. Days away grew into weeks away, and weeks became months as the Lyceum seasons went on.

For some things she made a special effort. On 4 December 1850 *The Day of Reckoning* opened. It was a 'heavier' piece than usual for the Lyceum at this time, closer to the mood of and themes of Adelphi melodrama than to Olympic burlettas. It gave them a challenge that realized a mature fruition of what they had begun together in *One Hour*.

A general press comment on *The Day of Reckoning* was that Madame had little to do – an objection that had been raised for some time by her admirers. It is true that that evening really belongs to the male lead, a dignified sadness being demanded of the heroine. But, as with the Chorus in *The Golden Fleece*, someone else in the part would have revealed the extent of Vestris's achievement. George Henry Lewes noted:

> '. . . They were a lady and gentleman such as we meet in drawing-rooms, graceful, quiet, well-bred, perfectly dressed, perfectly oblivious of the footlights . . . If you wish to see really perfect acting, rush to the Lyceum and be astonished at *The Day of Reckoning* . . . Oh, what a contrast between the natural manner of these two and the stage manner and stage life of all the rest.'

The last comment is a telling revelation of what was happening, or rather not happening, to the company without the watchful eye of Madame.

More significantly, Lewes saw in this play the transformation of the 'clever mimic' and 'lively caricaturist' into a 'fine comedian' and 'portrait painter'. From Mathews's early promise as the 'airy and fascinating' *jeune premier* who in *One Hour* 'seated opposite Madame Vestris, and made to subdue his restless impatience while he held her skeins of silk – a *very* drawing-room version of Hercules at the feet of Omphale' to *The Day of Reckoning*: 'Imagine a Count D'Orsay destitute alike of principle and of feeling, the incarnation of heartless elegance, cool yet agreeable, admirable in all the externals which make men admired in society, and hateful in all the qualities tested by the serious trials of life: such was the Count presented by Charles Mathews . . . Whether the pit really understood this presentation, and felt it as a rare specimen of art, I cannot say . . .'

Madame's protegé had arrived – as at home in French or English companies. If the seasons had made sufficient money, Eliza could have stayed at home or watched from the auditorium (though it is doubtful if that would have consoled her much).

During her intermittent appearances she saw changes of faces and of policy reflected on the playbills, which still claimed her as manageress. Planché, although providing material for all the seasons at the Lyceum, gradually wrote less for them and his personal attendances at the theatre became rare. Mathews was largely doing his own editing and quite a bit of writing. As adviser he had George Henry Lewes whose knowledge of the French theatre was more up-to-date in sympathy, if not as wide in experience as Planché's.

The importation – more often smuggling – of French plays had become a flourishing theatrical side industry taking advantage of the fashion for 'items from the French'. 'Spies' were paid by English managements to copy down the plays as they were acted – or even to steal prompt books – get them across the channel and deliver them for translation, usually more of a transmogrification.

(The pattern of this literary piracy was echoed almost identically in this century by the 'sketchers' who smuggled information from the Paris fashion houses to London and New York.) The copyright treaty eventually signed between Britain and France in January 1852 ended the piracy, but not the importation. It just increased managerial costs.

The adapter for Mathews was Lewes (billed as 'Slingsby Lawrence') who had his own little nook at the Lyceum in which to do his work. It should be urged that the French style of comedy was admirably suited to Mathews's personality and technique, and his problem was the apparent impossibility of finding a native playwright who could both match his style and be prolific enough to meet the never-ending demand for new material. There was unfortunately no one who could do for Lyceum comedy what Planché had done for Olympic burletta.

Planché, still writing and still prolific, could still be relied upon to provide material for a 'spectacular', but it was his imagination rather than his writing that the management banked upon. The humour now had a dated air, a heavy-handedness and a 'literary' turn that was too staid for nimble Mathews and the younger bloods in the audience. Planché's wit also assumed a modicum of education in the audience, a supposition that was more justified in the pits of the then patent theatres or the boxes at the Olympic than in the less predictable auditorium of the Lyceum. Easier means of transport, and advertising, in an ever-expanding London, made the business of entertainment more competitive and less exclusive than it had been, particularly light entertainment. Much less obviously but no less certainly than in France, the lower classes in Britain were finding their individuality and their voices. Individuality was emphasized in the personal appearance and an easy arrogance. Dexterity of speech rather than extent of perception was looked for and aimed at; emotional reactions rather than logical inferences determined responses to moods and situations. Mathews with his dapper appearance and easy air of comradeship with the lads in his pit benches, was the actor for the age. He excelled in characters who lightly concealed a good heart with a roguish, quick-witted playfulness and a studied carelessness in their well-cut clothes:

'In our juvenile apprehensions he was the beau-ideal of elegance. We studied his costumes with ardent devotion. We envied him his tailor, and "made him our pattern to live and die". We could see no faults in him; and all the criticisms which our elders passed on him grated harshly in our ears as the croaking of "fogies".' (Lewes)

Only French playwrights were providing just the material for his line of business.

Although she had been instrumental in bringing about the kind of theatre that suited Mathews and the French style, Madame was no longer the actress

DRAMATIS PERSONÆ.

(From Original Play-bill.)

THE FIRST PART.

Entirely original, founded on the third and fourth books of "The Argonautics," a poem by the late Apollonius Rhodius, Esq., Principal Librarian to His Egyptian Majesty Ptolemy Evergetes, Professor of Greek Poetry in the Royal College of Alexandria, &c., &c., and entitled

JASON IN COLCHIS.

ÆETES, KING OF COLCHIS (Possessor of the original Golden Fleece)	MR. JAMES BLAND
JASON (Commander of "The Argo," and son of Æson, the deposed King of Iolchos) ...	MISS P. HORTON
ANONYMOUS (Captain of the Royal Guards) ...	MR. CAULFIELD
MEDEA (Daughter of Æetes, an *enchanting* creature)	MADAME VESTRIS

ARGONAUTS (*i.e.*, crew of "The Argo")—By a *number* of Young Persons under *Fifty*.

Colchian Nobles, Sages, Guards, &c.

THE SECOND PART.

Very freely translated from the popular Tragedy of Euripides, and particularly adapted to the Haymarket stage, under the title of

MEDEA IN CORINTH.

CREON (King of Corinth)	MR. JAMES B

(Who, by particular desire, and on this occasion only, has obligingly consented to be twice the King he usually is at this season.)

JASON (Married but not settled, exceedingly classical, but very far from correct)	MISS P. HOR
MEDEA (Jason's lawfully wedded Wife, and mother of two fine boys, both likely to do well, which is more than can be said of their parents)	MADAME VE
MERMEROS ⎫ (the two fine boys aforesaid) ⎰	MASTER ELD
PHERES ⎭ ⎱	MASTER YOU
PSUCHE (a good old soul—Nurse to the two fine boys aforesaid)	MISS CARRE

Corinthians, Guards, &c.

N.B.—The Public is respectfully informed that, in order to p this Grand Classical Work in a style which may defy competi any other establishment, the Lessee has, regardless of expense, e

MR. CHARLES MATHEWS

to represent the whole body of the Chorus, rendering at least fif male voices entirely unnecessary.

The stage, which has been constructed after the approved of the revived Greek Theatre, will be partially raised, but the p admission remain exactly as before. It is also requisite to obser frequent change of scene being contrary to the usage of the Greek Drama, several of the most

SPLENDID PICTORIAL EFFECTS

Will be left entirely to the imagination of the audienc

for the age. Ease of manner, the warm heart under the playful exterior, the science of dress, all these were a part of her own stock in trade and theories of performance. But older, though still largely French, guidelines had taken her through her career. Guidelines that belonged to the 'ancien régime' rather than to newer and more revolutionary times. Orderliness, the importance of trivia, the ritual of dress, the 'sang froid' of the public images, the privacy of the boudoir (where the same guidelines prevailed), the skilful wearing of a mask without ever denying that it was a mask: these were the things that influenced Madame's use of her intelligence.

She would not have accepted Hamlet's rejection of 'seems' or the insistence of Burns that 'a man's a man for a' that'. She would have endorsed Burke's maxim that 'vice itself lost half its evil by losing all its grossness' and Lady Blessington's cool 'There are so few before whom one would condescend to appear otherwise than happy'.

The long public 'confessions' published by Mathews at the time of his financial difficulties cannot have pleased her – any more than the retention of the pit benches. She had herself made public statements, as has been noted, but their tone was very different, 'more like a speech from the throne' as a wag had once commented! Mathews probably wrote the last few public addresses for her but, when those addresses became more in the nature of official explanations of difficulties, she left their delivery to him. This was only partly dictated by the social consideration that it seemed more fitting for the husband to speak, for until the later years of the Lyceum, press and public spoke of the Lyceum as 'Vestris's theatre'.

She certainly 'commanded' a public following over a long career, and was certainly popular as well as the darling of the 'nobility'. Her 'aristocratic' attitudes gave her a certain aloofness which her professional personality transformed into a fascination. Sir Walter Scott in 1840 added the word 'glamour' to the popular vocabulary. Like Madame's stage practices, the word has been much abused and debased since that time but in its original sense it applied to her, for she had 'a delusive or alluring charm' (O.E.D.).

Charles Mathews's popularity was a different thing. Anything but aloof, he cleverly persuaded his audiences that here was no mystery, here was 'one of the boys' who might have wandered in from the club or lightly sprung up upon the stage from the pit. There was no question of 'commanding' popularity:

'Indeed, the personal regard which the public feels for him is something extraordinary when we consider that it is not within the scope of his powers to move us by kindling any of our deeper sympathies . . . the feeling was not inaptly expressed by an elderly gentleman in the boxes of the Lyceum on the fall of the curtain one night . . . "And to think of such a man being in difficulties! There ought to be a public subscription got up to pay his debts."' (Lewes)

These comments are not to deny the Mathews's skill in playing together. In the scripts carefully made for them, the two were able to blend their approaches, largely because their effects were in many ways similar, particularly an assured 'naturalness'. But it should be remembered that they *were* special scripts, either new or adapted, and that it was extremely difficult for any dramatist to get them to see his rather than their views of a play.

The troubles with Boucicault that have been mentioned cannot have been the only instances of this kind of problem, and something similar might well have been at least partly to blame for the break with Webster.

During the Lyceum seasons Eliza continued to perform when she could with Charles in those pieces that her aging appearance could still carry beside his youthful looks. The new pieces in which they appeared together took account of this change, in mood as well as content — as in *The Day of Reckoning*.

For the rest she appeared in Planché pieces, extravaganzas and fairy-tale plays that were familiar ground, such as *The King of the Peacocks* and *King Charming*. All in all she played in about a fifth of the hundred or so productions (old and new) that were put on during the seven seasons that she was able to appear at the Lyceum, not acting at all in the last, the eighth season. For the longer running pieces in which she was involved she only played for part of the run. Her indisposition, usually attributed to 'hoarseness', indicates a chronic development of earlier trouble, and it was possibly cancer of the throat.

*   *   *

The visual side of things at the Lyceum was mainly in the hands of William Roxby Beverley, a painter from an acting family whose background left him with no respect for actors and even less for authors. As a stage decorator and the kind of artist who treats the theatre as a one-man exhibition for his experiments, Beverley cannot claim the over-emphasized interest given to Inigo Jones before him and Edward Gordon Craig after him. He saw the stage as a series of two-dimensional canvases for him to embellish, resenting three-dimensional scenery as being even more intrusive than three-dimensional actors. His happiest moments were when he could dispense with actors altogether, leaving his scenery to make an unadulterated effect upon his audiences: '. . . in Planché's *King of the Peacocks* I effected the "hit" of the play by a pure piece of scenic art, without a soul on the stage' Beverley said in an interview for the *Sunday Times* in 1885. 'To end an act with merely a beautiful fanciful scene, with no dramatis personae visible was daring. But those were the days when imagination in scenic art was valued.'

214

FRENCH PLAYS.
Mme. Vestris' Royal Olympic Theatre.

Positively the Last Night but one of Mademoiselle LEON-TINE FAY, and Monsieur VOLNYS.

The Managers beg leave to announce to the Nobility, Gentry, Subscribers to the French Plays, and the Public in general, that there will be *No Performance this Evening, Monday, the* 27th *July.*—Those parties who have taken Private Boxes and Stalls, for the representation of the celebrated piece *LE TARTUFFE,* may retain them for Wednesday Evening, or on application at the Box-office have their Money returned.

WEDNESDAY, July 29th, 1835, *for the Benefit of*

MONSIEUR VOLNYS,

AND FOR THIS NIGHT ONLY,

Molière's celebrated Comedy, in Five Acts, called

Le Tartuffe; ou, L'imposteur.

Mademoiselle Leontine Fay remplira le Rôle d'*Élmire;* M. Volnys celui de *Tartuffe.*

After which a Variety of Singing and Dancing, by several Eminent Performers.

To conclude with, by DESIRE,

L'AMI GRANDET.

Mlle. Leontine Fay remplira le rôle de *La Duchesse de Langeais.* M. Volnys celui de *L'Ami Grandet,* (his Original Character.)

FRIDAY, Ju'y 31st, 1835, *for the Benefit of*

MONS. PELISSIE.

On which occasion the Principal singers and Dancers of the King's Theatre have kindly offered their services.

Application for Subscription and Tickets to be made to Mr. Last, at the Box Office (open from 10 till 4 o'Clock, and at the Theatre during the Performance.

Doors open at Seven o'Clock—Performances begin at half-past Seven.

DRAMATIS PERSONÆ.

CHARMING THE FIRST (King of the Fan-sea Isles, an immortal personage) ... ... MADAME VESTRIS

H...CKT THE HUNDREDTH (King of ...ayne) ... ... MR. FRANK MATTHEWS

... Queen and Second Wife) ... MRS. FRANK MATTHEWS

...LORINA (Daughter of King ...y his First Wife) ... MISS JULIA ST. GEORGE

...NA (Daughter of Queen ...irst Husband) ... ... MISS MARTINDALE

...m King Charming) .. MR. HARCOURT

... Page) ... ... MISS HUNT

... ... MR. SUTER

.. .. MR. BELLINGHAM

...T ... ... MR. BURT

... ... MR. DE COURCY

...ysician ... MR. H. HORNCASTLE

...orn, Spirit of Ether, his

... MRS. C. HORN

...s ELLIS

...c.

KING CHARMING.

92

PROGRAMME OF SCENERY.

By Mr. W. Beverley, Mr. Meadows, and Assistants.

ACT FIRST.

Hall of Audience in the Castle of King Henpeckt.

GARDEN OF THE CASTLE.

ABODE OF THE FAIRY SOUSSIO.

FLORINA'S CHAMBER.

THE CYPRESS GROVE.

With a Necromantic Excursion to the Fan-sea Islands!

ACT SECOND.

HAUNT OF THE FAIRIES.

GRAND FAIRY QUADRILLE, GALOP, AND EVERY COUNTRY DANCE,

Being an Industrious Exhibition of

THE STEPS OF ALL NATIONS,

By Miss ROSINA WRIGHT,

Assisted by Mesdames Burbidge, Mars, Maile, Maurice, Wadham, Hunt, C. Hunt, Edwards, Ford, Webber, Clarkson, Gale, Martineuz, Dring.

Gates of King Charming's Palace.

WHISPERING GALLERY & HALL OF ECHOES IN THE PALACE.

KING CHARMING'S CABINET.

A SCENE OF DESTRUCTION,

Succeeded by the

Glorious Restoration of King Charming to Throne of Fan-sea.

When performers were used for such production numbers they were usually appendages to the scene, holding up draperies or lights, closing a vista as a living statue or peopling a cloud formation: in other words the functions of actor and scene were reversed.

Beverley condemned 'built-up' scenes. 'I condemn all this straining after realism entirely, because it serves no artistic purpose.' What was such a man doing in a theatre with Vestris's name on the bills? The answer lies in his own comment that it was Mathews's confidence in his projects that enabled them to be done. But as far as Madame was concerned, however beautiful the painting, the method was a return to everything she had worked to change.

The public clapped the pretty pictures. Planché might quietly protest backstage and George Henry Lewes might warn in the press that such baubles could not save a theatre in the long run, but Beverley kept and increased his influence and prestige, his name eventually dominating the playbills in huge letters.

With so many pounds going to support Beverley's whims, the funds left over for creditors (some of them patient since 1838) were constantly dwindling. The Mathewses had cut personal expenditure for some years, living within £1,000 a year between them, and the people at the theatre were paid.

The length of the seasons were extended to make more money, some of them lasting almost a year, with brief breaks of a few weeks, either because of Madame's illness or else to provide the management with excuses to reduce or adjust the company – an old theatrical device, but one that Madame had never used when she was in control.

Another economy that was tried was the retaining of the same playbill for a succession of nights, instead of offering a constant variety of bills and so needing to retain a number of irregularly used performers. This practice, which eventually developed into the 'long run' familiar today, also meant that some of the backstage pressure of work was eased for technicians and actors. A constantly changing bill makes for constant rehearsal and much-moved scenery needs renovation and repair – especially with a visual reputation to keep up.

Economy and novelty were aimed at in introducing one long play for the evening instead of a series of plays of varying length. In the fifth season *A Chain of Events* in eight acts was presented, while the following season *A Strange History* offered nine acts for the evening's bill. The titles are indicative of the kind of stories involved: themes that could offer no less variety for the eyes but which could use the same company of players throughout the evening. *A Chain of Events* played for fifty-nine consecutive performances. It was in fact no novelty for the story had been done at the Adelphi as *The Queen of the Market*, and both versions had been taken from the Parisian success *Les Dames de Les Halles*.

The success of the Lyceum production was mainly due to the ambitious staging which outdid both the Adelphi and the Parisian productions. The playbills promised, and the management provided, eight visual links for their chain:

A Street in Paris
Storm at Sea
Therese's Shop
Bonneau's House
Apartment of the Marquis de Melcy
A Room at Therese's
Market of the Innocents, with the Fountain by Moonlight
Holiday Fête
Illuminated Saloon Looking Into the Court of the Palais Royal

The Fountain was real, and to prove it some poor actor was nightly tumbled into the water, a vulgarity that the *Morning Chronicle* thought unsuitable for 'a house of the class and the pretensions of the Lyceum' (3 April 1852), and that the box patrons possibly felt to be a case of the mice playing now that the cat was so often away.

The novelty, together with the leading actress, Laura Keene, had gone by the time of the play's revival for eight performances in the next season, and *A Strange History* survived only eleven showings. Lyceum audiences didn't want to concentrate so long on any one piece but the notion was eventually to become, like the long run, the accepted thing.

It is hard to say how far Madame had a say in these innovations but it is doubtful if she was much involved. Their personal expenses at this time were for doctors and for morphine.

As if the failure of the expensive *A Strange History* were not enough, the weather contrived the death blow for Mathews's management. Heavy snow kept the audiences away for a couple of weeks that would normally have done well for the pantomime, and the box office couldn't stand it. At five o'clock on Tuesday evening 7 February 1854 Mathews was arrested for debt. A full house at the Lyceum was asked to accept a substitute reading for Mathews owing to his 'indisposition'. The audience would not accept this, got their money back and went home. These were the days before understudies, but it is doubtful whether audiences would have accepted anyone else playing Mathews's part.

The company, understandably, panicked. When, having sent a message that he would be with them, he arrived at the theatre the next evening, Mathews found that another audience had been sent home and only a small band of loyal actors were waiting for the boss. He recalled the company and continued the season but by April was once again compelled to initiate bankruptcy proceedings.

And once again was demonstrated the exceptional goodwill and affection that these two performers engendered in their public. Personal letters of support and sympathetic comments in the press were augmented by practical help, from the offer of a £5 loan to the concern of a group of men who considered taking over the business side of things for Mathews, leaving him to control the artistic side. It must often have struck business people as a puzzling phenomenon: continued popularity and apparent success combined with constant financial troubles. It seemed to be an obvious case of a good asset mismanaged and so a potential money-maker for the right operator. (There were to be similar feelings about the Beecham seasons at Covent Garden which absorbed a fortune.) Appointing someone to look into his affairs, those interested in taking over were satisfied that a series of misfortunes rather than personal extravagance and bad judgement were at the root of the trouble. Arnold, the Lyceum landlord, not only renewed the lease but subsidized it to the tune of £500. A subscription was raised and Mathews took a life insurance to cover it.

For the five weeks that it took to negotiate some kind of settlement, the Lyceum performers, technicians, workmen and women were all at liberty to take offers that came to such skilled people. They could not be certain whether Mathews could employ them again but without exception they waited to see if he could still use them.

Mr Charles Mathews in announcing the re-opening of the Lyceum for Monday 5 June 1854, could 'not resist the opportunity' of publicly thanking everyone in the Establishment for their loyalty and friendship, and he may be forgiven his indulgence in putting a long notice on the playbills to this effect.

Thirty-nine years, within a few days, after her début at the King's, Madame Vestris appeared in her last new play: an adaptation by George Henry Lewes of Scribe's *La Joie Fait Peur*, given the good English title *Sunshine Through the Clouds*. Twelve nights before, Scribe's play had closed at the St James's where it had been successful in its original production brought over from Paris (where it had played for fifty nights).

The play was enthusiastically received and Madame given an ovation. The press echoed the enthusiasm, *The Times* giving a careful comparison between the French and English performances: 'The Lyceum has wisely aimed at an exact imitation of the French manner' which extended to the interpretation of the performers. 'This adoption bespoke care and intelligence, but, nevertheless, it suggested the belief that the imitation of externals was not accompanied by a thorough conception of internal character. On the other hand, the performance of the mother, by Madame Vestris stands far above that of the rest, and is, to a certain extent, an original creation . . .'

So she was still pioneering: having got the set to work with her she could bring greater economy to acting – imply rather than assert – ready for Ibsen to do for acting what she had done for staging: relating all the parts to each other and to the play. The comparison with Ibsen is justified. Other playwrights were to prepare the British public before they could take the Norwegian giant, but it was Ibsen who took the implications of Madame's kind of staging

THE LYCEUM THEATRE – Exterior and Interior

to its fullest extent. One of the 'prophets' for Ibsen's plays was Tom Robertson, who was in some of the later Lyceum seasons, seeing little of Madame but well aware of her influence and approach. It is probable that had he shared the best of her time he would have begun his real work earlier. However, he made the most of his time in the prompter's box at the Lyceum.

Her début had been for the Benefit of Armand, in a German opera with an Italian libretto. Her final performance was also a Benefit, to support Charles, in a French play translated into English.

An exceptional Benefit was arranged for the Mathewses on 26 July 1854. An overcrowded house — at increased prices — saw an unprecedented collection of leading players giving their services. The gesture of rival managers releasing their star attractions for this occasion was the greatest professional tribute that could have been paid to Eliza and Charles, complementing the personal tribute of the loyalty of their employees.

Sunshine Through the Clouds was the play chosen for Vestris to appear in at the Benefit. The success of the play and of the evening was gratifying, though it is probable that she knew, with the same infallible intuition that had foretold the end of the Covent Garden project, that Charles would never lead her forward to meet another series of calls demanding her appearance.

15

Afterpiece

That is really the end of the story. There were to follow two years for most of which Eliza was at her house in Fulham confined either to her bed or her chair.

In March of 1855 Mathews finally gave up the lone struggle to keep the Lyceum going. 'The long and serious illness of Mrs. Mathews, which has unfortunately deprived him of her assistance in the Management, as well as of her Talent on the stage (both of which he has ever found indispensable to the welfare of the enterprise)' combined with lack of capital to compel a retreat.

There followed a round of performing for Mathews in other London theatres and long tours in the provinces. There was no shortage of work for the popular actor, but all his earnings were entailed and he was given allowances from them. In this way Charles was able to keep Eliza medically attended and reasonably nursed. When on tour, he never failed to write to her every day. He must have missed her. Touring is a strange business: the busy public hours in the evening contrasting sharply with the lonely hours of the days and nights.

Taking a hasty supper after a long rehearsal at Preston on 4 July 1856, Mathews was arrested for debt and taken in the pouring rain to Lancaster Castle prison. But for the timely arrival of the balance of some money from the previous engagement at Rochdale, he would have spent his twenty-six days there as he had spent his first night: on dirty straw in a stone room with twenty-one other prisoners.

There was a daily exchange of letters between Fulham and Lancaster, of which only his survive. The arrest was a further shock to an already dying Eliza, but she resolved to attempt a visit to him. He had to use all his powers of persuasion to prevent the mad attempt. It would 'bring you to your grave' he wrote and could not even bear the thought of her in the midst of turnkeys, prisoners, and convicts. The further relapse that she suffered at the time of this exchange ruled out any question of her not complying.

She rallied by the end of the month and was sitting up when he arrived home on 2 August, to be with her for the last six days of her life.

Like all troupers, she had wanted to die in harness, to fall dead after the fall of the curtain on a successful evening. So she had told her old friend John Laurie. The protracted pain of her epilogue with Charles is no concern of anyone but themselves. The outline has been given only to round off the story and to emphasize the courage of both of them.

She died at midnight on Friday and it was not until the following Monday 11 August that the news was published. The immediate reactions were personal and affectionate. *The Times's* comment is representative of others:

'It is some consolation for her loss that death relieved her from a state of lingering and hopeless suffering, for few will be more sincerely regretted than the gifted daughter [sic] of the engraver Bartolozzi.'

The obituaries in the periodicals and more permanent publications, for instance *Bentley's Miscellany*, the *Gentleman's Magazine*, and the *Annual Register* all make the points that few women had had so much publicity and prominence in the public eye, and that her reputation was 'little short of European'.

She would have been pleased, generally, with what was said of her. To be so well written up in the *Gentleman's Magazine* (which had announced her marriages and always treated her gallantly) would have especially pleased her. In common with other notices of her life the *Gentleman's Magazine* could not avoid reference to the indiscretions of her 'salad days', but salacious speculation is nicely put in its place:

'. . . so was it the habit of the flaneurs and diners-out of twenty years ago, to attribute the most romantic anecdotes of boundless extravagance or bizarre behaviour to Madame Vestris. In creating for her this unenviable notoriety, jealousy had no small share. It is well-known that in the eyes of the mean-spirited, there is nothing so criminal as success, and we regret that in the theatrical profession the truth of this axiom is too frequently elucidated.'

No one was so ungallant as to allude to the autumnal frenzy of the love for Edward.

Planché in his *Recollections and Reflections* follows the mention of her death with:

'. . . since which period no one has ever appeared possessing that peculiar combination of personal attractions and professional ability which, for so many years, made her the most popular actress and manager of her day.'

And that is the note to end on. The 'fascinating little Vestris' with her Italian looks and French manners, taking her Bavarian broom to sweep away all the mess from the auditorium and the junk from the stage; and Madame, watch in hand and staff attentive: and, later, with a young heart accompanying her older head to epitomize her theatrical achievement in *Grist to the Mill*:

'At her first entrance into the dilapidated old château, when the drama was moving somewhat slowly, her appearance was like a gleam of sunshine thrown on a dusky ruin.'

APPENDIX A

Elliston and Management

Theatrical management, in common with other professional pursuits, was an individual business in the nineteenth century. Success depended upon the skill, cunning and foresight of the man at the top. (Joint management had never proved successful.) 'Undeserved odium' was inevitable. Elliston took the immediate view, that 'the show must go on, and go on tonight'. Academic considerations of the possible long-term effects of the show put on, or the manner in which it was advertised, could not conern him in his overcrowded days and did little to disturb his indulgent nights.

To those uninvolved or unable to imagine the complexities of management Elliston was always a problem. The witty lampooned him with such items as the mock playbill:

PUFFIANA;

OR,

EVERY GENTLEMAN HIS OWN TRUMPETER.

Respectfully Inscribed, without Permission,

TO THAT

PRINCE OF PUFFERS,

AND PARAGON OF PERFORMERS,

ROBERT WILLIAM ELLISTON, ESQ.

LESSEE AND EXHIBITOR

OF THE PATENT PUPPET SHOW, THEATRE ROYAL DRURY-LANE:

CONTAINING

SUNDRY SPECIMENS OF THE MOST APPROVED STYLES OF PUFFING,

AS USED BY THE FIRST LOTTERY OFFICES,

MEDICAL BOARDS, AND BLACKING WAREHOUSES, IN THE UNITED KINGDOM.

BY

GALE GULL'EM, Q. T. Z.

MEMBER OF THE ROYAL COLLEGE OF COZENERS.

The scholarly were nonplussed and made their objections known: 'The friends of Dr. Busby assert that although he enjoys the appointment of reader to Mr. Elliston, not one of the various pieces which have hitherto been produced were submitted to his inspection.' (*Theatrical Inquisitor* March 1820)

These instances might be considered examples of deserved odium. To balance the record two cases of undeserved odium may be cited.

Edmund Kean opened as King Lear in 1820. He had seen an effect at a mechanical exhibition in Spring Gardens: a device for raising an artificial storm. The machine produced wind and water effects in a specially constructed setting, and he wanted Elliston to have the machine set up for the storm scenes in *King Lear*. Elliston protested that Edmund Kean needed no such tricks, and he was concerned about the cost involved. But Kean insisted and special scenery was made, involving the use of thousands of 'leaves' and other items to be animated by the 'wind', and the installation of troughs and gutters for the 'cascade' of water. Raymond comments on the 'magnitude and ruinous expense of the undertaking'.

Every notice of the play described the storm effect at great length, spending comparatively few words on Kean's Lear, (not one of his better performances it seems). Such an effect, vulgar as some thought, was attributed, of course, to Elliston. The judicious grieved and the wags chanted: 'Blow, Bob, and crack your cheeks.' and *The Times* advised: 'The machinery may be transferred to the next new pantomime.'

A second case concerned the building rather than the stage. Raymond (*Memoirs of Elliston*, London 1844) gives the following account of how Drury Lane came to have its still-existing portico:

'During the recess, Elliston projected a portico, for the grand entrance from Brydges Street to his theatre, which, if carred into effect in conformity with his design, would have been useful, ornamental, and executed at a reasonable expense. The difficulties he had to encounter in the completion of the hideous covered way which now defaces the elevation of Drury Lane, were innumerable. First, the parish (for what earthly reason no one can tell) violently opposed the measure; the district surveyor next threw rubbish in the way. Mr. Soane then puzzled both the question and the district surveyor, and introduced a Mr. Spiller, who perplexed all parties. Between the latter two, the excresence now protruding into Brydges Street from the wall of the theatre, was fomented. Elliston had nothing in the world to do with it – except, indeed, paying the expenses, which literally amounted to the enormous sum of £1,050! A foundation was laid which might have supported a church tower, in which loads of money returned to their mother earth, but no mine of wealth opened to poor Elliston. The sum for which Mr. Hardwick would have contracted to execute Elliston's first design, was three hundred pounds.'

Raymond also reminds us that the vagaries of managements were more than matched by the ruses of the actors:

'Elliston was much annoyed by a conspiracy in the Theatre, in the nature of "a strike" among the actors. This strike took place on the question of "the sick clause", a privilege which had been lately much abused by SICK ACTORS not being able to play, whenever whitebait offered an engagement at Greenwich, or any part of the drama being deemed too heavy for the stomach. A meeting was convened on the subject, at which Mr. Calcraft presided; but nothing could be done for poor Elliston. The "aegrotat" was a stubborn disease, and there was no cure for it. Actors were, as usual, armed with medical certificates under all kinds of indispositions, so that a clean bill was rarely seen within the walls of Drury.

'A melo-drama, called *Therese*, was produced, in which Miss Kelly was the heroine – and inimitable, indeed, was her acting. On a certain occasion, *Giovanni* having been advertised for presentation, Madame Vestris is sick, and sure enough there is a certificate to prove it. *Giovanni* is consequently given up, and *Therese* put up. Within two hours Miss Kelly is sick, and there is another certificate, equally clear and satisfactory. *Harlequin versus Shakespeare* . . . is the last substitute for the night's entertainment, when Munden (Joe Snip) has most unaccountably a sudden attack of gout – he is sick; on which all doubts are removed by a certificate to the direct fact. We have known a lady so cruelly affected with this endemic, that she could not act her part, and, on the very night in question, indulging her egritude behind the scenes, by contemptuously criticising her impromtu substitute in the character. *O si SICK omnes!*'

APPENDIX B

The Monopoly

From 1660 to 1843 a law, based on the granting of a charter by Charles II to William d'Avenant and Charles Killigrew, prevented any theatres other than Covent Garden or Drury Lane from presenting Shakespeare or any other play *as a play*. Known as the Monopoly, this ruling, together with Walpole's Licensing Act of 1737, must take most of the blame for the decline and the restriction of dramatic writing in Britain during the eighteenth and early nineteenth centuries.

Covent Garden and Drury Lane were known as the 'major' houses. Other theatres, with the exception of the King's, which was not interested in presenting plays, were known as the 'minors'. In 1766, a Royal Patent was given to the Haymarket for the summer months only. Thus it became a third Theatre Royal in London, taking over when the majors were closed.

In order to keep within the law, the minors were obliged to put on entertainments involving music and songs. These entertainments were given a variety of names: burlesque; burletta; extravaganza etc., all different in form but essentially similar in kind, the English descendants of the *burla* of the Commedia dell'arte. The *burle* were extended versions of the usual short comic interludes given by the Italian comedians. Practical jokes (including trick scenery and properties), knockabout clowning, indelicate innuendoes, and parody were the usual ingredients.

Parody and scenic effects were the lines chiefly developed by the English minor theatres, though the dignity of the majors was affronted by the impudence of the minors when Shakespeare was 'adapted' as an 'operatic' or musical offering. The laughter and spectacle of the minors proved more lucrative than the solemnity and austerity of the majors. Still clinging to their 'rights', the majors competed for the public by adding the minor kind of entertainment to their own bills. The comparative costs of mounting such pieces in their much larger theatres left the majors with mounting bills of another kind, and so the silly business went on.

The Monopoly was an ill wind for dramatic writing in England but, by the challenge that it offered to the minors, it blew some good European appendages on to the British dramatic muse; notably an Italian eye and a French ear. Madame Vestris, by birth and experience, was peculiarly suited to assist in the operation.

It should be noted that the origins of burlesque-type entertainments and melodrama were in no way similar. The Parisian melodrama was imported and adapted for the London stage, and its conventions and assumptions, especially the scenic and musical elements, became mingled with those of burlesque. The transformation from Republican virtues to constitutional respectability was stage-managed by the British love of compromise, or intellectual laziness, whichever view you happen to take.

APPENDIX C

'The Bride of Messina'

This play is worth a separate word. In 1804 Schiller wrote *Die Braut von Messina*. The most fascinating of his plays, it was a boldly imaginative attempt, under the influence of Goethe, to bring the classical idea of tragedy back into dramatic writing. Taking his structural ideas from the Greeks (more specifically, Sophocles), he used an observing and commenting chorus. Taking his emotional attitude from Racine he almost arrived at that fusion of lucidity and mystery, that inter-relationship between light and shade, that Camus so aptly defined as the true area of tragedy. Schiller's avowed purpose was the declaration of 'open and honourable warfare against naturalism in art'; to bring the old 'poetical' standards back to 'transform' the increasingly sordid world. In *Die Braut* he worked too hard for his aim. Had he used the more detached (now sometimes called 'epic' or 'Brechtian') approach that five years earlier he had taken with his trilogy on the Thirty Years' War, *Wallenstein*, the result might have been nearer his goal. As it stands, *Die Braut* remains one of the most important European plays of the nineteenth century, for both its longing look backwards and its prophetic look forwards in style.

Coleridge translated *Wallenstein* in 1800. Part of his valiant and Quixotic crusade to bring us intellectually into Europe, Coleridge's translation made Schiller's name known in Britain.

Schiller's *Die Braut* was 'translated' (nothing as vigorous as rape took place) by Sheridan Knowles's attempt to combine the tedious style he thought apt for a Theatre Royal tragedy with the sentimental implication and 'moments' that the ladies in the house expected from him. This indigestible piece was iced by Madame to look as inviting as a wedding feast: a consummation devoutly to be missed by anyone concerned for the revival of dramatic writing in Britannia's realms.

It is interesting to consider Madame's handling of this play with the later production of *The Golden Fleece*, in which she appeared as Medea, at the Haymarket. Planché's parody and the handling of it by both Vestris and Mathews were, in their own way and in a strictly limited sense, doing for comedy some of the things that Schiller was aiming for in tragedy.

SELECTED BIBLIOGRAPHY

Newspapers and periodicals are indicated in the text when quotations and references are used (see Index).

PUBLISHED MATERIAL

Anderson, James R., *An Actor's Life*, London 1902

Bunn, Alfred, *The Stage, Both Before and Behind the Curtain* (3 vols), London 1840

Chubb, William, *Memoirs of the Public and Private Life, etc., of Madame Vestris*, etc. London 1830(?)
(This is one of many, attributed to various authors and publishers, printed at about this time. An admonitory tone and prim style was adopted to explain and excuse the grubby envy)

Coleman, John, *Players and Playwrights I have Known*, London 1888

Crabb Robinson, Henry, *The London Theatre 1811–1866*, London 1966 (selections from the diary of H.C.R. edited for The Society for Theatre Research by Eluned Brown)

Duncombe, T. H., *The Life and Correspondence of Thomas Slingsby Duncombe* (2 vols), London 1868
(An account, by his son, of one of Vestris's early admirers and supporters whose infatuation was not shared by his heir)

Ebers, John, *Seven Years of the King's Theatre*, London 1828

Forster, John, and Lewes, George Henry, *Dramatic Essays*, London 1896

Hunt, Leigh, *Autobiography and Reminiscences* (3 vols), London 1850

Lewes, George Henry, *On Actors and the Art of Acting*, London 1875

Mackintosh, Matthew (Old Stager), *Stage Reminiscences*, Glasgow 1866

Macready, William Charles, *Diaries and Reminiscences*, edited by Sir Frederick Pollock (2 vols), London 1875

Marston, Westland, *Our Recent Actors* (2 vols), London 1888

Mathews, Charles James, *The Life of Charles James Mathews*, edited by Charles Dickens (2 vols), London 1879

Oxberry, William and Mrs Catherine, *Oxberry's Dramatic Biography* (5 vols), Volume 5, London 1826

Pearce, Charles E, *Madame Vestris and her Times*, London 1923

Planché, James Robinson, *Recollections and Reflections* (2 vols), London 1872

Troubridge, St Vincent, *The Benefit System in the British Theatre*, London 1967

Tuer, Andrew W., *Bartolozzi and his Works*, London 1885

232

Vandenhoff, George, *An Actor's Notebook; or, The Green-Room and Stage*, London 1865

Watson, Ernest Bradlee, *Sheridan to Robertson, a Study of the Nineteenth-Century Stage*, Harvard 1926

Waitzkin, Leo, *The Witch of Wych Street*, Harvard 1933

ARTICLES

Armstrong, William, 'Madame Vestris: A Centenary Appreciation', *Theatre Notebook*, Vol. XI, London, Autumn 1956

Butler, James H., (i) 'The Ill-Fated American Theatrical Tour of Charles James Mathews and his wife, Madame Vestris', *Theatre Research/Recherches Théâtrales*, Paris, Vol. VIII, No. 1, 1966

(ii) 'An Examination of the Plays Produced by Madame Vestris during her Management of The Olympic Theatre in London from January 3 1831 to May 31 1839', *Theatre Survey*, Vol. X, No. 2, Pittsburgh, November 1969

UNPUBLISHED MATERIAL

Mathews Family Papers at Princeton University

Haugen, Clair O., *Covent Garden and the Lyceum under the Charles J. Mathews's*, thesis for the University of Wisconsin 1968

FRENCH PUBLICATIONS

Pixerécourt, Guilbert de, (i) *Guerre au Mélodrame!!!* under nom de plume 'Le Bonhomme du Marais', Paris 1818

(ii) 'Le Mélodrame', Article in *Paris ou le Livre des Cent-et-Un*, Tme 6, Paris 1832

(iii) 'Dernieres Réflexions de L'auteur sur le Mélodrame'. Article in *Theatre Choisi*, Tme IV, Paris 1843

Ginisty, Paul, *Mélodrame, Paris* 1910

Hartog, Willie G., *Guilbert de Pixerécourt*, Paris 1913

INDEX

Changing Your World

Growing a Plan
One Story at a Time

Follow Me

[25] Those who love their life in this world will lose it. Those who care nothing for their life in this world will keep it for eternity. [26] Anyone who wants to serve me must follow me, because my servants must be where I am. And the Father will honor anyone who serves me.

John 12:25-26, NLT

Printed in the United States of America
By Bingham Bend Publishers

Book Design © 2020 Susan Heslup

Ordering Information:
This book may be purchased in paperback or Kindle from Amazon.com
Or in paperback from walteralbritton7@gmail.com

Changing Your World/ Walter Albritton – 1st ed.

ISBN 979-8-5764-9650-1

Dedicated To

Toby Warren

Founder and Chief Executive Officer,
National Leadership Centers for Excellence,
Auburn, Alabama

A true Game Changer to whom God has given a gigantic vision
of how kindness can overcome incivility and save America
from hatred and violence

Tirelessly inspiring fellow Americans of all races to love one another
and work together to achieve "a more perfect union" for our nation

Devoting his life to building bridges of friendship

Dear Friend and Brother in Christ whose life continually
sharpens my own

Toby's favorite Bible verse:

As iron sharpens iron, so one person sharpens another.
Proverbs 27:17 (NIV)

To learn more about how you can help achieve "a more perfect
union" for America, and secure helpful information regarding
Civility in America, you may email Toby at
twarren@ustrust1787.org

CONTENTS

AFTERWORD

ABOUT WALTER ALBRITTON

OTHER BOOKS BY WALTER ALBRITTON

It's a challenging task to write the foreword to a book by a popular and well-known United Methodist preacher who needs no introduction. Everyone, it seems, knows the Rev. Walter Albritton.

My name is Ed Williams, and I am a retired journalism professor at Auburn University. I've always told my students that when you write a newspaper article about someone, to try and tell the reader something about the person that the reader doesn't already know. I think the same goes for the forewords of books by preachers – especially those who are as well known, loved and respected as the Rev. Walter Albritton.

Not long after I retired from the journalism faculty at Auburn University in 2013 my pastor, Dr. George Mathison at Auburn United Methodist Church, asked if I would introduce and welcome Brother Walter to our church one Sunday morning. Brother George was going to be out of town, and he asked Brother Walter to preach at all three services at AUMC.

If you know the Rev. Walter Albritton, you know that he is a master storyteller. I have read and enjoyed his Sunday columns, Altar Call, in The Opelika-Auburn News for years. Brother Walter told me that he has been telling stories in the local newspaper for 31 years. He shared with me an email from a reader who thanked him for "writing with authenticity" and for giving people "hope, joy, laughter, all while talking about God."

Brother Walter told me that he has been writing a newspaper column since 1963 when the late Ed Dannelly, editor of The Andalusia Star-News, allowed him to begin writing a weekly column titled "For Saints and Other Sinners." In his newspaper columns, he says he tries to show readers how "the good news of Jesus enlivens every aspect of human life".

I served as Brother Walter's sponsor on the Walk to Emmaus spiritual retreat some years back, and I feel that I know him pretty well. But in writing this foreword I needed to learn even more about this man of God.

So I did what all reporters do in the 21st century. I looked him up on Facebook. Yes, Walter Albritton has a Facebook page. He is an active user of the Internet and even has a Twitter account. Brother Walter lists the Bible as his favorite book. Not surprising. But there's more. According to Facebook, he loves singing, God, being a pastor, prayer, and ... ice cream!

I also Googled him on the Internet and found a webpage of Walter's sermons and columns that he writes each Sunday for our local newspaper. But any reporter will tell you that the best way to learn about people is just to ask simple, direct questions.

I always told my students that the best thing about being a journalist is that you get to ask questions that are none of your business. So I emailed Walter some personal questions. Questions like, How old are you? How long have you been married? Where did you meet your wife? What made you decide to be a preacher? Did you know John Ed and George Mathison when they were little boys?

Well, Rev. Walter Albritton is 88 years old, he's from Wetumpka, Alabama, he's been preaching for 70 years. He met his childhood sweetheart, Dean Brown, in the first grade. They were married June 1, 1952, 68 years, and they were blessed with five sons, 12 grandchildren and 17 great grandchildren. He pastored four churches during his senior year at Auburn.

One of my favorite stories in this book is "Daddy, Where is God?" – a sweet remembrance of the Albrittons' little boy David who died of leukemia when he was 3 years old. Drawing us closer – when I learned from Brother Walter that David and I both were born the same year, 1953.

Walter retired from Trinity United Methodist Church in Opelika in 2002 at age 70 after serving 48 years in the Alabama-West Florida Conference. He didn't like being retired, he had both knees replaced, and he joined the staff of St. James United Methodist Church in Montgomery as associate pastor of congregational care.

Walter was 13 when Brother Si Mathison, his wife Miss Mary, and sons John Ed and George moved to Wetumpka in 1945. John Ed says that Walter taught him how to play basketball. During the five years that the Mathisons were in Wetumpka, Walter was influenced by Brother Si to become a Christian and finally to accept the call to ministry. George and Walter have been prayer partners for more than 50 years.

Walter felt drawn to journalism and attended and graduated from Auburn University with a major in English and minors in journalism and speech. He was elected editor of the campus newspaper, The Auburn Plainsman, in the early 1950s. Brother Walter and I have things in common. I am a journalism major (not at Auburn), and I served as the faculty adviser of The Plainsman for 23 of the 30 years that I taught at Auburn.

Walter Albritton has a great sense of humor. He likes to laugh, and he makes others laugh. When I went by the Albritton home to drive Brother Walter to the Walk to Emmaus at Lake Martin, I noticed a cross stitch on the wall in the Albritton home that quotes a verse from Proverbs 17:22: "A merry heart doeth good like a medicine, but a broken spirit dries up the bones."

Rev. Walter Albritton, pastor, preacher, storyteller, encourager and friend, I have been blessed by our enduring friendship. Proverbs 27:17 tells us, "As iron sharpens iron, so one man sharpens another." God bless you and thank you, Brother Walter, for sharpening me.

It's a great honor to write this foreword for what you say will be your last book, Brother Walter. It is my prayer that others will be blessed and encouraged by the stories that you share. I was, and I know that they will be.

Ed Williams
Journalism professor emeritus
Auburn University
Nov. 18, 2020

Our world is in trouble. It needs change. If that is true, and I believe it is, then the question I must answer is this: Am I changing my world? I have one life to live. Am I using it to change the world?

Like everyone, you too have but one life. Are you using your life to change your world? That's the question I invite you to answer as you read the stories in this book. After each story I will invite you to pause, meditate on what you read, and ask yourself this question: How did this story help me change my life? Then write down one word as your answer, one word that you can use to build a plan for the way you can use your life to change your world.

As you read these stories, imagine that Christ is sitting beside you in a comfortable place in your home. Imagine that he is asking you these questions:

Who are you? What are you doing with your life? Where are you heading?

At the end of the book there is a page where you can write down a Seven Point Plan for Changing Your World. Reflect on all the words you have composed at the end of each story. Use those words to build your Seven Point Plan. Then ask Christ to help you begin executing your plan!

The year 2020 will always be known as the year of the COVID-19 pandemic. Early in the year the virus began impacting the entire world as millions of people fell victims of the deadly disease. As the year comes to a close, there have been more than 60 million cases worldwide, and more than a million and a half deaths.

Without warning our lives were suddenly changed by masks, hand-washing, social distancing, quarantine and the fear of death. Millions have lost jobs. Over 100,000 businesses have closed, never to reopen. And while vaccines are promised to be available soon, the virus is getting worse again, all across America and all across the world.

While we have struggled with the effect of the virus, the political scene in America has never been worse. Our nation has never been more divided and civility has been replaced with hatred, violence and name-calling the likes of which most of us have never witnessed. Politically speaking, we have lost the art of listening respectfully to those whose opinions differ from our own. Our world needs changing!

It has been against this background that I have continued writing this year. I have felt a desperate need to encourage my fellow Americans to practice kindness as an antidote to the incivility that is crippling our society. I have joined hands with Toby Warren to invite our fellow citizens to work for racial harmony and work together to achieve "a more perfect union." Under Toby's leadership, marvelous plans are underway that will involve hundreds of key people across America engaged in creating "a more perfect union".

I have added my voice to those who are pleading for an end to the systemic racism that has motivated much of the violence and hatred that has erupted like an open sewer on the streets of our major cities. These are some of the ways I am working to change my world.

Having devoted my life to serving Christ, I am convinced that those who follow Christ can and must play a major role in ending racism and creating a society where people of all races can enjoy justice and fairness. Christ followers understand that we are called to love God and love our neighbors. This indeed is the business of the King! And if we are willing to deny ourselves and follow where Christ leads, we can contribute to the healing of our land by making the love of our neighbors a primary concern.

I shall thank God if reading this book inspires even a few people to become true followers of Christ, for that is the desperate need of our nation – men and women who obey Christ, love God, love their neighbors of all races, and work together to build "a more perfect union" for the next generation. My prayer, dear reader, is that you will be one of those Christ followers God uses to change our world so that His will may be done in it. Please, join the ranks of those who are using their lives to change our world!

Walter Albritton, sjc

The Cabin
Wetumpka, Alabama
December, 2020

CHANGING YOUR
World

Growing a Plan
One Story at a Time

WALTER ALBRITTON

Changing Your World

In our time, some Christians identify themselves as "Christ Followers." The term appeals to me because it delivers more meaning than simply describing oneself as a "Christian." It subtly conveys the truth that Christ is alive and I am following him.

When Dean and I were in a boat on the beautiful Sea of Galilee, I wondered what it was like that day when four fishermen heard Jesus say, "Come, follow me." Peter, Andrew, James and John were ordinary men, fishing for a living, and tending their nets. Their way of life was abruptly interrupted by Jesus' words, "Follow me." They could hardly have understood what it would mean to follow Jesus but, amazingly, "At once they left their nets and followed him."

The gospels describe how the other disciples left what they were doing and accepted Jesus' invitation to follow him. Levi the tax collector, for example, was sitting at his tax booth, minding his own business, when Jesus walked by, stopped and said simply to Levi, "Follow me." Immediately, "Levi got up and followed him."

When Jesus began his ministry, walking from one town to another, preaching, teaching and healing, large crowds began following him. That soon became a problem because so many people want to touch him so they might be healed. So Mark tells us in his Gospel, "Because of the crowd he (Jesus) told his disciples to have a small boat ready for him, to keep the people from crowding him."

After his resurrection more and more people began following Jesus until today the number of adherents of Christianity is 2.4 billion, though not all of them are serious "Christ Followers." The question that begs to be answered is why the early disciples followed Jesus and why millions follow him today.

The best answer for me is the magnetism of Jesus. There is something magnetic about the person and presence of Jesus. Some hear the call early in life and rise up and follow him. Others feel a tugging at the heart, often for years, which culminates in a decision to begin following Jesus. All who follow Christ seriously sense that God is up to something and they long to share in what He is doing.

What does it mean to follow Christ? What does it mean to follow anyone? To follow another means much more than to "trail" someone; its deeper meaning is to admire, enjoy, support, respect and obey that person. Think of the rich significance that has for Christ Followers! Christ is a Person! He is alive! He is the ultimate example of how to live! Obedience strengthens our connection to him! The more that we love and serve him, "the sweeter he grows"!

Following Christ involves more than a dispassionate connection to the Christian faith. True followers are "all in" about loving, serving and obeying Christ. With hearts changed by the undeserved grace of God, they experience a new life of purpose and power. The Source of this new life is their union with the living Christ, the Vine who provides life to all who are connected to him.

John Wesley described genuine followers of Christ as "Altogether Christians," in contrast to those who were "Almost

Christians." Wesley helped us understand that some people are Christians in name only; they hang around the water but never get wet. When they jump in and allow their hearts to be transformed by the love of God, they become serious about "holiness of heart and life." They move from being lackadaisical disciples to becoming deeply serious about living for Christ in every arena of life.

A halfhearted Christian may "prefer" Christianity over the other religions of the world. An authentic Christ Follower has joyfully embraced the truth that Christ is the "one and only Son of God" who can save us from our sins, give us the gift of eternal life and use our witness to love others into the Kingdom of God.

If you ask, what is your life like if you follow Christ in today's world, this is my answer:

1. *You grasp the essentials of the gospel.*

You believe that Jesus is the Son of God who lived, suffered, died on the cross and was resurrected by the power of God. You believe there is no salvation apart from Christ and that by trusting him you can be baptized, cleansed of your sins and receive the gift of eternal life. You heard him call your name. You answered his call, surrendered your life to him and trusted him for salvation. You received from him the gift of the Holy Spirit who now guides your life. You still have flaws and you don't live a perfect life but you have a growing desire to please Christ in all you say and do.

2. *You live with continual gratitude for God's mercy.*

Why is "Amazing Grace" the song most loved by Christians across the world? Because we all identify with the phrase, "Amazing grace, how sweet the sound, that saved a wretch like me." You never forget the joy of hearing the living Christ say to you, "Your sins are forgiven." There is a song I love deeply because it expresses how I feel about the grace that saved me from my sins. These are the inspiring words of that song: "I stand amazed in the presence of Jesus the Nazarene, and wonder how he could love me, a sinner, condemned, unclean. How marvelous! How wonderful! And my song shall ever be: How marvelous! How wonderful is my Savior's love for me!" The wonder of wonders is that Jesus does love me despite my sins, and it is his love that keeps changing me and filling my heart with gratitude for my salvation.

3. *You have a constant desire to worship the Lord.*

You find yourself wanting to praise God every day, not just on Sunday. You want to give him glory, to thank him for your blessings, especially for his mercy in getting you connected to Christ. You enjoy reading the Bible more than ever. You are feeding on his Word and as you read the scriptures, you find yourself praising God for the peace and joy of knowing Christ. You delight in praising him in the morning, at noontime and in the evening! Your heart is continually filled with praise for his lovingkindness!

4. *You want other people to know Christ.*

You don't want to be obnoxious but you want to witness to your faith and your love for Christ. You want to love others into the kingdom of God. Knowing that Jesus taught the early disciples to "fish for men," you want him to teach you how to be his witness. More and more you care deeply for others to find the joy and peace that Christ alone can give to the human heart. As you grow in grace, you find yourself more and more willing to tell others, even strangers, about what Jesus has done for you, and what he means to you. And whenever you share your love for him, you give the Holy Spirit the opportunity to whisper in your listener's ear, "Perhaps it is time for me to ask Jesus to change my life!"

5. *You live in perpetual surrender to Christ.*

You surrendered to Christ at the beginning of your journey but you discovered that following Christ requires daily surrender. You take seriously what he said about the cross: "If anyone desires to come after me, let him deny himself, and take up his cross, and follow me." So you ask him to show you how to do that daily. In the face of hardship, even bewildering circumstances, you learn to say to yourself, "If with tears I must serve Christ, then with tears I will serve him. I belong to him. He belongs to me. Whatever he asks of me, I will do it with the strength he gives me." Then, often in the midst of heartache, you find that he gives you joy and peace you never dreamed of having. This reinforces your desire to honor Christ in every way possible.

6. *You are unwilling to settle for a nominal relationship to Christ.*

The more you follow Christ, and enjoy the strength he provides, the more you want to be the best you can be for him. A weak, pathetic relationship to Christ is out of the question. You are inspired by the zeal of other Christians – like for example that of C. T. Studd. A wealthy Englishman, he surrendered to Christ and sold everything so he could take the gospel to the world.

Studd went first to China, then to India, and in retirement to Sudan. Your heart is pulsating as you read Studd's last words: "Too long have we been waiting for one another to begin! The time for waiting is past! Should such men as we fear? Before the whole world, yes before the sleepy, lukewarm, faithless, namby-pamby Christian world, we will dare to trust our God, and we will do it with his joy unspeakable singing aloud in our hearts. We will a thousand times sooner die trusting only in our God than live trusting in man." Hearing of such passion to serve Christ drives you to your knees to rededicate your life to his work.

Recently my friend Maxie Dunnam suggested that during the isolation of Covid 19 we might be blessed by spending time reading again The Pilgrim's Progress, the great classic by John Bunyan. "Live," Maxie said, "with that character with a 'Strong Countenance.' It is this character in the book who, looking at the difficulties of living the Christian life, boldly said, "Set down my name, sir. For I have looked this whole thing in the face; and cost me what it may, I mean to have Christlikeness, and will." That, I thought, is the attitude of true followers of Christ: Set down my name, sir! Whatever the cost, my aim in life is Christlikeness! Yes!

Maxie went on to say: "Here is commitment! And this is our need. It is only in such devotion that our religious experience becomes vital, real and meaningful. Aren't we more interested in comfort than challenge? Security than salvation? Rather than committing our lives completely to God, we become bargain hunters in the basement of pale piety and moldy morals. We go on searching for a watered-down religion that offers little and demands less. With only a halfhearted desire for God and the whole truth, we are satisfied with that which is only tinged with 'full' Christianity. We are fearsome of the God who demands sacrifice. We shy away from the call of Christ who makes it distinct and demanding: 'If any man would come after me, let him deny himself, and take up his cross daily, and follow me.'"

Yes, Maxie, true Christ followers are not satisfied with a watered-down religion! Like the character with a "Strong Countenance," they have decided whatever the cost, they will deny themselves and follow Christ on the pathway that leads to Christlikeness! As I read Maxie's words, I felt like standing up and saying to my Lord, "Set down my name, sir! I am all in – all the way!"

Does Christ still invite his disciples to follow him? His missionary servant Albert Schweitzer answered that question boldly when he penned these words:

"He comes to us as One unknown, without a name, as of old, by the lakeside, He came to those men who knew Him not. He speaks to us the same words: 'Follow thou me!' and sets us to the tasks which He has to fulfill for our time. He commands. And to those who obey Him, whether they be wise or simple, He will reveal himself in the toils, the conflicts, the sufferings which they shall pass through in His fellowship, and, as an ineffable mystery, they shall learn in their own experience Who He is."

Over 70 years of ministry I have closed many worship services by asking people to respond to Christ by making their own the decision that of a simple song; so dear reader, if you are not already a Christ Follower, today I offer you that same opportunity. Christ is alive. He invites you to follow him in today's world. He wants to use your witness and your gifts to change the world. To follow him, you must obey him. In this moment you can choose to let these words become the desire of your heart:

> I have decided to follow Jesus;
> I have decided to follow Jesus;
> I have decided to follow Jesus;
> No turning back, no turning back.

> Tho' none go with me, I still will follow,
> Tho' none go with me I still will follow,
> Tho' none go with me, I still will follow;
> No turning back, no turning back.

> My cross I'll carry, till I see Jesus;
> My cross I'll carry till I see Jesus,
> My cross I'll carry till I see Jesus;
> No turning back, No turning back.

> The world behind me, the cross before me,
> The world behind me, the cross before me;
> The world behind me, the cross before me;
> No turning back, no turning back.

It's a decision that will change your world!

One Word: _____
How did this story help me change my life?

The Business of the King

One of my great delights in life is to find a poem that stirs my soul. I have stored several in my memory bank. When boredom comes calling, I don't need an energy drink to rejuvenate my mind and body. A little poem packed with truth restores my enthusiasm for life. Today, I want to share one of those treasures with you and apply its power to the coronavirus problems we all face. Get ready for a blessing! Here it is:

Life can never be dull again
Once we've thrown our windows open wide
And whispered to ourselves this wondrous thing,
We are wanted for the business of the King!

The isolation made necessary by COVID-19 has been exasperating. We are tired of being stuck at home, weary of waiting for businesses to reopen. Some of us have the advantage of sharing the frustration with a spouse. Others of us are alone which must make the seclusion even more difficult. We do find some relief from boredom when a family member or a friend drops by with food or medicine, always standing 10 feet away. But whether you live in Germany, South America or Alabama, you are pleading for deliverance from this isolation curse.

Though I struggle like everyone else with being homebound, I realize it is necessary for my own safety and that of my family and friends. To ignore the CDC health guidelines would be foolish. We can find a way to recover from the collapse of our economy but there is no recovery from death. So for whatever time is necessary, we all need to do what our health experts recommend. Social distancing may be aggravating but it could save your life or the life of a loved one.

I find some comfort in remembering that our isolation is nothing compared to the isolation of thousands of death-row inmates in our prisons. Most of them are isolated in a small cell with no windows for 23 hours a day. And the sad reality is that a few of them are innocent, awaiting execution for a crime they did not commit. If you doubt that, I suggest you read the eye-opening book Just Mercy by Bryan Stevenson. Every person who believes in fairness and justice for all should read this book.

The best medicine I have found for the monotony of isolation is to celebrate the truth of my little power poem. Life's dullness is overpowered by the "wondrous" truth that "we are wanted for the business of the King." There is more to life than birth, work, retirement and death. Nothing could be duller than to grow up, earn enough money to buy a pile of stuff, guard it for a while, then die and be buried in a shallow grave – and never experience the thrill of knowing and serving the King, whose name is Jesus!

The unseen world is more "real" than the world we can see and touch. That unseen world is the Kingdom of God. God sent His son Jesus into the physical world to reveal to us the invisible Kingdom. During his earthly ministry Jesus invited us to live in the Kingdom and to serve Him for He is the King of the Kingdom. Today, as the living Christ, He invites us to accept his invitation to work with Him in "the business of the King." Few things thrill my soul more than the amazing thought that God "wants me" for the business of His Son! And while my role is that of a pastor, that is but one of a thousand ways one may serve King Jesus. Men and women in almost every profession may engage in the King's business!

What is this business? It is to share the good news of God's love. John said it perfectly: "God so loved the world that he gave his one and only Son, that whoever believes in him shall not perish but have eternal life" (3:16). Millions of people still do not know that Jesus died for their sins, that their sins were forgiven when Jesus was nailed to that cruel cross, and that by surrendering to Jesus, and living in the Kingdom, they may begin living the eternal life that stretches beyond the grave!

The business of the King is to make Jesus known and loved. It is to witness to the ways our lives have been changed, and are being changed, by the transforming power of the living Christ. It is to help people see that the true meaning of life is not found in eating, drinking and playing around but in finding ways to love people into the Kingdom of God. It is to help others discover that meaning and joy are found in loving God and loving our neighbors as we love ourselves.

Must we wallow in dullness and frustration because we are sheltered in our homes for a time? No! A thousand times No! We can grow our faith forward by reading and studying God's Word. We can spend time in intercessory prayer, lifting up the sick, praying for our heroes who are on the front lines of service. We can encourage others with phone calls, cards, letters and gifts of food and flowers. We can find creative ways to make our love known to family and friends. We can pray for a worldwide spiritual awakening. We are not helpless because we are isolated. We can be about the business of the King!

Now repeat that little poem 10 times until you have memorized it. Then, the next time dullness comes calling, celebrate the truth that you are wanted for the business of the King! Say it to yourself: "I am wanted for the business of the King!" You are – so get busy! Obey the King's commands. Choose to follow King Jesus boldly in every situation. Despite the suffering of our broken world, obedience will lead to joy and peace.

One Word: _____
How did this story help me change my life?

3

Daddy, Where is God?

I remember it as though it was yesterday. I was driving our car. Our son David, almost three, was standing on the front seat beside me, his left arm around my neck. He broke the silence suddenly by asking, "Daddy, where is God?"

The little boy's question stunned me. David had heard me and his mother speak often about God so it must have dawned on him that he had never seen God. Now he wanted his daddy to tell him where God was. Though it would have been true, I figured it would be of little help to tell him that God is everywhere so I replied, "Son, God is in heaven."

"Where is heaven?" he asked. "Heaven is a real place somewhere in the world but we cannot see it until we die," I responded, inwardly hoping he would be satisfied and stop asking me these profound questions. I was only 23 at the time, ill-equipped to explain to a child or anyone the omnipresence of God. Thankfully, he had no more questions that day. He must have realized his Dad had few answers.

David died a few months later. Since his death, for 64 years, I have known and felt the presence of God in my life, some days

13

more remarkably than others. If asked David's question these days, I would answer by describing some of the "holy moments" of my life when God's presence seemed extraordinarily real.

One of those moments occurred on the day David died. He died in my arms about 4:30 in the morning. Dean and I had been up all night tending to David as he suffered restlessly. As David breathed his last breath, Dean roused from fitful sleeping and said to me, "It's time for his medicine." With a broken heart I replied, "Honey, he won't need any more medicine." The sun was rising as I laid his lifeless body on the bed.

Within two hours, there was a knock on our front door. I thought it was the undertaker whom I had called. But it was one of my seminary professors whom I had not called. A tall, blond Swede, Doctor Nels Ferre said, "I have come to see David." I said, "Sir, David died a little while ago." He said, "I know; that's why I have come." I am still not sure how he found out; I am content to believe God sent him.

Going into the bedroom with us, Doctor Ferre quickly lifted David's body up in his arms and prayed a simple prayer, thanking God for giving David to us for three years and offering him back to God. I have not seen that done before or since, but it was stunningly beautiful. Then, after putting David's body back on the bed, and putting his arms around Dean and me, he said, "I have come this morning to tell you that God hurts like you hurt." After praying for us, he went on his way.

Where was God? God was in our home that morning, having sent one of his servants to remind us that God had not used leukemia to kill David but he was hurting with us in our sorrow. Our home was hell that morning but God met us there, in the hallways of hell, and led us out into the sunshine of his eternal love. God was there that morning. I know it.

For some reason God likes to manifest Himself in our home as He did when David died. Several years later, after God had gifted us with four more sons, our marriage had become a disaster. Outbursts of anger spoiled every day. We were sick and tired of each other. Then one day when we were in the kitchen exchanging insults, we fell to our knees beside the breakfast table, crying and asking each other for forgiveness, and pleading with God to save our marriage. It became a holy moment of reconciliation, a moment of relief and great joy. Where was God? He was in that kitchen gluing our broken relationship back together. I knew He was present then and I still know it.

God came to our home on another less dramatic occasion when our sons were teenagers. A stranger knocked on our front door early one Saturday morning. He told me his name and asked if he could speak with me for a few minutes. Inside he shared that his teenage son was a drinking partner with one of my sons.

"Last night, he came home drunk again at 2:00 am so I decided to whip him. That turned out to be a mistake because he wound up beating the hell out of me." I realized then why there were fresh scratches on his face. He paused, wiping tears from his cheeks. Then he said, "I guess you are not happy with your son's drinking, and you being a preacher, maybe you can help me figure out what to do. I am at my wits' end."

We talked and prayed together for an hour. We met again several times, praying together and asking God to help us become the fathers our sons needed us to be. The man and I became good friends.

He and his family did not attend church anywhere. Six months later he led his family down to the altar one Sunday morning and they gave their lives to Jesus. Our sons did not stop drinking right away but we, their fathers, became good friends, brothers in Christ, and God helped us become better and wiser fathers. Our sons would later become responsible men.

I can close my eyes and still hear that man knocking on my door. Only a compassionate God, who wanted the best for us and our sons, could have brought us together that Saturday morning. Where was God? He was knocking on our door so that two frustrated fathers could help each other find the grace we needed to guide our sons in the ways of the Lord.

If you, like little David, are wondering where God is, you don't need to go to some church to find Him. He is probably in your home, ready to help you. If He is not there now, then listen because that is probably Him knocking on your door. Let Him in. You will be amazed at what He can do once you are ready to let Him help you. He has the power to change you and make you a true follower of Christ. Let Him do it!

One Word: _____
How did this story help me change my life?

4

He Just Stood There Watching

Along with millions of others, I watched the shocking video of Minneapolis police officer Derek Chauvin kneeling on the neck of George Floyd. I was horrified to watch an officer of the law cruelly killing a man who, with his last breath, kept pleading, "I can't breathe! I can't breathe."

The video showed that Floyd was no threat since his hands were handcuffed behind his back. I figured that any second the officer would remove his knee, but he did not. I learned later that he kept his knee pressed down on Floyd's neck for eight minutes and 46 seconds. I winced as I tried to imagine how excruciating the man's pain must have been.

Equally disturbing to me about the video was the sight of three fellow officers standing nearby, observing officer Chauvin's cruelty, and doing nothing. I kept thinking that the one officer standing nearest Floyd would reach down and insist that Chauvin remove his knee from Floyd's neck but he did not. He just stood there, watching. He just stood there, when he could have saved a man's life. I wanted to shout, "Do something, man; do something! Stop this deliberate cruelty!" But he just stood there, watching.

Officer Chauvin's brutal cruelty has resulted, finally, in his arrest for murder. Though all four officers were fired, the culpability of the other three officers should lead to their arrest as well. All four officers share responsibility for George Floyd's death but what troubles me deeply is the picture of the officer who stood there, watching and listening to Floyd begging for help, and did nothing. He just stood there, watching.

I thought about the Apostle Paul, arguably the greatest missionary of the Christian faith. When Paul was a young man, he did what the "silent" police officer did; he just stood there watching a man being stoned to death. Perhaps it was his guilt from doing nothing that caused Paul to describe himself as "the chief of sinners." You can sense the lingering pain of that hour as he spoke about it in the Acts of the Apostles (22:20, ESV), "*And when the blood of Stephen your witness was being shed, I myself was standing by and approving and watching over the garments of those who killed him.*" Thankfully, by the grace of God, Paul later came under the life-changing influence of Stephen's Lord, Jesus, and eventually died himself a martyr of the Christian faith.

I thought of the disciples of Jesus. They, too, stood there watching (or hiding) as Jesus was cruelly beaten and finally crucified. Like the silent Minneapolis police officer, they never said a mumbling word. They just stood there, watching.

I thought of Pilate, the Roman governor in Jerusalem who could have refused to endorse the crucifixion of Jesus. Instead Pilate yielded to the mob's demand to "Crucify him!" and "washed his hands" to declare himself innocent of Jesus' death. I thought about how the coronavirus has forced us to wash our hands a thousand times this spring, and wondered how many of us have washed our hands a thousand times in the face of the systemic racial injustice that continues to pollute our culture. Too many of us have, in silence, looked the other way, ignoring the undeserved suffering of fellow human beings.

I thought of what Martin Luther King Jr. said about silence during the racial turmoil of his time. His words remain disturbing:

"Our lives begin to end the day we become silent about things that matter."

"In the end we will remember not the words of our enemies, but the silence of our friends."

"There comes a time when silence is betrayal."

"History will have to record that the greatest tragedy of this period of social transition was not the strident clamor of the bad people, but the appalling silence of the good people."

The troubling truth of King's words reminds us of the familiar words of Edmund Burke who said, "The only thing necessary for the triumph of evil is for good men to do nothing."

It is likely true that the accumulated silence of several generations has sparked the widespread protests that have erupted since George Floyd's murder, and the recent killing of several other black persons by white men. Unfortunately, some protests have become violent in major cities across America, resulting in deaths, injuries, looting, demonstrators fighting with law enforcement personnel and buildings and property being destroyed by fires. Angry mobs continue to fan the flames of hatred and anger. Peaceful protests can lead to change; violence only exacerbates the problem.

I thought about my own silence for there have been times when I too have just stood there, watching. I should have spoken up, taken a stand, but I left the fight to others. Looking back, I realize there were times when I should have denounced the racial injustice that persists in our white-dominated culture. I have asked God to forgive me and put steel in my backbone.

Racism, of course, is a universal problem; it exists in all the world's cultures. To find a solution, we must determine the cause of racism. Ultimately, the answer can be summed up in one word, the word sin. Racism, then, is but one expression of man's defiance of the eternal laws of God.

Since racism is a human sin, there are racists in every ethnic group in the world. People of every race struggle with good versus evil so there are good people and evil people of every color. Christians find victory over evil through faith in Jesus Christ. When we receive God's forgiveness for our sins by yielding to the Lordship of Jesus, we begin to see people differently. We see people not as blacks, whites, Hispanics or Orientals, but as persons for whom Jesus died. We value every human life no matter the color of the skin. We see every person as potentially a brother or sister in Christ. We become willing to stand in the gap for the oppressed and disenfranchised. We find ways to express love in good deeds as well as words.

God sent His Son Jesus into the world to die for our sins and open the door to the Kingdom of God for all people. It is the business of those who have found their way into God's Kingdom to invite and welcome all people to join them in living a life of obedience to the eternal laws of God. Kingdom life involves primarily loving God and loving one another. And loving one another will lead us to oppose evil and work for a system that provides equality and justice for all people.

We cannot hate another person and love God. While hatred empowers evil and causes suffering, in the end hatred will lose because God is love and love wins. That is eternal truth – love wins! Martin Luther King Jr affirmed that truth by grounding his fight for justice on nonviolence rather than hatred for white oppressors. Doctor King put it this way, "Hate cannot drive out hate, only love can do that." He was right.

Why should good people speak out against bigotry, prejudice and injustice? Because God has taught us that it is His will for us to value every life and respect the dignity of every human being, regardless of their race or social status. To practice, support or tolerate racial injustice is to defy almighty God. If the chaos in America today has taught us anything, it is that the time has come for white Christians to come out of the closet of silence and oppose racial injustice wherever it exists in our society.

I have dear friends whose skin color is not white like mine. My age reminds me that I do not have much time left to stand up for the dignity and worth of every person. But, God willing, I intend to continue building bridges of friendship across racial lines as well as opposing racial injustice more aggressively. I will be silent at times, but only because I need to listen more sensitively to my black brothers and sisters. Listening compassionately will let them know that I am ashamed of the ways they have been mistreated and hurt by the prejudice and injustice of white people like me. When I listen, really listen, I begin to understand the pain prejudice has inflicted upon my black brothers and sisters.

One day my stammering tongue will lie silent in the grave. But until then, I will ask God for the wisdom to use it wisely and lovingly, in the hope that I can inspire a few people to practice daily the advice Saint Paul gave to his friends in Ephesus: "And be kind to one another, tenderhearted, forgiving one another, even as God in Christ forgave you."

Ultimately, evil can be overcome by acts of kindness practiced in the name of Jesus by good people of all races. When we do that intentionally, every day, in simple ways, we can make a difference. And surely none of us wants to be remembered as a person who just stood there, watching. If we are willing, we can live so that we will be remembered as true followers of Christ.

One Word: _____
How did this story help me change my life?

5

Neutralizing Racism

A unifying phrase emerged early during the COVID-19 pandemic. For two months now we have seen these words many times: "We are all in this together." The word "we" includes all human beings; for the entire world is in the grip of the deadly coronavirus. The phrase implies that since we are all in the same boat, we had better learn how to row together.

Another phrase that caught my attention was this: "We are all on the same team." In this fight to overcome the virus, we need to think of ourselves as brothers and sisters, not as whites or blacks or Hispanics or any other race or ethnicity.

The murder of George Floyd has given new meaning to these phrases. The nationwide protests against racism involve us all, for the sin of racism is a worldwide problem. If there was ever a time when we all need to work together to eradicate racism, it is now. This is a time for us to be fellow Americans, regardless of race or faith or political alliance. We are all in this together!

In recent days many statements have been written and shared. While opinions can be helpful, rhetoric will not remove racism. Repentance and forgiveness are needed. Hearts changed by the grace of God are needed. Silence must be replaced with a demand for justice for all. The "power brokers" in business, the government and the church must lead the way for change – or get out of the way. Those who continue to stand in the middle of the road are likely to get run over. Change is coming! It must come! Without significant change, the future of our nation is in peril.

But what I am writing is, after all, just more rhetoric. So in my remaining space I want to offer practical suggestions as to how ordinary citizens can facilitate the eradication of racism. My list is not exhaustive; allow it to stimulate your own list of things you can do to help remove racism from our society.

One, examine your heart. Ask God to show you the truth about how you think and relate to persons of another color. If there is any racism in your heart, ask God to forgive you and change your heart so you can begin loving people regardless of their skin color.

Two, resolve to judge others on the basis of their character, not their skin color. Base your opinions of others on their deeds, not their race.

Three, be done with inflammatory language that demeans people of color. Show respect for the value, dignity and worth of every person. Speak about others as you would have them speak about you.

Four, love your neighbors. Because of the coronavirus, we can show love for our neighbors by wearing a mask. But go beyond that; find other simple ways to express love for your neighbors. Initiate conversations with neighbors and friends about our need to treat all people fairly and put an end to injustice and racial discrimination. We have ignored the subject for generations, far too long.

Five, pray daily that God will heal our land of the sin of racism. Pray that our leaders will move forward with specific plans to eradicate racism from our society. Pray for our pastors to provide the spiritual leadership needed for this crucial hour in America. Pray for the men and women serving in law enforcement. Most of our police officers, troopers, sheriffs and others are good people who deserve our support. Though the "bad apples" must no longer be tolerated, we need to recognize and applaud those who are fair to all people, regardless of their race.

Six, talk to your children (and grandchildren) about racism. Listen to your children. Listen patiently to their opinions; invite them to share their experiences. Every person, young and old, has something to bring to the table. Pray with your family, asking God to reveal ways each of us can make a difference.

Seven, resolve to stop being silent about racist practices. When you see people being mistreated because of their skin color, speak up. Write or call your representatives in the state legislature and Congress and urge them to support changes in laws and policies that will help eradicate racism in our society. Make your voice heard.

Eight, in your daily routine look for simple ways to practice civility in every situation. Be polite to people, even strangers. Since love can overcome hatred, practice acts of kindness toward others, especially people of another race. Kindness has the power to defeat incivility.

Nine, make an effort to build bridges of friendship with persons of another race. This may give you the opportunity to listen to the heartbeat of someone who endures daily the cruelty of discrimination. The "haves" can help build a better world by truly listening to the "have nots."

Ten, donate money, food or clothing to an agency that is helping the poor. For example, the Mercy House at 2412 Council

Street in Montgomery. The number is 334-676-3040. (Don't ask them to come after your gift; go over there and become friends with the good folks who run the place.) If you are able, make a significant financial gift on a regular basis to a ministry like Mercy House.

Eleven, volunteer a few hours of your time to serve in a local ministry by sweeping floors, washing dishes or serving food. Go beyond words and smiles; do something that makes you look like a caring human being. Some of us need to get out of our gated communities and get our hands dirty helping the poor.

Twelve, recommend Jesus to others. He alone can change our hearts. Faith in Jesus cannot co-exist with racism. I repeat – Faith in Jesus cannot co-exist with racism! The ground is level at the foot of the cross. Jesus shed His blood on that cross so that our sins could be forgiven and so we could live in the Kingdom as brothers and sisters.

Though Satan is using racism to divide and destroy our nation, we need not yield to his demonic forces that hold us in bondage. We can turn to God and find the strength to recognize evil among us and neutralize it with justice, love and peace. Our survival is doubtful if we continue to tolerate racism. It can be overcome, however, when enough of us decide to neutralize systemic racism and work together to build a system that provides justice and equality for all people. Thus shall we honor God and prepare a better world for our descendants. True followers of Christ can lead the way to a society that is free of racism.

One Word: _____
How did this story help me change my life?

6

Changing the Culture of Cruelty

Life in America today presents us with this disturbing irony: how kind we can be as individuals and how cruel we can be en masse. Individually we may practice kindness, but collectively, we encourage unkindness when we condone it with our silence.

My friend Bill Brown brought this paradox to my attention in a kind response to my recent article on encouraging kindness. A retired journalist and distinguished newspaper editor, Bill deplores with me the proliferating incivility of our day.

Sadly, we must acknowledge that the art of cruelty (the opposite of kindness) is being practiced before us daily by most of the candidates for public office, including the president. Even sadder is the reality that many of us are encouraging this incivility, some by our cheers and some by our silence. "We the people" could diminish this culture of cruelty by insisting that our leaders stop publicly demeaning one another.

Bill wonders, as I do, why so many people are encouraging unkindness, unwittingly of course, by condoning it with their silence. Bill raises a good question: "Is it the cloak of anonymity that allows us to act out our basest impulses?"

While we are all tempted to hide behind the cloak of anonymity, the question raises a deeper issue, that of our relationship to God. Our base, or vile, impulses spring from our "lower nature" and the Bible has a lot to say about that.

Consider, for example, what Paul says in Romans 8: *"If men comply with their lower nature, their thoughts are shaped by the lower nature; if with their spiritual nature, by the spiritual. Thoughts shaped by the lower nature mean death; thoughts shaped by the spiritual mean life and peace. For thoughts shaped by the lower nature mean a state of enmity to God"* (Weymouth).

Think of it as a matter of life or death. Cruelty, a thought aroused by the lower nature, leads to death. Kindness, a thought inspired by the spiritual nature, leads to life and peace. The ultimate question is whether we desire or disdain the will of God.
The will of God for Jesus was the "food" which sustained him. Jesus said to his disciples, "My food is to do the will of him who sent me and to finish his work." If the will of God was food for Jesus, then it is life-giving food for us as well. As E. Stanley Jones says, "We are made for the will of God as the body is made for food. Everything else is poison!"

The culture of cruelty in America is poisoning our society. It can destroy us because it makes us enemies with God, the Source of the life and peace we all seek. If we refuse to drink this poison and instead feed on the will of God, this food will provide all the sustenance we need for a life shaped by our higher nature. We are made to live by this higher nature, not our lower.

As a Methodist I have been reminded often of the sound advice John Wesley offered the early Methodists about voting. He urged people to do three things:

1. *To vote, without fee or reward, for the person they judged most worthy;*

2. *To speak no evil of the person they voted against;* and

3. *To take care their spirits were not sharpened against those who voted on the other side.* Excellent advice 250 years ago and still excellent for today.

Imagine the impact we could have on our culture of cruelty if thousands of us followed Wesley's advice today, and did so because we believed it to be the will of God. We would not eliminate unkindness in the public arena but we could surely weaken its insidious effect on the unity of our nation.

The Psalmist said what I need to remember to say every morning: "I desire to do your will, O my God; your law is within my heart (Psalm 40:8). If I greet every sunrise with that desire in my heart, I will always choose kindness over cruelty, bitterness and vulgarity.

It helps me, and should help us all, to remember how Jesus explained who will enter the kingdom of heaven. He said it will be "those who do the will of my heavenly Father."

Let us then choose kindness instead of cruelty because it is the will of God. To do anything else is to swallow poison. We are truly alive when we live by the will of God. We wither and die when we spurn the will of God.

In a letter written from a prison two thousand years ago, the Apostle Paul admonished his friends in Philippi to practice kindness for the ultimate reason: because God had forgiven their sins. Paul's inspiring words invited them, and invite us, to embrace kindness as the way God wants us to live:

"Be kind to one another, tenderhearted, forgiving one another, as God in Christ forgave you."

May God bless America with people who choose to live like that!

One Word: _____

How did this story help me change my life?

7

Settling Disputes Without Violence

The media remind us daily of the abhorrent political divisiveness that exists in America. The division is so ugly that one wonders if "a more perfect Union" can be achieved in our lifetime, though the hope for it does persist in the minds of many peace-loving citizens.

Political dissension, however, is not a new phenomenon in America. Historians remind us that our first president, George Washington, was so "bruised and disillusioned" by his critics that he said to a friend during his second term in office, "No man was ever more tired of public life, or more devoutly wished for retirement, than I do." Washington spent an inordinate amount of time "refereeing" the fierce and continuing quarrels between two of his cabinet members, Alexander Hamilton and Thomas Jefferson. Each man was the primary spokesperson for the two major political divisions of that era and constantly vilified each other.

The good news is that America slowly became a great nation despite the schism that threatened to throttle the birth of a new nation. Somehow, men and women of goodwill found a way to let unity prevail. Perhaps this can inspire hope that men and women of our day can resolve their differences and work together in the pursuit of "a more perfect Union."

Students of the Bible understand that differences can be settled without resorting to violence and hatred. An inspiring story in the 15th chapter of the Acts of the Apostles is a good example of how disputes may be settled amiably for the common good.

There arose in the church in Antioch a dispute about circumcision. As more and more Gentiles began embracing Christ as Lord, some of the Jewish converts insisted that Gentiles could not be saved unless they were circumcised. This resulted in a sharp dispute in the Antioch church so they sent Paul and Barnabas to Jerusalem to seek a solution from the apostles and elders.

In Jerusalem the matter was hotly debated. After much discussion, Peter got up and pled with the group to agree that circumcision was a "yoke" no longer necessary because God had purified the hearts of the Gentiles by faith. "We believe," Peter insisted, "it is through the grace of our Lord Jesus that we are saved, just as they are."

At this point Barnabas and Paul shared with the group "the miraculous signs and wonders God has done among the Gentiles through them." A great silence came over the group as Barnabas and Paul spoke. Then James stood and urged the group to "not make it difficult for the Gentiles who are turning to God" by insisting that they be circumcised. So persuasive was James that his judgment inspired concurrence.

Embracing accord, the apostles and elders drafted a letter stating their opinion and sent two disciples to deliver the epistle in person to the Antioch congregation. The letter was received with great joy and the two disciples who read it "said much to encourage and strengthen the brothers." Unity was preserved and the door to salvation was now more widely opened to Gentiles.

One may observe that in settling this serious dispute, neither side found it necessary to vilify the other. When goodwill is valued, people can share differences of opinion without denigrating those who disagree. In the centuries since Peter and Paul, the church has grown when Christians resolved their differences and worked together. On the other hand, disputing and despicable criticism of others have always stifled growth and unity.

Because we are all flawed, tranquility cannot be realized without the practice of forgiveness. In Romans Paul admonishes us, "If it is possible, as much as depends on you, live peaceably with all men." To live peaceably with others we must be willing to extend mercy to people with whom we disagree. Disputes are seldom settled until mercy is extended. This becomes all the more important when we recall that Jesus reminded us that we cannot receive God's mercy unless we are willing to extend mercy to others.

There is a lesson here for us and our fellow American citizens. We can sow the seeds of dissension and remain divided, fomenting a culture of hatred and violence, or we can find ways to reconcile our differences and, with goodwill, mercy and kindness, work together to achieve "a more perfect Union." The future of our nation depends upon the choice made by "we, the people."

One Word: _____
How did this story help me change my life?

8

Time for Some Down On Our Knees Praying

Methodists by and large have usually received the holy sacrament while kneeling at an altar rail. Only the few who were unable to kneel were given the elements while standing. The virus madness has changed all that. These days some pastors deliver the sacrament through a car window during a "drive by" communion service. This serves to remind us that what matters is not the position of the body but the attitude of the soul as a believer partakes of this means of grace.

Growing up a Methodist I did not perceive kneeling to receive the sacrament as kneeling to pray. But on Sunday nights the pastor often "opened the altar for prayer" by inviting one and all to come kneel and pray while quiet music was played. Though doing so was often meaningful to me, that was about the only time I ever saw people kneeling to pray.

When our children were small, I often knelt beside their bed to pray for and with them. But my kneeling was not so much out of reverence as it was simply a convenient way to be near each child while praying.

Then God began showing me that earnest prayer born out of great need may often drive us to our knees in prayer. I hasten to say that what matters most in prayer is the attitude of the heart, not one's posture in prayer. Even so, there is something about praying on our knees that symbolizes reverence, humility and our desperate desire for the help and mercy that God alone can provide.

Three times when I was in desperate need myself, God sent men to pray for me, and every time, each man dropped on his knees beside me to pray. Neither man knew the nature of my need, only that God had told them to go pray for me. The sense of God's presence was an overwhelming blessing as God met my need. Joy flooded my soul. I began to believe that God wanted me to go to my knees more often in prayer, especially when I was praying for individuals who had come to me with a great need for God's mercy and guidance.

The Bible gives us several examples of men praying on their knees. In First Kings we find King Solomon crying out to God for Israel in a powerful prayer, the kind of prayer we should be praying for our nation. When Solomon finished praying, "he rose from before the altar of the Lord, where he had been kneeling with his hands stretched out toward heaven."

In another poignant scene we find the reformer and prophet Ezra, so ashamed of the disgraceful sins of Israel that he fell on his knees praying "with my hands spread out to the Lord my God." His stirring prayer of repentance is yet another example of the kind of prayer we Americans should be praying for our country.

When Daniel learned that anyone who prayed to any god other than King Darius would be put to death, his faith did not cave in to fear. Instead, the Bible tells us, three times a day Daniel "got down on his knees and prayed, giving thanks to his God, just as he had done before." Though he was thrown into the lions' den, Daniel's faith was rewarded when God's angel "shut the mouths of the lions."

In the New Testament several people knelt at the feet of Jesus, begging for help or healing. Filled with compassion, Jesus reached out and touched them. Blind men were blessed with sight. Lepers were healed. The lame began to walk. The deaf began to hear. The mute began to speak. The response of Jesus reveals the compassion of God since Jesus, in his own words, was doing what his Father had sent him to do.

These stories suggest a few questions: Have you ever felt so desperate for God's help that you fell on your knees praying? Or have you ever felt such shame for the sins of our nation that you fell on your knees praying? Or have you ever felt so stirred by the love of God that you fell on your knees praying? Or have you ever felt such gratitude for the grace of God that you fell on your knees praying?

Two dear friends of mine found their son dead in his bed at age 34. When they called on me to help them, I fell on my knees praying that God would heal their broken hearts. In time, God did that, gloriously. I fell on my knees thanking the Lord for that healing work of grace.

When a tornado killed a young lawyer's wife and four children, he renounced his faith in God. The next day a friend of mine drove 300 miles to tell the young lawyer that he loved him.

My friend said that when he walked into the lawyer's home, the man's faith "came rushing back" when he saw my friend's face. Tears streaming down his face, the lawyer said, "I knew instantly that only God could cause a man to come so far to share my sorrow." When my friend told me that story, I felt like falling on my knees to praise God.

I can see C. S. Lewis falling on his knees praising God for his salvation on the day he became a Christian. Lewis said, "I was probably the most surprised atheist on the planet when suddenly there was someone else in the room – and I knew it was Jesus!" He would later describe his conversion as being "surprised by joy." So many times I find the joy of the Lord so wonderful that I feel like falling on my knees praying.

I felt like that one day when I met Dewey in the Rain Forest of Ecuador. Dewey, one of the Waodani tribesmen who killed five American missionaries in 1956, had been won to Christ by the widows of those missionaries. Less than five feet tall, Dewey was now a Christian and pastor of a little church there in the Rain Forest. We shook hands but could not understand each other because of the language barrier. But when I said the word "Jesus," Dewey grinned, pointed to the sky and embraced me. We were brothers – through Jesus! I felt like dropping to my knees on the grass and thanking Jesus for such a moment.

Peter must have felt a sense of desperation when the disciples called him to Joppa the day Tabitha died. When Peter arrived, they took him into the upstairs room where the woman's dead body been washed and placed. What could he do, Peter must have thought. The woman is dead. But Peter knew he served a great and mighty God so with no hesitation he got down on his knees and began praying. Soon, to the amazement of those who had been crying, Tabitha was up on her feet, alive and well. Peter must have felt like falling on his knees again, to praise God for answering his prayer.

In Paul's Letter to the Ephesians is one of the most beautiful prayers in the Bible. After reminding his Ephesians friends that through faith in Christ they may approach God with freedom and confidence, he begins his inspiring prayer with these words: "For this reason I kneel before the Father, from whom his whole family in heaven and on earth derives its name." Evidently Paul found it needful sometimes to fall on his knees praying.

There are, of course, other ways we can use our knees. "Taking a knee" as a sign of protest has become popular since Colin Kaepernick did so in 2016 with his National Anthem defiance. Unfortunately many have been duped into embracing the radical "Black Lives Matter" movement without realizing that the goal of its leaders is more anarchy than reformation of the government.

While peaceful protests can sometimes force changes that are needed in our society, protests that are not grounded in man's accountability to God will accomplish little good. We need to add prayer to protests. In other words, if God is not in it, then we had better not do it. And God is not in it if there is violence, stealing, killing, and destruction of property. That most Americans understand this should give us hope for the future.

The Apostle Paul tells us in his Letter to the Philippians that one day we will fall on our knees to acknowledge what God has done. These words are part of Paul's marvelous tribute to Jesus in chapter two: *"For this reason also, God highly exalted Him, and bestowed on Him the name which is above every name, so that at the name of Jesus every knee will bow, of those who are in heaven and on earth and under the earth, and that every tongue will confess that Jesus Christ is Lord, to the glory of God the Father."*

In the meantime, we can rejoice that our great and mighty God is saying to us today what He said to Israel years ago:

"If my people, who are called by my name, will humble themselves and pray and seek my face and turn from their wicked ways, then I will hear from heaven, and I will forgive their sin and will heal their land." (2 Chronicles 7:14) Surely the time has come for God's people of all races to treat one another with love and respect and do some "down on our knees" praying, and praying with the attitude that meets God's requirements for the healing of our land.

One Word: _____

How did this story help me change my life?

9

The Thin Blue Line

Violent crime since the murder of George Floyd in May has led hundreds of police officers to file for retirement. In New York State alone, more than 500 officers have decided to retire, citing lack of respect, the loss of overtime pay and the clamor to defund the police.

This is alarming news at a time when lawlessness is rampant in major cities across our nation. Yet who can blame these officers? Few of us would want a job that requires you to risk your life every day while angry people ridicule you, throw eggs and bricks at you and torch your police car while bystanders applaud such deeds.

But while the decision to retire is understandable, we all know chaos will rule and ruin our country without responsible law enforcement. The truth is, a peaceful society cannot exist without police. So those of us who care about our nation need to send a message to our law enforcement personnel, and the message is this: We need you! Don't leave us now because we need you more than ever!

Overwhelming violence is not new. Ages ago the Prophet Habakkuk cried out to God with a plea that sounds like our own today:

"How long, O Lord, must I call for help, but you do not listen? Or cry out to you, 'Violence!' but you do not save? Why do you make me look at injustice? Why do you tolerate wrong? Destruction and violence are before me; there is strife, and conflict abounds. Therefore the law is paralyzed, and justice never prevails. The wicked hem in the righteous, so that justice is perverted."

The Lord answered Habakkuk's complaint, advising him that a time of judgment was coming. Interestingly, one of the sins requiring God's punishment was bloodshed. This is what the Lord said: "Woe to him who builds a city with bloodshed and establishes a city by crime!" Then come these memorable words: "For the earth will be filled with the knowledge of the glory of the Lord, as the waters cover the sea."

Habakkuk's response is captivating. While he pleads, "in wrath remember mercy," he also declares his decision to remain faithful to God no matter what. Few words in the Bible are more inspiring than these by the prophet:

"Though the fig tree does not bud and there are no grapes on the vines, though the olive crop fails and the fields produce no food, though there are no sheep in the pen and no cattle in the stalls, yet I will rejoice in the Lord, I will be joyful in God my Savior."

What strength Habakkuk had! To pronounce correctly the prophet's name, you must use the word "back." So you pronounce his name this way: "Huh-back-kuk." In the prophet's back was a strong backbone, a backbone with steel in it. There was no Jell-O in it!

Habakkuk saw hard times coming. God was going to punish the people for their sins. But Habakkuk's faith was not shaken. He believed God was in control and nothing would destroy the joy God gives to those who trust him.

The little word "yet" is a powerful word. God's people are "Yet people." No matter how difficult the times, God's people will say, "Yet will I rejoice in the Lord, I will rejoice in the God of my salvation!"

There is no doubt there are some "bad" police officers who need to be removed from law enforcement. But the majority of the police are decent, God-fearing public servants who need our support, respect, affirmation and prayers. They need people with strong backbone who will stand with them in the face of the hate, violence and ridicule they are facing today.

And now more than ever, our nation needs police officers with steel in their backbone, men and women who will say, despite the dangers facing us, yet will we stay the course and do our part to save America from the chaos threatening to divide and destroy us. How desperately our country needs good people who refuse to quit because times are hard!

Dare we not pray for such a thin blue line to emerge with new strength and resolve in our time?

One Word: _____
How did this story help me change my life?

10

Why Does God Allow the Coronavirus?

Most people will agree that the coronavirus is not "the will of God." God has not released this terrible pandemic to punish us for our sins or to "thin" the population of the world. But assuming this is true, it is perfectly reasonable to ask why God is allowing this virus to kill thousands, perhaps millions, of people.

This question brings to mind Saint Paul's thorn in the flesh. Why did God allow a thorn in the flesh to torment Paul? Paul's answer to that question, given in his second letter to the Corinthians, is helpful but somewhat puzzling. Because he had received *"wonderful revelations"* from God, Paul says God gave him a thorn in his flesh to keep him from *"becoming proud."* He describes the thorn as *"a messenger from Satan to torment me."*

Paul goes on to explain that *"three different times"* he *"begged the Lord"* to take away this thorn, but God did not do so. Instead, each time God answered Paul by saying, *"My grace is all you need. My power works best in weakness."*

Paul's response was surprisingly positive: *"So now I am glad to boast about my weaknesses, so that the power of Christ can work through me. That's why I take pleasure in my weaknesses, and in the insults, hardships, persecutions, and troubles that I suffer for Christ. For when I am weak, then I am strong."*

These words reveal a dramatic change in Paul's perspective. One minute he is asking God to end Satan's torment in his body. The next he is declaring his confidence that although God has refused his request, God will give him the grace to overcome his hardships. And that grace, Paul says, is all he needs. That amazing insight about suffering may well be one of the great secrets of life.

Across the ages followers of Christ have been inspired by Paul's attitude. While he did ask for deliverance from his thorn three times, there is no indication that he asked a fourth time. Instead he began believing that God's grace was sufficient for him, or all that he needed to accept the suffering he endured while serving Christ. He learned to "delight" in his weaknesses, hardships and troubles. He discovered that he could experience the power of Christ working through him in the midst of suffering. Christ's followers have, like Paul, have made that same discovery, finding that God's grace was sufficient for them also.

Somewhere along life's journey I began to realize that our problems can make us better people – if we learn to appropriate God's grace in the midst of the hardships we are facing. To do that we must, like Paul, choose to believe that God can give us the spiritual strength to endure the troubles we are facing. When we do that, we will have moments of great joy when we can testify that God provided "all we needed" to survive our hardships. E. Stanley Jones called that "victorious living"! And it is – victory that is ours only by the grace of God.

The good news about grace is that it is available to one and all. The most unworthy among us may receive God's grace because it is unmerited and undeserved. Paul called himself "the chief" of sinners, indicating that if God was willing to give it to him, then it is available to anyone willing to surrender to Christ and trust Him.

Trusting Christ involves the willingness to *"boast of our weaknesses."* That is not easy to do. We are sons and daughters of a culture that values impressive credentials and counterfeit honors. We covet the adulation of our peers. At one time Paul was like that, but he changed. He lost confidence in his achievements and began to value only one thing – "knowing Christ."

Here is the secret of obtaining this power called grace. Our perspective, desires and values must change. This happens when our faith in God becomes serious, when we decide to cherish our acceptance by God and no longer thirst for "the applause of men." A more mature faith helps us grasp at least some understanding of why God allows suffering and how He uses it in our lives.

Like Paul's thorn in the flesh, the coronavirus is a mystery. Why does God allow it? How will God use it? Is God allowing this virus to give us time to stop trusting in "things" and turn to the living God? Is He allowing this virus in the hope that we will reexamine our values and realize that relationships are more important than possessions? Is God using this suffering to remind us that the true meaning of life is not found in cell phones and computers but in loving God and loving our neighbors as we love ourselves?

Perhaps God will use this suffering to help us turn in our weakness to depend on Him rather than ourselves. This "invisible enemy" has revealed our desperate need of help. Will our fear of this enemy cause us to humble ourselves and pray as the Psalmist prayed, *"O Lord my God, I called to you for help and you healed me"*?

Faith could lead us out of fear and inspire us to declare with the Psalmist: "God is our refuge and strength, an ever-present help in trouble. Therefore we will not fear, though the earth give way and the mountains fall into the heart of the sea, though its waters roar and foam and the mountains quake with their surging."

Like Paul, we may beg God to deliver us from our thorns in the flesh. And if He says no as He did to Paul, we can follow Paul's inspiring example. Paul did not give up on God because He said no. He learned to depend not on himself but on the grace of God. That grace kept expanding Paul's faith so that despite his suffering, and with his execution looming before him, Paul could declare, *"No, in all these things we are more than conquerors through him who loved us. For I am convinced that neither death nor life, neither angels nor demons, neither the present nor the future, nor any powers, neither height nor depth, nor anything else in all creation, will be able to separate us from the love of God that is in Christ Jesus our Lord."*

What a faith! Whenever I read those words, my heart cries out to God to give me a faith like that! With a faith like Paul's I can face my suffering with peace and without fear.

Jesus understood that the world was filled with hardships. Some of his words, spoken to his disciples a few days before his crucifixion, are startling as we endure these days of isolation in our homes: *"A time is coming, and has come, when you will be scattered each to his own home.... I have told you these things, so that in me you may have peace. In this world you will have trouble. But take heart! I have overcome the world."*

In the Easter season we celebrate the resurrection of Jesus. Millions shout "He is Risen!" He is alive! We rejoice because Jesus defeated death and gave us the promise of eternal life. His resurrection gives us hope when we face the troubles of this perilous world. In this year of the Coronavirus pandemic, we need not wait until Easter to celebrate the resurrection. Suffering and death will not have the last word! Death is not the end. Hope is greater than fear and God has filled our hearts with hope.

In these troubling days, we need to strictly obey the health guidelines we have been given. We need to pray for deliverance from this terrible virus, and pray that the great scientists of the world will soon produce a vaccine. However, our greatest need is not a vaccine for COVID-19; our greatest need is to humble ourselves, turn in repentance to God, receive his grace and find comfort in the peace that only Jesus can give.

One Word: _____
How did this story help me change my life?

Solving Problems by Listening

One of my favorite stories is about an old man who lived his final years in the home of his son and his wife. They had a daily routine. Every afternoon about five o'clock the old man went for a walk, always returning by six when the three of them had supper together. One day the old man was 45 minutes late returning for supper. With worried faces, his son and his wife asked if there had been a problem. "No," the old man replied, "I just ran into a man who would not stop listening to me!"

Listening is a fine art. You may smile at that old man but the truth is, you do feel blessed when someone stops talking long enough to really listen to you. Some people never stop talking. They are the "motor mouths" who think the rest of us have nothing better to do than to listen to what they have to say. Listening is not in their game plan.

Jesus knew what it was like to have people in his audience who paid little attention to his teaching. To get their attention,

Jesus used a bit of subtle humor when he said, "He who has ears, let him hear." People must have smiled at his words, "He who has ears." Everyone has ears. Everyone also knows that the words of a speaker can "go in one ear and out the other." Jesus was inviting people to pay attention, really listen, to what he was saying.

Recent translations have improved the words of Jesus in the King James Version: "Who hath ears to hear, let him hear." Goodspeed has him say: "Let him who has ears listen!" The NRSV: "Let anyone with ears listen!" The Living Bible offers the clearest version yet: "Anyone who is willing to hear should listen and understand!" It would be fair to say that Jesus was saying was, "Hey, listen up now, this is important!"

In these days of protests in America, some peaceful and some violent, we are all realizing the importance of listening. It is not a lesson for white people alone; all of us, whatever the color of our skin, must learn to listen to one another. We need to talk to one another and we need to listen to one another. That will open up opportunities to love one another and work together to create a better world.

When it comes to the protests, we must not refuse to listen because some evil people are using the protests as a smokescreen for looting, stealing, destroying property, and even murder. Just as it is wrong to condemn all law enforcement personnel because some of them are bad apples, it is also wrong to condemn all the protestors because some of them are committed to violence and destruction. So it is imperative that we listen and learn what the vast majority of the protestors are saying – and work to make the changes that justice and fairness demand.

Even more important, we need to listen to what God is saying. The Bible implores us to listen to God. In the Book of Revelation, Christ says to the seven churches: *Anyone who is willing to hear should **listen** to the Spirit and understand what the Spirit* *is saying to the churches."* It is fascinating to recall what transpired on the Mount of Transfiguration. There Moses and Elijah appeared with Jesus to confirm his role as the Messiah. There his countenance was transfigured with divine glory. But even more significant was what God said: "This is my beloved Son; **listen** to him." Jesus urged the people to listen to what he said, and God the Father commanded us to listen to Jesus. And what is Jesus saying to us now, who are caught up in the conflict that is ripping our nation apart? I hear Jesus saying this to us:

"Everyone who listens to the Father and learns from him comes to me. No one has seen the Father except the one who is from God; only he has seen the Father. I tell you the truth, he who believes has everlasting life. I am the bread of life." (John 6)

"You have heard that it was said, 'Love your neighbor and hate your enemy.' But I tell you: Love your enemies and pray for those who persecute you." (Matthew 5)

"Then the King will say to those on his right, 'Come, you who are blessed by my Father; take your inheritance, the kingdom prepared for you since the creation of the world. For I was hungry and you gave me something to eat, I was thirsty and you gave me something to drink, I was a stranger and you invited me in, I needed clothes and you clothed me, I was sick and you looked after me, I was in prison and you came to visit me." (Matthew 25)

"My command is this: Love each other as I have loved you....You are my friends if you do what I command." (John 15)

Serious effort is necessary for us truly to listen, understand and obey. We must want to hear what Jesus is saying and how it applies to us. We must shut out the multitude of other "voices" clamoring for our attention. Only then can we really hear Jesus. At the last, when God draws the curtain upon the stage of time, it is certain that we will hear his voice. There will be no wax in our ears then. Either we will hear him say, "Depart from me, I never knew you;" or we will hear him say, "Welcome home, good and faithful servant."

When Jesus walked the dusty roads of Nazareth, his disciples were "hard of hearing." We are much like them. Eventually, those first century disciples listened and understood Jesus; then as they obeyed him, the Jesus Movement spread across the world. It is still spreading, offering hope and salvation to all people everywhere.

It is not too late for us to get the wax out of our ears and listen and learn from each other. We must not turn a deaf ear either to what hurting people are saying or to what God is saying. This is our day, our turn, to listen, learn, obey and love in ways that please God. If you will pause and quietly listen, really listen, you may hear the inner voice saying again, "Let anyone with ears listen!"

One Word: _____
How did this story help me change my life?

12

We Will Get Through This!

In times like these, hope enables us to affirm to ourselves and others, "We will get through this!" When spoken with courageous faith, those words can help hurting people believe they can handle their pain and move on.

When her husband died at age 41, Sarah Brown said those words to her two young daughters, Dean and Dot. In the lean years that followed, the girls never forgot their mother's determination to "make it" through the devastating loss of their father. Her grit gave them hope for their future. With the Lord's help, they made it through some tough days.

Two things always come to mind when I think about the word "through." The first is the 23rd Psalm in which we find this powerful word of hope: "Even though I walk through the valley of the shadow of death, I will fear no evil, for you are with me; your rod and your staff, they comfort me." King David's faith makes me want to shout!

His time to endure the darkness of the valley was at hand, but he did not plan to stop in it, or stay in it; he was determined to go **through** it! Sooner or later, suffering comes to each of us. But we have a choice. We can sit in it and pity our plight or we can walk on. We can believe that by the grace of God, we are going to walk through whatever valley we have to face. We can also choose, like David did, to believe that the Lord will be with us. And such faith overcomes our fear of evil so we can walk on unafraid.

I call this "the Through Principle." It can be applied to any horrendous situation that is thrust upon us. Instead of thinking of ourselves as victims, we can stand up and say to all who are listening, "We will get through this!"

The second thing that the word "through" brings to mind is the stirring song by Andrae Crouch, "Through It All." Crouch wrote and sang many wonderful songs but none touched my heart like this one:

I've had many tears and sorrows,
I've had questions for tomorrow,
there's been times I didn't know right from wrong.
But in every situation,
God gave me blessed consolation,
that my trials come to only make me strong.
Through it all,
through it all,
I've learned to trust in Jesus,
I've learned to trust in God.
Through it all,
through it all,
I've learned to depend upon His Word.
I've been to lots of places,
I've seen a lot of faces

there's been times I felt so all alone.
But in my lonely hours,
yes, those precious lonely hours,
Jesus lets me know that I was His own

Reflect on the inspiring faith Crouch shares in this song:

1. In every difficult situation God consoled me.
2. God has used my trials to make me strong.
3. Through it all, I have learned to trust in God and depend upon His Word.
4. Jesus has made my lonely hours precious with His Presence.
5. I have learned that I can depend on God no matter what I must face.

That is the kind of faith we all need during the trying times of our lives, faith that inspires us to grit our teeth and say, "We will get through this!" When Saint Paul grew weary of his "thorn in the flesh," he heard the Lord say, "My grace is sufficient for you." Though God allowed Paul to endure much suffering, Paul made his way through it all. His faith never wavered because he was confident that God's grace was all he needed.

In these days of social turmoil in America, and the uncertainty created by the novel coronavirus, we dare not think of ourselves as victims. We dare not think that we shall stay immersed in the pain and darkness of this valley. We must believe that, by the grace of God, we are going to walk through this valley!

We can work together to overcome racism. We can follow the health guidelines to protect ourselves and others from the deadly virus. We can defeat hatred with love. We can practice kindness in every situation. We can be peacemakers with our lips and our lives. We can trust God and rely on His Word. Together, we can create a better world for the next generation. We can walk on, resolutely saying to one and all, "We will get through this!"

One Word: _____
How did this story help me change my life?

13

God is Full of Surprises

The most important three-word sentence you will ever read is this: "God is love." That simple statement is found in the writing of John in the Bible. This truth is important because it reveals the nature of God. Love is the greatest attribute of God, a love God revealed when he sent his Son Jesus die on the cross for our sins.

The most important three-word sentence you can ever repeat is "Jesus loves me." Those are the beginning words of a simple song known all over the world.

Nothing you will ever learn is more important than the truth of those six words: God is love. Jesus loves me. When you respond to the love of Jesus, and surrender your life to him, you begin discovering many more wonderful things about God.

You discover, for example, that God is full of surprises, which some people, mistakenly I think, call coincidences. Over the years I have come to enjoy God's delightful surprises, one of which has been to introduce me to a "dynamite" disciple of Jesus. As you reflect on some ways God has surprised you, let me share one of my cherished surprises.

One summer when we were living in Demopolis, Alabama, a church member came to me on a Sunday morning with an unusual request. "There is a retired missionary visiting our church today, a charming person," my friend said. Would I please recognize her during worship and let her "say a word"?

As any pastor can tell you, it is rather dangerous to give the microphone to a stranger during a worship service. However, that day I felt no sense of alarm and agreed to honor the request. I knew nothing about the woman except her name. I had no idea where she had served as a missionary. So before the morning prayer, as a gesture of kindness to an elderly servant of God, I invited Julia Lake Kellersberger to offer a word of greeting to our people.

What happened when she took the mike was stunning. For about five minutes the little woman's "greeting" electrified the congregation – and me. We were spellbound, wanting her to keep on talking. I knew immediately that her brief comments were more exciting than any sermon I had preached in months. To this day I have wished I had had the good sense to surrender my sermon time to her that morning.

What did she say that was so stirring? Actually, it was no so much what she said as it was the manner in which she said it. How can I explain it? She simply radiated the presence, the joy, the glory of God! She was aglow with energy and enthusiasm. Expecting to see a weary, tottering old woman, I saw a radiant, captivating person who was totally alive!

I felt like talking off my shoes when she described where she had served. I knew I was standing on holy ground when she shared that with her husband, Eugene, a missionary and a medical doctor, she had served leprosy colonies in Central Africa for 24 years. That was the culminating chapter of their ministry; combining the years of their service, they served over a hundred years as missionaries in 27 countries on five continents. Together they visited and raised funds for leper colonies around the world.

Julia was 83 the Sunday she visited our church. Her husband had died but not before they had retired and spent several years at a retirement home in south Florida. She had driven her small Toyota to return to her roots, having been born in west Alabama on a farm near Linden. You will get a taste of her joyful spirit in the introduction to her delightful book, *The Bush is Burning*:

"As a child on a cotton plantation in the Deep South, I would swing high over our split-rail fence and wonder what lay beyond our neighbor's pasture. I did not like that fence! It kept me from seeing far enough. Later, when *Don't Fence Me In* became a popular song, I claimed it for my own. I want no fences, whether traditional, geographical or spiritual. I am Alabama-born but I am not Alabama-bound. I am proud to be a southerner unrestricted by the Mason-Dixon line and an American with global citizenship. The Master Architect broke down the middle wall of partition between me and all people, and I refuse to be re-fenced by man-made pickets. My circumscriptions are limited only by the firmament of heaven, the sunrise and the sunset. I do as I please, but I please to do the will of God for my life. That is why I have peace in my soul, joy in my heart and a song on my lips."

While Julia was visiting "her roots" for a few weeks, my wife and I accepted her invitation to share a meal in the little camper friends had provided during her visit. We enjoyed the "volcano" meal she prepared for us – mostly Mexican food stacked on a plate. Beside each plate was a tiny surprise wrapped in aluminum foil – an Alka Seltzer tablet which she claimed we would need after eating the volcano!

After the meal, and a brief conversation, Julia grasped our hands, slipped to her knees and began praying. The little camper suddenly seemed filled with the presence of God as Julia praised

Jesus and asked the Lord to bless each of us with a clear vision of His will for our lives.

Once again I did not want her to stop talking; the more she talked, the nearer God seemed.

Julia returned to her "mini-mansion" in south Florida and spent her last years "proclaiming the good news not with my lips but with my life." Responding to a rumor that Julia had died, a friend called to see if she was dead. "Not yet!" She replied. Amused by this call, Julia commented, "If any of us, regardless of our age, considers our work to be finished, then we are finished. We might as well put a sign over our door, 'Gone out of business.' Life is immortal until our life's work is done."

That last sentence had stuck with Julia all her life. Very sick as a baby, she was told the story of how she almost died one night. Her mother had rocked her in her arms all night, fearing Julia would not live until morning. That morning a visiting pastor cheered her weary mother with these words: "Daughter, your child is not going to die yet. Her lungs are too strong. God is working out his purpose, and her life is immortal until her life's work is done."

Finally, at age 89, Julia's work was done and in her own words, she moved into her "maxi-mansion" in the New Jerusalem, not needing a moving van because "all of my earthly possessions can be packed into my car, with room to spare." She had said to me, at age 83, "The older I get, I want more and more of less and less."

Today, I celebrate the goodness of God, the Father of our Lord Jesus, who continually surprises me by introducing me to some of his "dynamite" disciples. I am a blessed man for having known his servant, Julia Lake Kellersberger. I am amazed at the difference one disciple can make in the life of another.

One Word: _____

How did this story help me change my life?

14

Finding the Strength to Finish Well

In these fourth quarter years of my life I have pondered often the need to finish well the journey of life. I do not want to finish poorly so, before the horn sounds the game's end, I keep asking for the wisdom to get it right. Examples and connections come to mind.

Examples are important. Some are good, some bad. God blessed me with several excellent examples of how life ought to be lived. My Dad was the first. His example of integrity has influenced every day of my life. The pastor of my teen years, Si Mathison, was another. His joyful spirit inspired me to say, "If that is what a real Christian is like, then I want to be one!"

The example of several other pastor friends helped shape the direction of my life. Some were older; some were my peers. In each one I saw a genuine love for Christ and a servant heart that I wanted to emulate. As much as anyone, Paul Duffey exemplified for me the kind, humble, loving way a pastor may live out his retirement years. Griffin Lloyd inspired me to seek a deeper life in Christ. Red Hildreth's homespun preaching stirred me to become a more persuasive preacher.

Poor examples are valuable, revealing mistakes we should try to avoid. The Bible's King Solomon is an interesting example. For many years Solomon served God well, providing wisdom lessons that found a place in the Bible. For much of his life Solomon was a good example. The problem is that, despite his great wisdom, he did not finish well. His life ended in disgrace.

Why did Solomon not finish well? The Bible explains it simply: "his wives led him astray." We find this sad commentary in First Kings, chapter 11: *"As Solomon grew old, his wives turned his heart after other gods, and his heart was not fully devoted to the Lord his God, as the heart of David his father had been."* How do we explain Solomon's failure? Perhaps his power as the king intoxicated him to the extent that he ignored God and made his own rules. The sad result is the story of a man who had it all but lost it before crossing the finish line.

For a great example of one who endured to the end and finished well, we can find no better example than that of the Apostle Paul. After enduring severe persecution, incarceration and hardship, Paul sat chained in a Roman prison. Aware that his execution was imminent, Paul could have moaned about how God had deserted him. Instead he wrote these inspiring words to Timothy:

"For I am already being poured out as a drink offering, and the time of my departure has come. I have fought the good fight, I have finished the race, I have kept the faith. Henceforth there is laid up for me the crown of righteousness, which the Lord, the righteous judge, will award to me on that Day, and not to me but also to all who have loved his appearing" (2 Timothy 4:6-8).

Connections are as important as good examples. The ultimate connection is, of course, our bond to Jesus. He is the Vine; we are the branches. God's plan, shared with us by Jesus, is that we bear fruit as his disciples. That happens only if we remain connected to Jesus. His explanation is very clear: *"Apart from me you can do nothing."* Here is much more than the key to life; there is no life in the Spirit apart from union with Christ.

The connection to Jesus results in other life-sustaining relationships. All who are in union with Christ make up the "koinonia," the Christ-centered fellowship of believers. So when we belong to Jesus, we belong to everyone else who belongs to Jesus. This dynamic fellowship of those for whom "Jesus is Lord" is the very heart of the church. All of every race and nation are welcome to share the life and joy of this greatest of all connections. Love for Christ and one another is the distinguishing mark of this fellowship.

The richness of this fellowship became apparent to me while traveling and meeting with groups of Christians in other nations. In South America, Central America, India, Nepal, China, Africa and Europe, I discovered this remarkable fellowship of love among those who were connected to Jesus and to one another. In each fellowship I was welcomed as a "brother" by the believers in each family of Christ followers.

The Bible never suggests that the Christian journey is a "Lone Ranger" experience. Jesus needed Peter, James and John and the other apostles. Paul needed Barnabas, Silas and Timothy. We all need other believers in our lives, people to whom we may turn for wise counsel, encouragement, guidance and, sometimes, correction.

For more than a decade I have met monthly with six other retired pastors (now meeting on Zoom). What began as a casual lunch meeting became a sacred bond. Our fellowship reinforces our gratitude for the grace of God and our hope for the future of the church. The "presence" of these servants of Christ in my life spurs me to keep the faith and not falter in the last lap.

Two men with whom I served as pastors in one church, Earl Ballard and Jimmy Allen, became "brothers" in the richest sense of that word. Our continuing relationship illustrates the remarkable value of connections. My bond with these two pastors is a continuing source of joy, inspiration and encouragement in all the seasons of life. I thank God for the sacred connections that strengthen me to keep the faith, fight the good fight and finish well!

Finally, I must acknowledge the incredible significance of the scriptures in my journey. These key verses inspire me to stay the course:

Matthew 11:28-29 – *Come to me, all you who are weary and burdened, and I will give you rest. Take my yoke upon you and learn from me....* I found that I must "come to Jesus" daily! Going to Jesus constantly is necessary for me to stay in all circumstances yoked to Him. His rest provides the strength to take the next step. Going to Jesus daily, in prayer, in holy communion, in reading and digesting the scriptures, opens my heart to receive his grace. He called me to serve Him and promised to be with me to the end. He is faithful. I can count on that!

Ephesians 3:32 – *And be kind to one another, tenderhearted, forgiving one another, even as God in Christ forgave you.* Kindness always honors Christ. Tenderhearted kindness is the trademark of His servants. And life is impossible without forgiveness.

Galatians 2:20 – *I have been crucified with Christ and I no longer live, but Christ lives in me. The life I now live in the body, I live by faith in the Son of God, who loved me and gave himself for me.* When I surrendered to Jesus, I became alive to God. I live in Christ. Christ lives in me. Outside of Christ, there is no life. Living in Christ is the only way to live!

Philippians 4:13 – *I can do all things through Christ who strengthens me.* This is my "life verse" and it reminds me that in Him alone can I find the strength to remain a "good and faithful servant." His strengthening presence empowers me to serve Him.

To finish well, as a servant of Jesus, I must remain connected to Him, to my friends who are fellow servants of Jesus, and to His Living Word which provides my soul with bread for the journey. Of one thing I am certain: I cannot finish well in my own strength. I must have help. But, thanks be to God, that help is available! Perhaps nothing expresses this truth better than these words introduced to me by my wife Dean, my dearest fellow servant of Jesus:

O Christ I cannot do without Thee!
I cannot stand alone;
I have no strength, no goodness
Nor wisdom of my own.
But Thou, O blessed Savior,
Art all in all to me,
And perfect strength in weakness
Is theirs who lean on Thee.

Until then, Glory!

One Word: _____
How did this story help me change my life?

15

The High Cost of Identifying with Christ

While Republicans and Democrats struggle for control in America, I remind myself that my primary business is to live a genuine Christian life. Whatever my political persuasion, I have no greater obligation than to honor Jesus in every way possible. And the truth is, in America I have great freedom to do that.

There are many countries where practicing the Christian faith is risky business. A ministry called "Open Doors" releases annually a list of the top 50 countries where Christian persecution is most severe and the level of persecution is increasing. Open Doors reports that more than 260 million Christians "experience high, very high or extreme persecution for following Jesus." One of every 8 Christians in the world lives in a culture where Christianity is illegal, forbidden or punished.

Last year 2,983 Christians were killed for their faith, 9,488 churches and Christian buildings were attacked, and 3,711 believers were detained without trial, arrested, and sentenced or imprisoned.

Not surprisingly, North Korea and Afghanistan top of the list of nations with the worst persecution of Christians. In North Korea there are some 50,000 Christians in prison or labor camps today. The Kim family controls every aspect of life in North Korea. Islamic extremism remains the dominant global driver of persecution.

How is persecution defined? The answer: Hostility experienced as a result of identifying with Christ. This can mean torture, imprisonment, loss of home and possessions, losing custody of children, beheadings, rape and even death. More vulnerable than men, women risk sexual violence, torture, forced marriage and much more.

These statistics may be boring but I mention them because each of these numbers represents a brother or sister who is a member of the global family of Christians. The believers who died for their faith last year, and every year, are "family." And while it has never been a "big day" for us in America, the first Sunday in November is the International Day of Prayer for the Persecuted Church.

Were Saint Paul, who was severely persecuted for his faith in Jesus, alive, he would no doubt encourage us pray for our persecuted brethren every day and not just in November. It was Paul who said to the Corinthians, *"And if one member suffers, all the members suffer with it; if one member is honored, all the members rejoice with it."*

More Christians died for their faith during the 20th Century than in all the previous 19 centuries combined. This disturbing fact reminds me to thank God for the freedom of worship we enjoy in America. In China thousands of Christians are not permitted to gather for worship. Believers meet in homes, often in secret, for fear of being arrested and persecuted. Though the deadly coronavirus has come to us from China, inspiring stories have also come from that nation.

One Chinese pastor was sentenced to 12 years in jail for refusing to stop preaching the gospel to his small congregation. He was forced to wade daily into the filthy waste system of his town. That was his "work" station. Every day the pastor went about his work with faith that stunned his captors. They would hear him singing while in the cesspool, "And He walks with me, and He talks with me, and He tells me I am His own, and the joy we share, as we tarry there, none other has ever known." What a witness! And from a stinking cesspool!

By the time the pastor was released, and resumed preaching, his church had tripled in size. God was at work in that pastor's suffering, working for good as He always does with those who love Him.

While we in America may not be severely persecuted for practicing our faith, there is still a price to be paid for identifying with Christ. We do well to remember that though we shall suffer, God permits suffering and often uses it to advance the gospel and to test and refine our faith. Every trial we face can become an opportunity to honor Christ with authentic faith.

I am inspired by people who remain strong and steady disciples of Jesus despite their trials and heartaches. My sisters Neva Williams and Margie Flomer are two such disciples who have remained winsome and positive believers despite the loss of their husbands. Neither has ever allowed self-pity in the door. Margie lost John some 30 years ago and has inspired our family by "living for others" rather than lamenting her loss. Her children and grandchildren adore her for her untiring self-giving. Margie taught students with special needs in the public school for 32 years.

When Neva's husband, Gene, learned he had incurable cancer, he wrote this inspiring letter to all who were praying for him: "The joy of God's love is so marvelous that the hard things in this life become manageable. I am in His wonderful hands and I am at perfect peace. Thank you for your love and prayers." His faith did not flinch in the face of death.

Neva has inspired our family by demonstrating that same positive faith in God. Though she had buried both her sons, as the result of accidents, and a little later her husband, Neva chose to spend the last 20 years, not as a grieving mother and widow, but a servant of others. How? By serving as a volunteer at the Montgomery Cancer Center where Gene received his final treatments. Like Margie, she has a servant heart.

When you say your prayers tonight, pray for all who suffer because of violence and persecution in our world. Ask the Lord Jesus to fill you with the joy that will give you a happy face as you move through the trials of your journey. Your face, and your faith, can inspire others to identify with the Christ who alone can help us end the persecution that exists in our fallen world.

One Word: _____
How did this story help me change my life?

16

Acts of Kindness Inspire Kindness

One billboard around town gets my attention. The billboard is blank except for three words in the center. The words are "Just Be Kind." That's all there is. No person or business claims credit for the statement.

Those words got me to thinking about myself. I write about kindness. I advocate kindness. I encourage others to be kind. But questions pop up when I take an honest look at myself. Am I practicing what I preach? Do I go out of my way to commit acts of kindness? In what ways am I being kind to the people whose lives I touch? I realized I did not have many good answers to my questions.

Jesus had a word or two to say about the matter. In his Sermon on the Mount Jesus said, "Not everyone who says to me, 'Lord, Lord,' will enter the kingdom of heaven, but only he who does the will of my Father who is in heaven." I know that applies to me, just as it applies to every Christ follow Jesus is saying, "Walter, you can talk or write about kindness all day but if you don't practice it, your words will mean nothing. Talk is simply talk, but being kind to others is the will of my Father, and doing His will is what matters."

So I started at home, looking for simple ways to be kind to my wife, Dean. Like charity, kindness must begin at home. Only when I have kindness in place at home can I with integrity practice kindness outside my home. And I have discovered something wonderful; the more I am intentionally kind to Dean, the more she responds with kindness to me. Kindness inspires kindness.

The more I thought about kindness, the more I realized that I know many kind people, folks who never write about it or talk about it; they just do it. Every day they are doing what the billboard suggests; they are just being kind. And there has never been a time when kindness was needed more in our nation.

Civility has been replaced with name-calling and vulgar language. Crowds of people cheer those who speak disrespectfully of others. Candidates for public office no longer discuss the merits of issues; instead they viciously attack one another with derogatory words. Kind words are seldom heard nor expected.

Yet kindness remains alive. Here and there we see it practiced and when we see it, it inspires us to practice it ourselves. You will be able to think of several examples in your own arena; I will cite one that inspired me.

When Hurricane Sally came through central Alabama recently, heavy rain and wind knocked the power out for hundreds of homes and businesses. When this happened in Opelika, my friend Martha Hill, who is 86 and widow, said she was relived a few hours later when the lights came back on.

Martha got to thinking about how the power was restored so quickly and realized it was because linemen of Opelika Power Service were out in the bad weather, risking their lives, to repair the broken lines. Recently a tree limb fell on a power line in Martha's neighborhood and started a fire. Men from the fire department and linemen from OPS again worked in bad weather to put out the fire and restore power within an hour.

This time Martha decided kindness was in order. She called her friend Edith Walker and suggested they invite their neighbors to join them in an act of kindness. They quickly raised enough money to purchase 40 loaves of sweet breads from her friend Anna Freeman who operates Serenity Farms & Bakery. The next day Martha and Edith delivered 20 loaves of Lemon Blueberry bread and 20 loaves of Banana bread to the linemen of Opelika Power Service. It was an expression of kindness by a grateful neighborhood. The OPS Director, Derek Lee, was so impressed he gave the two ladies a tour of the center.

So, while I was thinking about kindness, and writing about kindness, Martha and Edith were out practicing kindness – kindness that tasted like delicious sweet bread on that day in Opelika. At her age, was it difficult for Martha to spearhead this act of kindness? Not at all. "You cannot imagine the joy I felt in showing kindness to these fine men who serve our community so well," Martha said.

Now, you dear reader, have been reading about kindness, and thinking about it. Hopefully, these few words have inspired you to get up and go practice kindness to prove my point – that kindness inspires kindness. People need it. You can do it. Have fun!

One Word: _____
How did this story help me change my life?

17

When You Don't Feel Like Singing

When I feel good and things are going my way, I feel like singing. I am a Christian and Christians sing. We sing because we are happy and free for we know His eye is on the sparrow. But when the bottom falls out, it is not easy to sing. So how do you sing when you feel like crying?

Before I try to answer that question, let me say a good word about crying. Crying is not bad; crying is good for you. When our little boy died, my wife did not start crying. Her sorrow was bottled up inside. Weeks went by and Dean became sick. Then a wise family doctor said to her, "Honey, if you don't start crying, this grief is going to kill you!" She began crying and was soon well – without taking any medicine "to calm her nerves." God created us with tear glands and tear ducts because our eyes require tears in order to function well every day. When trouble comes, our tears moisten the soil of the soul so that hope can grow within us.

There must, of course, be an end to crying because we are brokenhearted. The Psalmist David understood this. He admitted, in Psalm 42, that his tears had been "his food day and night," but he realized he had to stop being downcast and put his hope in God. His sobbing turned to a "cry" for mercy. Then David rejoiced for God "heard his cry" for mercy and "put a new song in my mouth." And that, beloved, is the answer! We can stop crying and start singing when the Lord's healing touch produces a new song in our hearts.

David did not gloss over his pain and despair but in the Psalms his basic advice is to praise the Lord and give thanks for his lovingkindness. He urges us to "sing to the Lord and tell of his wonderful acts." Such singing, even with a few tears in our eyes, helps us move through our heartache as the Lord is healing our hearts. When we determine to sing, the Lord helps us to continue singing as we sing through the pain.

I love the phrase, "He keeps me singing as I go." It is in a song penned by Luther Bridges titled "There's within my heart a Melody." This is the chorus: "Jesus, Jesus, Jesus, sweetest name I know, fills my every longing, keeps me singing as I go." In the second verse Bridges reminds us of a great truth – that when life falls apart, Jesus can heal the broken strings of our hearts and put a redeeming melody in our hearts. That verse says it all: "All my life was wrecked by sin and strife, discord filled my heart with pain; Jesus swept across the broken strings, stirred the slumbering chords again."

Across the years trouble and discord have often filled my heart with pain but time and again I have surrendered my pain to Jesus and he has put a new song in my heart. At 88 I am asking Him to do it again so I can continue to testify with Luther Bridges that He keeps me singing as I go.

Reading the Holy Scriptures helps me regain an eternal perspective. There is no doubt that Paul and Silas cried when they were stripped and beaten. Luke describes in Acts 16 how the two men were stripped and severely flogged, thrown into prison and their feet fastened in stocks. Yes, they cried in pain when they were beaten. But they stopped crying. And what Luke says seems incredible: "About midnight Paul and Silas were praying and singing hymns to God"!

Stories like that stir me to believe that I too can sing when I am hurting. And there are so many songs that help us do what David said do – "sing to the Lord and tell of his wonderful acts." When my burdens seem more than I can handle, I can sing "Jesus took my Burden." Its chorus lifts my spirit: "Yes, Jesus took my burden I could no longer bear. Yes, Jesus took my burden in answer to my prayer; my anxious fears subsided, my spirit was made strong, for Jesus took my burden and left me with a song." Yes, when I cry for mercy, He takes my burden!

A song like "Great is Thy Faithfulness" restores my soul. So often I have needed "pardon for sin and a peace that endureth." I have needed his dear presence "to cheer and to guide." I have needed "strength for today and bright hope for tomorrow." And when I turned to Jesus, He met my need. I tremble when I sing the words, "All I have needed thy hand hath provided"! Oh, yes! His hand! His hand! Great is the Lord's faithfulness!

When apathy stops me from singing, the Spirit gently reminds me to start singing the song that puts me back in the game. It is a simple song titled "Others." Its words remind me why God sent Jesus into the world: "Lord, help me live from day to day, in such a self-forgetful way, that even when I kneel to pray, my prayer shall be for others." One of the Lord's "wonderful acts" is reminding us that when we reach out to others who need a word of cheer, our own broken hearts are being healed. God does not save us so we can go to heaven; he saves us so we can bring others with us on our way to heaven.

I dearly love the song, "Until Then," by Stuart Hamblen. It reminds me that heartaches are stepping stones on the road to heaven. When my load is heavy, Hamblen's words help me stop whining and start singing again: "My heart can sing when I pause to remember a heartache here is but a stepping stone, along a trail that's winding always upward; this troubled world is not my final home. But until then my heart will go on singing; until then with joy I'll carry on, until the day my eyes behold the city, until the day God calls me home." Oh Yes!

Now, if you want a faith that can keep you singing, it all boils down to this: surrender to Jesus. That is the secret. When we surrender to Jesus, he begins living in our heart and gives us a faith that keeps us singing – until he calls us home. Salvation is in Jesus. Life is in Jesus. Either you are in Jesus or you are not. Either you are alive to God or you are dead in sin. And the only way to get in Jesus is by surrendering your life to him.

When you surrender to Jesus and let him live in you, and you live in him, he gives you the grace to keep on singing no matter your circumstances. You will find incredible joy in Jesus and you will find yourself singing, "He is Lord, He is Lord; He is risen from the dead and He is Lord! Every knee shall bow, every tongue confess that Jesus Christ is Lord!"

I have absolute confidence that if you surrender to Jesus, he will put a new song in your heart and give you the grace to keep on singing even when your cheeks are stained with tears. He has done it for me. He will do it for you. Glory!

One Word: _____
How did this story help me change my life?

18

Choosing the Right Coat

Christians who boldly stand up against injustice must be sure they are properly dressed. Their success in opposing wrongdoing will be limited if they are not "clothed" with humility.

New Testament writers Peter and Paul both counsel Christ followers to *"clothe themselves"* with humility because *"God opposes the proud but gives grace to the humble."*

Paul, in his Letter to the Colossians, speaks of Christian virtues as though each was a garment to be worn, a coat perhaps. He urges his friends to "put on" kindness, humility, meekness, and *"above all, put on love."*

Humility, then, is a choice but not the only choice. Arrogance is another coat on the rack, but one which the Bible counsels us not to put on. In fact Jesus repeatedly warns against pride. In one parable Jesus describes the striking difference between a tax collector and an arrogant Pharisee. When the Pharisee prayed, he thanked God for his superiority over evildoers. The tax collector prayed humbly, *"God, have mercy on me, a sinner."*

Jesus explains the lesson of the parable with these words: *"I tell you, this sinner, not the Pharisee, returned home justified before God. For those who exalt themselves will be humbled, and those who humble themselves will be exalted."* The message is clear: God rewards the humble but humiliates the proud.

That warning teaches us that humility is a lovely coat while arrogance is an ugly and dangerous garment to wear. To know the grave danger of pride we have but to read a few of Solomon's Proverbs:

"Pride leads to disgrace, but with humility comes wisdom" (11:2).

"Pride only breeds quarrels, but wisdom is found in those who take advice" (13:10).

"Pride goes before destruction, a haughty spirit before a fall" (16:18).

"Pride ends in humiliation, while humility brings honor" (29:23).

It is no accident that when Peter urges us to humble ourselves before God that he speaks immediately about our enemy, the devil. Satan does indeed prowl around us "like a roaring lion," and one way he "devours" us is by tempting us to think we are superior to others. White supremacy is but one example of how Satan has deceived some of us into ignoring Paul's sage advice: *"Do not think of yourself more highly than you ought."*

Though some scripture may seem ambiguous to us, what Paul says to the Romans is quite clear: *"Do not be proud, but be willing to associate with people of low position. Do not be conceited."*

Why such a strong warning from the Bible against pride? Because arrogance is self-destructive as well as ugly. It will destroy you; it separates you from people – and from God. Wear a pompous coat and you will soon lose the respect of the people you thought were your friends. People will not want to be around you because a haughty spirit is repulsive.

If we are to successfully resist and defeat the devil, we must constantly refuse to throw the ugly cloak of arrogance around our shoulders. When we pick out the clothes to wear each day, we must always reach for the garment of humility and put it on. It is the dress code God has chosen for His children.

Remember that every day as you relate to others, sharing your opinions and doing what you do. This truth you can take to the bank: nobody, absolutely no one, will be glad to see you if you are wearing the obnoxious coat of arrogance. If you are wearing one now, take it off and stuff it in the burning barrel. Don't take it to the Salvation Army; all the folks there have better sense than to wear it. Some of them are eating soup there because they did not take the Bible's warning seriously.

Speaking of taking the Bible seriously, consider the current plight of our nation in light of what God said one day to King Solomon: *"If my people, who are called by my name, will humble themselves and pray and seek my face and turn from their wicked ways, then I will hear from heaven, and I will forgive their sin and will heal their land"* (2 Chronicles 7:14).

Think through what God said. He did not expect or ask Solomon to heal the land. The healing of the land depended upon what God's people did. If, God says, if **my people** will humble themselves and repent of their wicked ways, then God would heal their land. This means that the solution is not in the hands of the President, or the Congress, or the Governors; it is in our hands. We, the people, must humble ourselves, repent and pray. To seek God's face means that we admit that nothing matters more than pleasing God!

It all begins with humility. The arrogant must become humble – and then pray. If, dear reader, you are one of God's people, then please humble yourself and pray. Pray for forgiveness for our wicked ways – and you know what they are. Then humbly trust God for the healing that America needs.

If enough of us, who are God's people, will choose daily to put on the coat of humility, and wear it in the midst of the evil and hatred that arrogance has bred among us, then surely God will hear our prayers and heal our land. There is no doubt this is our best hope for the future.

One Word: _____
How did this story help me change my life?

19

You are One of Us Now

The coronavirus has changed our lives in countless ways. Sunday mornings are different. Four months ago I preached in front of an audience, looking into the eyes of the people who had gathered for worship. Now I preach while looking into a camera with no one else in the room. It is a strange and difficult experience.

I sorely miss the contact with people. In earlier days I stood at the door at the end of worship services, shaking hands and greeting people. Most people smiled and walked on, eager to get to lunch. Some offered a kind word, such as "Liked your sermon," or "Good message pastor." They were being "nice" but what I longed to hear was a word from someone whose heart God had touched. Like the man who one Sunday gripped my hand with both of his and, with tears in his eyes, said "Brother Walter, the Lord met my need today."

On another Sunday a woman blessed me by saying, "I want you to know that as our service began today, I asked the Lord to speak to me. He did, and that's why I went forward and give my life to Jesus." Comments like that will inspire most any preacher to get excited about the high privilege of preaching the gospel. What any preacher worth his salt wants is not being told he preached a "nice" sermon but learning that his sermon helped a few people get connected or reconnected to Jesus. Preaching at its best allows people to hear a fresh word from God.

While I have been encouraged by many people as they were leaving church, I have also been shocked and discouraged. In my preaching I have sometimes alluded to my own sins and the joy of receiving God's forgiveness. After doing so one Sunday, a woman twice my age took my hand and said with disgust, "I find it very disappointing to learn that my pastor is a sinner!" She walked on briskly, not waiting for an answer and leaving me speechless.

That experience made me aware that there are a few people who do not understand that pastors hurt, bleed and cry – and disobey God – like the rest of the human race. Yes, pastors cry too. On rare occasions I have wept during a sermon. One Sunday I broke down and cried while sharing how much it hurt to see our little boy suffer and die with leukemia. My tears were spontaneous. I did not have "cry here" in my sermon notes.

After the worship service a man in his mid-sixties, ignoring my offer to shake hands, embraced me with a bear hug. Then, with tears in his eyes, he said, "You are one of us now; we know you hurt like we do." I was too deeply moved to speak so I just embraced him again as tears moistened my own cheeks.

Three years later that man's oldest son had major surgery. I was in the hospital waiting room with my friend and his wife when the doctor walked in and shared the dreaded news that their son had died on the operating table. "He had a massive heart attack during surgery and we could not save him," the doctor said. There, in that small consultation room, we wept together again – and reached out to God for help. I thanked God for the bonding of my heart with my friend's heart, in years past, so that I could share the awful anguish of those sad moments. Sometimes God uses pain and tears to help us move from casual to creative relationships in which the love of God may be known and shared.

God has a way of using hard times to bless those who trust Him. Our brokenness can be the doorway to blessings. I experienced that in my own family. During his teen years one of my sons had a drinking problem. One Saturday morning a man unknown to me appeared at my door. He introduced himself by explaining that his son was a drinking buddy of one of my sons. He said, "A few hours ago, about three o'clock this morning, my son came home drunk. I got angry and decided to beat the hell out of him, but it turned out that he beat the hell out of me."

I had noticed several bruises on his face and realized now why his face was a mess. He continued by saying, "I came to see you thinking that you being a preacher with the same problem I have that you might could help me." Stunned, I said to the man, "Well, my friend, I don't think I can help you, but I know someone who can help both of us, so come on in and let's talk to the good Lord about our boys."

Thus began a relationship with another man who reached out to me because he felt I was "one of us." The Lord was teaching me that being vulnerable about my flaws opens the way for people to identify with me – and more importantly with the God who hurts when His children hurt.

That time of prayer and sharing was the beginning of a good friendship. We prayed together, talked together, and grew spiritually together. I believe the Lord helped us become better fathers because we shared a common burden. And a few months later the man, together with his wife and sons, walked down the aisle of our church to give their lives to Jesus.

You will understand then why on Sunday mornings, when I am listening to a video sermon on my television screen, I long to stand at the church door again and shake hands with someone who says, "Pastor, the Lord met my need today."

How long, O Lord, how long?

One Word: _____

How did this story help me change my life?

20

Saying Goodbye to a Dying Friend

The older I get the more I realize how little I know. There are so many things nobody ever told me. For example, how do you tell a dying friend goodbye? During the past decade I have had to do that several times. Each time I felt like I was flying by the seat of my pants.

I remember how strangely uncomfortable I felt standing beside the hospital bed of my dying sister, then my wife's sister, then my father, and later my mother. I struggled to know what to say – to either family members or the person dying.

It seems cowardly to hide behind cliches like "silence is golden" or "just being present is enough." I know some are content to say nothing and assume that "the ministry of presence" is sufficient. That may be true but I still long to come up with at least a few words that might comfort, encourage and inspire faith. When I am the one dying, I hope my family and friends will say something to bless me, and not just stand by with their hands in their pockets waiting for me to take my last breath.

Some loquacious people do not have my problem. And their ceaseless talking makes me want to scream. I confess that it troubles me to encounter a talkative friend or relative quoting scripture and trying to get someone saved in their last hour. I think the time for such pleading is probably past, but then, who am I to judge?

I am big on holding hands. I have spent hours holding the hand of dying family members and friends. Occasionally I spoke of times past, of joyous memories we shared, but later I felt regret. For example, I still regret not telling my dad and my mother how grateful I was for the lessons they taught me and the examples they were for me.

One lovely spring day Shirley and Al called from Alaska. After a few pleasantries, Al's voice broke as he began telling us that Shirley had only a few weeks to live. At that moment, I realized they were calling to tell us goodbye. Shirley's faith was strong. She assured us she was at peace with God and would be waiting for us on the other side. But words failed me. Finally, I was able to tell Shirley I loved her and that her friendship had blessed my life. Was that enough? I don't know. Shirley died in less than a month.

Two years later the phone rang again. Now it was Al's turn to say goodbye. "I have terminal cancer," he said softly, "and my doctor says I don't have much time left." Again, words seemed caught in my throat. Al had been one of my dearest friends for forty years. I should have told him how much he had meant to me but the words never came from my lips. I did manage to tell Al that his strong faith would see him through to the end and that I was sure we would see each other again. A few weeks later word came that Al had died and I thought of so many things I wished I had said to him.

In the mail one day was a letter from a dear friend in Pensacola. The envelope was blue with snowflakes on it. Inside, the letter was dated September 13 but Irene's greeting was strange.

She began by writing, "Merry Christmas and Happy New Year!" Not exactly what you would expect from a letter written in mid-September. I read on, "I am sending this greeting early because if I wait, it may be too late. My pancreatic cancer is spreading and my time is not."

Tears hindered my reading the next lines for a moment. Then I almost laughed as Irene's faith jumped off the page. She said, "The good news is that I am not in pain, I feel great, and I am enjoying living with my daughter and her family." Then she scribbled a bold "HOORAY!" Her letter ended with these words: "My time is short. However, it is a happy time and I thank you for being my friends. Happy Holidays! See you over there!"

Immediately my wife and I both wrote Irene a letter and mailed them the next day. We thanked her for her marvelous faith, her wonderful friendship, and the precious ways she had been a blessing to us. We thanked her for the memories, especially those of times when her contagious laughter had us in stitches. Over the years her laughter had triggered so many moments of joy in our hearts. She was genuine to the core and always full of the joy of the Lord.

But guess what? Irene died the day before our letters arrived! I had finally gotten some words together to share with a dying friend – but they arrived too late. So you can understand why I want to do a better job of saying goodbye to the next dying friend who calls me for a final conversation.

Until then, my prayer will be simple: "Lord, help me know what to say and how to say it helpfully. And please, Lord, do save me from saying too much!"

One Word: _____
How did this story help me change my life?

Showing Faith by What You Do

In these pandemic days of protests, tension and turmoil, there is a lot of talk. The media have filled the airwaves and newspapers with so much talk that many of us are weary of "listening to the news." I have done my share of adding to the mountain of rhetoric that the coronavirus and racism have spawned.

All this talk caused me to recall what the biblical writer James has to say about faith and deeds. Granted, there are some passages in the Bible that are difficult to understand. But the Book of James is an exception. Here is an example of how James wrote with such clarity that no one can miss his meaning:

"What good is it, my brothers, if a man claims to have faith but has no deeds? Can such faith save him? Suppose a brother or sister is without clothes and daily food. If one of you says to him, 'Go, I wish you well; keep warm and well fed,' but does nothing about his physical needs, what good is it? In the same way, faith by itself, if it is not accompanied by action, is dead. But someone will say, 'You have faith; I have deeds.' Show me your faith without deeds, and I will show you my faith by what I do."

Neither talk nor faith will feed a person who is hungry. As the nationwide debate about what "to do" continues in the street and in Congress, we need to remember that many of our neighbors are hungry and many others are living in fear. We dare not forget these neighbors while we argue endlessly about solutions to our problems.

A picture of two women delivering cakes to firemen got me to thinking about the good people who are serving others while some of us write and talk about issues. I did not recognize the women at first; they had facemasks on. Then I saw their names and smiled for they are dear friends of mine, Martha Hill and Jennifer Jones.

When I asked why they were giving cakes to the firemen, Martha said, "We actually began with the Opelika Police Department. We heard the morale of the Police Department was low because of recent hostility toward the police so we got Kelly Cox to bake several large pound cakes. We delivered the cakes to the police with a note of appreciation from our church (Trinity Methodist)."

Sharing cakes with the police got Martha thinking about the firemen. Finding out there are 75 firemen, she quickly raised $525 from several women in her church. This was enough to get Kelly Cox to make 75 cakes which Martha and Jennifer delivered to the firemen.

I had to ask, who is Kelly Cox? It turns out Kelly has a cottage baking business in Opelika named Honeycomb Sweets. She got the name for her business from a Bible verse, Proverbs 16:24, "Gracious words are a honeycomb, sweet to the soul and healing to the bones." You will love this: Kelly's specialty, the cakes she baked for the firemen, are called "kindness cakes." (You can reach Kelly on Instagram or Facebook or by calling 334-524-4815.)

Kelly not only loves to bake; she also enjoys sharing as well as selling her cakes. Last week she baked a bunch of cakes and delivered them to people in her neighborhood. "The world felt so dark that I decided to make some happy tummies," she said. "Braxton (her husband) and I delivered cakes, leaving some on doorsteps. We knocked on doors and said, 'Have a good day.' It's a ministry to make people happy. It's not about the food, it's about sharing a little sweetness."

After sharing kindness cakes with over 100 police and fire personnel, Martha decided to deliver even more cakes to her friends at the Post Office. Why? "Well," Martha replied, "during the lonely winter days I would sometimes go to the Post Office just to be around my friends there and have them lift my spirit."

Martha is only 84. She copes with the sorrow of losing her husband Hoyt four years ago by offering kindness to the men and women who put their lives on the line every day for the people of her community. James would say, "Way to go, Martha; you show me your faith by what you do!" Martha tells me there are many others in her church offering kindness to others in a ministry called "Feeding God's Children." Hundreds of meals are being provided to children and others in the community who need food.

Martha also shares in a project in her neighborhood to show appreciation to the Sanitation Department workers. "We found out that the same four men regularly serve us by picking up garbage, trash and recycle items. So we collected homemade and store-bought goodies which we shared to show our appreciation for them," Martha said. "We even gave a gift card and some gifts to our mail carrier!"

In Montgomery, Mercy House is showing mercy to hundreds of people in an impoverished neighborhood of west Montgomery. A ministry of New Walk of Life Church on Council Street, Mercy House serves 100 hot meals a day to hungry people; in addition,

200 snack bags given out every day. Every week 70 families are given enough food to feed a family of five for a week. Pastor Ken Austin says, "We can do this only because of the generous support of caring people in the River Region."

Youth of the church are awarded money for A's and B's on their report cards. Pastor Austin tells me that during the night following busy fourth of July activities, he had the "honor" of getting out of bed and delivering food to a family that called and said, "Pastor, we don't have anything to eat."

The deeds described above are only a few of the many expressions of love which are going on all around us, for there are many good Americans whose faith is not dead and useless. We dare not focus so much on the "bad news" that we miss seeing the good deeds of our fellow Americans, deeds that can inspire us to practice good deeds ourselves.

Opinions matter. Words are important. But James would remind us, in the heat of the ugly debate going on in our nation, words without action, without deeds, are useless. Words will not warm a man who needs a coat. Words will not quiet the growling of a hungry man's stomach.

For many years I have sung a fine hymn in worship with others that our friend James would enjoy singing with us. The song, "Lead On, O King Eternal," includes this verse: *"Lead on, O King eternal, till sin's fierce war shall cease, and holiness shall whisper the sweet amen of peace. For not with swords loud clashing, nor roll of stirring drums; with deeds of love and mercy the heavenly kingdom comes."* That final phrase is bold-faced in my memory box for it says it all.

The talk with continue until all our stammering tongues lie silent in the grave. In the meantime, genuine faith will reveal itself in deeds of love and mercy for faith without deeds of love is fraudulent.

One Word: _____
How did this story help me change my life?

In the Right Place at the Right Time

Few things in life are more wonderful than being in the right place at the right time. I find it refreshing to re-call some of those times in my life and thank God for put-ting me where I needed to be.

Do I really believe that almighty God, the creator of heav-en and earth, arranges for his servants to be in a certain place at a certain time? Seems impossible, doesn't it? After all, there are nearly 8 billion people living on earth today. Well, though it may seem like "a bit of a stretch," I believe it. I believe it because I have experienced it several times. I will explain.

When our four sons were small, we stopped at a motel in Tarpon Springs, Florida one night during a vacation. The boys had insisted that I find a motel with a swimming pool, so I did, and soon we were all in the pool.

At one point I heard someone say, "What's wrong with Tim?" I looked around and saw Tim, who was six years old, floating motionless, head down in the water about 15 feet away. The boys said later than I "parted the water" racing to rescue Tim and pull him out of the pool.

Remembering nothing about the procedure for CPR, I turned Tim on his stomach and slapped his back a few times until he began spitting up water. We thought he had drowned but he regained consciousness and began breathing again. God had spared his life. I was in the right place at the right time.

One morning years ago , while driving to the post office, I found myself stopping at the home of a widow in our church. I had not planned to stop. I got out of the car and began walking up the sidewalk toward the woman's front door. I had no idea why I was going to see her. Before I could reach the door, the woman burst out the door crying, and saying to me, "Thank God you are here! I just received word that my son has been killed in Vietnam!" I shared her grief as best I could and prayed with her. I was stunned as I drove away, realizing that God had put me in the right place at the right time.

Back in the days when Methodists still practiced visitation evangelism, I met and prayed with six men who left the church to go visiting, two by two. As the odd man out, I started to my car to go visiting alone when another man walked up and said, "Pastor, the Lord told me I needed to go visiting with you tonight."

We got in my car and drove away, not knowing where we might go. I knew my friend had found victory over alcohol addiction so I suggested we go visit Mike, a man with a serious drinking problem. It would be a "cold call," since we had not called ahead. Before I could ring the doorbell at his home, his wife opened the door and said, "Oh Thank God you've come! Mike is in the back, on his knees, praying that someone would come help him!"

My companion witnessed to Mike about how the Lord had helped him stop drinking and find new life in Christ. We prayed with Mike and that night he gave his heart to Jesus and invited Him to help him overcome his addiction. In the months that followed, Mike became a new man in Christ. His decision helped him restore his marriage and regain the respect of his children. I knew that night I was in the right place at the right time.

One night, about midnight, a woman called, waking me up, to tell me that her neighbor was going to kill himself. "I thought you would want to know," she said, "since he is a member of your church." I dressed and went to the man's home, not having ever met him. The door was open but no one responded when I knocked and called out. So I walked in, speaking loudly, "Is anyone home?"

I found Jim (not his real name) in his bedroom. He was sitting on the side of the bed, a weary, broken man, holding in his lap a 38 revolver. I introduced myself as his pastor. He spoke slowly, like a man without hope. "Preacher, my wife left me for another man. She took both the kids with her. I am an alcoholic. My drinking has destroyed my family. The bank is foreclosing on my home. I've lost my job. I have nothing else to live for."

Nothing in my seminary training had prepared me for such a moment. I decided to keep him talking in the hope that I might think of something to say. He kept talking and after several minutes seemed to have relaxed a bit. Finally, I sat down beside him and promised to come back the next day and help him figure out what to do next. I assured him that God loved him and did not want him to take his own life. Then, ever so gently, I asked him to give me the gun.

He said nothing and did not move. The silence was deafening, until at last, he said, "OK," and handed me the gun. He agreed to get some much needed sleep and I drove home, a fully loaded pistol on the seat beside me. In the months that followed, several men in our church helped him save his home, get his job back, and manage the pain of losing his family. The help and love of those men saved Jim's life. I knew that night I had been in the right place at the right time.

Leukemia claimed the life of our son David in his third year. For eight long months we watched helplessly as the disease slowly robbed him of life. Finally, during his last night, my wife and I took turns rocking him in a chair beside our bed. About five o'clock, as the morning light was breaking, he died in my arms. I could have been somewhere else, miles away, or sleeping fitfully nearby. But I was there with him, holding him in my arms as he breathed his last breath. Graciously, God had me in the right place at the right time.

Though precarious, and often bewildering, life is precious. And few experiences are more exhilarating than those moments when you know that God has you in the right place at the right time. For such a gift, no one will ever be more grateful than I am.

One Word: _____
How did this story help me change my life?

Making a Difference When Hearts are Broken

When our friends lose a loved one, we want them to know we care about their pain. We do that in different ways. We may send cards, flowers or sometimes a book about grief. We may attend the funeral or the visitation. We may call to offer our condolences in a more personal way.

My friend Ed Williams has taught me an additional way to offer sympathy to those who are struggling with sorrow. Ed often sends others a unique blessing – the gift of his memories of the deceased. Having taught journalism at Auburn University for almost 30 years, Ed has stored in his memory bank many precious memories of his students. Since retirement, he enjoys rich friendship by keeping in touch with many of his students. When death invades their ranks, Ed sometimes offers the gift of memories he can recall.

Ed's memories extend back into the years he spent in the newspaper business before he became an Auburn professor. Gifted with a remarkable memory, Ed can recall events and conversations with many friends made in several Alabama towns. One of those friends died recently at the young age of 36, a man named Wilson Pippin. He and his family were special friends of Ed's for many years. Ed had visited in their home many times and Ed had known Wilson since he was a little boy.

When Wilson died, his mother Babs called Ed and asked him to select a scripture for the funeral that reminded him of Wilson when he was a young boy. Ed chose a verse from Psalms 127 – *"Children are a gift from the LORD; they are a real blessing"* (Good News Translation). The family's pastor used that verse in his eulogy in the memorial service at the Methodist Church in Lagrange, Georgia in October.

Ed explained to Babs and her husband Mike that he believed God gave Wilson to them as a gift for 36 years before taking him home. And, he added, "Wilson was also a blessing and a gift to me and thousands of others who came into his life." But Ed did more than provide a verse of scripture; he shared with the family the gift of his memories of Wilson.

He recalled a time after a visit with the family that they had gone to breakfast at the Waysider Restaurant. Wilson was a young boy and Ed was carrying him. Wilson turned to a man, a stranger, in the restaurant "and in his chirpy, friendly little voice said, 'This is my Uncle Ed." That Ed would remember that after so many years reveals how much that moment meant to Ed.

Ed shared about the time he took Wilson to an Auburn football game. "Wilson never met a stranger so he talked nonstop to a stranger, the man sitting next to him. At halftime the man swapped places with his wife. Wilson understood why. He said to Ed, 'He is not very friendly.'"

"One time at Christmas," Ed said, "we were sitting on the deck at the Pippin house in Selma, and Wilson was about 10 when he sang every single word of that Garth Brooks song 'Papa Loved Mama, Mama Loved Men.' A perfect rendition, every word, even down to the Garth Brooks twang. It was so cute and of course before the days of video cell phones. I wish I had a recording of it."

Ed also shared about the tender moment experienced when he was leaving to come home after a Christmas visit with the Pippins. "Wilson," he recalled, "put his arms around my neck and squeezed and held so tight and for so long I thought he would never let go. He was an affectionate little boy, and he always gave me that bear hug. I wish that I could hug him today. Precious memories!"

I can only imagine the difference it made to Wilson's parents for Ed to send them the gift of his memories. If we were to follow Ed's example, surely it would be a blessing to our friends when they are struggling with grief. As the song says, precious memories do linger, and for that we can be thankful. Perhaps they linger so we can share them as a gift to hurting people.

One Word: _____

How did this story help me change my life?

We Need Each Other

The incessant demand to "reopen" our society is fueled by much more than the looming economic crisis. Yes, people want to get back to work; they need to make money to pay their bills. The "stay at home" order is crippling businesses; people are suffering and they are frightened by an uncertain future. But our restlessness cannot be resolved by money alone.

Greater even than our need of money, as great as it is, is our need of fellowship. We are not made to live alone. The need to belong is a universal human need. The familiar saying, "No man is an island," is an eternal truth. Human beings are "hard-wired" to need other human beings. An old song expresses what we all know to be true: "People who need people are the luckiest people in the world." And the greater truth is that there are no people who do not need people.

Many years ago my wife gave me an anniversary gift that cost her one dollar. It was a small wooden plaque on which two rabbits were painted along with the words, "We Need Each Other." That plaque meant the world to me because it symbolized a new day in our marriage. We had gone through a few troubled years in which we sometimes expressed our frustration with each other by pretending we did not need each other. With the Lord's help, we overcame that dreadful attitude and found great joy in affirming our need of each other.

In these sunset years of our lives, and especially during the coronavirus pandemic, we have realized even more how much we need each other. I need Dean. She needs me. We need each other. And while the gift of life remains ours, we shall continually praise God for allowing us to meet needs in each other's life.

During these days when church buildings have been closed, the human need for meaningful fellowship remains real. And there is no more beautiful name for the church than "a fellowship of believers." The church at its best is a fellowship, a loving, redemptive fellowship. The authentic church is a gathering of friends who come together to love and encourage one another, worship and praise God together and enjoy the rich "fellowship of believers."

Reopening our churches for worship, so we can sit on pews or chairs six feet apart, will not satisfy our deep need for fellowship. As great as our need for "public" worship may be, greater still is our need for the refreshing, life-giving fellowship that occurs when "two or three are gathered together" in the name of Jesus, and He is present "in the midst of them." Like many of my friends, I long for the joy of meeting again with a few brothers and sisters to break bread together, study the scriptures, share our burdens and pray together.

Church should be a fellowship where people, despite their weaknesses, may love and be loved. It is not a fellowship of perfect people but a gathering of flawed people, each of whom is accepted despite their flaws. Though some people may find meaningful fellowship in a bar or tavern, a more transforming fellowship is available in a church. There, hopefully, there is always an atmosphere of forgiveness. There we are taught that because God has forgiven us in spite of our sins, we can forgive others in spite of their sins. To feel accepted despite our shortcomings is truly unspeakable joy.

The true church offers more than fellowship with people; it provides fellowship with the Father, the Son and the Holy Spirit. In the company of believers we learn that God promises us a fellowship that extends into eternity, a relationship that lasts forever. That is why you will find Christians singing joyfully, "What a fellowship, what a joy divine, leaning on the everlasting arms."

Yes, indeed, we are hard-wired with the need to belong, the need for fellowship with other human beings. And it was God who did the wiring. He made us with this universal need and He provided "the fellowship of believers" to meet this need. Since many of our brothers and sisters remain outside this rich fellowship, surely we need to say to our world what the Apostle John said to his own: "We proclaim to you what we have seen and heard, so that you may have fellowship with us. And our fellowship is with the Father and with his Son, Jesus Christ."

Imagine what God could do with our testimony if we Christians were willing to say to all our neighbors who remain outside the fellowship of believers, "We Need Each Other."

One Word: _____
How did this story help me change my life?

When Hands Become Tools of Blessing

The word "hand" is found 1500 times in the Bible. When Cain killed Abel, the ground opened to receive Abel's blood "from the hand" of his brother. Moses took the staff of God in his hand. When Moses' hands grew tired, Aaron and Hur held his hands up.

Though the Bible teaches us that God is a spirit, it also speaks figuratively of God's hand. The "right hand" of the Lord was "majestic in power." The Lord "stretched out his hand" many times against the enemies of Israel. Isaiah heard the Lord saying that He would strengthen and help him "with my righteous right hand."

Jesus spoke of the hands of his Father. Dying on the cross, Jesus cried out with a loud voice, "Father, into thy hands I commit my spirit." The early church grew because "the Lord's hand was with them."

Popular hymns and songs help us praise God for the blessings of His hands. One hymn especially comes to mind: "Great is Thy Faithfulness." My soul rejoices every time I sing the words,

"Morning by morning new mercies I see; all I have needed Thy hand hath provided; great is Thy faithfulness, Lord, unto me."

Another hymn that touches the heart is "Precious Lord, Take My Hand." During many hard times, I have found comfort in singing, "Take my hand, precious Lord, lead me home." And who is not blessed by the singing of "He's got the whole world in His hands" or "Put your hand in the hand of the man from Galilee"?

Since biblical times, placing your hand on the head of another person has been a sign of blessing. The Hebrew word for "to consecrate" means "to fill the hand," intimating that without consecration we have little or nothing to offer God. When bishops ordain elders in the church, they place their hands on the heads of the elders while praying prayers of consecration. When my young sons fell asleep in their beds at night, I would often kneel beside them and pray aloud a prayer of blessing for them, with my hands resting gently on their heads.

Love is often expressed by the simple gesture of holding hands. It was a special moment when I finally dared to hold Dean's hand when we began dating as teenagers. Years later, when our four-year-old son Steve was facing surgery, he asked me to hold his hand. Sometimes, when a loved one is dying, and words are stuck in our throat, we offer our love by holding hands.

The gospels tell us that when Jesus was healing the sick, he often "laid his hand" on them and healed them. Mothers brought their babies to Jesus, asking him to place his hands on them. On one occasion, in a synagogue, Jesus encountered a man with a withered hand. When Jesus told the man to stretch out his hand, the man stretched it out and it was healed.

Hands can be useful or useless. When they are idle, they become "the devil's workshop." The devil is defeated when we use our hands for loving purposes rather than violent ones. The man whose withered hand Jesus healed could thereafter use his hand to bless others. Dedicated to Jesus, our hands become tools of blessing.

When I was knocking on death's door because of an embolism, caring doctors and nurses used their hands to treat and comfort me. When you are too weak to wipe your own brow, the tender caress of a kind nurse makes you glad to be alive. Because of the nurses I have known, I never tire of singing the praises of the nursing profession. They are the unsung heroes of our society – because their hands make a difference.

Look around and you will see hands consecrated to Jesus using chain saws, preparing food for the elderly and the poor, sewing baby blankets, repairing a roof damaged by a storm, delivering care packages and food to the needy, assembling worship videos to be seen by people unable to attend church, preparing lessons for children unable to be in a classroom – all at work to honor the Christ!

When a friend of mine was struggling with a fatal illness, and unable to help himself, his friend John went to his home and rubbed his back and legs several times a week. John was a trained nurse and knew how to use his hands to bless a dying friend.

Helen Keller was liberated from blindness by a dedicated caregiver. Describing this dramatic rescue later, Keller wrote, "I was groping in darkness, like a ship lost at sea. One day I stretched out my hand and someone took it – someone who would teach me all things, but more than that, would love me." Helen's life was changed because Ann Sullivan took her hand.

An American tourist, visiting Albert Schweitzer at his hospital in Africa, was stunned to see the famous doctor using a wheelbarrow on the grounds. He expressed his amazement by asking Schweitzer, "Sir, how is it that you are pushing a wheelbarrow?" The good doctor calmly replied, "With two hands."

In these maddening days of the coronavirus pandemic, consider what you are doing with your hands. You can sit on your hands and do nothing but whine about our bleak circumstances. You can raise your hands in protest of what others are doing – or not doing. Or you can think creatively of simple ways to use your hands to make a difference.

Dedicated to Jesus, our hands can become a blessing. So let's get off our hands and work together with our heroes on the front lines whose hands are hard at work helping us get through this tough time. We will get through it – if we stretch out our hands. All hands on deck!

One Word: _____
How did this story help me change my life?

What Little I Know about God

The coronavirus pandemic has raised many questions for which there are no definitive answers. Some people say that God is using this lethal virus to punish us for our sins. Others disagree, insisting that God is using the virus to shake us loose from selfish and pathetic priorities. I am reluctant to argue the subject because I know so little about God.

That has not always been the case with me. When I was a brash young seminary student, I sometimes stayed up until midnight passionately debating theology with fellow students. I was quick to share my opinions but ignorant of how little I knew about God. Eventually my studies led me into the classroom of Dr. Nels Ferre who was teaching a six-months course on Systematic Theology at Vanderbilt University.

Doctor Ferre plunged us into the teachings of Karl Barth, Emil Brunner and Paul Tillich. Challenging to say the least for a country boy from Elmore County. But Ferre was a reputable theologian himself and instructed us to read several of his own books, one of which was titled *The Christian Understanding of God.*

In that book Ferre fervently speaks of our Creator as "the suffering God." The death of Jesus on the cross was the supreme revelation of God "suffering to save a sinful world." At the time I read that observation, I was too dense to grasp its full meaning. It was simply theology, talk about God, much of which sparked no excitement in me.

That, however, changed dramatically within a few months. It happened that while studying systemic theology under Doctor Ferre, our son David was suffering with leukemia. I was introduced to suffering in ways I had never experienced it. David's treatment, which would prolong his life but not save it, was frequent blood transfusions. Then two years old, my son begged me not to let the nurses "stick me" again. Believing it was necessary, I let them "stick" him again and again. He suffered and I suffered.

During the several months of David's illness, our pastor, crippled by rheumatoid arthritis, visited us often. I can still hear the sound of his crutches on the steps leading up to the door of our home. I can still see Tom Chappell on the floor playing with David. I can still see the pain in his face as he endured the suffering of moving his deformed body.

On the morning that David died in my arms, Nels Ferre became more than my systematic theology professor. He was the first person to come to our home only a couple of hours after David died. I still don't know how he learned of David's death. But there he was, a tall smiling Swede embracing us and lifting David's lifeless body off the bed as though offering him to God and thanking God for our son's three years with us. Then he took us in his arms and said, "I have come this morning to tell you that God hurts like you hurt." Later on I would realize that on that morning Nels Ferre became the messenger God sent to save us from drinking at the fountain of bitterness.

Over the following five years, baffled by why a loving God would ignore my prayers and let our little boy die, I struggled to understand who God was. I was "running on empty," and trying in my own strength to become an effective pastor. Then I met E. Stanley Jones with whom I shared my frustration. He prayed that God would give me a spiritual breakthrough and God did. I began to affirm that the living Christ was in me and I was in Him. Brother Stanley inspired me to believe that I could find all the energy I needed by living in Christ, and that He would speak to me by way of His "Inner Voice."

So, for 60 years, I have been listening to the Inner Voice of Christ and He has taught me what little I know about God. I can sum it all up in three basic affirmations.

First, there is a loving God who hurts like his children hurt. That loving God is the Father of our Lord Jesus. Far more than some abstract "Power," He is "the suffering God" to whom I was introduced by Nels Ferre.

Second, there is a loving God who is eager to forgive our sins and save us from the debilitating guilt of our misdoings. David's medicine during his illness caused him to become irritable at times. One day, a few weeks before he died, he threw in the floor the tray of food Dean had prepared for him. I picked the food up, then picked David up and walked up the street with him in my arms in misting rain. I did not scold him but held him close.

As I walked along, he put his arms around my neck, and said, "Daddy, I'm sorry." I hugged him close, as tears flowed down my cheeks, and replied, "It's alright son." Only a loving God could have given a suffering father and son such a moment. But time and again, across the years, I have witnessed this loving God give such transforming moments to his suffering children. He is far more ready to forgive than we are, and longs for his children to repent and say to Him, "Father, I'm sorry."

Finally, there is a loving God who is eager to empower His children to comfort hurting people. The course of our lives is often changed by the example of others. For 60 years I have wanted to be a man like Tom Chappell, a man who could ignore his own suffering long enough to comfort others in their suffering. For 60 years I have wanted to be a man like Nels Ferre, a man who could put his arms around hurting people and tell them that God hurts like they hurt.

When I consider what little I know about God, I believe I hear the Inner Voice telling me not to waste time debating God but to get busy, while it is day, serving the loving God who is hurting with us during this terrible coronavirus pandemic. There are hurting people all around us; let's not "burn daylight" but do what we can, while we can, to share the comfort He has given us with others.

One Word: _____
How did this story help me change my life?

27

O God, Where are You?

Deaths from the coronavirus continue to rise in the United States and across the world. Fear of death by this dread disease remains rampant among us. It will help us to remember that about 8,000 people die every day in the US from all causes. Heart disease and cancer are the leading causes of death. And accidents kill thousands every year.

Death, of course, is more than a statistic. It is a personal matter to each of us. Most of us know someone who has died of an accident, an overdose, suicide or manslaughter. The death of a friend or a family member usually shocks us. We don't understand why people die before they are old; it does not seem right for a child to be taken. And death shocks us because it reminds us that we too will die sometime.

In recent days death has disturbed me greatly. My friend Gloria's husband died of heart disease. Another friend's 12-year-old grandson was killed accidentally while on a turkey hunt. Then my dear friend Will died in his sleep at age 60. I was in tears when his son called with the news of his dad's passing. Like his wife, Gayle, my dear cousin, our family loved Will and were not ready for him to leave us. Yes, death is a personal matter!

Today I am thinking about a young mother who lost her only child shortly after Mother's Day many years ago. She and her husband, both only 24 years old, struggled to understand why God would allow a wonderful little boy to die when he was only three years old.

The mother wrestled with the basic questions begging to be answered when a child dies with an incurable disease: "Where are you God?" "Why did you let my little boy die?" "What is the meaning of life?" "How can I live without this precious child who has been my life?" "Who will help me with this emptiness in my life?" She expressed her despair and her search for hope in this little poem titled "In Time of Sorrow":

O God, where are you?
My world suddenly has lost all meaning.
As I stood there beside the grave,
I couldn't help asking,
Lord, what is the meaning of life?
How can I live in a world without this one
Who has been my very life?
I know so little about you, God,
But I dare to make one earnest plea –
That this dear one has not died in vain.
Help me in my sorrow to discover
The real meaning of life.
Lord, I feel so empty.
Yet I sense somehow that
You can become my fullness.
Fill me, while I cling to my faith
In Jesus your Son,
In whose name I pray. Amen.

The mother who wrote that did what the Psalmist had done – she cried out to God for help. David had said, in Psalm 61, "I will cry unto thee, when my heart is overwhelmed." God helped David and He helped that mother. She took her broken heart to Jesus who gave her healing and hope. She did not find answers to all her questions but she found God. And God helped her grow in faith until she could pen these lines:

If in this world of darkness
I can light a fire,
If I can cause one child to smile,
That is my desire.
To forget whatever may be my pain,
To brighten small, sad eyes
Is my fondest aim.

Today I gladly salute that mother who moved from overwhelming sorrow to enjoy several years of dressing like a clown whose antics and funny face made many children happy. For 68 years I have watched as Christ brightened her own sad eyes and gave her the strength to put her pain aside and spend her days serving others. In so doing she found the victory over death that Christ gives to those who love and serve Him. Thanks be to God that victory is available to all who struggle with death and sorrow!

When death invades our ranks, the wisest step we can take is to turn our grief over to the One who says to all who are broken-hearted, "Let not your heart be troubled...." He alone can rescue us from sadness and fill us with the joy of His peace.

One Word: _____
How did this story help me change my life?

28

Praying for God to Heal Our Land

Annually, by law, our nation observes a National Day of Prayer on the first Thursday of May. So, on that day, millions of Americans honor that law by uniting in prayer, not in a single observance somewhere but in hundreds of gatherings at different times of the day in every state of the union.

It would not be unreasonable to ask why such a day is fixed on our calendars. Should we not pray every day for our country? Why did congress pass such a law? Is not prayer more a personal matter that something to be legislated?

A bit of research reveals that even before the colonies declared their independence from England, leaders of the colonists in several states proclaimed a day for prayer and thanksgiving, in the fall, and a day for prayer and fasting in the spring or summer.

With some exceptions, the presidents of our nation have always called upon our citizens to turn to God in prayer, and to do so on certain days of the year. Thomas Jefferson was one of those exceptions. Jefferson did not follow the example of George

Washington and John Adams by proclaiming a day of prayer; he felt prayer was a personal matter and that the state should not be involved.

Harry S. Truman in 1952 signed the bill establishing a National Day of Prayer and requiring each subsequent president to proclaim a National Day of Prayer at a date of his choice. Then, in 1988, Ronald Reagan signed an amendment to the law specifying that the National Day of Prayer would be held on the first Thursday of May each year.

Reagan helped clarify the purpose of the day when he declared, "From General Washington's struggle at Valley Forge to the present, this Nation has fervently sought and received divine guidance as it pursued the course of history. This occasion provides our Nation with an opportunity to further recognize the source of our blessings, and to seek His help for the challenges we face today and in the future."

I first participated in a National Day of Prayer observance as a pastor while serving in Pensacola, Florida, in 1989. About a hundred people gathered at noon on the courthouse steps as several pastors and civic leaders offered prayers and invited the people to pray together. I felt inspired by the unusual nature of the occasion; it was first time I had gathered to pray with people of many different religions, different races, rich and poor, influential and ordinary citizens – all fellow Americans.

While Easter and Christmas are Christian observances, the National Day of Prayer is more inclusive, a day designed for "adherents of all great religions" to unite in prayer. When congressional leaders established this event, they expressed the hope that the observance might "one day bring renewed respect for God to all the peoples of the world."

I have fond memories of gathering in front of the courthouse with fellow citizens in Opelika during National Day of

Prayer observances. It always felt good to put aside our political, ethnic and religious differences and come together as fellow citizens calling upon God to continue guarding, guiding and blessing America. The feeling is reminiscent of the way the soul is stirred when one sings "God Bless America" with fellow citizens at community events.

The theme for the 2020 National Day of Prayer, "Pray God's Glory Across the Earth," is a phrase taken from an oft-quoted verse in the Book of Habakkuk – *"For the earth will be filled with the knowledge of the glory of the Lord, as the waters cover the sea."*

If I were speaking or praying in such a gathering, I would call attention to the words, "will be filled" in the prophetic words of the prophet. There is no hesitancy, no doubt but absolute confidence that "the earth will be filled with the knowledge of the glory of the Lord." Habakkuk is saying the Lord's goals for the world will happen; his purposes will be fulfilled. God's will shall not be thwarted!

Then I would go to Jesus, by way of Saint Paul. In his Second Letter to the Corinthians, 2:6, Paul uses Habakkuk's phrase when he writes, *"For God, who said, 'Let light shine out of darkness,' made his light shine in our hearts to give us the light of the knowledge of the glory of God in the face of Christ."*

Here Paul gives us the answer as to how Habakkuk's prophecy will be fulfilled. It will happen as God's people help all the people of the earth to become aware that the fullness of God's glory is found "in the face of Christ." Christians have a mission – to help people "see" God the Father in the face of our Lord Jesus! In Christ's own words, "Anyone who has seen me has seen the Father."

How can Christians persuade people to believe this? By loving people, all people, those near and far away. People cannot be driven into the Kingdom; they can be loved into it.

How is love expressed? Not so much by words as by actions. Actions to defend the defenseless and provide justice for the poor. Actions that provide food, clothes, shelter and jobs for the poor. Actions that demand equal rights for all citizens regardless of their race. Actions that reveal genuine love and respect for "the least of our brothers and sisters." Actions by leaders whose laws reflect their agreement with the Prophet Amos that justice needs to "roll on like a river, righteousness like a never-failing stream"!

Actually any day is a good day for Christians to pray that God will hear our prayers, heal our nation and help us make known to all the earth's people that the awareness of the glory of God has been revealed in the face of Jesus Christ.
God bless America!

One Word: _____
How did this story help me change my life?

Lessons of the Mighty Oak Trees

We built our little cabin 60 years ago in a grove of pines and oaks near the Tallapoosa River. Most of the pines were harvested years ago, the proceeds helping us raise four sons. We have enjoyed what the Prophet Hosea called "the pleasant shade of oaks." Such shade provided by several large oak trees has blessed our home all these years.

In the early hours of the Monday after the 2020 Easter, two of those stately oak trees came crashing to the earth in our front yard. Crushed beneath the trees were our 20-foot flagpole, the American flag attached to it and our outdoor light powered by Central Alabama Electric Cooperative. The Scuppernong Grape vines nearby survived with minor damage to the wooden frame supporting them.

Some trees have shallow root systems and are easily uprooted. I have always heard that oak trees have deep root systems and that "contrary winds" force the oak tree to send its roots deeper.

The unearthed roots of our largest oak seemed rather weak to me, so I asked our son Tim for his thoughts about the tree. (Tim is the federal government's State Forester for Alabama, working with USDA.) Oak trees, he said, have a lifespan of 150 to 250 years; he estimated our tree may have been 85 years old.

Tim explained that in a mature hardwood forest, the root strength of trees is greater because of the proximity of nearby trees or "neighbor" trees. Our tree had no neighbor to the southwest so its root system was weaker and thus more vulnerable to fierce wind. Tim observed that people have more strength to endure the storms of life when they are standing beside their neighbors rather than living in isolation.

The oak trees in our neck of the woods appear to be exactly like the Bible describes them: "great" and "mighty." Isaiah writes of men who will be called "oaks of righteousness," men who will "be like great oaks that the Lord has planted for his own glory."

Songwriters have borrowed this idea from the Bible and written songs about men who, "like mighty oak trees," have been faithful friends. Hank Williams Jr. sings one of those songs that depicts his "mighty oak tree" friends who have "stood by him" and are "rooted way down deep" in his soul. They are "strong and always there when I needed them the most." The song ends with hope that others are "lucky enough to find mighty oak trees like those rowdy friends of mine." I reckon most any man would feel blessed if his friends thought he was like a mighty oak tree friend. One might question the use of the word "rowdy" though Hank Junior did use the word advantageously in his career as a singer.

Since Mama Dean and I did not hear the oak trees fall in the night, it was a shocking sight to behold when I opened the front door Monday morning. The powerful wind that brought them down must have done so swiftly, in only a few seconds. Strangely, our home, only 30 feet away from the trees, was not damaged.

The wind chimes hanging beside the porch were untouched by the mighty wind. Trees nearby had few if any broken limbs. The wind simply dipped down, clobbered my two oak trees, and went on its merry way, destroying nothing else in our neighborhood.

All day I pondered what lessons we might learn from the loss of the oaks. It was a day of sobering thoughts. Had the wind slammed the trees down 30 feet to the right, our family might have been planning our funeral on Monday. Our bedroom is the corner of the house nearest the big oaks that fell. I spent some time thanking the Lord that we had not been injured or killed by those mighty oaks.

Knowing from weather reports that the storm would descend upon us shortly after midnight, we had gone to bed actually thinking about the danger of those oaks falling on us. I remember saying just before we went to sleep, "Lord, our lives are in your hands so we will not be afraid." We awoke the next morning as usual. We had been spared.

So this is our first lesson: **When you awaken from a night's rest, greet each new day with thanksgiving to God for the precious gift of life.** No matter your age, you should take seriously the brevity of life. You do that by living each day to the fullest, thankful that Jesus came to give us an abundant life. Thank God for your life. Love those around you. Forgive those who have hurt you. Refuse to be bored or boring. Be happy with what you have. Look beyond your trouble and think of ways you can help others with their troubles. Be ready to depart this life for you are here one day, and gone tomorrow!

The second lesson: **Enjoy the simple blessings of life, like the shade of great oak trees, and don't take these blessings for granted.** You can have them one day and they can be gone the next. Never fret because you lack the money to fly to Hawaii for a vacation; just enjoy what you have and be thankful for it. If the isolation brought on by the coronavirus has taught us anything, it is that we can find true joy in a simpler way of life. Doing without some things we thought we had to have has helped reassess our values. So we can applaud what someone said recently, "Those of us who have much should learn to live more simply so others can simply live."

The third lesson: **When the storms of life are raging, nothing matters more than the assurance that the Lord is standing with you, an ever present help in time of trouble.** Over the years I have enjoyed singing Charles Tindley's inspiring song, "Stand By Me." These words stir my soul: "When the storms of life are raging, stand by me. When the world is tossing me, like a ship upon the sea, thou who rulest wind and water, stand by me." The storms do come. As they come, the wisest thing we can do is to ask the Lord to help us face them bravely as we find strength in His presence. And remembering Tim's advice, we can find additional strength by standing in the company of our neighbors, loving and assisting them as we are able.

The fourth lesson: **Though trouble comes to us all, almighty God, our heavenly Father, is still in control of the world.** As the songwriter says, "This is my Father's world: why should my heart be sad? The Lord is King; let the heavens ring! God reigns; let the earth be glad!" Oak trees live; oak trees die. The coronavirus lives and it too will die. Fear grips us; fear is overcome. We struggle with adversity; we get through adversity.

In the meantime, we shall be wise to ponder questions of eternal significance: What can I do to sink my roots deeper into the mind and will of God? How can I demonstrate my love of God? How can I better love my neighbors? How can I honor Christ in my daily life? How can I make a difference in the lives of my family and friends? The more we ask Him, the more God is willing to show us how to live out our days in ways that please Him.

One Word: _____

How did this story help me change my life?

30

Walking in the Park with Jesus

Memories of walking with our children in Centennial Park in Nashville are most precious to me. We lived in Nashville twice and loved Music City. There were no sidewalks on the streets where we lived so on weekends and holidays we often found our way to Centennial Park.

There we fed the ducks in a large pond, rambled through and around the Parthenon and let the boys crawl up into the cab of the large train engine. We marveled at the beautiful flowers everywhere. The boys romped on open fields. Sometimes we found a table and enjoyed a picnic lunch.

One of our fondest hours was the day Dean and I spent a few hours in the park with our dear friend, Sister Maria, a Roman Catholic nun. After walking a while, we sat and talked, mostly about our grief over the death of our son. Maria's gentle questions soon led me to tears, and to my surprise I began sobbing. The catharsis of that hour was transforming for me, an unexpected gift of God while strolling in a park. I know now that, spiritually, Jesus was in Maria, ministering to me through her.

I have often wondered what it would have been like to walk in a park with Jesus. He would have been gentle and caring, like Sister Maria. He loved flowers and birds and it was mostly out-doors, and on hillsides, where Jesus taught the crowds who came eagerly to hear him. I can imagine sitting across from Jesus under a shade tree, and hearing him say:

"Walter, don't worry about things – food, drink, and clothes. For you already have life and a body – and they are far more im-portant than what to eat and wear. Look at the birds! They don't worry about what to eat – they don't need to sow or reap or store up food – for your heavenly Father feeds them. And you, Walter, are far more valuable to him than they are."

When he paused, I might have said to him, "Well, Lord, I realize that I should not worry but I don't know how to stop wor-rying. Isn't it just human to worry? Doesn't everybody worry?"

I can hear Jesus replying, "Walter, will all your worries add a single moment to your life? And why worry about your clothes? Look at the field lilies! They don't worry about theirs. Yet King Solomon in all his glory was not clothed as beautifully as they. And if God cares so wonderfully for flowers that are here today and gone tomorrow, won't he more surely care for you, a man of little faith?"

I might have replied, "I see your point, Lord. I must confess that I stay too busy to pay much attention to birds and flowers. I guess I need to stop and smell the roses and let them teach me to trust God more and put an end to my useless worrying."

Smiling, Jesus may have replied, "You've got it Walter! So don't worry at all about having food and clothing. Why be like the heathen? For they take pride in all these things and are deeply concerned about them. But your heavenly Father already knows perfectly well that you need them, and he will give them to you if you give him first place in your life and live as he wants you too So don't be anxious about tomorrow. God will take care of your tomorrow too. Live one day at a time, Walter."

Such a walk in the park with Jesus would put a new spring in my step, a new joy in my heart. I would look for someone to whom I could say, "You know, Jesus was 'a man of sorrows, acquainted with grief,' but he was also a man filled with joy and a contagious peace. He could relax in a lovely meadow and trust his Father to meet his needs."

I would remember that time in the park for the rest of my life and I would be forever telling people what I learned from Jesus. I would sum up what he told me in these simple words:

1. Don't worry about things.
2. Relax and enjoy the quiet beauty outdoors.
3. Trust your heavenly Father to meet your needs.
4. Put God first.
5. Live one day at a time.

And I would remember all this by quietly singing the simple song that goes like this: *"One day at a time, sweet Jesus. That's all I'm asking from you. Just give me the strength to do every day what I have to do. Yesterday's gone sweet Jesus. And tomorrow may never be mine. Lord, help me today, show me the way, one day at a time."*

Nashville is far away now and I don't travel much anymore. I don't reckon I will ever walk in Centennial Park again. But sometimes I sit on the porch, and start singing that song, and imagine that Jesus is talking to me. The more he says, the more I want to listen, and, as the sun is setting, I let him bless me like he used to in Nashville.

It seems like, as the years roll on, I need that more and more.

One Word: _____

How did this story help me change my life?

31

Facing Our Greatest Fear

Are you afraid to die? If you are, then welcome to the club. Most people fear death. It's normal to do so. Some say it is our greatest fear. Others say it is a matter of age. The older you get, the more reconciled you are to the inevitability of dying. You are not as fearful as you once were.

When I was younger, I was sometimes flippant about dying. I remember saying, "At 75, I realize I have lived half of my life already." But people seemed only slightly amused at my presumption that I would live to be 150. Sometimes I would get a laugh by quipping, "The average of death is one per person." And you could always get a laugh by telling the story of the preacher who said to his congregation, "Stand up if you want to go to heaven." Everyone stood up except one old man. So the preacher asked the man, "Sir, are we to understand that you do not wish to go to heaven?" To which the man replied, "Oh no sir, I do want to go to heaven; I just thought you were getting up a load to go today!"

Now, at 88, I realize every day that I am around third base and about ready to slide across home plate. Every person born into this world is going to die. I am no exception. But, like the old man in the story, I would rather not leave for heaven today.

No matter your age, in these days you cannot avoid thinking about death when across the world thousands are dying as victims of the coronavirus. The dreadful COVID-19 is no respecter of persons. People of all ages are contracting the invisible virus. The death toll is rising as the virus spreads globally. The respected health expert, Dr. Anthony Fauci, has predicted there may be as many as 200,000 deaths in the United States.

In the face of such a crisis, every preacher is advising the flock to have faith and resist fear. While that is a laudable message that stimulates hope, we may still recognize that fear does have its value. Fear can motivate us to leave a lasting legacy. Fear can remind us, in the words of an old song, that "my living shall not be in vain if I can help somebody." Fear provokes us to reevaluate our values. We begin to see more clearly what really matters. That we cannot worship in "Easter clothes" or have an Easter egg hunt become small problems. Fear can spur us to stand up and face fear and make the most of whatever time we have left.

Fear can also prompt us to search the scriptures and find there a solid foundation for faith in the eternal life promised by Jesus. Eternal life is a gift of God that begins here and extends beyond the grave. Here, by choosing to live in the kingdom of God, we experience an abundant life that gets even better in the life to come. Our eternal soul lives on in heaven. Where is heaven? It's where Jesus is – and we shall have the joy of being with Him there!

The writer of Hebrews gives us the good news that we can be delivered from the fear of death. Read the second chapter and rejoice in this truth: When Jesus died on the cross, he broke the power of the devil, who holds the power of death, so that He could "free those who all their lives were held in slavery by their fear of death." When fear of death tries to get control of my mind, I tell it I am no longer its slave because my Savior's death set me free! Am I worthy of having the Son of God die for me? No! Saint Paul explains in Romans why Jesus died: "God demonstrates his own love for us in this: While we were still sinners, Christ died for us." And, as Paul says, while "the wages of sin is death, the gift of God is eternal life in Christ Jesus our Lord."

That gift of God was authenticated by the resurrection of Jesus from the grave. And choosing to believe in the resurrection of Jesus helps us overcome the fear of death. Are the sceptics right? Is the resurrection of Jesus a myth? Each of us must decide. Faith says Jesus was raised from the dead by the power of God. Doubt says it did not happen.

Actually it is difficult not to believe in the resurrection. To disprove the resurrection, you must explain why the tomb was empty, why the body was missing, and most of all, how his disciples overcame their fear of the Romans and began preaching the resurrection. As Peter explained at Pentecost, "God has raised this Jesus to life, and we are all witnesses of the fact." The resurrection of Jesus was a "fact" to the disciples. All but John believed it so strongly that they were willing to die rather than stop proclaiming this fact. Their testimony was sealed with their own blood!

Sceptics must also explain Christ's appearances after the resurrection. People saw him. They touched him. They saw the scars in his hands and on His body. His disciples ate a breakfast that Jesus prepared for them. On one occasion He even appeared to 500 people. His disciples were so convinced of his resurrection that they came out of hiding; they were changed men! No longer huddling in fear for their lives, they began proclaiming Christ's resurrection publicly. That is almost impossible to explain unless Jesus was truly alive. The evidence is overwhelmingly in favor of the resurrection!

Faith that overcomes the fear of death is found the liturgy of the Sacrament of Holy Communion. In one powerful section, the pastor says, "In remembrance of these your mighty acts in Jesus Christ, we offer ourselves in praise and thanksgiving as a holy and living sacrifice, in union with Christ's offering for us, as we proclaim the mystery of faith." Then the people respond together, saying "Christ has died; Christ is risen; Christ will come again." Every time I say those words with fellow believers, I feel faith surging in my soul! And the fear of death whimpers into the shadows again!

On this day we call Easter Sunday, millions of Christians are celebrating the resurrection of Jesus in strange new ways. Fear of the deadly coronavirus prevents us from gathering in our churches to sing together our great resurrection hymns. We are hunkered down in our homes, victims of fear like the disciples of Jesus following his crucifixion. Fear of death caused them to hide behind locked doors. Easter reminds us that what happened to those disciples can happen to us. While the fearful disciples were meeting, Jesus walked through those locked doors! His words to them are words we need to hear him say to us: "Jesus came and stood among them and said, 'Peace be with you!'" (John 20:19). Nothing helps us overcome the fear of death more that hearing our resurrected Savior whisper in our hearts, "Fear not! Peace be with you!"

The certainty of death awaits each of us. One way to prepare ourselves for the day of our departure is to observe how other believers face death without fear. My encounters with several Christians facing death have helped me to overcome my fear of dying. Carla is one inspiring example. I had met Carla and Dwayne, her devoted husband, when I preached in their church in a little town in Texas. We became good friends.

Carla had been struggling with cancer. Mother of three children, she had battled the dread disease for eight years but her gallant fight was coming to an end. Realizing that death was near, she called me from her hospital bed with an urgent, heartrending request. "We have been good friends. Will you come and assist my pastor with my funeral? I don't want a sad funeral; I want it to be a victorious celebration of my life." Gladly I agreed to come.

Her courageous spirit touched me deeply. My voice broke as I asked her to talk to me about what I might share in her funeral eulogy. She whispered hoarsely, "Tell everyone I have kept the faith though it was not easy. My suffering has seemed unfair, especially to my children, but I have peace with God and I know where I am going."

Carla told me that in her months of suffering, she had clung to one precious passage of scripture, "Be joyful always, pray continually; give thanks in all circumstances, for this is God's will for you in Christ Jesus" (1 Thessalonians 5:16-18). I think of her when I read that verse. My eyes were filled with tears as I told her goodbye. I knew I would never hear her voice again this side of heaven.

In that holy moment I believed the Lord was giving me a message through that heartbreaking phone call from Carla. He was saying, "Death is not the end of a life like Carla's. After her wasted body is buried in a simple grave, her soul will live on with me because I have given her the gift of eternal life." I thanked the Lord for His words of hope and for the way Carla's courage had strengthened my own faith. His grace enabled me to fly to Texas and help Dwayne and her family celebrate her life here and God's gift of eternal life that did not end with her funeral. Dwayne and I remain close friends and he, like me, is nearing home plate but still sharing Carla's strong faith in the love of God.

Carla's faith, and the robust faith of many others facing death, helps me today to stand up like a child of God and say YES to faith and NO to the fear of death. Years ago, in the company of a small band of believers, my heart was filled to overflowing as I learned to sing this uplifting chorus:

> *I will not be afraid,*
> *I will not be afraid,*
> *I will look upward*
> *And travel onward,*
> *And not be afraid.*

> *He says He will be with me;*
> *He says He will be with me;*
> *He goes before me,*
> *And is beside me,*
> *So I'm not afraid.*

When fear of death comes knocking on my door, I sing that song – and Christ gives me the victory! He is Risen! Hallelujah!

One Word: _____
How did this story help me change my life?

The World's Greatest Treasure

One summer a young boy spent a week with his grandmother. His parents were good people but had no use for the church. When his grandmother took the boy to church, everything about the worship service was new to him. He was doing fine until the preacher stepped up to the pulpit and began preaching with a loud, booming voice.

Frightened by the pastor's shouting, the boy asked with a trembling voice, "Grandmother, will that man hurt us if he gets out of that box?" Drawing the boy closer to her side, Grandmother assured her grandson that the preacher was not going to hurt them.

Isolated for many days now, in this "box" we call our home, I confess that I am a bit scared of the coronavirus. Like millions of others, I wonder if the virus is going to hurt me or kill me, or my wife, or a family member, or a friend. And like the little boy, I am asking questions. Two questions actually.

First, what I am going to do if this sequestration lasts for several more weeks? Here is my answer: I will continue what I am doing now – thanking God for the treasure I have found. That treasure is not my wife Dean, though she has been a treasured gift from God for almost 68 years. That treasure is Jesus, the greatest of all the world's treasures. Fortunately, Dean and I found this wonderful treasure together and finding it was the greatest thing that ever happened to us. That treasure became the focus of our life together.

This is not a new idea. I got it from Saint Paul. Read his letters and you find him saying in a hundred different ways that Jesus was his greatest treasure, God's "unspeakable gift." Jesus preached often about the kingdom of God; he called the kingdom a treasure for which a man would sell everything he possessed in order to obtain it.

And what is the kingdom of God? It is that realm of life in which Jesus is the King, that way of life in which the servants of King Jesus find purpose, power and peace for the living of this earthly life – and joyous hope for the life beyond death. When Paul encountered Jesus and surrendered to him, he began living in the kingdom of God – and so do all who become followers of Jesus.

When Jesus is our treasure, we can face whatever comes up knowing that He will see us through it. Isolated? Yes, but not alone for He is with us. Troubled and anxious? Yes, but His peace breaks the grip of fear. Weary? Yes, but He renews our strength. Fearful of dying? Yes, but that fear is overcome by His assurance that on the other side of death He will welcome us home to our eternal reward. Paul calls this reward "our inheritance" which we will share with all the saints of God who now enjoy the "eternal life" that Jesus promised us.

As we await release from this strange seclusion, we realize that our earthly treasures are likely diminishing. The virus is robbing us of our earthly "wealth." But this is a good time to remember that our true wealth was never our earthly possessions. The word "earthly" reminds us that we ourselves are but clay. Paul reminds us that it is in "earthen" vessels, or "jars of clay," that we have this treasure. We are mortal beings, here for a little while and gone. Life may never again be as good as we had it before this maddening virus began sweeping the earth. But we who are believers will still have our treasure! We will still have Jesus! And Jesus will be enough!

Paul says it much better than I can. As you read his powerful words, you may find your heart beating faster. Read this slowly, allowing it to sink into your subconscious mind. Pause now and then to rejoice and celebrate the great truth of what you are reading:

"But now we have this treasure in jars of clay to show that this all-surpassing power is from God and not from us. We are hard pressed on every side, but not crushed; perplexed, but not in despair; persecuted, but not abandoned; struck down, but not destroyed. We always carry in our body the death of Jesus, so that the life of Jesus may also be revealed in our body. For we who are alive are always being given over to death for Jesus' sake. So then, death is at work in us, but life is at work in you.

"It is written, 'I believed; therefore I have spoken.' With that same spirit of faith we also believe and therefore speak, because we know that the one who raised the Lord Jesus from the dead will also raise us up with Jesus and present us with you in his presence. All this is for your benefit, so that the grace that is reaching more and more people may cause thanksgiving to overflow to the glory of God.

"Therefore we do not lose heart. Though outwardly we are wasting away, yet inwardly we are being renewed day by day. For our light and momentary troubles are achieving for us an eternal glory that far

outweighs them all. So we fix our eyes not on what is seen, but on what is unseen. For what is seen is temporary, but what is unseen is eternal." (2 Corinthians 4:7-18, NIV)

The truth of Paul's words, vibrating in my mind, make me want to shout! I am perplexed but I am not in despair! I will not lose heart! I will fix my eyes on what is unseen, the true treasure of this life! I will look upward and travel onward! And He will go with me!

Martin Luther's great treasure was also Jesus. He lived and served God in a time when a great plague was devastating Europe. But he did not lose heart! Read again his great hymn, "A Mighty Fortress is Our God." The song is a mighty testament of faith in God. Though we must struggle with the "Prince of Darkness," we will not tremble for we can "endure his rage," confident that "one little word" shall ensure his doom! That that one little word is Jesus! In these days when everything is being shaken, Jesus will give us the courage to sing with Luther, "Let goods and kindred go, this mortal life also; the body they may kill; God's truth abideth still; his kingdom is forever"! That is good news at a time when the daily news is about suffering and death!

The second question I am asking is this: What will I do when I get out of this box, this perplexing confinement? I will continue as long as I have breath to encourage others to find this treasure and live in the kingdom of God. The coronavirus will not be the last problem the human race will face. But whatever the problems, there will be no greater treasure that Jesus. He is the unchanging reality in this world of chaos.

To live in the kingdom of God is to love God supremely and to love our neighbors. We cannot do that without help. Jesus gives us that help. When He is our treasure, He enables us to do His will, and to do even the impossible. He reveals to us how to love and encourage our family and friends. He helps us know how to pray and during these strange days, we have more time to pray than ever! And though we cannot socialize, we can still express love through cards, letters, books, gifts and telephone calls. These are channels of love available to us while we remain in the box!

Let me ask you one question. Do you have this treasure? Rejoice if you do! And if you do not have it, will you ask your heavenly Father to give it to you? He will be delighted to give it to you, for more than anything He wants you to live victoriously in this life and be ready to enjoy your eternal inheritance on the other side! Jesus alone can make that an unchanging reality in this changing world!

One Word: _____
How did this story help me change my life?

If I Can Help Somebody

Everywhere you turn, you find good advice concerning the terrifying coronavirus that is sweeping the world and producing global fear. Brilliant health experts are advising us daily how to avoid this deadly disease.

Taking this advice seriously, and at the insistence of our family, my wife and I are hunkering down for whatever spell is necessary to guard our health. At age 88, we would be foolish to do otherwise.

Like everyone else, I am looking for words of comfort and reassurance that will help us deal with fear. The Bible, of course, is a great help for many of us. It is comforting to remind ourselves that the God who "created the heavens and the earth" is still the Ruler of his world. This is a great time to sing the great hymn, "This is My Father's World." Our heavenly Father is the source of love and life. It is not His will that people die of sickness; otherwise, His Son Jesus would not gone around healing the sick during his earthly ministry.

I have found solace in these unsettling days by reminding myself that while one day I am going to die, God has given me the blessed assurance that my Lord Jesus has prepared a place for my soul in the Father's House. The Bible calls that place "a house in heaven not made with hands, eternal in the heavens." While I am not eager to die, I know that this world is not my home so until He calls me home, "my heart will go on singing and with joy I will carry on!"

My friends Ed Williams and Jere Beasley share daily online a word of scripture and a comforting thought or a brief prayer that blesses hundreds of people. A few days ago, this one winged hope into my heart:

"*When Jesus woke up [in the storm-tossed boat], he rebuked the wind and said to the waves, 'Silence! Be still!' Suddenly the wind stopped, and there was a great calm.*" – Mark 4:39.

"*O God, my Father in heaven, give me faith to believe that Jesus can calm my heart and help me through my storms. In Jesus' name, I pray Amen.*"

That day I found it helpful to ask King Jesus to calm my heart and remove from it any hear of the coronavirus. The power of Jesus is greater than any plague the devil may release in the world. How do I know that? The Bible "tells me so." Faith is strengthened by remembering what John said: "He who is in you is greater than he who is in the world." Yes!

Like most people, we find it strange to be confined to our home for weeks. Isolation on such a large scale has made the world much smaller. The coronavirus pandemic is not merely an American problem; it is a problem for humanity. Globally, the fear of this awful virus is uniting people of all nations in a common search for deliverance. One's religion, or political alignment, pales in significance, forcing people of different persuasions to work together in a common cause. Hopefully, once this problem is past, world leaders will see other creative ways to work together.

Not wanting to become couch potatoes, my wife and I have asked what we might do to help others while sequestered in our home. Dean said with a laugh, "I'm glad we like each other since we must be together 24-7!" I agreed with a smile.

One idea of helping others that came to us is this: make telephone calls to the elderly, offering words of cheer, comfort and hope. The virus is highly contagious but it cannot be transmitted through the telephone! We know this can make a difference because we have experienced it. Several friends have telephoned us, and others have emailed us, asking "Are you and Dean OK?" That simple gesture blessed us so we have called several elderly friends to share our love and concern. The elderly, after all, are the ones who are at the greatest risk of dying from exposure to COVID-19.

As Dean and I were discussing "helping somebody," she recalled a time 60 years ago when we were dining in the Roosevelt Hotel in New Orleans and heard the singer Roberta Sherwood singing in the Blue Room. We can still close our eyes and remember her singing the poignant words of one song that found a home in our hearts:

> *If I can help somebody as I pass along,*
> *If I can cheer somebody with a word or a song,*
> *If I can show somebody he is travelling wrong,*
> *Then my living shall not be in vain!*

> *Then my living shall not be in vain,*
> *Then my living shall not be in vain!*
> *If I can help somebody as I pass along,*
> *Then my living shall not be in vain!*

> *If I can do my duty as a Christian oft,*
> *If I can bring back beauty to a world up wrought,*

If I can spread love's message that the Master taught,
Then my living shall not be in vain!

May I humbly suggest that your living will not be in vain if you will "help somebody," an elderly family member or friend, with a caring phone call until this perplexing time is past. Whatever the outcome, this too shall pass. Until that day, let us do whatever we can, as long as we have breath, to help somebody. That will be the best use of our time no matter how much we have left.

One Word: _____
How did this story help me change my life?

The Energy and Power of Passion

When I told my father that God had called me to preach, he looked at me intently and said, "Well, if you are going to be a preacher, be a good one!" He never explained what he meant but his words filled me with passion to become "a good one."

I soon learned that one can seldom achieve success without passion. My early passion to become an effective preacher led me to realize that success would elude me unless I was passionate about the gospel and its power to turn people from sin to new life in Christ. During my seminary education I quickly observed that the effective preachers, the "good" ones, had passion while the poor preachers had little or no passion. Preachers without passion were boring; those with passion stirred people to respond to God.

So how does one preach with passion? Every preacher has to determine his or her own answer to that question. For me, it boiled down to this: Preach always about one of the basic issues of life, having asked the Lord to put one of those issues on your heart. Then through diligent prayer and study, prepare well a sermon you will not have to "read" to your congregation.

Passion becomes energy and power when the preacher's words come from the heart as he or she looks into the eyes of the people while preaching. Passion is conveyed to the audience through eye contact. The less eye contact, the less effective the preaching.

Can you imagine the Apostle Peter having to look constantly at a manuscript while preaching at Pentecost? Would you suppose the Apostle Paul, when preaching at Athens about the city's unknown God, was continually thumbing through his notes on some podium? Hardly!

Think of Jesus preaching about the Beatitudes on a hillside in Galilee. Try to imagine him pausing in his preaching and saying to one of the apostles, "Hey James, hand me my sermon notes; I think there was one more beatitude I wanted to mention to the people."

Is it too much to expect a preacher to spend the time necessary to be prepared to stand up and speak passionately for 20 minutes about the most important ideas the human mind can ever consider?

To study the life of Christ is to observe a man of passion. There is no evidence that he was ever apathetic, aloof, indifferent or stoic. His words were compelling and challenging: "Repent for the kingdom of heaven is near;" "Follow me;" "Go into all the world;" "Your sins are forgiven;" "Seek and you will find;" "Love your enemies;" "Bless those who curse you;" "You cannot serve both God and money;" "Stretch out your hand;" "You will be my witnesses;" "Rise up and walk." The gospels portray Jesus as a man of passion, emotion, conviction and enthusiasm. And he is the perfect model for the way we should live – with passion in every arena of life, not just preaching.

The happiest people are those who are passionate about their work. Sam Walton, the creator of the Wal-Mart Empire, said it best: "If you love your work, you'll be out there every day trying to do it the best you possibly can, and pretty soon everybody around will catch the passion from you - like a fever." Ask yourself: Is your attitude toward your work contagious! It is if you love what you are doing!

Passion is a trait we admire in others, whether in business, law, athletics, medicine, education or any arena. Passionate people are engaged in life; they are seriously devoted to their values and causes. A salesman who is not passionate about what he is selling will soon lose his job. Businesses want passionate salespeople.

A Christian oncologist advised his nursing staff: "You were not hired for your ability but for your attitude. You are here not to earn a paycheck but to serve our patients and to do so with compassion." Compassion is love wrapped up in passion.

Life without passion is like sipping lukewarm water when you could be drinking sweet iced tea. There is enough apathy in the world; what the word needs is more passion. Hurting people will never find solace in the aloofness of their neighbors. People who are truly alive find it impossible to be indifferent to the pain of others. Asked why he chose to live as a missionary doctor in impoverished Africa, Albert Schweitzer replied, "There is a great load of pain in the world and I decided that I must get under my share of that pain." That was a passionate decision!

Moderation or self-control is a good thing as, for example, in the drinking of alcohol. But moderation is also dangerous. C. S. Lewis reminds us that "a moderated religion is as good as no religion at all." People without passion for their faith are likely to settle for nominal Christianity instead of a passionate Christianity.

Restraint can lead to boredom. Bored preachers will deliver boring sermons. The Preacher, in the Old Testament book of Ecclesiastes, tells us, without feeling, that there is a time to be born and a time to die. But passionate questions emerge when we probe the meaning of our life. Why were we born? What is the purpose of life? What happens when we die? Is the grave the end? How do we deal with the dread of death?

The brevity of life should stimulate passion about the way we spend our days. On any given day we know not how much more time we have to live. That should motivate us to make the best use possible of the time we have left. We are wise to passionately remember that any time is always the right time to do the right thing for the right purpose.

If we have become lethargic, while there is time we can flee from aloofness and come alive! We can resist stoicism and begin to care deeply about the hurting people around us. Though we may not imitate Jesus perfectly, we can at least try! The more we try, the more likely God will give us the passion needed to live with a contagious enthusiasm that will become a valuable legacy for those we leave behind. Choose to live with passion as long as you have breath!

One Word: _____
How did this story help me change my life?

When You Pray

Search the gospels and you will find that Jesus assumed his disciples would pray. On several occasions, he began teaching moments with the three words, "When you pray." If we are to learn to pray correctly, we will need to pay attention to the instructions Jesus gave his disciples about praying. So, let's look at five of Jesus' teachings.

One, Jesus said, "**When you pray**, do not be like the hypocrites, for they love to pray standing in the synagogues and on the street corners to be seen by others." Here is a stern warning not to make prayer a spectacle, hoping to be seen and admired by others.

Two, Jesus said, "**When you pray**, go into your room, close the door and pray to your Father." Thus does Jesus teach us that prayer can be an intimate, personal conversation with our loving heavenly Father. While we can, and should, pray with others, we should also establish the habit of talking with God alone, in a private place.

Three, Jesus said, "**When you pray**, do not keep on babbling like pagans, for they think they will be heard because of their many words." Authentic prayer, then, does not require an abundance of words. I once heard a man pray aloud in a meeting for more than 15 minutes. He prayed so long that I got bored and started timing his prayer. My friend Mary Webster said that once she prayed alone for three hours and uttered only two words, "Help me." Babbling on and on then while praying is to pray like a pagan, not like a child of God.

Four, Jesus said, "**When you stand praying**, if you hold anything against anyone, forgive them, so that your Father in heaven may forgive you your sins." More than once Jesus reminds us that if we have an unforgiving spirit, we might as well not pray. To pray correctly includes seeking God's forgiveness for our sins, but God will not forgive our sins until we have forgiven those who have sinned against us.

Five, Jesus said, "**When you pray**, say 'Father, hallowed be your name, your kingdom come." What follows is Luke's version of the "Lord's Prayer." Here is the revolutionary idea introduced to the people of God by Jesus, that our prayers are to be directed to "our Father." While many today are staunchly opposed to addressing God with the masculine word, "Father," it remains unshakably true that Jesus taught us to do so. That is an irrefutable fact.

Early in my Christian life I struggled to know how to pray alone with God. I had no instructions about how to do it. Should I pray aloud or silently? Should I close my eyes? Bow my head? Gradually I learned a few "patterns" for prayer, like the ACTS plan: Begin with adoration, followed by confession, thanksgiving, and finally supplication. That is a good plan because it begins with the adoration of God and puts requests for yourself last.

It was E. Stanley Jones, however, who helped me most with the process of a quiet time of prayer. His plan was simple enough: "In your prayer hour, take your Testament and a pen." That makes sense. How does God speak to us? Mainly, through the holy scriptures. Of course, His Spirit can speak directly to our spirit in our quiet time; sometimes we may hear the "Inner Voice" speak profoundly to our needs. But on a day to day basis, the best way to "hear" God, and to communicate with God, is to read the Bible, especially the New Testament, constantly asking these questions: "What is God saying to me in this passage of scripture?" "What would happen if I took this lesson seriously?" "How can I apply this teaching in my daily life?"

We do not "worship" the Bible though it is our finest book. We may call it "The Book" for it is indeed the greatest book ever written. The Bible teaches us that Jesus is the Word of God so when we read the words of the Bible, we can ask these words to take us to the Word. Then, we may invite the living Word of God, Jesus Himself, to speak his word of guidance, correction or comfort to our seeking hearts.

There are words in the Bible that can change our lives from time to time – words such as hope, grace, forgiveness, peace, joy, love. E. Stanly Jones says God has "gone into those words and He comes out of those words" to meet our needs when we need them. Brother Stanley admits that all his life he would often press his lips to some verse on the page that touched his heart. Laughing, he says that "through that verse I kiss my Father's cheek!" I love that! And like Brother Stanley, we too can often see God's face shining through holy words of scripture.

There have been several moments in my life when I knew God was speaking directly to me through some sacred words of scripture. It was like the Lord was calling my name! I can identify with the Chinese Christian, Doctor Lo, who homesick and discouraged, turned to his New Testament for comfort. The first words his eyes fell on was Matthew 28:20, "Lo, I am with you always."

So, when you pray, you may enrich your quiet time alone with God by doing more than closing your eyes and praying. You may read precious words of scripture and invite your Father to speak to you through those words. Use your pen to make notes that may well be God's message to you. Write down what you are "hearing" Him say to you. Then, thanking Him for fresh words of hope and guidance, arise and get busy living like He tells you to live, knowing that Christ will indeed be with you always!

One Word: _____
How did this story help me change my life?

Please Lord, Teach Us All to Pray

Before he was crucified, Jesus spent three years in ministry with his disciples by his side. He taught them by word and by example. The kingdom of God was the focus of his teaching. The disciples asked many questions and made many requests. The one request with which most of us can identify is this one: "Lord, teach us to pray."

As children we are taught many things, such as reading, writing and arithmetic. But I do not remember anyone ever offering to teach me to pray when I was growing up. My siblings and I were taught the importance of prayer by the example of our parents. My father always prayed this simple prayer at every mealtime: "Bless, O Lord, this food to our use and ourselves to Thy service, for Christ's sake, Amen." It is the only prayer I ever heard him pray, but hearing him pray it a thousand times convinced me that he was a praying man.

I don't remember ever hearing my mother pray aloud. She left that up to Daddy. But I know she prayed for she was a godly woman whose faith was implicit in the way she lived her life. I am certain that God blessed me in a hundred ways in answer to my mother's prayers. I remember Mama reading Bible stories to me. I have often wondered if she taught me that well-known children's prayer:

Now I lay me down to sleep,
I pray the Lord my soul to keep.
If I should die before I wake,
I pray the Lord my soul to take.

The prayer is so frightening that I think had I been taught it as a child, I would still remember going to sleep with the dread that I might die before I woke.

When our children was small, we taught them to pray at mealtime and at bedtime. This is one of the first prayers we taught them to pray before they were able to construct one of their own:

God is great, God is good.
Let us thank Him for our food.
By His Hand we are fed.
Thank you for our daily bread.

Another prayer we used often at mealtime was this one: "Be present at our table Lord, be here and everywhere adored; these creatures bless and grant that we may feast In Paradise with Thee." As the children grew older, I realized that they thought the best prayers were short prayers, "lest the gravy get cold."

Prayers can be funny. This Irish Blessing is an example:

May those who love us, love us.
And those who don't love us,
May God turn their hearts.
And if He doesn't turn their hearts,
May He turn their ankles,
So we may know them by their limping!

The Serenity Prayer, made popular by Alcoholics Anonymous, is a marvelous prayer worthy of being prayed anytime by saints as well as sinners: *"God grant me the serenity to accept the things I cannot change, courage to change the things I can, and wisdom to know the difference."* That, of course, is but one sentence of the complete prayer, though the basic idea has spawned this parody: *"Lord, grant me the serenity to accept stupid people the way they are, courage to maintain my self-control, and wisdom to know that if I act on it, I will go to jail."*

This is another humorous prayer: *"Dear Lord, so far today I am doing alright. I have not gossiped, lost my temper, been greedy, grumpy, nasty, selfish or self-indulgent. I have not whined, complained, cursed, or eaten any chocolate. I have charged nothing on my credit card. But I will be getting out of bed in a minute and I will really need your help then. Amen."*

Prayers can be selfish. In the wonderful movie "Shenandoah," Jimmy Stuart plays the role of an arrogant Virginia farmer who prays this prayer at mealtime: *"Lord, we cleared this land. We plowed it, sowed it and harvested it. We cooked the harvest. It wouldn't be here – we wouldn't be eating it – if we hadn't done it all ourselves. We worked dog-bone hard for every crumb and morsel. But we thank you just the same anyway, Lord, for this food we are about to eat. Amen."* Definitely not a model prayer.

One way to learn to pray, once you get serious about it, is to read, pray and study the 650 prayers that are in the Bible. The most well-known prayer of the Bible is the Lord's Prayer. It is significant that Jesus gave this prayer to his disciples in response to their request to teach them to pray. About the prayer, Jesus said, "This is how you should pray." I believe he meant more than "Repeat these words when you pray." The prayer is a model because of several basic assumptions embedded in the prayer. I shall mention but two. One, when you pray, think of God as "our

Father," and yourself as his beloved child. Two, a forgiving spirit is necessary for your prayers to be authentic. That is implicit in the words, "Forgive us our debts (or sins) as we also have forgiven our debtors." As we study this prayer, and the other prayers of the Bible, God Himself become our Teacher. Thus does he "teach us to pray."

Many of Saint Paul's prayers are worthy of imitating. I love what he says to the Philippians: *"I thank my God every time I remember you. In all my prayers for all of you, I always pray with joy because of your partnership in the gospel from the first day until now, being confident of this, that he who began a good work in you will carry it on to completion until the day of Christ Jesus."*

The Psalms of the Old Testament are prayers that have been sung and prayed with great benefit for centuries. Praying some of the Psalms can set your soul on fire. Next time you want to do some real praying, read Psalm 103 as your own prayer, praying earnestly, *"Bless the Lord, O my soul; and all that is within me, bless His holy name! Bless the Lord, O my soul, and forget not all His benefits: who forgives all your iniquities, who heals all your diseases, who redeems your life from destruction, who crowns you with lovingkindness and tender mercies, who satisfies your mouth with good things, so that your youth is renewed like the eagle's."*

If that kind of praying does not light your fire, then your wood is wet! Come to think of it: I believe praying Psalm 51 might make even wet wood burn. You begin praying this Psalm prayer by saying, "Have mercy upon me, O God." Christians who pray prayers like that can expect God to do a new work of grace in their hearts.

Prayers can be especially meaningful at those times when dear friends are departing our presence on a long journey to somewhere else in the world. On such occasions my wife and I like to embrace our friends and offer a brief prayer, thanking God for the love that binds us, and asking God to give them safe travel home. Here is a prayer of blessing you would not likely pray on such an occasion, but it does suggest the warmth and tenderness that help parting prayers touch the heart:

May the road rise up to meet you.
May the wind be always at your back.
May the sun shine warm upon your face,
And rains fall soft upon your fields.
And, until we meet again,
May God hold you in the palm of his hand.

One Word: _____
How did this story help me change my life?

God Uses Altar Calls to Change Lives

During 70 years of preaching I have given what we preachers call "altar calls" more than 3,000 times. An altar call is usually an invitation to come forward, to the altar, and accept Jesus Christ as Savior. On some occasions the call may be an invitation to join the church or to give one's life or resources to some ministry of the church. It is always a personal call designed to motivate individuals to respond to God.

One night during a worship service, a woman came in, off the street, and took a seat in a back pew. Her only clothing was a thin cotton dress, nothing more. When she began talking to herself, it was obvious she was somewhat inebriated and distraught. My wife got up from her seat, went over to comfort the woman and sitting beside her, put her arm around her. She calmed down. As soon as I gave the altar call, the woman, whose name was Gracie, asked my wife if she could go to the altar and Dean said, "I'll go with you." Praying for her, we saw not only tears but red bruises on her face and learned that she had been severely beaten by the man with whom she had been living. Gracie was not dramatically "changed" at the altar that night but the love she found there gave her hope for the future. Several caring women went out of their way to help her find a way out of the darkness and make a fresh start. Gracie soon joined the Navy and began a new life as a disciple of Jesus.

I have had several men tell me that when the invitation was given, they gripped the back of the pew and resisted the impulse to go forward. They knew God was calling but they refused to give up and walk down front. James Moore, a pastor, tells the story of a young man who did that in his church, then felt guilty about it and called Moore on Sunday afternoon to confess how badly he felt about staying glued to the pew.

The young man told Moore that it happened to him on consecutive Sundays. He said, "I just grabbed hold of the back of the pew and held on for dear life, and then it was too late; the service ended. I walked out of church disgusted with myself. I knew deep in my heart that God wanted me to go down and commit myself to Christ but I fought it off – both times. But I promised God if I ever felt that way again, I would seize the moment and act on it boldly."

He paused, and then went on, "It happened again this morning and I have been miserable all afternoon. But before I called you, I said a prayer and promised God that I was going to get baptized before the sun goes down tonight – so pastor, will you baptize me before the sun goes down tonight?" Pastor Moore quickly replied, "Of course I will." To which the young man responded, "I forgot to mention I promised God I would get baptized by immersion! I feel so dirty and I want to be washed clean!"

Now the pastor was perplexed. Like most Methodist churches, his church did not have a baptismal pool so he explained that he would have to make arrangements with a Baptist church to use their baptistry and they might have to wait until the next day for his baptism. "Oh, no," the young man replied, "I promised God I would get baptized by immersion before the sun goes down today! So, if you cannot baptize me, I'll have to find somebody else who will."

Even more perplexed now, Moore did not know what to say. Then the young man said, "Pastor, you have a swimming pool at the church; can you baptize me in it?" Moore sealed the deal saying, "Yes! Meet me at the pool at 5:00 o'clock!"

On the way to the church pool, Moore started sweating as questions vibrated in his brain. Was it "legal" to baptize someone in a swimming pool? What if his bishop found out about it? Why didn't the seminary teach me how to handle this?

The pastor's questions vanished when he saw the young man waiting at the pool for him. "I'll never forget the look on his face, his sense of urgency, his intensity, his resolve and his gratitude. At that moment I didn't care what the letter of the law of the church said, I just knew Jesus wanted me to baptize that young man so I did! The next Sunday he finally found the courage to come to the altar at the end of the service and made his public confession of faith in Christ."

I have had my share of life-changing moments at the altar. Once on a Saturday night my phone rang about 9:00 p.m. It was Frank calling. When I first met Frank, I learned that he despised churches and preachers. But the Holy Spirit got hold of Frank and softened his heart until, on that Saturday night his angry spirit melted in the warmth of God's love.

Frank was still a bit rough around the edges so his voice was a little blunt that night when he called me. "Preacher," he said, "You know I have never had much use for churches but lately I have been thinking it's about time for me to get right with the Lord.

Tomorrow is my birthday and I was wondering if you would baptize me in church tomorrow?" The next day, my heart pounding with joy, I baptized Frank on his 65th birthday while tears stained his cheeks and mine.

Experiences like that at the altar will inspire any pastor to keep on making altar calls. If you happen to be in church one Sunday when I am preaching, don't grab the back of the pew in front of you and resist the impulse to come forward. I would love to meet you at the altar, on our knees, and let God do a fresh work of grace in your heart and mine. Believe me, I know from experience, the altar is a wonderful place to do business with God.

One Word: _____
How did this story help me change my life?

38

What Makes a Sermon Worth Hearing?

The worship service had ended. I had preached once again. As was my custom, I stood at the exit to greet my parishioners as they departed for lunch. Some would shake my hand and just smile. Others might say, "I enjoyed your sermon, pastor." One woman startled me. She just looked at me for a few seconds and then said, "You know, pastor, some of your sermons are better than others." As she walked away, I replied, "Truer words were never spoken!"

Every pastor dreads preaching an irrelevant or boring sermon. The primary way to prevent such preaching is to always choose subjects about which you can preach with passion, subjects that deal with the real issues of life. Even if your listeners are not inspired by your message, they will appreciate your fervor. So, for me, if I am not passionate about my subject, I am not ready to preach.

I soon wearied of hearing people say they "enjoyed" my sermons. While I wanted people to "like" my preaching, my goal was not for them to "enjoy" the sermon. One Sunday I finally heard the response I longed for when a man, with tears in his eyes, gripped my hand and said, "Pastor, the Lord met my need today!" Those words thrilled my soul! That day I realized that truly good preaching helps people connect with Jesus at some point of need in their lives.

Excellence in preaching has been a consuming desire of mine for 70 years – and it remains my goal. This aspiration gripped me when I was a young pastor meeting with my new church leaders. I invited them to share what they expected of me as their new preacher. Their expectations did not surprise me. "Visit the sick." "Visit us in our homes." "Win new people to Christ so we can grow." "Be available when you are needed." Finally, one man dropped the hammer on me when he said, "I would like for you to have something to say that is worth hearing when you stand up to preach." I received his words as a message from God to take preaching seriously and pay whatever price was necessary to be fully prepared when I stood behind the sacred desk.

So what is preaching that is "worth hearing"? It is more than great oratory though eloquence need not be eschewed. Good preaching is more than impressive talk about God; it is preaching that motivates people to connect with God, preaching that inspires people to believe that God wants to connect with them.

Quotations by Mother Teresa are plentiful. One that brings me to my knees is this: "People ought to be able to meet Jesus in us." By "us" the saintly nun meant Christians in general and that includes preachers. So excellent preaching permits people to meet Jesus. You know your preaching is effective not when people say they enjoyed your sermon but when they say, "I want to know your Jesus; he spoke to me while you were preaching."

I learned that the more vulnerable I became in sharing my own flaws, the more my preaching allowed people to meet Jesus. People want a real person in the pulpit, someone with whom they can identify, someone who hurts and bleeds like they do. I discovered that the more I told the truth about the hurts and heartaches of my life and my family, the more God energized my preaching and inspired people to connect with Jesus in ways that I had connected with Him. So, to paraphrase Mother Teresa, "People ought to be able to meet Jesus in their pastor's preaching."

The truly effective preacher cannot succeed without the help of a team of brothers and sisters who are "in his balcony" come hell or high water. Years ago a man named Don Bennett climbed Mount Rainier in Washington, 14,410 feet to the summit. He made the climb on one leg and two crutches, becoming the first amputee to climb that mountain. Asked to share the most important lesson he learned, he spoke of his team that helped him to realize his dream, and said, "You can't do it alone."

My preaching moved to a higher level after I invited a few men to meet with me at 6 a.m. on Sunday mornings. At the altar of the church, we shared our hearts with one another and prayed for each other. They prayed for me – to preach the Word that people needed to hear, and as one man prayed, "Lord, help our pastor preach what we need to hear whether we like it or not!" The prayers of a small group of faithful men and women, who love Jesus and love their pastor, can make the difference as to whether there will be Jell-0 or steel in the pastor's backbone.

A pastor does not need to climb Mount Rainier to realize that without God's help, and the help of others, he or she can never preach sermons that are worth hearing, sermons in which people can meet Jesus. Thankfully, that help is available for the asking!

So you're not a preacher. You don't preach sermons. Well, you are not off the hook if you consider yourself a Christian. That's because people should be able to meet Jesus in you. Mother Teresa said it and I believe it!

One Word: _____
How did this story help me change my life?

39

Refuse to Live in Bondage to Fear

Should I live that long, my next birthday will be number 89. Sometimes I wonder if the coronavirus will take me out before that birthday. After all, in the past six months the virus has claimed the lives of 163,000 people in the United States and many of them have been old folks like me.

You may wonder if this is fear or realism for me. Honestly, some of both I think. So it is fair to ask me, how do you deal with this fear when it comes knocking on your door. Here's how: I tell fear to keep walking because I am resolved not to live in bondage to fear. Instead, I choose to live with confidence in the future. This confidence is a gift of God to the children of God and I am a child of God through faith in Jesus Christ.

Does my confidence in the future lead me to think I am not going to die? No, on the contrary, I know I am going to die. But my life is in the hands of my heavenly Father who has already numbered the days of my earthly life. And as Stuart Hamlin says

163

in one of his songs that I love dearly, "Until then, with joy I'll carry on."

Confidence springs from receiving the gift of eternal life. In the first of his three letters, John says, "God has given us eternal life, and this life is in his Son." This gracious gift is available to all who by faith embrace Jesus Christ as Savior and Lord. And eternal life does not begin in heaven; it begins here and continues in our life beyond the death of our body.

One of my beloved mentors was Thomas Carruth. Tom was a man of prayer and as Christlike a man as I have ever known. One day I asked him the secret of his prayer life. He replied, "If I have a secret, it is that I have read the letters of John more than 3,000 times. I read them every day. The more I read John's words, the more I am motivated to pray, and to love people with the love of Jesus. To love and to pray is the way of the Master."

I am blessed because Tom touched my life and taught me to treasure the confident faith of John, the beloved apostle. John lived, and wrote, with confidence. He was certain that Jesus is the Christ, and that everyone who believes that he is, has been born of God. Eternal life is in the Son, and those who have the Son have, present tense, this life. This is one of the foundational truths of the Christian faith.

John's confidence was so complete that he insisted that those who believe may know that they have eternal life. So, a believer can receive assurance of salvation beyond any doubt. This assurance enables believers to sing joyously with Fanny Crosby, "Blessed assurance, Jesus is mine! O what a foretaste of glory divine! Heir of salvation, purchase of God, born in his Spirit, washed in his blood."

Some would have you believe that if you drink a certain beer on the beach that "It doesn't get any better than this!" But here is something far greater than the sweet taste of that beer – the joy of knowing your sins forgiven amidst the thrill of realizing that, saved by grace, you are now a child of God!

When by faith we embrace Jesus as the Son of God and trust him for our salvation, he fills us with joy unspeakable, sends us out into the world with a sense of mission, and gives us the strength to serve him. We are amazed to discover the Lord has broken any chains that had bound us to the past. We are free because we have become alive to God.

And there is more! As we begin living into eternal life, we realize that our joy here is but a "foretaste" of the greater joy that awaits us in heaven. So the rest of our days may be lived in the blessed assurance that eternal life is ours now and forever – because he who has the Son has life! Such confidence allows even a poor boy from Elmore County the privilege of declaring, I will not live in bondage to fear!

One Word: _____
How did this story help me change my life?

40

Make People Feel Good about Themselves

I miss Ben. He died at 84 in 2016. We were friends for 60 years. We were preachers. We never lived in the same town so when we got together we talked for hours – about heartaches and blessings, the sweetness and sorrows of our families, faith discoveries, the keys to church renewal, books we were reading and books we were writing, and the current issues facing the world.

Looking back since Ben's passing, it dawned on me that there was never a meeting with Ben that left me with negative feelings about myself or him. Every encounter was stimulating, positive and encouraging. In the last decade of his life we met often and never with an agenda. It was, I think, what Solomon called iron sharpening iron – "As iron sharpens iron, so a friend sharpens a friend" (Proverbs 27:17). Ben had a way of making me feel good about myself, my potential, and my future. Conversations with him generated hope in my soul. I like to believe he felt the same way about me.

Not every encounter with other people is like that. Now and then you walk away from someone feeling disgusted, disturbed or even angry. You can only pray that you never have that same effect on someone else. The truth is, the way we relate to the people we encounter can make a huge difference in their lives. So if you want that difference to be helpful and not hurtful, these suggestions may be helpful:

One, encourage people. The value of encouragement is enormous. Everybody needs it. Everybody can give it. Nobody lives well without it. Look every day for someone you can encourage. If the clerk who takes my money for a purchase smiles, I usually say, "Thank you for your smile." It is a small way to encourage someone who is probably struggling to make ends meet.

Two, be kind to people. Yes, our culture has become impersonal. But be friendly anyway. Refuse to be return indifference with indifference. A friendly comment spoken with kindness can sometimes change a person's attitude. Rudeness is the behavior of callous people. Choose to be polite, gracious and courteous to everyone you meet. It will make you feel better about yourself and your kindness could inspire others to follow your example.

Three, say "Thank you." Thank the people who serve you. I asked my waitress in a restaurant if there was anything I could ask God to do for her. She looked at me for a few seconds, then burst into tears. "Yes," she said, "please ask God to help me; I am going through a bitter divorce." I took her hand and prayed for her quietly. As I started to leave, she thanked me for my prayer.

Four, smile at people. A frown requires more energy than a smile. So save your energy and smile even when you are hurting. Usually you will get a smile in return. I smile a lot because I don't want a stranger passing me to say, "There goes an old sourpuss; he must have heartburn." We have a choice when we meet people.

We can frown, stare indifferently or smile. A friendly smile is always the best choice.

Five, affirm people. Commend them. Before most people can do their best, they need to hear someone say, "You've got what it takes!" Never be demeaning or "talk down" to someone. Leave it to lesser souls to belittle people. Find gracious ways to offer others the gift of affirmation. Your support could tip the scales in favor of their success. .

Six, forgive people. You hurt people. People hurt you. That's life. An unforgiving spirit leads to misery. Harsh words unwisely spoken had wounded my friendship with a relative. I tried to ignore it for months. Finally, I swallowed my pride and asked him to forgive me. He did and we have been good friends ever since. Harsh words separate people. But the separation need not be permanent. Pride is an infection of the soul for which forgiveness is the only medicine. Ask the person you have hurt for forgiveness. Forgive the person who has hurt you. There is no other way to peace. So forgive – and live!

Seven, pray for people. Pray for your family and your friends. Pray for your colleagues. Pray for the Congress. Pray for the President. Pray for our nation. Pray for the persecuted. Pray for the people in prisons. Pray for understanding. Pray that your kindness will allow people to see Jesus in you. Pray that everyone you meet with find joy and peace by trusting Jesus as Savior and Lord. Pray for the poor, especially the homeless. Pray for God to show you ways to be a blessing. Thank God even for your aches and pains; they remind you that you are alive, and life is a precious gift.

There are people in your life who need you. They need your encouragement, your kindness, your prayers, perhaps your forgiveness. You have what it takes to make a huge difference in their lives. I didn't know this when I was young. A lot of years passed before I made this discovery. But I know it now and that's why I am making an effort to be the kind of person who makes other people feel good about themselves. I invite you to join me in this endeavor to be a Christian worthy of the name.

One Word: _____
How did this story help me change my life?

You Can Overcome Nagging Regret

A popular American writer, aware that his death was imminent, and reflecting upon his life, wrote in his final essay, "I have no regrets." Upon reading that, I wondered how any thinking person could make such a statement. Surely it was said in jest. Everyone has regrets since none of us is perfect. So it is inevitable that we will make our share of poor decisions.

After much pondering, I have changed my mind. I understand now how this writer could come to the end of his life with no regrets. There is only one explanation. He had given his regrets to God and in the warm sunshine of God's forgiveness, his regrets had melted away. And that is what each of us must do – and can do – if we are to overcome the harassing regrets that have the power to ruin our lives.

Regret is real. It is a normal human emotion. All of us understand what Harriet Beecher Stowe was talking about when she said, "The bitterest tears shed over graves are for words left unsaid and deeds left undone." Is there anyone of us who has not stood beside an open grave and felt the pain of such regret? If you know you need to initiate the recovery of a broken relationship, do you not think of that every day? The longer you put off what you need to do, the more you allow your neglect to turn into an irritating regret.

The dictionary defines regret as "sorrow aroused by circumstances beyond one's control or power to repair." Such sorrow is a common human experience. You know what I mean. You uttered words you cannot recall, words that haunt you. You made mistakes you cannot change or fix. And the sorrow over deeds you cannot change can rob you of the joy available in the present hour.

The writer Fulton Oursler used the chilling picture of crucifixion to remind us how regret can ruin our lives: "Many of us crucify ourselves between two thieves – regret for the past and fear of the future." I much prefer the humor of Will Rogers who said with a smile, "Don't let yesterday use up too much of today."

Carl Sandburg, the famous American poet, wrote a poem about regret that I wish I had never read. Some say he wrote it about his wife, Lillian, but I don't believe that. I think she would have left him and their goats had that been true. His poem, titled "MAG," is so disturbing that I am reluctant to share it but I do so because it describes the destructive power of regret. Here it is:

I wish to God I never saw you, Mag.
I wish you never quit your job and came along with me.
I wish we never bought a license and a white dress
For you to get married in the day we ran off to a minister
And told him we would love each other and take care of
each other
Always and always long as the sun and the rain lasts anywhere.
Yes, I'm wishing now you lived somewhere away from here

And I was a bum on the bumpers a thousand miles away
dead broke.
I wish the kids had never come
And rent and coal and clothes to pay for
And a grocery man calling for cash,
Every day cash for beans and prunes.
I wish to God I never saw you, Mag.
I wish to God the kids had never come.

If Mag was a real person, I hope she never had such demeaning regret spewed upon her in spoken words or in writing. However, the more I ponder this poem, the more I think that Sandburg is simply describing the devastating effect of regret. It can destroy a person, a marriage, a family. Though Mag and her husband are probably fictitious persons, I think that here and there I have met Mag and her husband, people who were living wretched lives under the weight of crushing circumstances.

When I have counseled such bewildered couples, I have always told them this: "God is not interested in your past. He allowed His Son to die on the cross so that your mistakes, your sins, could be forgiven. If you will let Him, He will remove your past as far as the east is from the west and give you the grace to handle your present problems and hope for your future."

No matter how overwhelming life may become, the best way to overcome nagging regrets is to give them to God and let the warm sunshine of His forgiveness melt them away. That solution has worked for me – and it continues to work. It is not complicated. It's called grace.

One Word: _____
How did this story help me change my life?

Preserved to the End of Time

Traditions change. Customs change. Habits change. Morals change. Laws change. Change is constant in every arena. Though some people resist change, to survive and thrive we must all learn to adapt to change.

Rituals of the church change. When I was in seminary 65 years ago, one professor insisted that we memorize the ritual for holy communion, a most difficult assignment. To my dismay, a few years later that ritual was changed. It seems the woods are full of "scholars" who stay busy updating rituals.

In my lifetime Methodist rituals have been changed several times. It may not surprise my younger colleagues to learn that I have not welcomed some of our ritual changes. At 88, it goes without saying that I am "old-fashioned," so I continue to prefer the "old" ritual for baptism which, thankfully, is still available. I prefer it mainly because it includes these stirring words:

"The church is of God, and will be preserved to the end of time, for the conduct of worship and the due administration of God's Word and Sacraments, the maintenance of Christian fellowship and discipline, the

edification of believers, and the conversion of the world. All, of every age and station, stand in need of the means of grace which it alone supplies."

The phrase, "Will be preserved to the end of time," says it all. That I believe. It is an important truth for the church to affirm. In the midst of a world that is constantly changing, we need to remind ourselves that nothing can stop the plan God has begun in the world through his church. In Christ God has opened the door to heaven for all who believe. No man can ever shut that door!

If every Christian church building in the world was destroyed today, tomorrow the Christian movement would be stronger than ever! The people whose hearts God has touched are not dependent upon bricks and mortar to finish the work Christ began. God can use buildings but his plan can be fulfilled without them.

Judaism is an example of how God works. Repeatedly the Jews have been crushed, defeated, enslaved and slaughtered. But God has continued to restore them by his mighty power. Israel belongs to God to the present hour.

Those who seek to destroy Israel must first defeat God and that will never happen. God is the sovereign ruler of the universe. He has ordained that in the end love wins and hate loses. Those who perpetuate hate and violence can inflict suffering upon millions but the ultimate victory belongs to God. The apostle Paul understood that. He was convinced that nothing, absolutely nothing, *"will be able to separate us from the love of God in Christ Jesus our Lord"* (Romans 8:39).

Long ago the ruthless King Nebuchadnezzar confiscated the sacred vessels of the temple. He destroyed the temple. No doubt he thought, "That is the end of Judah and the end of the Judahites. They are finished." But old Neb was wrong. God always has the last word. God had a plan, a plan that can be assaulted but not thwarted by recalcitrant men.

The prophet Jeremiah understood this plan. He knew God could not be defeated. The prophet was convinced that God's power was so great that he could even use the pagan King Cyrus to accomplish his purposes – and God did! When Cyrus came to power over Babylonia he gave the exiled Jews the freedom to worship the God of their choice. They began to worship Yahweh more faithfully than ever before. Exile had taught them the foolishness of worshipping pagan gods.

With no temple to use for worship the Jews developed synagogue worship. In these small groups they began to love the Holy Scriptures more than ever. The Jews became a people of the book, and that book was God's Word. Out of that environment God brought forth his only Son Jesus, the Messiah for whom the Jews had waited so long. God does mighty things with people who meet and study his Word – and then practice its truth.

God used the exile of the Jews for their good and his glory. Slowly they realized that God had a plan and that his plans cannot be ultimately stymied.

The prophet Ezra tells in Second Chronicles of a mighty moment among the Jews. My heart skips a beat when I read it! The priests and heads of families "got ready to go up and rebuild the house of the Lord in Jerusalem"! They got ready! Why? Because God stirred their spirits! The power of God was so real that even King Cyrus' heart was stirred. He returned to the Jews the vessels that King Nebuchadnezzar had desecrated by using them in pagan worship.

We live in a time when God's people need their hearts stirred again by the Spirit of God. We are prone to forget that God is still on the throne. The evil and violence in the world rob us of hope. Discouragement causes us to take a dim view of the church. Then we become apathetic.

But the good news is that God will not leave us alone. He finds us in the darkness of our disobedience and restores our hope that his plan for the world will not fail. He raises up another Ezra who motivates us to "get ready" to do God's bidding. He energizes us to do our part in completing His plan.

When God stirs us to action we get busy doing his will – forgiving and loving one another and sharing Christ with our neighbors. We find the divine energy to do our part, no matter how small, to help the kingdoms of this world become the Kingdom of our Lord and of his Christ!

Only then – when almighty God has stirred us out of our lethargy – will we have the courage to face even the worst of times with joy and hope. Only then will we find the enthusiasm to sing our faith as George Frederic Handel sang it: Hallelujah! Hallelujah! *Hallelujah! Hallelujah! Hallelujah! For the Lord God Omnipotent reigneth. Hallelujah! Hallelujah! Hallelujah! Hallelujah!*

And if we add the word "Glory" to all those "Hallelujahs," I believe Brother George would offer his approval with a smile—and another joyful Hallelujah!

One Word: _____
How did this story help me change my life?

Your Sins Are Forgiven

Jesus was a supper guest at the home of Simon, one of the Pharisees. A woman who had lived a sinful life interrupted the meal. Standing behind Jesus, she began to wet his feet with her tears. Then, to the dismay of the Pharisee, the woman wiped the feet of Jesus with her hair, kissed his feet and poured expensive perfume on them.

Simon was infuriated that Jesus would allow such a sinner to even touch him. Sensing Simon's angry attitude, Jesus raised an interesting question with his host. First he described two men who owed money to another man. One owed a large amount, the other a small amount. Neither had the money to pay their debt so the man canceled both debts. "Which of them," Jesus asked Simon, "will love him more?"

Simon replied with the obvious answer, "I suppose the one who had the bigger debt canceled." After commending Simon for his answer, Jesus invited him to take a new look at the sinful woman as he compared Simon's inconsiderate welcome into his home with the lavish welcome of the woman. Because her many sins had been forgiven, Jesus said, "she has shown me much love."

Then, to Simon, Jesus spoke the stinging words: "A person who is forgiven little shows only little love."

Turning to the woman, Jesus said tenderly, "Your sins are forgiven." Imagine how she must have felt at that moment. Surely those were the most beautiful words she had ever heard. She had known the pain of being despised, of having people look at her as though she was a piece of trash. Now this captivating teacher, in whom she saw the love of God, had spoken with liberating authority the transforming words, "Your sins are forgiven." Those words birthed life-giving hope for her future in her heart.

Given the fact that we are all sinners, in need of God's mercy, are those four words not the words each of us needs desperately to hear from God? There are other beautiful words. If you tell me, "God loves you," I realize that is good news. But knowing God loves me does not set me free from the devastating guilt of my sins. So good news only becomes great news when I hear the Lord responding to my repentance by saying, "Walter, your sins are forgiven." That is the liberating, holy moment of a lifetime!

As we travel life's journey, we can look through the windshield at the future or we can look at the past in the rear view mirror. Looking at past wrongs can be paralyzing. Guilt may overwhelm us when we recall the shameful deeds of our youth. Will a just God forgive us?

Such pondering can result in bondage to the past. We are not free to enjoy life today. Guilt prevents us from inhaling the pure joy of knowing that we are alive by the pleasure of the God who made us and also loves us. So our most desperate need is what Jesus gave the sinful woman -- God's forgiveness for our sins.

The gospels make it abundantly clear that we cannot obtain God's forgiveness simply by asking for it. We must first forgive those who have sinned against us. If we are unwilling to forgive someone who has hurt us, we cannot enjoy God's forgiveness for our sins. In the words of Jesus, "if you do not forgive men their sins, your Father will not forgive your sins".

This is an uncomfortable truth if you are estranged from someone who has sinned against you. But if you are to have peace with God, you must forgive that person – and the sooner the better since you know not when your own life with end. Three little words can end the agony of estrangement. Those words are "I forgive you," three of the sweetest words in the English language.

Is there someone in your life who needs to hear those words from your lips? If so, you know what you need to do. Grab yourself by the nape of the neck, swallow your pride, and go do it! You can do it – and the Lord will help you do it.

Saint Paul understood the necessity of forgiveness. Writing to the Ephesians, Paul urged them to "get rid of all bitterness, rage and anger, brawling and slander, along with every form of malice." He followed that with one of the most profound admonitions in the Bible: "Be kind and compassionate to one another, forgiving each other, just as in Christ God forgave you." So nothing, absolutely nothing, strengthens your relationship with God more than your willingness to forgive those who have sinned against you.

Many great truths can be summed up in few words: "God loves you;" "God forgives you." Those words are like proclamations of the Church. But proclamations do not change our hearts and give us peace with God. That only happens when we become willing to say the beautiful words, "I forgive you," to someone who has hurt us. Saying that to someone is like saying what Jesus said to the sinful woman: "Your sins are forgiven." That gives God the opportunity to do what He does best: reconcile and heal our relationships.

At the center of Christianity is a cross, an ugly cross upon which Jesus died. Why did he die? So that all who believe in him might receive forgiveness for their sins. In a sense, when Jesus was dying upon that cross, God was saying to the world: "Your sins are forgiven."

The living Christ, loose in the world since his resurrection, is forever empowering people of all races to forgive one another and to experience the joy of knowing their sins are forgiven. Millions of people have not heard this good news. Think of the people around you. There is likely someone in bondage who would be blessed to have you, as a caring friend, share the good news that their sins are forgiven. Hearing the words, "Your sins are forgiven," could very well convince some miserable person that God really does love them.

One Word: _____
How did this story help me change my life?

44

Finding the Grit to Handle Adversity

New beginnings can be welcomed with joy and anticipation. But some things do not change. Mystery remains. None of us knows what the future holds for us.

The optimist believes wonderful days are ahead. The pessimist believes disaster is just around the corner. Actually, in one sense both are right because life is a mix of joy and sorrow, pleasure and pain, wonder and bewilderment. Year after year, we all experience the good, the bad, and the ugly.

Whatever else each new year brings, it will bring to each of us our portion of pain, trouble and fear. To live victoriously we must find the grit to handle well whatever adversities we shall face.

For me, singing provides the grit I need to face my difficulties and fears. My inspiration for this conviction comes from the Bible. Though Job suffered greatly, he knew a God who gave him "songs in the night." I know that same God and he has given me songs in the night.

Some nights I toss and turn, unable to sleep and I start thinking about dying. Fear disturbs me. Is what Jesus said about preparing a place for me in the Father's House really true or does life end when the body is lowered into a grave? Disturbing thoughts sometimes trouble my soul in the night hours.

During those nights, instead of fretting, I start singing – in my soul so I won't awaken my dear wife. Songs I learned growing up in church flood my mind – like "Living for Jesus," with these words in the refrain:

> *O Jesus, Lord and Savior, I give myself to Thee,*
> *For Thou, in Thy atonement, didst give Thyself for me;*
> *I own no other Master, my heart shall be Thy throne;*
> *My life I give, henceforth to live, O Christ, for Thee alone.*

I sing that refrain again and again. I repeat several times the words, "My heart shall be Thy Throne"! Then I recall and sing the first verse:

> *Living for Jesus, a life that is true,*
> *Striving to please Him in all that I do;*
> *Yielding allegiance, glad-hearted and free,*
> *This is the pathway of blessing for me.*

After singing that a time or two, I affirm that I am living for Jesus and doing so is a "pathway of blessing for me." I am not a victim of my fears; I am on the pathway of blessing that leads to heaven! And I tell "Fear" not to slam the door on his way out of my house! If I am not soon asleep, I start singing another song that is precious to me:

My heart can sing when I pause to remember
A heartache here is but a stepping stone
Along a path that's winding always upward
This troubled world is not my final home
But until then my heart will go on singing
Until then with joy I'll carry on
Until the day my eyes behold my Savior
Until the day God calls me home

I love that song. My heartaches are stepping stones on that pathway of blessing that is leading me home – to my home in my Father' House – and until then, by the grace of God "with joy I'll carry one"! My troubles are nothing compared to the joy awaiting me on the other side.

I must admit that singing songs in the night is not original with me. I learned it from Paul and Silas. The Bible tells us those two men had been stripped and beaten – "severely flogged" Doctor Luke tells us. Thrown in to a stinking prison, their feet fastened in stocks, Paul and Silas were not fretting about their pain and trouble. About midnight they began "singing hymns to God"! Glory be!

If Paul and Silas could find the grit to do that, Walter can do it too! You can do it too! Even if you "can't carry a tune in a bucket," you can still sing in your soul! So get ready. Adversity is coming. Fear is knocking on your door. But when you start singing songs in the night about living for Jesus, and carrying on with joy until God calls you home, the peace and joy of victory will be yours!

One Word: _____
How did this story help me change my life?

45

One Small Thread in God's Tapestry

Mary, the mother of Jesus, gets much attention during the holy season of Christmas. She deserves it. Her beautiful faith in God's plan of salvation shines like a light penetrating the world's darkness. Her unflinching obedience to God remains the example of the ages for believers.

But let's not overlook Joseph. He deserves some attention for he also is a model for Christ followers. His situation is unique but his opportunity to obey God is universal. The eternal destiny of every person is caught up in one's willingness to trust and obey God.

In his Gospel, Matthew tells us that Joseph received his instructions from an angel in a dream. Lesser men might have dismissed the advice. Joseph, however, obeyed the angel, doing what he believed God wanted him to do. He gave up his plan to end his commitment to Mary; instead he brought her into his home and cared for her.

Our own plans are often hampered by our pride. We believe we know what is best. We need no one's counsel, much less the counsel of God. We want to be able to say, "I did it my way." So God tests our faith every time he says, "Do it my way, not your way. My way is best, even though you may not understand it."

We should not expect Joseph is comprehend how this infant would "save his people from their sins." Nevertheless, he follows instructions and names the baby Jesus, thus embracing his role in the miraculous birth. Simply put, he obeyed God.

Few of us comprehend all that God is doing in the events of our lives. God does not require that we understand. He does require obedience. He required it of Joseph and he requires it of us today. Joseph was an ordinary man called to serve God. God still calls ordinary people to do what he asks them to do. And each of us must decide whether we will live life God's way or our way.

The flight from Bethlehem into Egypt is another example of Joseph's obedience. Once again his instructions come from an angel in a dream. Joseph must act quickly to save Jesus from death at the hands of wicked Herod the Great. Losing no time, Joseph leaves in the night and escorts his little family to safety in Egypt.

After some time had passed, the angel is busy again, instructing Joseph to take Mary and Jesus into Israel. Those who wished to kill Jesus are now dead. So Joseph carries out his orders, taking Mary and Jesus back to their home in Nazareth.

The scriptures tell us little of what transpired during Jesus' childhood. We may assume that Mary and Joseph taught Jesus, and their other children, how to love and honor God as they grew up in the humble home of a carpenter. We can imagine Jesus learning patience in the skill of carpentry as he assisted in constructing fine oxen yokes.

Joseph was not a prominent man. He was an ordinary man. This should get our attention for the Bible shows us that God chooses common people to do his will. He calls people in different ways. Sometimes he has used angels, sometimes dreams. And what He once did, he can do again, if he chooses. But his methods are limitless. He can reach the heart of a man or a woman by a thousand stairways.

Joseph is an example of how we can respond to God. God may speak to us in many ways: through the scriptures, a sermon, circumstances, the words of a trusted friend or the Inner Voice. When he speaks, we can listen and obey. What he asks of us are usually not impressive things but little things, simple things. We need not grasp "the big picture." It will be enough simply to embrace the tasks at hand and do what He asks us to do. To use the words of Mother Teresa, we can do "small things with great love." When we do that, not caring who gets the credit, God's work is done in God's way to God's glory.

God used the ordinary man Joseph to help the world see Jesus. In these days God wants to use our quiet, humble deeds of love and kindness to show Jesus to the world. People can see Jesus in our ordinary, everyday lives, when we do our best to follow the directions God has given us for living. They will see Jesus when we forgive one another, when we are kind rather than mean, and when we share what we have with the least of our brethren.

No task is small in the eyes of God. No duty God assigns is insignificant. In the grand scheme of things, God will take the obedience of ordinary people and knit it into something beautiful. My obedience, your obedience, can become one small thread in the exquisite tapestry God is weaving with our lives. We shall be wise to follow Joseph's example of obedience.

One Word: _____
How did this story help me change my life?

46

Focus On Your Blessings

When someone asks me how I am doing, I sometimes reply, "I am blessed." I picked that up from a good friend in Opelika. That was his constant answer, even when he was suffering from the cancer that took his life. He never complained or called attention to his pain. His simple response was his way of staying focused on his blessings instead of discussing his problems.

My friend had it right. He taught me to focus on my blessings. When I do that, I refrain from constantly seeking pity for my troubles. It's not because nobody wants to hear about them; true friends do care. The key word is "constantly" – me and you. If you will share your difficulties with only a few close friends, the rest of your time can be used to share hope and joy with the people around you. The truth is, most of us enjoy being around people who, despite their misfortunes, are positive and hopeful about the future. That attitude springs from the conviction that your blessings are much greater than your trials.

Many songs are stored in my memory bank but there is none better than the one composed by Johnson Oatman Jr. titled "Count

Your Blessings." If you want help to overcome your burdens, then just start doing what Oatman invites us to do in his song:

Count your many blessings – name them one by one;
And it will surprise you what the Lord hath done

Counting your blessings is a healthy exercise anytime of the year, not just during the Thanksgiving season. To focus on your blessings will not make your problems go away but it can help you walk away from self-pity. Positive thinking helps you overcome the depression brought on by your troubles. And that is good medicine for your soul.

When I begin counting my blessings I think of my family, especially my wife Dean. We met in the first grade at age six. She does not remember it but I am sure I overheard her tell the girl beside her, "I am going to marry that boy one day!" Well, even if she did not say it, I am so thankful that 14 years later she did walk down the aisle and become my wife. No man has ever been married to a more supportive and loving woman than Dean has been for me. Truth is, we had some rocky times but together we learned to "lean on Jesus" and found the grace to repent, forgive and grow. Through 68 plus years Dean has always been the strong one, weathering some storms that would have wrecked weaker souls.

My four sons, their wives and their families, are precious blessings. In these sunset years, few things thrill me more than a phone call from one of them. Their love and concern for "Mean Granny Dean" and me means the world to us. We call their names in prayer during our morning devotions, asking the Lord to guard and guide each one in the ways of the Lord. And talk about joy! That's what fills our hearts when one of our grandchildren calls to say, "How you doing Grampa and Grandma?" Facetime with the great grandchildren is a precious gift of modern technology.

I am thankful for our church. The people of the Saint James United Methodist Church have indulged my preaching for 17 years and only a few have slept through my sermons. Of course whenever I see someone sleeping while I am preaching, I just assume they trust me and are not really bored.

Preaching for me remains a great privilege; it has never been drudgery or duty. I don't have to preach; I get to preach. At Saint James Dean and I have shared a rich fellowship with some of the finest disciples of Jesus I have ever known. They are our dear brothers and sisters in Christ.

Our years at Saint James have been enriched by the privilege of serving Christ there alongside our son Steve, his wife Amy, their two sons Jake and Josh, and my brother Seth and his wife Pearl. Every pastor needs a brother like Seth. His support and encouragement have touched me deeply. After a worship service, when most of the people are walking out and making their way to lunch, my brother Seth, who sings in our choir, will stay long enough to hug me and say, "Good sermon brother!" What a brother! I reckon you can imagine how much it blesses me to have my brother and his wife cheering me on.

Since my retirement we have come to know and love many of the dear people in our son Matt's church, Wetumpka First Methodist. Pastor Matt has to run to keep up with the Christ followers in that church. It is truly a Good Samaritan Church because those folks know how to practice compassion. And, despite the Covid pandemic, the church is growing, spiritually as well as numerically. I reckon you can tell that I am proud of my home church, the folks who recommended me for the ministry 70 years ago!

My list of blessings must include my two sisters, Neva Williams and Margie Flomer. God has blessed us with the precious gift of living in harmony with one another. I cherish our relationship with them and their families and praise God for giving me two sisters who love and serve the Lord. Together we often thank God for our sister Laurida, who departed this life more than 20 years ago, but left us with precious memories of the joy and courage that filled her heart.

Each Thanksgiving Day we share a meal at the old home place where I was born. Steve and Amy live there now, having bought and remodeled the place after my parents died. I count it a rare blessing to enjoy a meal in the home where I grew up. For many years my parents hosted a Thanksgiving Day meal for our family. Some of my dearest memories were made at my mother's table. In recent years Steve and Amy have hosted the Thanksgiving Day gathering now attended by about 100 family and friends. We will sit around many tables, talk of old times and lament the way things have changed. I am thankful that Steve and Amy continue the tradition of gathering at Papa's place, now Steve's place and Amy's place, for Thanksgiving.

The blessings I count are mostly people, not things. So many people have made a difference in my life, like Sunday School teachers and pastors who influenced my faith as a child, people who encouraged me to believe that God had a plan for my life. Most of the good things I have experienced happened because caring people took an interest in me and opened doors of opportunity for me. Many of them are in heaven now and in a quiet moment I can hear them still cheering for me.

My list of blessings has to include the men with whom I share lunch almost every week. They are friends and fellow disciples of Jesus whose encouragement and love I need. In addition, I must thank God for the men and women who have met weekly in our home as a Life Group. Together we have studied God's Word, shared a simple meal, prayed and encouraged one another. We have shared our struggles and, now and then, shed a few tears together. The love and friendship we have shared is one of the greatest treasures of my life.

Most of us stay busy. We live in the fast lane, rushing here and there. Now and then the sweetness of life can be restored by taking the time to focus on our blessings. It is wise to stop and smell the roses. Tell friends and family members how much you love them. Notice the small blessings. If the only food in your refrigerator is one quart of milk, instead of complaining, thank God the milk is not sour and think of someone with whom you can share it.

As you think of all God has done for you, remember this: He is not done blessing you! Give Him a chance and He will give you more blessings than you can count! And if you really want to enjoy a great life, ignore your troubles and start sharing your blessings with someone who has less than you do. When you do, you will discover why Jesus said, "It is more blessed to give than to receive."

One Word: _____
How did this story help me change my life?

Honoring Our Veterans

Veterans Day is an important day in America. Every November 11 is a national holiday when countless tributes are paid to our military veterans. It is a good thing to honor the men and women who have made many sacrifices to serve our nation and preserve the freedoms we enjoy. I have two sons who served our country proudly, one in the Navy and the other in the Air Force. Some of my grandchildren are veterans.

During the Second World War my Uncle Luke Johnson served as an Air Force pilot. I was nine years old when the United States entered the war. My mother obtained her brother's address so I could write him. It's hard to describe what it meant to me as a young boy to receive a letter, and sometimes pictures of his B-17 Flying Fortress bomber, from Uncle Luke. I was awestruck by his taking the time to write me. When I saw newsreel pictures of our American fighter planes, I imagined myself flying the P-47 Thunderbolt in combat.

Last Monday I got to thinking about the debt we owe to veterans other than our military veterans. For example, the men and women who are veteran Sunday School teachers in our churches.

I grew up in the church so I am indebted to many men and women who taught me as a child, a youth and an adult. Though the Sunday School teaching ministry is not as strong today as it once was in our churches, I can testify that my faith was shaped and strengthened by those who taught me.

Most Sunday School teachers have received little training in theology. They learn the faith through Bible study and listening to Sunday sermons. But like me, some of them learned how to teach by spending years in Sunday School classes taught by people whose faith they admired. Those who become excellent teachers of the Word are those who "stay in the Word" studying and seeking the help of the Holy Spirit, the Great Teacher of us all.

Howard Hendricks loves to tell about the great lesson about teaching he learned as a college student. He worked in the college dining hall and on his way to work at 5:30 every morning he walked past the home of one of his professors. Through a window he could see the professor studying at his desk. At night Howard stayed late in the library studying. On his way home home he would see the light on and his professor still studying. One day he asked him, "What keeps you studying? You never seem to stop." His answer: "Son, I would rather have my students drink from a running stream than a stagnant pool." God rewards those who study his Word.

The most effective teachers are not those who acquire the most knowledge through diligent study, but those who also love their students. Wise teachers know that the best way to win a student to Christ is to love them into the Kingdom. When teachers love their students, they pray for them. When one teacher was asked the secret of his success with his class, he pulled out a little black book. On each page he had a picture of each of the boys in his junior high class. Under each name, there were notes the teacher had made like "having trouble with math," "his parents have no interest in church," or "would like to become a missionary." Said the teacher: "I pray over these pages every day and I can hardly wait for Sunday to see what God has been doing in their lives."

For 17 years I have observed and admired the teachers of adult Sunday School classes at Saint James United Methodist Church. They are the real heroes of the church. Many of them are seasoned veterans of the "war" Satan has launched to win the minds of people who are not sold out to Jesus.

Some of these teachers have been on the firing line for 20 or 30 years, longer than the average veteran has served in the military. These veteran teachers take seriously the truth that all who become disciples of Jesus are under orders to carry out the Great Commission – to go into all the world spreading spiritual holiness, making disciples, baptizing them, and teaching them what Jesus said. These teachers understand that God wants to use them to expose and overcome the corruption constantly at work in our fallen world – and to lead unbelievers to faith in Christ. They know that as trustees of the faith, they are to guard it and pass it on to other faithful disciples who will keep the chain strong until Christ returns.

My good friend Cecil Spear spent his life working as a civil engineer in the steel business. When it seemed wise to move from Montgomery to Auburn a few years ago, Cecil did not want to give up his turn as a rotating teacher in his Sunday School class. So every second Sunday he drives from Auburn to teach the class and worship with his lifelong friends at Saint James. Fellow class members welcome his teaching because they know he is a faithful veteran who loves them and for years has sought to "correctly handle the word of truth." The Greek word translated as "reliable" or "faithful" means one who is believing, one who is loyal, one who can be depended upon. Like his fellow teachers, Cecil knows that the privilege of teaching is a sacred trust. He and the others are doing what Paul urged Timothy to do in 1 Timothy 6:20 – "guard the trust that has been entrusted to you."

Effective teaching is hard work but it does have its rewards. The teacher's example in "walking like he talks" can influence his students to "hear God" speaking in the scripture lessons and inspire them to give up living on the periphery of life and surrender to the Lordship of Christ. When that happens, you realize that the best rewards of teaching are eternal rewards.

A chaplain, ministering to a wounded soldier who knew he was dying, listened intently as the soldier asked him to write a letter to his Sunday School teacher. He said, "Tell her I died a Christian because of what she taught me. The memory of her earnest pleas and the warmth of her love as she asked us to accept Jesus has stayed with me. Tell her I will meet her in heaven."

The chaplain sent the message to the teacher and soon received this reply: "May God forgive me. Just last month I resigned as a teacher because I felt my teaching had been fruitless. How I regret my lack of faith! I have asked my pastor to let me go back to teaching a class." Perhaps this story will inspire some teacher who has become "weary in well doing" to refuse to give up and get back on the firing line as a faithful teacher.

Pause for a moment. Recall the names and faces of your Sunday School teachers. Then give thanks for these veteran servants of God who deserve to be honored for their faithful work as guardians of the truth. Many of us can say, with grateful hearts, "It was my Sunday School teacher who inspired me to fall in love with Jesus." For some of us, we owe our teachers a debt we can never repay.

One Word: _____
How did this story help me change my life?

Because the Daffodils are Blooming Again

S arah's daffodils are blooming again. The lovely yellow and white flowers spring up every January to grace our lawn on into February. They remind me to give thanks once again for Sarah, Dean's mother. She planted our daffodils.

Sarah departed this life 21 years ago, but her little daffodils are still blessing me. That dear woman loved to work in the yard. Giver her a rake and she was in heaven. I wish she was still here. I don't like rakes or yardwork. But I do love her daffodils.

The lawnmower cuts the daffodils down. Grass grows over the green stems. You don't know the daffodils are there in the fall. But, though dormant, they are still there, waiting until January to burst up out of the ground. I can almost hear them shouting, "Take heart old man, we are here again!" They do so encourage me. Their arrival stirs my confidence in the promises of God.

A phrase too glib for you? Well, let me explain. Consider just one of God's promises, this one from Ezekiel: *"And I will send down the showers in their season; they shall be showers of blessing. And the trees of the field shall yield their fruit, and the earth shall yield its increase, and they shall be secure in their land; and they shall know that I am the Lord"* (34:26-27).

The daffodils rise up and bloom because God says do it. Dormancy is part of God's plan. Spring arrives on His schedule. Trees yield their fruit because God says, "Yield your fruit." The seasons change because God says, "Change." Things happen when God speaks. Remember how Genesis puts it: "God said, 'Let there be light,' and there was light."

So, because the daffodils are blooming again, I need not be discouraged as I wait for the harvest God has promised. Yes, life is a struggle. Winter is hard. But my labor, and your labor, will not be in vain. Spring will come. God will, in His own good time, bring forth fruit from our labor. He is, after all, the Lord of the harvest!

Are there times when I am bewildered by difficult circumstances? Are there times when I do not understand what God is doing? Are there people for whom I have been praying still living in darkness? Yes! But I need not despair for the daffodils are blooming again! So, I will not yield to the demon of discouragement. I will continue to trust and serve God no matter how difficult the winter may be.

When I was 29, my life was radically changed by an encounter with E. Stanley Jones. God used Jones to rescue me from the harsh winter that had come upon my soul. As Christ spoke to me through Brother Stanley, a spiritual springtime set my soul free. Joy and peace began blooming in my soul! I came alive to God in ways I had never been alive.

Who was E. Stanley Jones? At the time I met him he was in the last decade of his life. A missionary to India, he was known across the world for proclaiming Jesus as The Way to God. His constant theme was "Jesus is Lord!" I was thrilled to discover how he found The Way to life in Christ. His story involves a preacher who knew what it meant to wait on God while being rebuffed by his fellow Methodists, especially Methodist hierarchy.

That preacher was Henry Clay Morrison, president of Asbury College and founder of Asbury Theological Seminary in Kentucky. Known as one of the greatest pulpit orators in America, Morrison was snubbed by some Methodist leaders who did not like his emphasis on holiness. Booked on one occasion to preach at large churches in Baltimore, Maryland, he arrived to discover that the presiding elder had directed the pastors to cancel the meetings.

Morrison had no place to preach – until the pastor of a small congregation in Baltimore dared to invite Morrison to preach in his church. Refusing to be discouraged, Morrison accepted the invitation. That night, after preaching to a small crowd, Morrison had only one person, a 14-year-old boy, to come forward at the end of the service. That boy was E. Stanley Jones who accepted Morrison's invitation to give his life to Christ.

Henry Clay Morrison had no way of knowing that night that his faithfulness would be rewarded with such a great harvest of souls through the ministry of E. Stanley Jones. By God's grace, Morrison lived to see that young man graduate from Asbury and become a missionary and evangelist who inspired thousands upon thousands across the world to accept Jesus as Lord of their lives.

Because the daffodils are blooming, I shall not lose heart. The chilly winds of winter will give way to spring and its showers of blessing. The Lord of the harvest, who faithfully keeps his promises, will reward the faithfulness of his children who choose to live as Christ followers today. You can bet your life on that!

One Word: _____
How did this story help me change my life?
+++

My Seven Point Plan for Changing My World

1. _____
   _____
   _____

2. _____
   _____
   _____

3. _____
   _____
   _____

4. _____
   _____
   _____

5. _____
   _____
   _____

6. _____
   _____
   _____

7. _____
   _____
   _____

AFTERWORD

Thank you for taking the time to read this book. I would love to sit on our front porch and visit with you for a while. We could talk about the joy of practicing random acts of kindness. You could tell me about times when you felt the sudden urge to offer kindness to a stranger or a friend. We could share how challenging, and yet rewarding, it is to live as Christ followers. We could discuss things we can do to promote racial harmony and overcome the incivility that is ripping apart the fabric of our nation. We could admit that though we struggle with the fear of death, our faith in the promises of our Lord helps us break the stranglehold of that fear.

When it comes to my writing, I freely admit that I am indebted to many dear friends whose encouragement and friendship enhance my thinking. Many of my convictions have been birthed by thought-provoking conversations with men and women who inspire me live as a genuine follower of Christ. Seeing others do it motivates me to believe that I can do it too. It is not easy to wake up every day and deny yourself, because the "self" keeps begging me to "eat, drink and be merry." So where can we find the power to continually take up our cross and follow Christ? I find that God releases that power to each of us through the fellowship of believers. And that does not need to be a large fellowship. It can be that "two or three together" intimacy, where we have fellowship with the Father, with the Son, and with a few others with whom we have bonded. It is in that affectionate relationship that "one person sharpens another as iron sharpens iron." So I thank God for the dear friends who love me enough to sharpen my thinking and quicken my desire to love God with all my heart and follow Christ wherever he leads me.

If you believe this book might have value for others, please go online at Amazon.com and compose a brief review of the book. Positive reviews are helpful in getting books into the hands of other people.

One final word. If you have not yet decided to deny yourself and live as a follower of Christ, you could do that right now, this very minute. Just get on your knees and surrender your life to Jesus. He will give you a new heart. His Inner Voice will guide you to find a fellowship in which you can grow into an authentic Christ follower. Believe me, you do not want to miss the joy and privilege of letting Christ use your witness and your gifts to change our world. Decide to become a Christ follower. Do it now. It is a decision you will never regret!

About Walter Albritton

Walter grew up on a farm near Wetumpka, Alabama. As a boy he milked two cows before school and again after coming home from school. He grew up with four wonderful siblings – his sisters Neva, Margie and Laurida (now blessing heaven with her laughter), and his brother Seth. Farm life was a blessing. Parents Walter and Caroline worked hard, loved God and lived with integrity. They raised cows, hogs, chickens, horses, mules, and rabbits. They grew their own vegetables in a huge garden. Mama loved flowers, had a hot house and grew Day lilies by the hundreds. Papa grew cotton, corn, oats and hay. Walter and Seth remember there was always work to do, fixing fences if nothing else.

Walter laughs and says one of the reasons he thanks God for calling him into the ministry is that he did not want to spend the rest of his life cleaning out the chicken house. He loved Josephine, the little horse he rode from age 12 until he went off to Auburn University but has seldom ridden a horse since.

Walter got his theological training at Vanderbilt University and Emory University. He and his wife Dean have five sons – David (already in heaven); Matt, Mark, Tim and Steve. They have 12 grandchildren and 17 great grandchildren. Walter and Dean live at the Cabin a half mile from the Tallapoosa River and about eight miles from Wetumpka.

Other Books By Walter Albritton

Living in Christ – the Only Way to Live

Life's Greatest Adventure – Serving Jesus Christ

Measure Your Life by Breathtaking Moments

When You Lose Someone You Love

God is Not Done with You

When Your Heart is Broken

The Great Secret

233 Days

If You Want to Walk on Water, You've Got to Get Out of Your Boat

Leaning Over the Banisters of Heaven

Life is Short So Laugh Often, Live Fully and Love Deeply

Just Get Over It and Move On!

Don't Let Go of the Rope!

The Four Gospels (Commentary on Selected Passages)

Paul's Letters (Commentary on Selected Passages)

Beacons of Hope (Comments on Selected Passages)

Available from Amazon.com
Or from walteralbritton7@gmail.com